Lecture Notes in Computer Science 3224

Commenced Publication in 1973
Founding and Former Series Editors:
Gerhard Goos, Juris Hartmanis, and Jan van Leeuwen

Erland Jonsson   Alfonso Valdes
Magnus Almgren (Eds.)

Recent Advances in Intrusion Detection

7th International Symposium, RAID 2004
Sophia Antipolis, France, September 15-17, 2004
Proceedings

 Springer

Volume Editors

Erland Jonsson
Magnus Almgren
Chalmers University of Technology
SE-412 96 Göteborg, Sweden
E-mail:{erland.jonsson, magnus.almgren}@ce.chalmers.se

Alfonso Valdes
SRI International
333 Ravenswood Ave., Menlo Park, CA 94025, USA
E-mail: alfonso.valdes@sri.com

Library of Congress Control Number: 2004111363

CR Subject Classification (1998): K.6.5, K.4, E.3, C.2, D.4.6

ISSN 0302-9743
ISBN 3-540-23123-4 Springer Berlin Heidelberg New York

Springer is a part of Springer Science+Business Media

springeronline.com

© Springer-Verlag Berlin Heidelberg 2004
Printed in Germany

Preface

On behalf of the Program Committee, it is our pleasure to present to you the proceedings of the 7th Symposium on Recent Advances in Intrusion Detection (RAID 2004), which took place in Sophia-Antipolis, French Riviera, France, September 15–17, 2004.

The symposium brought together leading researchers and practitioners from academia, government and industry to discuss intrusion detection from research as well as commercial perspectives. We also encouraged discussions that addressed issues that arise when studying intrusion detection, including information gathering and monitoring, from a wider perspective. Thus, we had sessions on detection of worms and viruses, attack analysis, and practical experience reports.

The RAID 2004 Program Committee received 118 paper submissions from all over the world. All submissions were carefully reviewed by several members of the Program Committee and selection was made on the basis of scientific novelty, importance to the field, and technical quality. Final selection took place at a meeting held May 24 in Paris, France. Fourteen papers and two practical experience reports were selected for presentation and publication in the conference proceedings. In addition, a number of papers describing work in progress were selected for presentation at the symposium. The keynote address was given by Bruce Schneier of Counterpane Systems. Håkan Kvarnström of TeliaSonera gave an invited talk on the topic "Fighting Fraud in Telecom Environments."

A successful symposium is the result of the joint effort of many people. In particular, we would like to thank all authors who submitted papers, whether accepted or not. Our thanks also go to the Program Committee members and additional reviewers for their hard work with the large number of submissions. In addition, we want to thank the General Chair, Refik Molva, for handling conference arrangements, Magnus Almgren for preparing the conference proceedings, Marc Dacier for finding support from our sponsors, Yves Roudier for maintaining the conference Web site, and Hervé Debar at France Télécom R&D for arranging the Program Committee meeting. Finally, we extend our thanks to the sponsors: SAP, France Télécom, and Conseil Régional Provence Alpes Côte d'Azur.

September 2004

Erland Jonsson
Alfonso Valdes

Organization

RAID 2004 was organized by Institut Eurécom and held in conjunction with ESORICS 2004.

Conference Chairs

General Chair	Refik Molva (Institut Eurécom, France)
Program Chairs	Erland Jonsson (Chalmers University of Technology, Sweden)
	Alfonso Valdes (SRI International, USA)
Publications Chair	Magnus Almgren (Chalmers University of Technology, Sweden)
Publicity Chair	Yves Roudier (Institut Eurécom, France)
Sponsor Chair	Marc Dacier (Institut Eurécom, France)

Program Committee

Tatsuya Baba	NTT Data Corporation, Japan
Lee Badger	DARPA, USA
Sungdeok Cha	Korea Advanced Institute of Science and Technology, Korea
Steven Cheung	SRI International, USA
Hervé Debar	France Télécom R&D, France
Simone Fischer-Hübner	Karlstad University, Sweden
Steven Furnell	University of Plymouth, UK
Dogan Kesdogan	RWTH Aachen, Germany
Christopher Kruegel	Technical University Vienna, Austria
Håkan Kvarnström	TeliaSonera AB, Sweden
Wenke Lee	Georgia Institute of Technology, USA
Roy A. Maxion	Carnegie Mellon University, USA
John McHugh	CMU/SEI CERT, USA
Ludovic Mé	Supélec, France
George Mohay	Queensland University of Technology, Australia
Vern Paxson	International Computer Science Institute and Lawrence Berkeley National Laboratory, USA
Giovanni Vigna	UCSB, USA
Andreas Wespi	IBM Zurich Research Laboratory, Switzerland
S. Felix Wu	UC Davis, USA
Diego Zamboni	IBM Zurich Research Laboratory, Switzerland

Steering Committee

Marc Dacier (Chair)	Institut Eurécom, France
Hervé Debar	France Télécom R&D, France
Deborah Frincke	Pacific Northwest National Laboratory, USA
Ming-Yuh Huang	The Boeing Company, USA
Wenke Lee	Georgia Institute of Technology, USA
Ludovic Mé	Supélec, France
Giovanni Vigna	UCSB, USA
Andreas Wespi	IBM Zurich Research Laboratory, Switzerland
S. Felix Wu	UC Davis, USA

Additional Reviewers

Magnus Almgren	Chalmers University of Technology, Sweden
Christophe Bidan	Supélec, France
Phil Brooke	University of Plymouth, UK
Sanghyun Cho	Korea Advanced Institute of Science and Technology, Korea
Andrew Clark	Queensland University of Technology, Australia
Chris Clark	Georgia Institute of Technology, USA
Marc Dacier	Institut Eurécom, France
Drew Dean	SRI International, USA
Maximillian Dornseif	RWTH Aachen, Germany
Bruno Dutertre	SRI International, USA
Ulrich Flegel	Dortmund University, Germany
Deborah Frincke	Pacific Northwest National Laboratory, USA
Anup Ghosh	DARPA, USA
Satoshi Hakomori	NTT Data Corporation, Japan
Jeffery P. Hansen	Carnegie Mellon University, USA
Anders Hansmats	TeliaSonera AB, Sweden
Hans Hedbom	Karlstad University, Sweden
Thorsten Holz	RWTH Aachen, Germany
Gary Hong	UC Davis, USA
Ming-Yuh Huang	The Boeing Company, USA
Klaus Julisch	IBM Zurich Research Laboratory, Switzerland
Jaeyeon Jung	Massachusetts Institute of Technology, USA
Kevin S. Killourhy	Carnegie Mellon University, USA
Hansung Kim	Korea Advanced Institute of Science and Technology, Korea
Oleg Kolesnikov	Georgia Institute of Technology, USA
Tobias Kölsch	RWTH Aachen, Germany
Takayoshi Kusaka	NTT Data Corporation, Japan

Additional Reviewers (continued)

Byunghee Lee	Korea Advanced Institute of Science and Technology, Korea
Stefan Lindskog	Karlstad University, Sweden
Emilie Lundin Barse	Chalmers University of Technology, Sweden
Shigeyuki Matsuda	NTT Data Corporation, Japan
Michael Meier	Brandenburg University of Technology Cottbus, Germany
Benjamin Morin	France Télécom R&D, France
Darren Mutz	UCSB, USA
Tadeusz Pietraszek	IBM Zurich Research Laboratory, Switzerland
Alexis Pimenidis	RWTH Aachen, Germany
Xinzhou Qin	Georgia Institute of Technology, USA
Rob Reeder	Carnegie Mellon University, USA
Will Robertson	UCSB, USA
Tim Seipold	RWTH Aachen, Germany
Jeongseok Seo	Korea Advanced Institute of Science and Technology, Korea
Hervé Sibert	France Télécom R&D, France
Kymie M.C. Tan	Carnegie Mellon University, USA
Axel Tanner	IBM Zurich Research Laboratory, Switzerland
Elvis Tombini	France Télécom R&D, France
Eric Totel	Supélec, France
Fredrik Valeur	UCSB, USA
Chris Vanden Berghe	IBM Zurich Research Laboratory, Switzerland
Jouni Viinikka	France Télécom R&D, France
Nicholas Weaver	International Computer Science Institute, USA
Ralf Wienzek	RWTH Aachen, Germany
Jacob Zimmerman	Supélec, France
Albin Zuccato	Karlstad University, Sweden

Table of Contents

Anomaly Detection

Formal Analysis for Intrusion Detection

Automatic Extraction of Accurate Application-Specific Sandboxing Policy

Lap Chung Lam and Tzi-cker Chiueh

Rether Networks, Inc.
99 Mark Tree RD Suite 301, Centereach NY 11720, USA
lclam@cs.sunysb.edu, chiueh@rether.com
http://www.rether.com

Abstract. One of the most dangerous cybersecurity threats is *control hijacking* attacks, which hijack the control of a victim application, and execute arbitrary system calls assuming the identity of the victim program's effective user. System call monitoring has been touted as an effective defense against control hijacking attacks because it could prevent remote attackers from inflicting damage upon a victim system even if they can successfully compromise certain applications running on the system. However, the Achilles' heel of the system call monitoring approach is the construction of accurate system call behavior model that minimizes false positives and negatives. This paper describes the design, implementation, and evaluation of a Program semantics-Aware Intrusion Detection system called *Paid*, which automatically derives an application-specific system call behavior model from the application's source code, and checks the application's run-time system call pattern against this model to thwart any control hijacking attacks. The per-application behavior model is in the form of the *sites* and *ordering* of system calls made in the application, as well as its partial control flow. Experiments on a fully working *Paid* prototype show that *Paid* can indeed stop attacks that exploit non-standard security holes, such as format string attacks that modify function pointers, and that the run-time latency and throughput penalty of *Paid* are under 11.66% and 10.44%, respectively, for a set of production-mode network server applications including Apache, Sendmail, Ftp daemon, etc.

Keywords: intrusion detection, system call graph, sandboxing, mimicry attack, non-deterministic finite state automaton

1 Introduction

Many computer security vulnerabilities arise from software bugs. One particular class of bugs allows remote attackers to hijack the control of victim programs and inflict damage upon victim machines. These *control hijacking* exploits are considered among the most dangerous cybersecurity threats because remote attackers can unilaterally mount an attack without requiring any special set-up or any actions on the part of victim users (unlike email attachment or web page download). Moreover, many production-mode network applications appear to be rife with software defects that expose such vulnerabilities. For example, in the

E. Jonsson et al. (Eds.): RAID 2004, LNCS 3224, pp. 1–20, 2004.

most recent quarterly CERT Advisory summary (03/2003) [4], seven out of ten vulnerabilities can lead to control hijacking attacks. As another example, the notorious SQL Slammer worm also relies on control hijacking attacks to duplicate and propagate itself epidemically across the net.

An effective way to defeat control-hijacking attacks is application-based anomaly intrusion detection. An application-based anomaly intrusion detection system closely monitors the activities of a process. If any activity deviates from the predefined acceptable behavior model, the system terminates the process or flags the activity as intrusion. The most common way to model the acceptable behavior of an application is to use system calls made by the application. The underlying assumption of the system call-based intrusion detection is that remote attackers can damage a victim system only by making malicious system calls once they hijack a victim application. Given that system call is the only means to inflict damage, it follows logically that by closely monitoring the system calls made by a network application at run time, it is possible to detect and prevent malicious system calls that attackers issue, and thus protect a computer system from attackers even if some of its network applications have been compromised. While the mechanics of system call-based anomaly intrusion detection is well understood, successful application of this technology requires an accurate system call model that minimizes false positives and negatives.

Wagner and Dean [22] first introduced the idea of using compiler to derive a call graph that can capture the system call ordering of an application. At run time, any system call that does not follow the statically derived order is considered as an act of intrusion and thus should be prohibited. A call graph derived from a program's control flow graph (CFG) is a non-deterministic finite-state automaton (NFA) due to such control constructs as if-then-else and function call/return. The degree of non-determinism determines the extent to which mimicry attack [23] is possible, through so-called impossible paths [22]. This paper describes the design, implementation, and evaluation of a Program semantics-Aware Intrusion Detection system called *Paid*, which consists of a compiler that can derive a deterministic finite-state automaton (DFA) model which captures the system call *sites*, system call *ordering*, and *partial control flow* from an application's source code, and an in-kernel run-time verifier that compares an application's run-time system call pattern against its statically derived system call model, even in the presence of function pointers, signals, and setjmp/longjmp calls. *Paid* features several unique techniques:

- *Paid* inlines each system call site in the program with its associated system call stub so that each system call is uniquely labeled by the return address of its corresponding int 0x80 instruction,
- *Paid* inlines each call in the application call graph to a function having multiple call sites with the function's call graph, thus eliminating the non-determinism associated with the exit point of such functions,
- *Paid* introduces a notify system call that its compiler component can use to inform its run-time verifier component of information that cannot be determined statically such as function pointers, signal delivery, and to eliminate whatever non-determinism that cannot be resolved through system call inlining and graph inlining, and

– *Paid* inserts random null system calls (which are also part of the system call graph) at compile time and performs run-time stack integrity check to prevent attackers from mounting mimicry attacks.

The combination of these techniques enables *Paid* to derive an accurate DFA system call graph model from the source code of application programs, which in turn minimizes the run-time checking overhead. However, the current *Paid* prototype has one drawback: it does not perform system call argument analysis. But we will include this feature in the next version of *Paid*.

2 Related Work

2.1 System Call-Based Sandboxing

Many recent anomaly detection systems [22, 8, 18, 13, 9, 24, 15, 17] defines normal behavior model using run-time application activities. Although such systems cannot stop all attacks, they can effectively detect and stop many control hijacking attacks. Among these systems, system call pattern has become the most popular choice for modeling application behavior. However, simply keeping track of system calls may not be sufficient because it cannot capture other program information such as user-level application states.

Wagner and Dean's work [22] advocated a compiler approach to derive three different system call models, callgraph model (NFA), abstract stack or pushdown automaton model (PDA), and digraph model. Among all three models, the PDA model, which models the stack operations to eliminate the impossible paths, is the most precise model, but it is also the most expensive model in terms of time and space in many cases. *Paid*'s DFA model represents a significant advance over their work. First, *Paid* uses `notify` system call, system call inlining, and graph inlining to reduce the degree of non-determinism in the input programs. Second, *Paid* uses stack integrity check and random insertion of null system calls to greatly raise the barrier for mimicry attacks. Third, *Paid* is more efficient than Wagner and Dean's system in run-time checking overhead. For example, for a single transaction, their PDA model took 42 minutes for `qpopper` and more than 1 hour for `sendmail`, whereas *Paid* only takes 0.040679 seconds for `qpopper` and 0.047133 seconds for `sendmail`.

Giffin et al. [9] extended Wagner's work to application binaries for secure remote execution. They used null system call to eliminate impossible paths in their NFA model by placing a null system call after a function call. *Paid* is different from this work because it places a null system call only where non-determinism cannot be resolved through graph inlining and system call stub inlining. As a result, *Paid* can use the DFA model to implement a simple and efficient runtime verifier inside the kernel. Giffin et al. also tried graph inlining, which they called automaton inlining. They found graph inlining increases the state space dramatically, but *Paid*'s implementation on Linux only increases the state space around 100%. This discrepancy is due to the `libc` library on Solaris. For example, for a single `socket` call, it only needs a single edge or transition on Linux, while it takes more than 100 edges on Solaris. They found numerous other library functions that share the same problem. Giffin's PDA model is similar to Wagner's model, and they used a bounded-stack to solve the infinite stack problem. However, when the stack is full, the PDA model eventually becomes a less precise NFA model. Giffin et al. also proposed a Dyck model [10] to solve non-determinism problem by placing a null system call before and after a function call to simulate stack operation. To reduce performance overhead, a null system call from a function call does not actually trap to the kernel if the function call itself does not make a system call.

Behavior blocking is a variation of system call-based intrusion detection. Behavior blocking systems run applications in a sandbox. All sandboxed applications can only have the privileges specified by the sandbox. Even if an application is hijacked, it cannot use more privileges than as specified. Existing behavior blocking systems include MAPbox [1], WindBox [3], Janus [11], and Consh [2]. The key issue of behavior blocking systems is to define an accurate sandboxing policy, which is what *Paid* is designed for.

Systems such as StackGuard [6], StackShield [21] and RAD [5, 16] tried to protect the return addresses on the stack, which are common targets of buffer overflow attacks. Non-executable stack [19] prevents applications from executing any code on the stack. Another problem is that they cannot prevent attacks that target function pointers. IBM's GCC extension [7] reorders local variables and places all pointer variables at lower addresses than buffers. This technique offers some protection against buffer overflow attacks, but not buffer underflow attacks. Purify [12] instruments binaries to check each memory access at run time. However, the performance degradation and the increased memory usage are the key issues that prevent Purify from being used in production mode. Kiriansky [14] checks every branch instruction to ensure that no illegal code can be executed.

3   Program Semantics-Aware Intrusion Detection

3.1   Overview

Paid includes a compiler that automatically derives a system call site flow graph or SCSFG from an application's source code, and a DFA-based run-time verifier that checks the legitimacy of each system call. To be efficient, the run-time verifier of *Paid* is embedded in the kernel to avoid the context-switching overhead associated with user-level system call monitors. The in-kernel verifier has to be simple so that it itself does not introduce additional vulnerabilities. It also needs to be fast so as to reduce the performance overheard visible to applications. Finally it should not consume much of the kernel memory. The key challenge of *Paid* is to minimize the degree of non-determinism in the derived SCSFG such that the number of checks that the run-time verifier needs to perform is minimized.

Once an application's SCSFG is known, the attacker can also use this information to mount a mimicry attack, in which the attacker follows a legitimate path through the application's SCSFG until it reaches a system call she needs to deal the fatal blow. For example, assume an application has a buffer overflow vulnerability and the system call sequence following the vulnerability point is {open, setreuid, write, close, exec}, and an attacker needs setreuid and exec for her attack. After the attacker hijacks the application's control using a buffer overflow attack, she can mimic the legitimate system call sequence by interleaving calls to open, write and close with those to setreuid and exec properly, thus successfully fooling any intrusion detection systems that check only system call ordering. To address mimicry attacks, *Paid* applies two simple techniques: stack integrity check and random insertion of null system calls. In the next version of *Paid*, we will add a comprehensive checking mechanism on system call arguments as well.

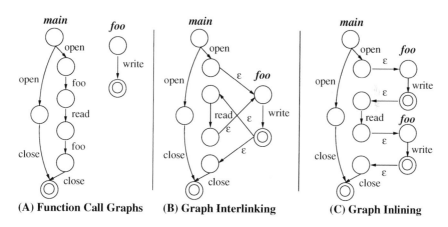

(A) Function Call Graphs   **(B) Graph Interlinking**   **(C) Graph Inlining**

Fig. 1. Graph interlinking and graph inlining are two alternative to constructing a whole-program system call graph from the system call graphs of individual functions

3.2   From NFA to DFA

The simplest way to construct a call graph for an application is to extract a local call graph for each function from the function's CFG, and then construct the final application call graph by linking per-function local call graphs using either *graph interlinking* or *graph inlining*, which are illustrated in Figure 1. A local call graph or an application call graph is naturally an NFA because of such control constructs as if-then-else and function call/return. To remove non-determinism, we employ the following techniques: 1) system call stub inlining, 2) graph inlining, and 3) insertion of notify system call.

One source of non-determinism is due to functions that have many call sites. For these functions, the number of out-going edges of the final state of their local call graph is more than one, as exemplified by the function foo in Figure 1(B). To eliminate this type of non-determinism, we use graph inlining as illustrated in Figure 1(C). In the application call graph, each call to a function with multiple call sites points to a unique duplicate of the function's call graph, thus ensuring that the final state of each such duplicated call graph have a single out-going edge. Graph inlining can significantly increase the state space if not applied carefully. We use an ε-transition removal algorithm to remove all non-system call edges from a function's CFG before merging the per-function call graphs.

Another source of non-determinism is due to control transfer constructs, such as `for loop`, `while loop` and `if-else-then`. One example of such problem is shown in Figure 1(C), where the program's control can go to two different states from the first state, at which an `open` system call is made. The reason for this non-determinism is that on a Linux system, system calls are made indirectly through system call stubs. Therefore, it is not possible to differentiate the open system call made in the then branch from that in the else branch. We address this problem by uniquely identifying each system call so that when a system call is made, the runtime checker knows who it is. More concretely, we inline every system call with its associated system call stub so that a system call can be uniquely identified with its return address.

System call stubs inlining does not completely solve the non-determinism problem due to flow control constructs, since it does not inline normal functions. An example of such non-determinism is shown as follows:

```
a()           b()           c()           main()
{             {             {             {
  open();       a();          a();          if(true)
}               read();       close();        b();
              }             }             else
                                            c();
                                        }
```

Since the functions a, b, and c are not inlined, the then branch and the else branch of `main` eventually lead to the same open system call even though the open system call stub is inlined. As another example, graph inlining cannot completely eliminate all non-determinism for recursive functions with multiple call sites, either. *Paid* introduces a new system call called `notify` to resolve whatever non-determinism is left after graph inlining and system call stub inlining are applied. The *Paid* compiler compiles an application in two passes. The first passes generates an NFA, and *Paid* visits every state of the NFA to detect non-determinism. When there is non-determinism, it traces back to the initial point that leads to the non-determinism and marks it accordingly. In the second pass the compiler inserts a `notify` call to each marked point to remove the corresponding non-determinism, and finally generates a DFA. Giffin et al [9, 10] used a similar idea to eliminate non-determinism due to multi-caller functions. However, blindly inserting `notify` calls can incur high performance overhead. *Paid* only inserts `notify` calls when non-determinism cannot be resolved by system call stub inlining and automaton inlining.

With system call stub inlining, graph inlining and `notify` system call insertion, the final call graph generated by the *Paid* compiler is actually a DFA, which we refer to as System Call Site Flow Graph or SCSFG. In addition to system call ordering, SCSFG also captures the exact location where each system call is made since all system call stubs are inlined. Also the final SCSFG does not contain any non system call, which reduces the state space dramatically since most of the function calls do not contain any system calls.

3.3   System Call Inlining

In Linux, system calls are made through system call stubs, and the actual trap instruction that transfers control to the kernel is `int $0x80` in the Intel X86 architecture. *Paid* inlines each system call site with the associated stub and the address of the instruction following int $0x80 becomes the unique label for the system call site. Figure 2(B) shows the result of inlining system call sites. LABEL_foo_0001 is the call site of the write system call in the *then* branch, and LABEL_foo_0003 is the call site of the write system call in the *else* branch. Figure 2(C) shows the SCSFG for the function foo, which includes a unique transition edge for each of the write system calls.

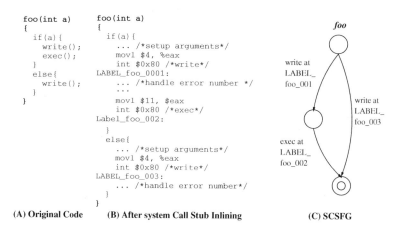

(A) Original Code   (B) After system Call Stub Inlining   (C) SCSFG

Fig. 2. After system call site inlining, the two write system calls can be distinguished based on their unique labels, as indicated by **LABEL_foo_0001** and **LABEL_foo_0003** in the result of inlining (B). Accordingly, the SCFG in (C) has two different write transition edges

System call site inlining is implemented via GCC front-end's function inlining mechanism. However, to exploit this mechanism, we need to rewrite all system call stubs so that they are suitable for inlining. Rewriting system call stubs turns out to be a time-consuming task because of various idiosyncrasies in the stubs. Some system call stubs such as open, read, and write are actually generated through scripts. Other system call stubs such as the exec family, the socket family, and clone need to be modified by hand so that they conform to the call stub convention used in GLIBC. Finally, the LIBIO library, which replaces the old standard I/O library in the new version of GLIBC, turns out to consume most of the rewriting effort. Although *Paid* does not inline normal functions, it chose to inline fopen and fwrite because they are important to system security. However, because fopen and fwrite use other functions in the LIBIO library and the actual open and write system call is made through a function pointer, we are forced to modify the whole LIBIO library so that function pointers are eliminated and the resulting functions are suitable for inlining.

To force GCC automatically to inline a function, the function has to be declared as always_inline, and the function has to be parsed before its callers. Therefore, all rewritten system call stubs are declared as always_inline, and are put in a header file called `syscall_inline.h`. The only modification to GCC for system call stub inlining is to make sure that the `syscall_inlined.h` is always loaded and parsed first before other header files and the original source file.

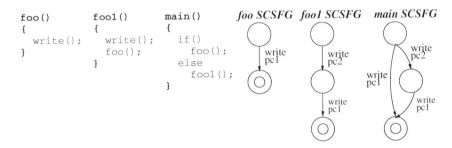

Fig. 3. *Paid's* compiler builds a SCSFG for each function, and the SCSFG for `main` represents the SCSFG for the entire program because of graphs inlining

3.4   Building System Call Site Flow Graph

Paid needs two passes to compile an application. The two passes are very similar except that during the first pass, *Paid* analyzes the resulting SCSFGs to find out where to insert notify calls to eliminate non-determinism. The second pass builds the final SCSFGs into a DFA model. *Paid's* compiler generates a call site flow graph (CSFG) for each function, which contains normal function calls and system calls in the function. Then starting with `main`'s CSFG, *Paid's* linker uses a depth first search algorithm to build a SCSFG for each function in a bottom up fashion. For example, if function `foo1` calls function `foo2`, `foo2`'s SCSFG is constructed first, and is then duplicated and inlined in the SCSFG of `foo1`. If the linker detects a recursive call chain, it inlines every function in the call chain and assigns the resulting graph as the call graph of the first function in the chain. For example, for the recursive call chain (a->b->c->a), the linker inlines the CSFG of c and b at their respective call sites and assigns the expanded graph to a. The result of inlining turns a call chain into a self-recursive call. After a SCSFG is generated, the linker uses a simple ε-transition removal algorithm to walk through the whole graph and remove all non-system-call nodes. In the end, each function's SCSFG contains only system call nodes, and an entry node and exit node. Because *Paid* inlines each function call graph, the SCSFG of `main` is the SCSFG for the whole program, which the run-time verifier uses to check each incoming system call. Finally, the linker stores all SCSFGs that contain at least one system call node, in an `.scsfg` section of the final ELF executable binary. Figure 3 shows a short program with its SCSFGs. It is still necessary to store the SCSFGs for individual functions because they may be needed when the main SCSFG is amended at run time, as described in the following subsection.

Many GLIBC functions are written in assembly language. We have to manually generate the CSFGs for those functions. The technique we use to generate CSFGs for functions written in assembly language is to compose dummy skeleton

C functions that preserve the call sequence of these functions, and then use the *Paid* compiler to compile the skeleton C functions. The CSFGs for the skeleton C functions are by construction the CSFGs for the assembly-code functions.

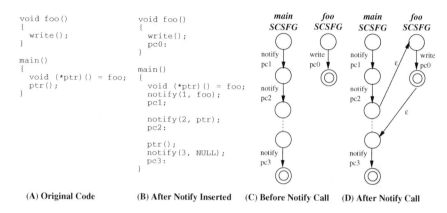

(A) Original Code   **(B) After Notify Inserted**   **(C) Before Notify Call**   **(D) After Notify Call**

Fig. 4. This demonstrates how a `notify` system call associated with a function pointer amends an application's SCSFG at run time. (C) shows the SCSFGs before `notify` is called. (D) shows how `notify` links the main SCSFG and the SCSFG of the target function, `foo`

3.5   Run-Time Notification

The original design of *Paid* assumes that the control flow graph of a program can be completely determined at compile time. This assumption is not valid because of branches whose target addresses cannot be determined statically, signals, unconventional control transfers such as setjmps/longjmps, etc. To solve this problem, *Paid* introduces a special run-time notification mechanism based on a special system call, `notify(int flag, unsigned address)`, which informs the run-time verifier of where the program control currently is at the time when the `notify` system call is made. *Paid* uses the `notify` system call for different purposes, each of which corresponds to a distinct value in the flag field. With the help of `notify`, *Paid*'s run-time verifier can synchronize with the monitored application across control transfers that cannot be determined at compile time. Because `notify` is a system call and is thus also subject to the same sandboxing control as other system calls, attackers cannot issue arbitrary `notify` system calls and modify the victim application's system call pattern.

Instead of applying pointer analysis, *Paid* inserts a `notify` system call before every function call that uses a function pointer. The actual value of the function pointer variable, or the entry point of the target function, is used as an argument to the `notify` system call, as shown by the second notify call in Figure 4(B). When a `notify` system call that *Paid*'s compiler inserts because of a function pointer traps into the kernel, and the target function's SCSFG has not been linked to the main SCSFG at the current execution point, the run-time verifier searches for the SCSFG of the target function and dynamically links the matched

SCSFG to the main SCSFG at the current execution point, as demonstrated by Figure 4(D). Because any function could potentially be the target of an indirect function call, *Paid* needs to store the SCSFGs for all functions. If a function is called from multiple call sites through a function pointer simultaneously, the main SCSFG may become an NFA. To avoid this, *Paid* also inserts a `notify` system call after every function call that uses a function pointer to inform the run-time verifier about which return path it should take. However, an attacker can overflow a function pointer to point to a desired existing function to exploit the attacks similar to return-to-libc attack. To reduce the attack possibilities, *Paid* also inserts a notify call at each location where a function's entry point is assigned to a function pointer, such as shown by the first notify call in Figure 4(B). The notify call informs the run-time verifier to mark the function, and the run-timer never links any unmarked function's SCSFG to the main SCSFG.

Setjmp and `longjmp` functions are for non-local control transfers. To handle `setjmp`/`longjmp` calls correctly, the *Paid* compiler inserts a `notify` call before each `setjmp` call, using the address of the jmp_buf object as an argument. The jmp_buf data structure is modified to include a pointer of the `notify` call in the SCSFG. The added pointer is also used to pass the corresponding `setjmp` return address to a `notify` call. When a `notify` system call due to `setjmp` is made, the run-time verifier first retrieves the `setjmp` return address from the jmp_buf and stores it in the current notify node, and then the verifier stores the current location, which is the address of the current `notify` node, in the jmp_buf object. *Paid*'s compiler also inserts a `notify` system call before a `longjmp call`, using the address of the jmp_buf as an argument. Upon a `notify` call due to `longjmp`, the run-time verifier retrieves the previous location from the jmp_buf object and links this location to the current location if the saved `setjmp` return address matches the `longjmp` destination address stored in the jmp_buf.

Signals are handled differently. For non-blocking signals, the kernel either ignores the signal, executes the default handler or invokes the user-supplied signal handler. In the first two cases no user code is executed and so no modifications are needed. However, if the application provides a signal handler, say `handle_signal`, the run-time verifier first creates a new system call node for the `sigreturn` system call, which is pushed on the user stack by the kernel, and links the new node to the final node of the SCSFG of `handle_signal`. Then the verifier saves the current SCSFG pointer in the new node, and changes the current SCSFG pointer to the entry node of the SCSFG of `handle_signal`. Finally, the `handle_signal` is executed. When `handle_signal` returns back to the kernel through the `sigreturn` system call, the run-time verifier restores the current SCSFG pointer from the one saved in the node corresponding to the `sigreturn` system call, and proceeds as normal.

3.6   Stack Integrity Check

System call stub inlining and sandboxing based on system call sites/ordering constraints force an attack code to jump to the actual system call sites in the program in order to issue a system call. However, when control is transferred to a system call site, it is not always possible for the attack code to grab the control back. To further strengthen the protection, *Paid*'s run-time verifier also checks the stack integrity by ensuring that all the return addresses in the stack are proper when a system call is made. If any return address is outside the original text segment, this indicates a control-hijacking attack may have occurred, because *Paid* explicitly forces all code regions to be read-only so that no attack code could be inserted into these regions. This simple stack integrity check greatly reduces the room that mimicry attacks have for maneuver as most such attacks need to make more than one system calls. Although GCC uses stack for function trampolines for nested functions, it does not affect the stack integrity check since function trampoline code does not make function calls. Also before executing a signal handler, Linux puts the `sigreturn` system call on the user stack and points the signal handler's return address to the `sigreturn` system call code in the stack. However, *Paid* can easily detects such return addresses by examing the code on the stack since the `sigreturn` invocation code is always the same.

3.7   Random Insertion of Null System Calls

To further improve the detection strength of *Paid* , *Paid* randomly inserts some null system calls into an application. A null system call is a `notify` system call that does not perform any operation. *Paid* randomly chooses some functions that do not lead to any system call between two consecutive system calls in a function call sequence to insert random `notify` call. For example, for the call sequence {`write`, `buf`, `a`, `b`, `c`, `exec`}, *Paid* may insert a `notify` call in the function `a` so that the new call sequence would be {`write`, `buf`, `a`, `notify`, `b`, `c`, `exec`}. Assuming that a buffer overflow happens in the function `buf`, the attack code cannot call `exec` directly since `notify` is before `exec` in the sequence, and the `notify` call is also included in the SCSFG. If the attacking code wants to call `exec`, it has to setup the stack to regain the control after it makes a `notify` call. However, since the verifier checks the stack when the `notify` is made, it detects the illegal return address on the stack and terminate the process. To make the remote attacks more difficult, one may be willing to recompile server applications and hide the binaries from the remote attackers. Since notify calls are inserted randomly, it is highly unlikely that an attack code can guess their existence and their call sites. Inserting null system calls provides the run-time verifier more observation points to monitor an application. Together with stack integrity check, it also forces attack code to follow more closely the application's original control flow.

   To randomly insert null system call, the first compilation pass analyzes the initial version of the SCSFGs and determines where to insert null system calls, and the second pass builds the final SCSFGs with random `notify` calls inserted. The exact algorithm for inserting null system calls in the current *Paid* prototype works as follows. For each two system calls A and B in an application SCSFG, if there exist a path from A to B where there is no other system call, *Paid* randomly chooses some functions that do not lead to any system call on the path to insert null system call. If the number of functions on a path is 2 to 4, the compiler randomly inserts a null system call into one of the functions. If the number of function calls is 5 to 7, it randomly inserts 2 null system calls; if the number is 8 and up, it inserts 3. Many paths may go through a same function;

however, *Paid* never inserts more than one null system calls in a function, and it always make sure that a null system call is inserted outside any loop.

Potentially an attacker can examine the binary to deduce the locations of these randomly inserted `notify` system calls. In practice, such attacks are unlikely because it is well known that perfect disassembly is not impossible on X86 architecture [16], due to the fact that distinguishing data and code is fundamentally undecidable, and *Paid* can randomly insert some dummy data into the instruction/text segment as an anti-disassembler technique.

3.8   Run-Time Verifier

Linux's binary loader is modified to load the `.scsfg` segment of an ELF binary into a randomly chosen region of its address space. That is, although the verifier performs system call-based sandboxing inside the kernel, the SCSFGs used in sandboxing reside in the user space, rather than in the kernel address space. To prevent attackers from accessing SCSFGs, the region at which the SCSFGs are stored is chosen randomly at load time. In addition, the SCSFG region is marked as read-only, so that it is not possible for an attacker to modify them without making system calls, which will be rejected because *Paid* checks every system call. When the run-time verifier needs to amend the main SCSFG due to a `notify` system call, it has to make the SCSFG region writable, and turns it back to read-only after the amendment. However, these operations are performed inside the kernel, and thus may override the region's read-only marking.

An *execution pointer* is added into Linux's `task_struct` to keep track of a process's current progress within its associated SCSFG. For each incoming system call, the verifier compares the system call number and the call site with each child of the node pointed to by the execution pointer. If a match is found, the execution pointer is moved to the matched node; otherwise, it indicates that an illegal system call is made, and the verifier simply terminates the process. Because a program's main SCSFG is a DFA, only a single execution pointer is needed and the SCSFG graph traversal implementation is extremely simple, only 45 lines of C code. Accordingly, the performance overhead of the run-time verifier is very small, as demonstrated in Section 5.

3.9   Support for Dynamically Linked Libraries

Paid treats the dynamically linked libraries as static linked libraries. It statically builds the SCSFGs for each DLL used by an application, and inlines the DLL SCSFGs to the main SCSFG of the application at the static linking time. However, for each DLL, there is a table to hold all call site addresses in the `.scsfg` segment. If a DLL is loaded at a different address than the preferred address, the loader will fix all its call site addresses in the associated table at load time. For libraries loaded by `dlopen` at run time, the pre-built SCSFGs of these libraries are copied to the application's own address space after the libraries are loaded. All library function calls via function pointers that are obtained by `dlsym` also rely on `notify` system calls, with an additional burden to fix call site addresses if a library is not loaded in the preferred location. The disadvantage of statically inlining the SCSFGs of the DLLs is that the resulting binaries cannot work with different versions of the same libraries.

3.10   Support for Threads

To support a multi-threaded application, *Paid* needs to maintain an execution pointer for each thread, and applies a mechanism similar to the way `setjmp/longjmp` is handled to switch the execution pointer at run time. At this point *Paid* does not support applications using user-level threads. However, this is not a limitation because most multi-threaded applications use kernel-level threads, which Linux supports through the `clone` system call. Although many applications use `pthread`, the `pthread` library of GLIBC actually uses kernel-level threads as well on Linux. We modified the `clone` and `fork` system calls so that the SCSFG region is copied when they are called.

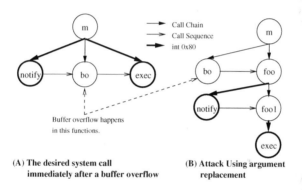

(A) The desired system call
immediately after a buffer overflow

(B) Attack Using argument
replacement

Fig. 5. This figure shows the two cases that *Paid* cannot handle. Figure (A) shows an attack that only needs a single system call and the desired system call is immediately after a buffer overflow. Figure (B) shows the argument replacement attack assuming that the arguments needed by `exec` are directly passed from the function `m` to the system call `exec` through the call chain. After the buffer overflow, the injected code sets up the desired arguments for the `foo` function, and then calls `foo` directly

4   Attack Analysis

Even though *Paid* uses several techniques to reduce the feasibility of mimicry attacks, there are two cases in which mimicry attacks are still possible as shown in Figure 5. First, if an attack code can compromise an application and then directly issue a damaging system call without requiring getting the control back, for example, when an `exec` system call immediately follows a buffer overflow vulnerability, *Paid* cannot stop this type of attacks. Second, if an attacker can mount an attack without making system calls explicitly, for example, by just manipulating the system call arguments of one or multiple legitimate system calls already in the program, *Paid* cannot stop this type of attacks, either. However, to the best of our knowledge these two types of attacks are very rare in practice.

Stack integrity check helps *Paid* to ensure that the stack state at the time a system call is made is proper. However, there is no guarantee that the monitored application indeed goes through the function call sequence as reflected in the chain of return addresses, because the attacker can easily doctor the stack frames before making any system call just to fool the stack integrity checking mechanism. None the less, stack integrity check at least greatly complicates the attack code, while incurring a relatively modest performance overhead, as shown in Section 6.

Because *Paid* embeds an application's SCSFG inside its binary file, and checks the application's run-time behavior against it, some ill-formed SCSFGs may cause *Paid*'s run-time verifier to misbehave, such as entering an infinite loop, thus leading to denial-of-service attacks. To the best of our knowledge, *Paid*'s run-time verifier does not have such weaknesses. As a second line of defense, *Paid* can perform run-time checks only for trusted applications, in a way similar to how only certain applications have their setuid bit turned on. Finally, the run-time verifier can include some self-monitoring capability, so that it can detect anomalous system call graphs and terminate the process.

5   Performance Evaluation

5.1   Prototype and Methodology

The current *Paid* compiler is derived from GCC 3.1 and GNU ld 2.11.94 (linker), and runs on Red Hat Linux 7.2. The *Paid* prototype can successfully compile the whole GLIBC (version 2.2.5), and production-mode network server programs implemented using `fork` or `clone` system call, such as Apache and Wu-ftp. For this study, we used as test programs the set of network server applications shown in Table 1, and compared *Paid*'s performance and space requirement with those of GCC 3.1 and Red Hat Linux 7.2, which represent the baseline case. To analyze detailed performance overhead, we conducted each experiment in four different configurations: plain *Paid* that only uses SCSFGs (plain *Paid*), *Paid* with stack integrity check (*Paid*/stack), *Paid* with random insertion of null system calls (*Paid*/random), and *Paid* with both stack integrity check and random null system calls (*Paid*/stack/random).

To test the performance of each server program, we used two client machines to continuously send 2000 requests to the tested server program. In addition, we modified the server machine's kernel to record the creation and termination time of each process. The throughput of a network server application is calculated by dividing 2000 by the time interval between the creation of the first forked process and the termination of the last forked process. The latency is calculated by taking the average of the run time used by the 2000 forked processes. The Apache web server program is handled separately in this study. We configured Apache to handle each incoming request with a single child process so that we could accurately measure the latency of each Web request.

The server machine is a 1.5-GHz P4 with 256MB memory, one client machine is a 300-MHz P2 with 128MB memory and the other client is a 1.1-GHz P3 with 512MB memory. They are connected through an isolated 100Mbps Ethernet link. All machines run Redhat Linux 7.2. To test http and ftp servers, the client machines continuously fetched a 1-KByte file from the server, and the two client programs were started simultaneously. In the case of pop3 server, the clients checked mails and retrieved a 1-KByte mail from the server. For the sendmail server, two clients continuously sent a 1-KByte mail to two different users. All client programs used in the test were modified in such a way that they continuously sent 1000 requests to the server. A new request was sent only after the previous one was completely finished. To speed up the request sending process, client programs simply discarded the data returned from the server. All network server programs tested were statically linked, and the modified GLIBC-2.2.5 library was recompiled by the *Paid* compiler.

5.2   Effectiveness

Two small programs with buffer overflow vulnerability were used to test the effectiveness of *Paid* in stopping attackers from making unauthorized system calls. The first program allows attackers to overflow the return address of one of its functions and point it to a piece of injected code that makes malicious system calls. *Paid*'s run-time checker successfully stopped the execution of the program since the injected system calls were not the next valid system calls in the original program's main SCSFG. The second program allows attackers to overflow a function pointer to point to a piece of dynamically injected code. Existing buffer overflow defense systems such as Stackguard/Stackshield and RAD cannot handle this type of attacks. However, the notify system call in *Paid* successfully detects this attack because the SCSFG of the injected code was not found in the original program's .scsfg segment. We also tested *Paid* on the "double free" vulnerability of wu-ftpd-2.6.0. The exploit script is based on the program written by TESO Security [20]. Again *Paid* is able to successfully stop this attack while the exploit successfully spawns a root shell from the ftpd that is compiled by the original GCC compiler.

5.3   Performance Overhead

Paid adds an extra .scsfg segment to an application's binary image to store all SCSFGs. The size of the .scsfg segment is expected to be large because it

Table 1. Characteristics of a set of popular network applications that are known to have buffer overflow vulnerability. The source code line count includes all the libraries used in the programs, excluding libc

Program Name	Lines of Code	Brief Description
Qpopper-4.0	32104	Pop3 server
Apache-1.3.20	51974	Web server
Sendmail-8.11.3	73612	Mail server
Wu-ftpd-2.6.0	28055	Ftp server
Proftpd-1.2.8	58620	Ftp server
Pure-ftpd-1.0.14	28182	Ftp server

Table 2. The binary image size and compilation time overhead of *Paid* compared with GCC. The absolute size of the `.scsfg` segment of each network application in bytes is also listed

Program Name	Plain Paid Binary Size Overhead	Plain Paid SCSFGs Size	Plain Paid Compile Time Overhead	Random Paid Binary size Overhead	Random Paid SCSFGs Size	Random Paid Compile Time Overhead
Qpopper-4.0	124.86%	798,780	119.30%	155.05%	996,840	121.00%
Apache-1.3.20	156.38%	1,338,739	232.98%	177.99%	1,529,224	247.92%
Sendmail-8.11.3	153.87%	1,845,208	198.15%	184.79%	2,073,524	211.53%
Wu-ftpd-2.6.0	149.47%	1,078,448	164.73%	173.04%	1,253,412	197.45%
Proftpd-1.2.8	178.02%	1,590,262	169.84%	194.12%	1,738,270	194.18%
pure-ftpd-1.0.14	116.27%	680,820	100.12%	128.85%	755,304	120.85%

contains the SCSFGs of all the functions in the application as well as in the libraries that the application links to. Because of the `.scsfg` segment, and because of system call inlining, the binary image of a network application compiled under the *Paid* compiler is much larger than that compiled under GCC. The binary image space overhead of the test applications ranges from 116.27% to 178.02% for the applications compiled by plain *Paid*, and from 128.85% to 194.12% for the applications compiled by *Paid* with random null system calls, as shown in Table 2. Most of the space overhead is indeed due to the `.scsfg` segment. The absolute size of this segment for each of the test network applications is also shown in Table 2. Note that this increase in binary size only stresses the user address space, but has no effect on the kernel address space size.

The *Paid* compiler also needs more time to extract the SCSFGs. Table 2 shows that the additional compilation time overhead of *Paid* when compared with GCC is from 100.12% to 232.98% for plain *Paid*, and from 120.85% to 247.92% for *Paid*/random. Under*Paid*'s compiler, compilation of applications takes two passes. Table 2 only shows the compilation time overhead of the second pass.

Table 3. The latency penalty of each network application compiled under *Paid* with different configurations when compared with the baseline case

Program	paid Latency Penalty	paid/stack Latency Penalty	paid/random Latency Penalty	paid/stack/rand Latency Penalty
Qpopper-4.0	5.69%	5.84%	6.42%	6.63%
Apache-1.3.20	5.14%	5.70%	6.93%	7.63%
Sendmail-8.11.3	7.31%	8.38%	10.32%	11.66%
Wu-ftpd-2.6.0	2.28%	2.76%	3.73%	4.58%
Proftpd-1.2.8	6.85%	7.63%	8.55%	9.85%
pure-ftpd-1.0.14	4.80%	5.33%	5.10%	7.58%

The performance overhead of *Paid* mainly comes from the additional check at each system call invocation. More specifically, it involves stack integrity check and the decision logic required to move to next DFA state. We measured the average latency penalty at each system call due to this check, and the results in

Table 5 show that this penalty is between 5.43% to 7.48%. However, the overall latency penalty of plain *Paid* compared to the base case (GCC + generic Linux) is smaller, as shown in Table 3 and Table 4, because each network application also spends a significant portion of its run time in the user space. As a result, the overall latency penalty of plain *Paid* ranges from 2.28% (wu-ftpd) to 7.31% (sendmail), and the throughput penalty ranges from 2.23% (Wu-ftpd) to 6.81% (Sendmail). These results demonstrate that despite the fact that *Paid* constructs a detailed per-application behavior model and checks it at run time, its run-time performance cost is really modest. This is also true for the *Paid*/stack/random configuration, which includes both stack check and random insertion of null system calls. The latency penalty for *Paid*/stack/random is from 4.58% (Wu-ftpd) to 11.66%(Sendmail), and the throughput latency penalty ranges from 4.38% (Wu-ftpd) to 10.44% (Sendmail).

Compared with plain *Paid*, *Paid*/Stack only increases the performance overhead slightly as shown in Table 3 and Table 4. The latency penalty of *Paid*/Stack ranges from 2.76% to 8.38%, and the throughput penalty ranges from 2.69% to 7.73%. This shows that checking the stack integrity at every system call is a relatively inexpensive verification mechanism. In contrast, *Paid*/random incurs more overhead than *Paid*/stack, because each null system call inserted incurs expensive context switching overhead. As the number of null system calls inserted increases, this overhead also increases, but the strength of protection against mimicry attacks also improves as attack codes are forced to follow more closely the application's original execution flow. The latency penalty for *Paid*/random ranges from 3.73% to 10.32%, and the throughput penalty ranges from 3.60% to 9.36%.

Table 4. The throughput penalty of each network application compiled under *Paid* with different configurations when compared with the baseline case

Program	paid Throughput Penalty	paid/stack Throughput Penalty	paid/random Throughput Penalty	paid/stack/rand Throughput Penalty
Qpopper-4.0	5.38%	5.52%	6.03%	6.22%
Apache-1.3.20	4.89%	5.39%	6.48%	7.09%
Sendmail-8.11.3	6.81%	7.73%	9.36%	10.44%
Wu-ftpd-2.6.0	2.23%	2.69%	3.60%	4.38%
Proftpd-1.2.8	6.41%	7.10%	7.87%	8.96%
pure-ftpd-1.0.14	4.58%	5.06%	4.85%	7.05%

One of the major concerns early in the development cycle of this project is the performance overhead associated with `notify` system calls, which are used to amend the main SCSFG at run time when functions are called through function pointers or other dynamic control transfers that cannot determine at compile time. Amending a SCSFG may take a non-negligible amount of time. In addition, the SCSFG region and the SCSFG's current execution point need to be copied to the child process as part of `fork` or `clone`. Copying of the SCSFG region actually does not incur serious performance overhead because Linux uses copy-on-write. However, when `notify` system calls are made, the SCSFG needs to be modified, and additional data copying is required to implement copy-on-write.

To study the impact of `notify` system calls due to function pointers on the application performance, we instrumented the *Paid* compiler and the run-time verifier to measure the `notify` system call frequency. Table 5 lists the number of `notify` calls inserted into each tested network application and the modified GLIBC statically. We also collected the actual number of `notify` calls made at run time. The number of dynamic `notify` calls includes both calls from the applications and the modified GLIBC. If the SCSFG of a function has been linked to the main SCSFG by a notify call at the same call site previously, the verifier does not need to search for the SCSFG again. The last column of the table shows the number of `notify` calls that actually need a full-scale search through the SCSFGs, or the number of `notify` cache misses.

The number of statically inserted `notify` calls ranges from 2 (wu-ftpd) to 247 (Apache), and the number of actual calls ranges from 92 (pure-ftpd) to 673 (Proftpd). The number of `notify` calls that need full SCSFG search ranges from 7 (wu-ftpd) to 33 (Proftpd). Even though Proftpd makes 673 `notify` calls at run time, its latency penalty is 9.85% and the throughput penalty is 8.96%. This low overhead mainly comes from the surprising low overhead associated with `notify` system calls. When SCSFG search is not needed, a `notify` system call only needs 1,745 CPU cycles. The average time requirement for a `notify` system call that needs SCSFG search is 3,383 CPU cycles. However, most of `notify` system calls do not need SCSFG search.

Table 5. The average per-system call latency penalty, the number of static and dynamic `notify` system calls, and the number of dynamic `notify` system calls that need full-scale SCSFG search

Program Name	Average System Call Overhead	Static Notify Count	Dynamic Notify Count	Notify Calls Need to Search for SCSFG
Qpopper-4.0	7.48%	111	49	7
Apache-1.3.20	5.61%	247	181	10
Sendmail-8.11.3	7.06%	69	386	16
Wu-ftpd-2.6.0	6.09%	2	99	7
Proftpd-1.2.8	6.89%	149	673	33
Pure-ftpd-1.0.14	5.43%	4	92	23
modified-GLIBC	N/A	604	N/A	N/A

6   Conclusion

System call-based intrusion detection provides the last line of defense against control-hijacking attacks because it limits what attackers can do even after they successfully compromise a victim application. The Achilles' heel of system call-based intrusion detection is how to efficiently and accurately derive a system call model that can be tailored to individual network applications. This paper describes the design, implementation, and evaluation of *Paid*, a fully operational compiler-based system call-based intrusion detection system that can automatically derive a highly accurate system call model from the source code of an arbitrary network application. One key feature of *Paid* is its ability to exploit run-time information to minimize the degree of non-determinism that is inherent in a pure static analysis approach to extracting system call graph. The other unique feature that sets *Paid* apart from all existing system call-based intrusion detection systems including commercial behavior blocking products, is its application of several techniques that together reduce the vulnerability window to mimicry attacks to a very small set of unlikely program patterns. As a result, we believe *Paid* represents one of the most comprehensive, robust, and precise host-based intrusion detection systems that are truly usable, scalable, and extensible. Performance measurements on a fully working *Paid* prototype show that the run-time latency and throughput penalty of *Paid* are under 11.66% and 10.44%, respectively, for a set of popular network applications including the Apache web server, the Sendmail SMTP server, a Pop3 server, the wu-ftpd FTP daemon, etc. Furthermore, by using a system call inlining technique, *Paid* dramatically reduces the run-time system call overhead. This excellent performance improvement mainly comes from the fact that the SCSFGs that *Paid*'s compiler generates is a DFA.

Currently, we are working on extending the *Paid* prototype in the following directions. First, we are developing compiler techniques that can capture system call arguments whose values can be statically determined or remain fixed after initialization. Being able to check system call arguments further shrinks the window of vulnerability to control-hijacking attacks. Second, we are exploring the feasibility of applying the same security policy extraction methodology on binary programs directly, so that even legacy applications whose source code is not available can enjoy the protection that *Paid* can provide.

References

1. A. Acharya and R. Mandar. Mapbox: Using parameterized behavior classes to confine untrusted applications. In *Proceedings of the Tenth USENIX Security Symposium*, 2000.
2. A. Alexandrov, P. Kmiec, and K. Schauser. Consh: A confined execution environment for internet computations. *In USENIX Ann. Technical Conf*, 99.
3. D. Balfanz and D. R. Simon. Windowbox: a simple security model for the connected desktop. In *Proceedings of the 4th USENIX Windows Systems Symposium*, pages 37–48, 2000.
4. CERT Corrdingation Center. Cert summary cs-2003-01. *http://www.cert.org/summaries/*, 2003.
5. T. cker Chiueh and F.-H. Hsu. Rad: A compiler time solution to buffer overflow attacks. In *Proceedings of International Conference on Distributed Computing Systems (ICDCS)*, Phoenix, Arizona, April 2001.
6. C. Cowan, C. Pu, D. Maier, H. Hinton, J. Walpole, P. Bakke, S. Beattie, A. Grier, P. Wagle, and Q. Zhang. Stackguard: Automatic adaptive detection and prevention of buffer-overflow attacks. In *Proceedings of the Seventh USENIX Security Symposium*, pages 63–78, San Antonio, Texas, January 1998.
7. H. Etho. Gcc extension for protecting applications from stack-smashing attacks. *http://www.trl.ibm.com/projects/security/ssp/*.
8. H. H. Feng, O. M. Kolesnikov, P. Fogla, W. Lee, and W. Gong. Anomaly detection using call stack information. In *Proceedings of the IEEE Symposium on Security and Privacy*, pages 62–76, Berkeley, CA, May 2003. IEE Press.

9. J. T. Giffin, S. Jha, and B. P. Miller. Detecting manipulated remote call streams. *USENIX Security Symposium*, August 2002.

10. J. T. Giffin, S. Jha, and B. P. Miller. Efficient context-sensitive intrusion detection. *11th Annual Network and Distributed System Security Symposium*, February 2004.

11. I. Goldberg, D. Wagner, R. Thomas, and E. A. Brewer. A secure environment for untrusted helper applications. In *Proceedings of the 6th Usenix Security Symposium*, San Jose, CA, USA, 1996.

12. R. Hastings and B. Joyce. Purify: Fast detection of memory leaks and access errors. In *Proceedings of the Winter USENIX Conference*, pages 125–136, 1992.

13. S. Hofmeyr, S. Forrest, and A. Somayaji. Intrusion detection using sequences of system calls. *Journal of Computer Security*, 6(3), 1998.

14. V. Kiriansky, D. Bruening, and S. Amarasinghe. Secure execution via program shepherding. *In 11th USENIX Security Symposium*, August 2002.

15. N. Nguyen, P. Reiher, and G. H. Kuenning. Detecting insider threats by monitoring system call activity. In *IEEE Information Assurance Workshop*, United States Military Academy West Point, New York, June 2003.

16. M. Prasad and T. cker Chiueh. A binary rewriting approach to stack-based buffer overflow attacks. In *Proceedings of 2003 USENIX Conference*, June 2003.

17. V. Prevelakis and D. Spinellis. Sandboxing applications. In *Proceedings of the FREENIX Track: 2001 USENIX Annual Technical Conference*, pages 119–126, Berkeley, CA, June 2001. USENIX Association.

18. R. Sekar, M. Bendre, P. Bollineni, and D. Dhurjati. A fast automaton-based method for detecting anomalous program behaviors. *IEEE Symposium on Security and Privacy*, pages 144–155, 2001.

19. Solar Designer. Non-executable user stack. *http://www.false.com/security/linux-stack/*.

20. TESO Security. x86/linux wu_ftpd remote root exploit. *http://packetstormsecurity.nl/0205-exploits/7350wurm.c.*

21. Vendicator. Stackshield: A "stack smashing" technique protection tool for linux. *http://www.angelfire.com/sk/stackshield/*.

22. D. Wagner and D. Dean. Intrusion detection via static analysis. In *Proceedings of the IEEE Symposium on Security and Privacy*, pages 156–169, Oakland, CA, May 2001. IEEE Press.

23. D. Wagner and P. Soto. Mimicry attacks on host-based intrusion detection systems. In *Proceedings of the 9th ACM Conference on Computer and Communications Security*, November 2002.

24. C. Warrender, S. Forrest, and B. Pearlmutter. Detecting intrusions using system calls: Alternative data models, May 1999.

Context Sensitive Anomaly Monitoring of Process Control Flow to Detect Mimicry Attacks and Impossible Paths*

Haizhi Xu, Wenliang Du, and Steve J. Chapin

Systems Assurance Institute, Syracuse University, Syracuse NY 13244, USA
{hxu02,wedu,chapin}@ecs.syr.edu

Abstract. Many intrusions amplify rights or circumvent defenses by issuing system calls in ways that the original process did not. Defense against these attacks emphasizes preventing attacking code from being introduced to the system and detecting or preventing execution of the injected code. Another approach, where this paper fits in, is to assume that both injection and execution have occurred, and to detect and prevent the executing code from subverting the target system. We propose a method using waypoints: marks along the normal execution path that a process must follow to successfully access operating system services. Waypoints actively log trustworthy context information as the program executes, allowing our anomaly monitor to both monitor control flow and restrict system call permissions to conform to the legitimate needs of application functions. We describe our design and implementation of waypoints and present results showing that waypoint-based anomaly monitors can detect a subset of mimicry attacks and impossible paths.

Keywords: anomaly detection, context sensitive, waypoint, control flow monitoring, mimicry attacks, impossible paths

1 Introduction

Common remote attacks on computer systems have exploited implementation errors to inject code into running processes. Buffer overflow attacks are the best-known example of this type of attacks. For years, people have been working on preventing, detecting, and tolerating these attacks [1–13]. Despite these efforts, current systems are not secure. Attackers frequently find new vulnerabilities and quickly develop adaptive methods that circumvent security mechanisms.

Host-based defense can take place at one of three stages: preventing code injection, preventing execution of the injected code, and detecting the attack after the injected code has begun execution. One class of detection mechanisms, execution-monitoring anomaly detection, compares a stream of observable events in the execution of a running process to a profile of "known-good" behavior, and raises alerts on deviations from the profile. While it is possible to treat each instruction executed by the process as an event for comparison to the profile, typical anomaly detectors use system calls [6, 14–17] or function calls [5, 18] as the granularity for events.

---

* This work was supported in part by a Syracuse University Graduate Fellowship Award.

E. Jonsson et al. (Eds.): RAID 2004, LNCS 3224, pp. 21–38, 2004.
© Springer-Verlag Berlin Heidelberg 2004

We focus our efforts on detecting attempts to subvert the system through the kernel API (the system call interface), assuming the attacking code has started to run. We monitor requests for system services (i.e., system calls) of running processes, and detect anomalous requests that could not occur as a result of executing the code in the original binary program image.

Two major problems that system-call based anomaly detection faces are mimicry attacks [12, 19] and impossible paths [12]. A mimicry attack interleaves the real attacking code with innocuous code, thereby impersonating a legitimate sequence of actions. For example, if the legitimate code has the system call sequence

```
getuid() ... open() ... execve()
```

and the attack has the sequence

```
getuid() ... execve()
```

the attacker can add a "no-op" system call to match the legitimate attack sequence:

```
getuid() ... open("/dev/null"...) ... execve().
```

We further divide mimicry attacks into global mimicry attacks and local mimicry attacks. Considering the minimum set of system calls necessary for the functionality of an application function, the system call sequence in a global mimicry attack combines the legal system calls of multiple functions, while a local mimicry attack uses the legal system calls of only the running function.

An impossible path is a control path (with a sequence of system calls) that will never be executed by the legal program, but is a legal path on the control flow graph of the program. Impossible paths can be generated due to the nature of the non-deterministic finite state automata (NDFSA). For example, when both location A and B can call function f(), function f() can return to either location A or B. The call graph for the program allows a return-into-others impossible path wherein location A calls function f(), but the return goes to location B, which behavior appears legal in the control flow graph. This example attack is similar to a return-into-lib(c) attack in that both of them modify the legal control path at the function return points.

This paper introduces our use of waypoints[1] for assisting anomaly monitoring. Waypoints are kernel-supported trustworthy markers on the execution path that the process must follow when making system calls. In this paper, we use function-level scoping as the context of a waypoint. If function C calls function D, then the active context is that of D; upon function return, the active context is again that of C. Waypoints provide control flow context for security checking, which supports call flow checking approaches such as that in Feng, et al. [5] and allows us to check whether the process being monitored has permission to make the requested system call in the context of the current waypoint.

---

[1] This terminology is borrowed from route planning using a GPS system, while the term is as old as navigation systems, meaning a specific location saved in the receiver's memory that is used along a planned route.

The work presented in this paper makes the following contributions:

1. Kernel-supported waypoints provide fine-grained trustworthy context information for on-line monitoring. Using this information, we can restrict a process to access only those system calls that appeared in the original program fragment associated with the waypoint context.

   Waypoints can change the granularity of intrusion detection systems that monitor system call sequences. The more waypoints we set between two system calls, the more precise control of that program path we can provide to the detector.

2. Using the context information, our anomaly monitor can detect global mimicry attacks that use permissions (i.e. allowed system calls) across multiple functions. Any system service request falling out of the permission set of the current context is abnormal.

3. Our anomaly monitor can detect return-into-others impossible paths attacks. We use waypoints to monitor the function call flow and to guarantee that callees return to the right locations.

In the next section, we describe our model of attacks in detail. Section 3 describes our design and implementation of waypoints and the waypoint-based system call monitor. In section 4 we present performance measurements of our approach. Section 5 summarizes related work. Section 6 discusses the limitations and our future work and gives our conclusions.

2   Attack Models

Once the exploit code has a chance to run, it can access the system interface in the following three ways, which we present in order of increasing code granularity:

1. Jumping to a system call instruction, or a series of such instructions, within the injected code itself. Many remote attacks use shellcode – a piece of binary code that executes a command shell for attackers [20]. Most shellcode issues system requests directly through pre-compiled binary code. In this case, the attacker relies on knowing the system call numbers and parameters at the time he compiles the attack code, which, in the presence of a near monoculture in system architecture and standardized operating systems, is a reasonable assumption. The control path in this case is fully under the control of the attacker, as he controls the location of the sensitive system call at the time of the code injection.

2. Transferring control to legitimate code elsewhere in the process; the target code can be at any link on the path to the system call instruction. The attacking code achieves its goal by executing from the target instruction forward to the desired system call. The attack can be achieved either by creating fake parameters and then jumping to a legitimate system call instruction, (e.g., making it appear that the argument to an existing execve() call was "/bin/sh"), or by jumping to a point on the path leading to an actual call (e.g. execve("/bin/sh")) in the original program. Locations used in the latter attack include a system call wrapper function in a system library such as libc, an entry in the procedure linkage table (PLT) using

the address in the corresponding global offset table (GOT), or an instruction in an application function that leads to calling the above entries. This is general form of the `return-into-lib(c)` attack [21], in which the corrupted return address on the stack forces a control transfer to a system call wrapper in the `libc` library. For the remainder of this paper we will refer to this type of attack as an low-level control transfer (LCT) attack. In contrast to defending against the shellcode attack, it is of paramount importance to protect the control path when defending against an LCT attack.

3. Calling an existing application function that performs the system call(s) that the attacking code requires. While this is a form of control transfer attack, we distinguish it from the LCT because the granularity of the attack is at the application function level, not at the level of the individual instruction or system call. In this case, the control path is the sequence of application-level function invocations leading to the function that contains the attacking call.

Mimicry attacks can be achieved by directly jumping to injected code that mimics a legal sequence of system calls or calling a sequence of lib(c) functions, which fall in the above category 1 and 2 attacks. Attackers can also use category 3 attacks (i.e. calling existing application functions), but this is easier to detect than the category 1 and 2 attacks by using call flow monitoring techniques. Attackers can also explore impossible paths to elude detection by using the above three categories attacking techniques.

While function call flow monitoring can reduce attacks in category 3, and non-executable data sections can block attacks in category 1, attacks using category 2 techniques are more difficult to detect because they use legitimate code to achieve malicious purposes. An important characteristic that attackers use is that the default protection model permits programs to invoke any system call from any function, but in actuality each system call is only invoked from a few locations in the legal code. While some previous work has exploited the idea of binding system calls or other security sensitive events with context [5, 18, 22–24], this paper explores this approach further. We introduce the concept of waypoints to provide trustworthy control flow information, and show how to apply the information in anomaly detection.

3 Waypoint-Based System Call Access Control

We observe that an application function – a function in an application program, not a library function – in general uses only a small subset of system service routines[2], but has the power to invoke any system call under the default Unix protection model. This practice violates the principle of least privilege, which restricts a function to only invoke systems calls that are necessary for its proper execution. For example, `execve()` is not used by many legitimate functions, especially in setuid root regions, but it is common for exploit code to invoke that system call within the scope (or equivalently, the stack frame) of any vulnerable function. Waypoints provide a mechanism for restricting program access to system calls and enforces least privilege.

---

[2] For example, in table 1 and 2 of section 3.3, only 3 out of 416 application functions being monitored require `execve()` legally.

3.1 Waypoint Design

A waypoint, located in the code section, is a trustworthy checkpoint on control flow. Waypoints can actively report control flow information in real-time to assist intrusion detection, rather than gathering the information only at system call time. People can assign security attributes to each waypoint or to a sequence of waypoints.

To achieve our goals, waypoints must embody the following properties:

1. Authentication

   Because we assume that an attack has successfully started executing, and the attack has the right to access the whole process image, it is possible that the attacking code can overwrite code pointers. Although the code section is usually read-only, dynamically-generated code will be located in memory with both read and write permissions. This means that attackers have the ability to generate waypoints within their own code, and we must therefore authenticate waypoints.

   We authenticate the waypoints by their locations. Waypoints are deployed before the process runs, such that the waypoint locations are registered at program loading time. In this way, we can catch false waypoints generated at run time.

2. Integrity

   Because attackers can access the whole process image, information generated at and describing waypoints (e.g., their privileges) should be kept away from malicious access. We store all waypoint-related data and code in the kernel.

3. Compatibility

   Our waypoints work directly on binary code, so the original code may be generated from different high-level languages or with different compilers.

A natural granularity for control flow monitoring is at the function level. To trace function call flow, we set up waypoints at function entrance and exit. We generate waypoints and their associated permissions on a per-function basis through static analysis.

At run time, we can construct a push-down automata of the waypoints that parallels the execution stack of the process. An <u>entrance waypoint</u> disables the permissions of the previous waypoint, pushes the entrance waypoint on top of the waypoint stack, and enables its permissions. A corresponding <u>exit waypoint</u> discards the top value on the waypoint stack and restores the permissions of the previous waypoint.

It is possible that we assign different permissions to different parts of a function. In this case, we need a <u>middle waypoint</u>. A middle waypoint does not change the waypoint stack. It only changes permissions for the waypoint.

We deploy waypoints only in the application code. Although we do not set waypoints in libraries, we are concerned about library function exploitation. We treat security relevant events (system requests) triggered by library functions as running in the context of the application function that initiated the library call(s).

The waypoint stack records a function call trace. Using this context information, our access monitor can detect attacks in two ways: (1) <u>flow monitoring</u> – Globally, waypoints comprise the function call trace for the process. We can construct legal waypoint paths for some security critical system requests (e.g. execve ( )), such that when such a system call is made, the program must have passed a legal path. Similar ideas on control flow monitoring have been proposed in [5, 25], therefore, we do not discuss this approach further in this paper. (2) <u>permission monitoring</u> – Locally, we use static analysis to determine the set of system calls (permissions) required for each function, and ensure system calls invoked in the context of a function appears in its permission set.

3.2   Waypoint Implementation

If a piece of code needs to perform a system request legally, then we say that the piece of code has a <u>permission</u> to issue the system request. To simplify the implementation, we use a set to describe permissions for a waypoint and store the permission sets in a bitmap table.

We generate waypoints and their corresponding permissions through static analysis. We introduce global control flow information by defining the number of times that a function can be invoked. Usually, an application function does not issue system requests directly. It calls system call wrappers in the C library instead. The application may call the wrapper functions indirectly by calling other library functions first. We build a (transitive) map between system call wrappers and system call numbers. Currently, we analyze the hierarchical functions manually. Our next step is to automate this whole procedure.

We deploy the access monitor, together with the waypoint stack and the permission bitmap table, in the operating system kernel, as shown in figure 1. There are two fields in an entry of the waypoint stack, one is the location of the waypoint, the other is extra information for access monitoring. Since we monitor application function call flow, we use this field to store the return address from the function. In one application function, there is one entry waypoint and one exit waypoint, the pair of which is stored in the bitmap table. Field "entries" in the bitmap table indicates how many times a waypoint can be passed. In our current implementation, we only distinguish between one entry and multiple entries to avoid malicious jump to prologue code and function main(), which usually contain some dangerous system calls and should be entered only once.

At a waypoint location, there should be some mechanism to trigger the waypoint code in the kernel. We can invoke the waypoint code at several locations: an exception handler, an unused system call number service routine, or a new soft interrupt handler. We insert an illegal opcode at the waypoint location and run our waypoint management code as an exception handler.

An attacker can overwrite the return address or other code pointer to redirect control to a piece of shellcode or a library function. We protect the return address by saving it on the waypoint stack when we pass the entrance waypoint. When a waypoint return is executed at the exit waypoint, the return address on the regular stack is compared with the saved value on the waypoint stack for return address corruption. The exit waypoint identifier must also match with the entrance waypoint identifier, since they come in pairs. If the attacking code uses an unpaired exit waypoint or a faked waypoint, the comparison will fail. If the attack forces return into a different address, although the control flow can be changed, the <u>active permission set</u> – the permission set belonging to the most recently activated waypoint – is not changed, because the expected exit waypoint has not passed. The attacking code will still be limited to the unchanged permissions.

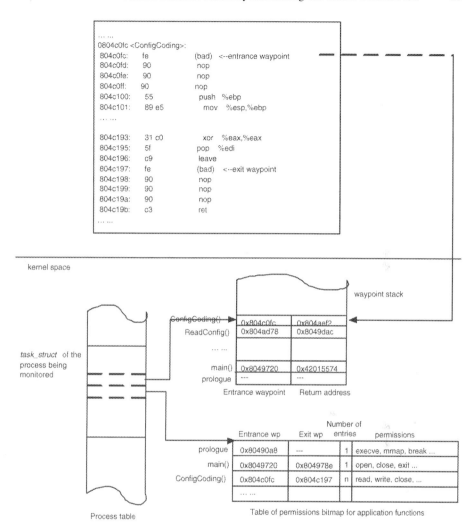

Fig. 1. Data structures needed for the waypoint-based access monitor: a waypoint stack and a table of permission bitmaps. The third column of the bitmap table indicates how many times a waypoint may be activated. The prologue code and function <u>main()</u> are allowed to run only one time during the process life. Function <u>ConfigCoding()</u> can be called unlimited times.

3.3   Monitoring Granularity

In our implementation, each waypoint causes a kernel trap, and each guarded function has at least two waypoints (an entrance/exit pair, plus optional middle waypoints). Thus, the performance of the system is dependent on the granularity of waypoint insertion. Our first implementation monitored every function, irrespective of whatever system calls the function contained. As reported in section 4, the overhead can be substantial.

Not all system calls are equally useful for subverting a system. We define <u>dangerous system calls</u> as those rated at threat level 1 in [26]. There are 22 dangerous system calls in Linux: chmod, fchmod, chown, fchown, lchown, execve, mount, rename, open, link, symlink, unlink, setuid, setresuid, setfsuid, setreuid, setgroups, setgid, setfsgid, setresgid, setregid, and create_module. Such system calls can be used to take full control of the system.

Table 1 and 2 show the number of functions containing dangerous system calls, and the permissions distribution. The tables show us that only a small portion of the application functions invoke dangerous system calls. Most functions call at most one dangerous system call, and no function calls more than three. Only three functions (two in tar and one in kon2) in the whole table require exec. Most functions invoking three dangerous system calls contain only file system-related calls such as open, symlink, and unlink.

Table 1. Number of functions invoking dangerous system calls, and the calls distribution. Only 12% (50) of functions in our analysis use dangerous system calls, while 1.2% (5) of them contains 3 dangeous calls.

program	# of applica- tion functions totally	# of functions containing dan- gerous system calls	containing 3 dangerous system calls	containing 2 dangerous system calls	containing 1 dangerous system calls
enscript	48	8	0	0	8
tar	165	26	3	3	20
gzip	92	6	1	3	2
kon2	111	10	1	5	4
totally	416	12%	1.2%	2.6%	8%

Table 2. Number of functions invoking dangerous system calls. For example, 20 functions in tar invokes open or rename. Only 0.7% (3) of all functions in our analysis call execve.

program	# of functions	create_module	execve	setu(/g)id	open/rename	chown(/mod)	link, sym(/un)link
enscript	48	0	0	0	8	0	0
tar	165	0	2	1	20	3	4
gzip	92	0	0	0	3	2	5
kon2	111	0	1	1	6	4	2
totally	416	0	0.7%	0.5%	9%	2.2%	2.6%

The distribution of dangerous system calls shows that partitioning of system call permissions should be effective. If an exploit happens within the context of one function, the attacker can use only those system calls authorized for that function, which significantly restricts the power of attack in gaining control of the system. Existing code-injection attacks exploit flaws in input routines, which do not, in general, have permission to call dangerous system calls. Open, however, is used widely in application functions (9% of application functions use it), requiring further restrictions to its parameters.

The numbers show that as an alternative of monitoring every function, we can monitor only functions containing dangerous system calls to detect subversions. In this case, we have a default permission set that allows all other system calls, and only deploy waypoints when switching between the general, default permissions and the strict, specific permissions associated with the function that uses dangerous system calls. This is a conscious trade-off of capability for performance; we no longer have a full waypoint stack in the kernel that reflects all function calls during program execution, but the overhead decreases significantly, as shown in figure 3 of section 4.

3.4 Waypoint-Based Anomaly Monitoring

After generating waypoints and their permission sets for a program, we monitor the program at run time. The procedure of the waypoint-based security monitor can be described in the following steps:

1. Marking a process with waypoints
   At the process initialization stage, we mark a process by setting a flag in its corresponding task_struct in the process table, indicating whether the process is being monitored or not. For a process being monitored, we set up a waypoint stack and create a table of permission bitmaps for the waypoints. The permission sets are generated statically.

2. Managing the waypoints at run time
   Waypoints are authenticated by their linear addresses. We implement the management procedure in an exception handler. When an exception is triggered, we first check whether it is a legitimate waypoint or not. A legitimate waypoint satisfies three conditions: (1) the process is being monitored; (2) the location of the exception (waypoint location) can be found in the legal waypoint list; and (3) the number of times that the waypoint is activated is less than or equal to the maximum allowed times. If the conditions are not satisfied, we pass control to the regular exception handler.

   After the verification, we manage the waypoint stack according to the type of the waypoint. If it is an entrance waypoint, we push it onto the waypoint stack and activate its permission set; if it is a middle waypoint, we only update the permissions; and if it is an exit waypoint, we pop the corresponding entrance waypoint from the stack and restore the previous permission set. After that, we emulate the original instruction if necessary, adjust the program counter to the location of the next instruction and return from the exception handling. To simplify implementation, we insert 4 nops at the waypoint locations and change the first nop to a waypoint instruction (i.e. a bad instruction in our implementation). In this way, we can avoid emulating the original instructions, because nops perform no operations.

3. Monitoring system requests

We implemented the access monitor as an in-kernel system call interceptor in front of the system call dispatcher. In terms of access control logic, the subject is the application function; the object is the system call number; and the operation is the system call request. After trapping into the kernel for a system call, the access control monitor first verifies whether the current process is being monitored or not. If yes, the monitor fetches the active waypoint from the top of the waypoint stack and its corresponding permission set from the permissions bitmap table. If the request belongs to the permission set, the monitor invokes the regular system service routine; otherwise, the monitor refuses the system call request and writes the violation information in the kernel log.

3.5   Implementation Issues

We have considered the following issues in our implementation:

1. monitoring offspring processes

We monitor the offspring processes the same way as we monitor the parent process. A child process inherits the monitor flag, the permission bitmap table, the waypoint stack, and the stack pointer from the parent process. If the child is allowed to run another program (e.g. by calling `execve()`), then the waypoint data structures of the new program will replace the current ones.

2. multiple-thread support

Linux uses light-weight processes to support threads efficiently. Monitoring a light-weight process is similar to monitoring an ordinary process, but requires a separate waypoint stack for every thread. Our current implementation does not support thread-based access monitoring.

3. number of passes

By restricting the number of times a waypoint can be passed during a process life time, we can monitor some global control flow characteristics efficiently. In particular, we allow the program prologue to start only one time, because it typically invokes dangerous system calls and is logically intended to run only once. We also allow `main()` to start only once per process execution.

4. non-structured control flow

Control flow does not always follow paths of function invocation. In the C/C++ languages, the `goto` statement performs an unconditional transfer of control to a named label, which must be in the current function. Because `goto` does not cross a function boundary, it does not affect function entrance and exit waypoints. However, it might jump across a middle waypoint, so we do not put any middle waypoints between a goto instruction and the corresponding target location.

`Setjmp` sets a jump point for a non-local goto, using a `jmp_buf` to store the current execution stack environment, while `longjmp` changes the control flow with the value in such a data structure. At the `setjmp` call, we use a waypoint to take a snapshot of the in-kernel waypoint stack and the `jmp_buf`, while at the `longjmp` location, a waypoint ensures that the target structure matches a `jmp_buf` in the kernel, and replaces the current waypoint stack with the corresponding snapshot.

5. permissions switch with a low-overhead policy

Under our low-overhead policy, we only monitor functions that invoke dangerous system calls. These functions may call one another, or call a function with only default permissions, or vice versa. Permissions are switched on the function call boundary. In the forward direction, where the caller has specific, elevated permissions, we use a middle waypoint to switch to the default permission set before calling, and switch the permissions back after returning. If the callee has specific, elevated permissions, regular entrance and exit waypoints will activate them.

6. the raw system interface

To control the target system, an attacker may use the raw system interface (e.g. /dev/mem and /dev/hda). This is an anomaly to most applications. Our waypoint-based defense will restrict the opportunities for the attacker to call open, but further defenses, e.g. parameter checking, are necessary for complete defense. Our current implementation does not employ parameter checking. See [5, 25–27] for further information on parameter monitoring.

3.6 Evasion Attacks and Defenses

Because the waypoint structures and code are located in the kernel, attackers cannot manipulate them directly. However, an adaptive attack may create an illegal instruction in the data sections as a fake waypoint or jump to the middle of a legitimate instruction (in an X86 system) to trigger the waypoint activation mechanism. As we explained in section 3.2, our waypoint management code can recognize the fake waypoints because all the legitimate waypoints are loaded into the kernel at load time. If an attack intentionally jumps over a waypoint, although it can change the control flow, the waypoint stack is not updated neither is the permission set.

Our waypoint mechanism was originally designed to counter attacks of category 1 (shellcode based attacks) and category 2 (LCT attacks) described in section 2, because these attacks bypass waypoints and therefore fail to acquire the associated permissions. Evasion attacks may use the category 3 attack (function granularity attacks), if these functions invoke the exact system calls and in the correct order, required by the attacker. For such programs, the low-overhead policy may not supply sufficient trace information to support function call flow monitoring, so full monitoring on function call path should be done.

If an attack launches a local mimicry attack, using one or a sequence of legitimate system calls of the current context, our mechanism cannot detect it. This is general case of abuse of the raw system interface mentioned above, and in similar fashion, we must employ complementary techniques. In our implementation, we adopt system interface randomization [2, 28] to counteract shellcode-based local mimicry attacks.

Existing implementations of system call number randomization [2] uses a permutation of the system call numbers. A simple permutation of the relatively small space (less than 256 system calls) allows attackers to guess the renumbering for a particular system call in 128 tries on average, or 255 guesses in the worst case.

To survive this brute force attack, we use a substitution cipher to map from 8-bit system call numbers to 32-bit numbers, thereby making a brute-force attack on the system impractical. In Linux, a system call number n is an unsigned 8-bit integer between

0 and 255, and is carried to the kernel in register %eax, a 32-bit register, of which 24 bits are unused. In our implementation, we make use of the whole register to carry the 32-bit system call number. We generate a one-to-one mapping between the 8-bit system call numbers and their corresponding 32-bit secrets. The access monitor restores the original number correspondingly upon a system call.

3.7   An Example

To demonstrate the effectiveness of our waypoint mechanism, we attacked a real application program in Linux, using both shellcode and return-into-lib(c) attacks. We chose kon2 version 0.3.9b as the target. kon2 is a Kanji emulator for the console. It is a setuid root application program. In version 0.3.9b, there is a buffer overflow vulnerability in function ConfigCoding() when using the -Coding command line parameter. This vulnerability, if appropriately exploited, can lead to local users being able to gain root privileges [29]. Part of the source code of the vulnerable function ConfigCoding() is shown in figure 2(a), with the vulnerable statement highlighted. Figure 2(b) shows its original binary code, and figure 2(c) shows the binary code with waypoints added.

To help the shellcode attack reach our waypoint mechanism, we disabled the system call renumbering and return address comparison features of our system during our experiment. In the following attack and defense experiment, we show how the waypoint mechanism can detect malicious system calls in both shellcode based and return-into-lib(c) based attacks.

- Attack 1: calling a system call instruction located in the shellcode
  In the attack, the return address of function ConfigCoding() is overflowed. In this experiment, the faked return address redirects to a piece of shellcode. Without our protection, the attacking code generated a shell. With our mechanisms deployed, the malicious system request execve(''/bin/sh'') was caught and the shell was not generated. At the location of the ret instruction, an exit waypoint is triggered, and the permissions for ConfigCoding()'s parent function (ReadConfig()) are activated. Because execve() is not among the permissions of ReadConfig(), the system request is denied. It is interesting to see that if the return address is overwritten, the malicious request is issued in the context of the parent function, because the malicious request is issued after the execution of instruction ret and the exit waypoint. If our mechanisms are fully deployed, the exit waypoint will guarantee that the return address is not faked.
- Attack 2: A low-level control transfer attack
  Recall that a low-level control transfer attack can redirect control to legitimate code for malicious purposes. In our experiment, we use the location of int execve (const char *filename, char *const argv[], char *const envp[]), a sensitive libc function, in the attacking code. Because neither ConfigCoding() nor its caller ReadConfig() have the permission to call system call execve(), the request is rejected by our monitor.
  Note, it is difficult to detect the return-into-lib(c) attacks. Program shepherding [25] ensures that library functions are called at only library entrance locations, and the

```
static int     ConfigCoding(const char *confstr)
{
    char reg[3][MAX_COLS]; <--Fixed size buffer  MAX_COLS=256
    int n, i;

    *reg[0] = *reg[1] = *reg[2] = '\0';
    sscanf(confstr, "%s %s %s", reg[0], reg[1], reg[2]);
    ^^^^^^^^^^^^^^^^^^^^^^^^^^^^^^^buffer overflow vulnerability here


    ... ...
    return SUCCESS;
}
```

(a) A buffer–overflow vulnerable function in kon2

```
0804c0fc <ConfigCoding>:
    804c0fc:      90              nop
    804c0fd:      90              nop
    804c0fe:      90              nop
    804c0ff:      90              nop
    804c100:      55              push   %ebp
    804c101:      89 e5            mov    %esp,%ebp
    ... ...

    804c193:      31 c0            xor    %eax,%eax
    804c195:      5f              pop    %edi
    804c196:      c9              leave
    804c197:      90              nop
    804c198:      90              nop
    804c199:      90              nop
    804c19a:      90              nop
    804c19b:      c3              ret
```

(b) the original binary code

```
0804c0fc <ConfigCoding>:
    804c0fc:      fe              (bad)  <--entrance waypoint
    804c0fd:      90              nop
    804c0fe:      90              nop
    804c0ff:      90              nop
    804c100:      55              push %ebp
    804c101:      89 e5            mov    %esp,%ebp
    ... ...

    804c193:      31 c0            xor    %eax,%eax
    804c195:      5f              pop    %edi
    804c196:      c9              leave
    804c197:      fe              (bad)  <--exit waypoint
    804c198:      90              nop
    804c199:      90              nop
    804c19a:      90              nop
    804c19b:      c3              ret
```

(c) the binary code with waypoints added

Fig. 2. A buffer overflow vulnerable function in kon2 and its waypoints.

library callee functions must exist in the external symbol table of the ELF format program. In kon2, because `execl()` and `execlp()` are used at other locations, there are corresponding entries in the external symbol table; so at any library entrance point, this request can pass the shepherding check. In addition, program shepherding monitors control flow only, so it is possible for an attack to compromise control flow related data (e.g. GOT), making the return-into-lib(c) attack realistic. In an IDS without control flow information, because `execve()` is used in the program, a mimicry attack may pass the check.

The only dangerous system call in the context of `ConfigCoding()` is `open()`. Within this context, the attacker does not have much freedom in gaining control of the system. Launching an `execve()` requires a global mimicry attack that crosses function boundaries, which is subject to both the call flow and permissions monitoring.

4   Overhead Measurement and Analysis

We measured the overhead of the waypoint-based access monitor on a system of Red-Hat Linux 9.0 (kernel version 2.4.20-8) on a 800MHz AMD Duron PC with 256MB memory.

The overhead of the waypoint-based access monitor has two main causes: waypoint registration in the exception handler and running the access monitor at each system call. The system call mapping is done before running, so it does not introduce any run-time overhead. The remapping at each system call is a binary search on a 256 entry table in our implementation. Because the remapping takes only tens of instructions, this overhead is negligible. The access monitor at the system call invocation compares the coming request number with the permission bitmap. These comparison operations cost little time. Therefore, the majority of the overhead is from the additional trap for the waypoint registration code in the exception handler, where caches and pipelines will be flushed.

Our measurement on a micro-benchmark program that calls a monitored function in a tight loop shows that the overhead for one waypoint invocation is 0.395 microseconds on average. This captures the cost of exception handling, but does not reveal overhead due to cache and pipeline flushing.

To better understand these effects on real applications, we tested a few well known GNU applications. We did not use real time, the time between program start and end, because the overhead can be hidden by the overwhelming I/O time. Instead, we use user time and sys time, the time that measures the process running in user mode and kernel mode, correspondingly. These time gives us an accurate understanding of the overhead.

As shown in figure 3, when we monitor all functions, the user time increases by about 10%–20%, but the system time increases dramatically. We attribute the increase in user time to the flushing of cache and pipelines. In the GNU programs we measured 3-5 times overhead due to our waypoint mechanism.

When we monitor only dangerous functions, the overhead is smaller than for monitoring all functions. Dangerous-function monitoring for `enscript`, `gzip` and `gunzip` introduces small overhead, but the overhead for `tar` is still high. In `gunzip`, there are only a few function calls for checking the zip file and for decompressing it.

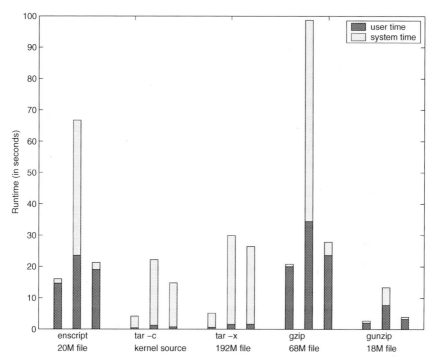

Fig. 3. Overhead of the waypoint-based access monitor. For every group, the left side bar shows the time of running the original program; the middle bar shows its running time under waypoint-based access monitoring for all functions; and the right side bar shows the result with monitoring only functions that invoke dangerous system calls.

Because there are only a few waypoint invocations in the entire program execution, the running time is close to the original running time. We conclude that the overhead depends on not only how many functions are monitored, but also how frequently these functions are invoked.

5   Related Work

There are three layers of defense in preventing attacks from subverting the system. The first layer of defense is to prevent the malicious data and code from being injected, typically by avoiding and tolerating implementation errors in the system. Existing techniques include language-based or compiler-based techniques, such as type checking [9, 30–32], or protecting data pointers [33] and format strings [3]. The second layer of defense is to prevent malicious code from being executed. Prevention methods include instruction set randomization [34, 35], non-executable stack and heap pages [8, 10], process image randomization [10, 13], and stack integrity guarding [4, 11]. The third layer of defense attempts to prevent the executing attack code from doing further harm though the system interface. Existing work at this stage includes anomaly detection [5, 6, 12, 24, 25, 27], process randomization [2, 10, 13, 28, 36], and instruction set randomization [34, 35].

Realizing that lack of context information in detection leads to certain false negatives possible (e.g., the impossible-path problem and the mimicry attacks), some anomaly monitors apply partial context information in anomaly detection [5, 24, 25]. The benefit of using context information is that control path information between two system call invocations can help detecting anomaly.

Retrieving user call stack information in system call interceptor [5] is promising in bringing function call flow information to the anomaly monitor. We explore this approach further by providing trustworthy control flow information to the monitor. One other difference is that while [5] emphasize the call stack signature at a system call invocation, we put much effort on guarding with the permissions of application functions. Program shepherding [25] uses an interpretor to monitor the control flow of a process. It enforces application code to call library functions only through certain library entrance points, and the target library function must be one of the external functions listed in the external symbol table of the application executable. Because program shepherding does not monitor the data flow, some control flow information, such as function pointers, may be overwritten. If the overwritten pointer happens to be a library entry point, and the attack chooses a library function that is used at any other locations in the program, the attack can pass the check. Context related permissions can help in this situation. [24] associates a system call with its invocation address. The return-into-lib(c) attack calls a library function, rather than a piece of shellcode. In this case, the locations do not provide enough control path information to the detector.

6   Conclusion

In this paper, we propose a new mechanism – waypoints – to provide trustworthy control flow information for anomaly monitoring. We demonstrated how to use our waypoint mechanism to detect global mimicry attacks. Our approach can also catch return-into-others impossible paths by guarding the return addresses. Implementing waypoints by kernel traps provides reliable control path information, but slows down an ordinary program by 3-5 times. As a trade-off, by monitoring only dangerous system calls, we can reduce the overhead by 16%-70%, but no longer monitor the complete function call path.

As noted in our discussion of access to the raw system interface, waypoint-based detection cannot find local mimicry attacks, because the function has the proper permissions required to invoke the dangerous system calls. In our current implementation, we associate a permission set with each waypoint, but a state machine can provide tighter monitoring than a set. We will also investigate the use of complementary techniques, such as parameter checking, to extend waypoints to defend against local mimicry attacks.

Impossible paths may be generated at multiple granularities. Our waypoint mechanism can detect only function-granular return-into-others impossible paths by guarding return addresses.

Our waypoint mechanism cannot directly detect attacks through interpreted code. Because we work at the binary code level, our mechanism does not "see" the interpreted code. Rather, it monitors the interpreter itself, and so only sees actions taken by the interpreter in response to directives in the interpreted code.

So far, we generate waypoints and their permissions statically, which does not support self-loading code. Our future work will be to support self-loading code by moving waypoint set up procedure (by code instrumentation) to program load time. Additional future work is to optimize performance. Some optimizations that we have discussed are hoisting waypoints out of loops and merging waypoints for several consecutively called functions.

Our prototype implementation of the waypoint mechanism for Linux X86 system may be downloaded from http://www.sai.syr.edu/projects.

Acknowledgments

We thank Kyung-suk Lhee and the anonymous referees for their helpful comments.

References

1. Baratloo, A., Tsai, T., Singh, N.: Libsafe: Protecting critical elements of stacks. Technical report, Avaya Labs Research (1999)
2. Chew, M., Song, D.: Mitigating buffer overflows by operating system randomization. Technical report, CMU department of computer science (2002)
3. Cowan, C., Barringer, M., Beattie, S., Kroah-Hartman, G., Frantzen, M., Lokier, J.: Format-Guard: Automatic Protection From printf Format String Vulnerabilities. In: proceedings of the 2001 USENIX Security Symposium, Washington D.C. (2001)
4. Cowan, C., Pu, C., Maier, D., Hinton, H., Walpole, J., Bakke, P., Beattie, S., Grier, A., Wagle, P., Zhang, Q.: StackGuard: Automatic Adaptive Detection and Prevention of Buffer-Overflow Attacks. In: Proceedings of the 7th USENIX Security Symposium, San Antonio, Texas (1998)
5. Feng, H.H., Kolesnikov, O.M., Fogla, P., Lee, W., Gong, W.: Anomaly Detection Using Call Stack Information. In: Proceedings of the 2003 IEEE Symposium on Security and Privacy, Berkeley, CA (2003)
6. Forrest, S., Hofmeyr, S.A., Somayaji, A., Longstaff, T.A.: A Sense of Self for Unix Processes. In: Proceedings of the 1996 IEEE Symposium on Security and Privacy. (1996)
7. Purczynski, W.: (kNoX – implementation of non-executable page protection mechanism)
8. Solar Designer: Non-Executable User Stack, (http://www.openwall.com/linux/)
9. Lhee, K., Chapin, S.J.: Type-Assisted Dynamic Buffer Overflow Detection. In: Proceedings of the 11th USENIX Security Symposium, San Francisco (2002)
10. the Pax team: design & implementation of PaX, (http://pageexec.virtualave.net/docs/index.html)
11. Vendicator: StackShield: A "stack smashing" technique protection tool for linux, (http://www.angelfire.com/sk/stackshield/)
12. Wagner, D., Dean, D.: Intrusion detection via static analysis. In: Proceedings of the 2001 IEEE Symposium on Security and Privacy. (2001)
13. Xu, J., Kalbarczyk, Z., Iyer, R.K.: Transparent Runtime Randomization for Security. In: Proceedings of the 22nd Symposium on Reliable and Distributed Systems (SRDS), Florence, Italy (2003)
14. Ghosh, A., Schwartzbard, A.: A study in using neural networks for anomaly and misuse detection. In: 8th USENIX security symposium. (1999)
15. Lee, W., Stolfo, S.: Data mining approaches for intrusion detection. In: 7th USENIX security symposium, San Antonio, TX (1998)

16. Warrender, C., Forrest, S., Pearlmutter, B.: Detecting Intrusions Using System Calls: Alternative Data Models. In: Proceedings of the 1999 IEEE Symposium on Security and Privacy. (1999)

17. Wespi, A., Dacier, M., Debar, H.: Intrusion detection using variable-length audit trail patterns. In: 3rd International workshop on the recent advances in intrusion detection. Volume LNCS 1907, Springer. (2000)

18. Abadi, M., Fournet, C.: Access control based on execution history. In: Proceedings of the 2003 Network and Distributed System Security Symposium. (2003)

19. Wagner, D., Soto, P.: Mimicry attacks on host-based intrusion detection systems. In: Proceedings of the 9th ACM Conference On Computer And Communication Security, Washington, DC, USA (2002)

20. Aleph One: Smashing The Stack For Fun And Profit. www.Phrack.org **49** (1996)

21. Nergal: The advanced return-into-lib(c) exploits. www.Phrack.org **58** (2001)

22. Box, D.: Essential .NET, Volume I: The Common Language Runtime. Addison Wesley (2002)

23. Gong, L., Ellison, G., Dageforde, M.: Inside Java 2 Platform Security: Architecture, API Design, and Implementation (2nd Edition). Addison Wesley (1999)

24. Sekar, R., Bendre, M., Dhurjati, D., Bollineni, P.: A fast automaton-based method for detecting anomalous program behaviors. In: Proceedings of the IEEE Symposium on Security and Privacy, IEEE Computer Society (2001) 144

25. Kiriansky, V., Bruening, D., Amarasinghe, S.: Secure execution via program shepherding. In: Proceedings of the 11th USENIX Security Symposium, San Francisco, CA (2002)

26. Bernaschi, M., Gabrielli, E., Mancini, L.V.: Enhancements to the linux kernel for blocking buffer overflow based attacks. In: 4th Linux showcase & conference. (2000)

27. Sekar, R., Venkatakrishnan, V., Basu, S., Bhatkar, S., DuVarney, D.C.: Model-carrying code: a practical approach for safe execution of untrusted applications. In: Proceedings of the nineteenth ACM symposium on Operating systems principles, ACM Press (2003) 15–28

28. Somayaji, A., Hofmeyr, S., Forrest, S.: Principles of a Computer Immune System. In: Proceedings of the 1997 New Security Paradigms Workshop, UK (1997)

29. Red Hat security: Updated kon2 packages fix buffer overflow (2003)

30. Ashcraft, K., Engler, D.R.: Using programmer-written compiler extensions to catch security holes. In: Proceedings of the 2002 IEEE Symposium on Security and Privacy, Oakland, CA (2002)

31. Necula, G.C.: Proof-carrying code. In: Proceedings of the 24th ACM SIGPLAN-SIGACT Symposium on Principles of Programming Langauges (POPL '97), Paris (1997) 106–119

32. Lhee, K., Chapin, S.J.: Buffer Overflow and Format String Overflow Vulnerabilities. Software – Practice & Experience **33** (2003) 423–460

33. Cowan, C., Beattie, S., Johansen, J., Wagle, P.: Pointguard: Protecting pointers from buffer overflow vulnerabilities. In: Proceedings of the 12th USENIX Security Symposium. (2003)

34. Barrantes, E.G., Ackley, D.H., Forrest, S., Palmer, T.S., Stefanovic, D., Zovi, D.D.: Randomized instruction set emulation to disrupt binary code injection attacks . In: Proceedings of the 10th ACM Conference On Computer And Communication Security. (2003)

35. Kc, G.S., Keromytis, A.D., Prevelakis, V.: Countering Code-Injection Attacks With Instruction-Set Randomization. In: Proceedings of the 10th ACM Conference On Computer And Communication Security. (2003)

36. Bhatkar, S., DuVarney, D.C., Sekar, R.: Address obfuscation: An efficient approach to combat a broad range of memory error exploits. In: Proceedings of the 12th USENIX Security Symposium, Washington D.C. (2003)

HoneyStat: Local Worm Detection Using Honeypots

David Dagon, Xinzhou Qin, Guofei Gu, Wenke Lee,
Julian Grizzard, John Levine, and Henry Owen

Georgia Institute of Technology
{dagon,xinzhou,guofei,wenke}@cc.gatech.edu
{grizzard,levine,henry.owen}@ece.gatech.edu

Abstract. Worm detection systems have traditionally used global strategies and focused on scan rates. The noise associated with this approach requires statistical techniques and large data sets (e.g., 2^{20} monitored machines) to yield timely alerts and avoid false positives. Worm detection techniques for smaller local networks have not been fully explored.

We consider how local networks can provide early detection and compliment global monitoring strategies. We describe HoneyStat, which uses modified honeypots to generate a highly accurate alert stream with low false positive rates. Unlike traditional highly-interactive honeypots, HoneyStat nodes are script-driven, automated, and cover a large IP space.

The HoneyStat nodes generate three classes of alerts: memory alerts (based on buffer overflow detection and process management), disk write alerts (such as writes to registry keys and critical files) and network alerts. Data collection is automated, and once an alert is issued, a time segment of previous traffic to the node is analyzed. A logit analysis determines what previous network activity explains the current honeypot alert. The result can indicate whether an automated or worm attack is present.

We demonstrate HoneyStat's improvements over previous worm detection techniques. First, using trace files from worm attacks on small networks, we demonstrate how it detects zero day worms. Second, we show how it detects multi vector worms that use combinations of ports to attack. Third, the alerts from HoneyStat provide more information than traditional IDS alerts, such as binary signatures, attack vectors, and attack rates. We also use extensive (year long) trace files to show how the logit analysis produces very low false positive rates.

Keywords: Honeypots, Intrusion Detection, Alert Correlation, Worm Detection

1 Introduction

Worm detection strategies have traditionally relied on artifacts incidental to the worm infection. For example, many researchers measure incoming scan rates (often using darknets) to indirectly detect worm outbreaks, e.g., [ZGGT03]. But since these techniques measure noise as well as attacks, they often use costly algorithms to identify worms. For example, [ZGGT03] suggests using a Kalman filter [Kal60] to detect worm attacks. In [QDG$^+$], this approach was found to work with a large data set but proved inappropriate for smaller networks.

E. Jonsson et al. (Eds.): RAID 2004, LNCS 3224, pp. 39–58, 2004.

To improve detection time and decrease errors caused by noise, the solution so far has been to increase monitoring efforts, and gather more data. The intuition is that with more data, statistical models perform better. Thus, researchers have suggested the creation of global monitoring centers [MSVS03], and collecting information from distributed sensors. These efforts are already yielding interesting results [YBJ04,Par04].

Although the need for global monitoring is obvious, the value this has for local networks is not entirely clear. For example, some local networks might have enough information to conclude a worm is active, based on additional information they are unwilling to share with other monitoring sites. Likewise, since global detection strategies require large amounts of sensor data, worm outbreaks may be detected only after local networks fall victim. Also, we see significant problems in gaining consensus among different networks, which frequently have competing and inconsistent policies regarding privacy, notification, and information sharing. Without doubt, aggregating information from distributed sensors makes good sense. However, our emphasis is on local networks and requires a complimentary approach. In addition to improving the *quantity* of monitoring data, researchers should work to improve the *quality* of the alert stream.

In this paper, we propose the use of honeypots to improve the accuracy of alerts generated for local intrusion detection systems. To motivate the discussion, we describe in Section 3 the worm infection cycle we observed in honeypots that led to the creation of HoneyStat. Since honeypots usually require labor-intensive management and review, we describe in Section 4 a deployment mechanism used to automate data collection. HoneyStat nodes collect three types of events: memory, disk write and network events. Section 4 describes these in detail, and discusses a way to compare and correlate intrusion events. Using logistic regression, we analyze previous network traffic to the honeypot to see what network traffic most explains the intrusion events. Intuitively, the logit analysis asks if there is a common set of network inputs that precede honeypot intrusions. Finding a pattern suggests the presence of an automated attack or worm.

To demonstrate HoneyStat's effectiveness, in Section 6, we describe our experience deploying HoneyStat nodes, and a retrospective analysis of network captures. We also use lengthy (year long) network trace files to analyze the false positive rate associated with the algorithm. The false positive rate is low, due to two influences: (a) the use of honeypots, which only produce alerts when there are successful attacks, and (b) the use of user-selected confidence intervals, which let one define a threshold for alerts. Finally, in Section 7, we analyze whether a local detection strategy with a low false positive rate (like HoneyStat) can make an effective worm detection tool. We consider the advantages this approach has for local networks.

2   Related Work

Honeypots. A honeypot is a vulnerable network decoy used for several purposes: (a) distracting attackers, (b) gathering early warnings about new attack techniques, (c) facilitating in-depth analysis of an adversary's strategies [Spi03,Sko02]. By design, a honeypot should not receive any network traffic, nor will it run any legitimate production services. This greatly reduces the problem of false positives and false negatives often found in other types of IDS systems.

Traditionally, honeypots have been used to gather intelligence about how human attackers operate [Spi03]. The labor-intensive log review required of traditional honeypots makes them unsuitable for a real-time IDS. In our experience, data capture and log analysis time can require a 1:40 ratio, meaning that a single hour of activity can require a week to fully decipher [LLO+03].

The closest work to our own is [LLO+03], which uses honeypots in an intrusion detection system. We have had great success at the Georgia Institute of Technology utilizing a Honeynet as an IDS tool, and have identified a large number of compromised systems on campus, mostly the result of worm-type exploits. Other researchers have started to look at honeypot alert aggregation techniques [JX04], but presume a centralized honeypot farming facility. Our simplified alert model allows for distributed honeypots, but is more focused on defending local networks.

Researchers have also considered using virtual honeypots, particularly with honeyd [Pro03]. Initially used to help prevent OS fingerprinting, honeyd is a network daemon that exhibits the TCP/IP stack behavior of different operating systems. It has since been extended to emulate some services (e.g., NetBIOS). Conceptually, honeyd is a daemon written using libpcap and libdnet. To emulate a service, honeyd requires researchers to write programs that completely copy the service's network behavior. Assuming one can write enough modules to emulate all aspects of an OS, a single machine can delay worms by inducing needless connections.

Recently, honeyd was offered as a way to detect and disable worms [Pro03]. We believe this approach has promise, but must overcome a significant hurdle before it is used as an early warning IDS. It is not clear how a daemon emulating a network service can catch zero day worms. If one knows a worm's attack pattern, it is possible to write modules that will behave like a vulnerable service. But before this is known, catching zero day worms requires emulating even the *presumably unknown* bugs in a network service. We were unable to find solutions to these limitations, and so do not consider virtual networks as a means of providing an improved alert stream. Instead, we used full honeypots.

More closely related to our work, [Kre03] suggested automatic binary signature extraction using honeypots. This work used honeyd, flow reconstruction, and pattern detection to generate IDS rules. The honeycomb approach also has promise, but uses a very simple algorithm (longest common substring) to correlate payloads. This makes it difficult to identify polymorphic worms and worms that use multiple attack vectors. Honeycomb was well suited for its stated purpose, however: extracting string signatures for automated updates to a firewall.

Worm Detection. Worm propagation and early detection have been active research topics in the security community. In worm propagation, researchers have proposed an epidemic model to study worm spreading, e.g., [Sta01,ZGT02,CGK03,WL03]. For early detection, researchers have proposed statistical models, e.g., Kalman Filter [ZGGT03], analyzing repeated outgoing connections [Wil02], ICMP messages collected at border routers to infer worm activity [BGB03] and victim counter-based detection algorithms [WVGK04]. All these approaches require a large deployment of sensors or a large monitoring IP space (e.g., 2^{20} IP addresses). Others suggest a "cyber Center for Disease Control" to coordinate data collection and analysis [SPN02]. Researchers have also proposed various data collection and monitoring architectures, e.g., "network telescopes" [Moo02b] and an "Internet Storm Center" [Ins].

Our objective is also to conduct early worm detection. However, considering the current difficulty and challenges in large space monitoring system (e.g., conflicts in data sharing, privacy, and coordinated responses), our detection mechanism is based on local networks, in particular, local honeypots for worm detection. In our prior work [QDG$^+$] we analyzed the current worm early detection algorithms, i.e., [ZGGT03] and [WVGK04], and found instability and high false positives when applying these techniques to local monitoring networks.

Event Correlation. Several techniques have been proposed for the alert/event correlation, e.g., pre-/post-condition-based pattern matching [NCR02,CM02,CLF03], chronicles formalism [MMDD02], clustering technique [DW01] and probabilistic-based correlation technique [VS01,GHH01]. All these techniques count on some prior knowledge of attack step relationships. Our approach is different in its need to detect *zero-day* worm attacks, and does not depend on prior knowledge of attack steps. Statistical alert correlation was presented in [QL03]. Our work is different in that our correlation analysis is based on variables collected over *short* observations. Time series-based analysis proposed in [QL03] is good for relatively long observation variables and requires a series of statistical tests in order to accurately correlate observations.

3   Worm Infection Cycles

If local networks do not have access to the volume of data used by global monitoring systems, what local resources can they use instead? Studying worm infections gives some insights, and identifies what data can be collected for use in a local IDS.

Model of Infection. A key assumption in our monitoring system is that the worm infection can be described in a systematic way. We first note that worms may take three types of actions during an infection phase. The Blaster worm is instructive, but we do not limit our model to this example. Blaster consists of a series of modules designed to infect a host [LUR03].

Memory Events. The infection process, illustrated in Figure 1(a), begins with a probe for a victim providing port 135 RPC services. The service is overflowed, and the victim spawns a shell listening on a port, usually 4444. (Later generations of the worm use different or even random ports.) This portion of the infection phase is characterized by memory events. No disk writes have taken place, and network activity cannot (yet) be characterized as abnormal, since the honeypot merely ACKs incoming packets. Still, a buffer overflow has taken place, and the infection has begun by corrupting a process.

Network Events. The Blaster shell remains open for only one connection and closes after the infection is completed. The shell is used to instruct the victim to download (often via tftp) an "egg" program. The egg can be obtained from the attacker, or a third party (such as a free website, or other compromised hosts.) The time delay between the initial exploit and the download of the egg is usually small in Blaster, but this may not always be the case. Exploits that wait a long period to download the egg risk having the service restarted, canceled, or infected by competing worms (e.g., Nachi). Nonetheless, some delay may occur between the overflow and the "egg" transfer. All during this time, other harmless network traffic may arrive. This portion of the infection phase is often characterized by network traffic. Downloading the egg for example requires the honeypot to initiate TCP (SYN) or UDP traffic. In some cases, however, the entire worm payload can be included in the initial attack packet [Sta01,Moo02a,ZGT02]. In such a case, network events may not be seen until much later.

Disk Events. Once the Blaster egg is downloaded, it is written to a directory so it may be activated upon reboot. Some worms (e.g., Witty [LUR04]) do not store the payload to disk, but do have other destructive disk operations. Not every worm creates disk operations.

These general categories of events, although present in Blaster, do not limit our analysis to just the August 2003 DCOM worm. A local detection strategy must anticipate future worms lacking some of these events.

Improved Data Capture. Traditional worm detection models deal with worm infection at either the start or end of the cycle shown in Figure 1(a). For example, models based on darknets consider only the rate and sometimes the origin of incoming scans, the traffic at the top of the diagram. The Destination Source Correlation (DSC) model [GSQ+04] also considers scans, but also tracks outgoing probes from the victim (traffic from the bottom of the diagram). The activity in the middle of the cycle (including memory and disk events) can be tracked.

Even if no buffer overflow is involved, as in the case of mail-based worms and LANMAN weak password guessing worms (e.g., pubstro worms), the infection still follows a general pattern: a small set of attack packets obtain initial results, and further network traffic follows, either from the egg deployment, or from subsequent scans.

Intrusion detection based only on incoming scan rates must address the potentially high rate of noise associated with darknets. As noted in Figure 1(a), every phase of the infection cycle may experience non-malicious network traffic. Statistical models that filter the noise (e.g., Kalman) require large data sets for input. It is no wonder, then, that scan-based worm detection algorithms have recently focused on distributed data collection.

4   HoneyStat Configuration and Deployment

The foregoing analysis of the worm infection cycle generally identified three classes of events that one might track in an IDS: memory, disk and network events. As noted above in Section 2, it is difficult to track all of these events in virtual honeypots or even in stateful firewalls. Networks focused on darknets, of course, have little chance of getting even complete network events, since they generally blackhole SYN packets, and never see the full TCP payload.

A complete system is needed to gather the worm cycle events and improve the data stream for an IDS. We therefore use a HoneyStat node, a minimal honeypot created in an emulator, and multihomed to cover a large address space. The deployment typically would not be interesting to attackers, because of its minimal resources (limited memory, limited drive size, etc.) Worms, however, are indiscriminating and use this configuration.

In practice, we can use VMware GSX Server as our honeypot platform. Currently, VMware GSX Server V3 can support up to 64 isolated virtual machines on a single hardware system [VMW04]. Mainstream operating systems (e.g. Windows, Linux, FreeBSD) all support multihoming. For example, Windows NT allows up to 32 IP addresses per interface. So if we use a GSX server with 64 virtual machines running windows and each windows having 32 IP addresses, then a single GSX machine can have $64 * 32 = 2^{11}$ IP addresses.

In practice, we found nodes with as little as 32MB RAM and 770MB virtual drives were more than adequate for capturing worms. Since the emulators were idle for the vast majority of time, many instances could be started on a single machine. Although slow and unusable from a user perspective, these virtual honeypots were able to respond to worms before any timeouts occur.

The honeypots remain idle until a *HoneyStat event* occurs. We define three types of events, corresponding to the worm infection cycle discussed in Section 3.

1. `MemoryEvent`. A honeypot can be configured to run buffer overflow protection software, such as a StackGuard [Inc03], or similar process-based monitoring tools. Likewise, Windows logs can be monitored for process failures and crashes. Any alert from these tools constitutes a HoneyStat event. Because there are no users, we found that one can use very simple anomaly detection techniques that would otherwise trigger enormous false positive rates on live systems. Since there are no users, even simple techinques work well.
2. `NetworkEvents`. The honeypots are configured to generate no outgoing traffic. If a honeypot generates SYN or UDP traffic, we consider it an event.
3. `DiskEvents`. Within the limits of the host system, we can also monitor honeypot disk activities and trap writes to key file areas. For example, writes to systems logs are expected, while writes to `C:\WINNT\SYSTEM32` are clearly events. In practice, we found that kqueue [Lem01] monitoring of flat virtual disks was reasonably efficient. One has to enumerate all directories and files of interest, however.

Data recorded during a HoneyStat event includes: (a) The OS/patch level of the host. (b) The type of event (memory, net, disk), and relevant capture data. For memory events, this includes stack state or any core, for network events this is the outgoing packet, and for disk events this includes a delta of the file changes, up to a size limit. (c) A trace file of all prior network activity, within a bound t_p, discussed in Section 5.

Based on our analysis in Section 3, we believe this to be a complete set of features necessary to observe worm behavior. However, new worms and evasive technologies will require us to revisit this heuristic list of features. Additionally, if HoneyStat is given a larger mission (e.g., e-mail virus detection or trojan analysis instead of just worm detection), then more detailed features must be extracted from the honeypots.

Once events are recorded, they are forwarded to an analysis node. This may be on the same machine hosting the honeypots, or (more likely) a central server that performs logging and propagates the events to other interested nodes. Figure 1(b) shows a conceptual view of one possible HoneyStat deployment. In general, the analysis node has a secure channel connecting it with the HoneyStat servers. Its primary job is to correlate alert events, perform statistical analysis, and issue alerts.

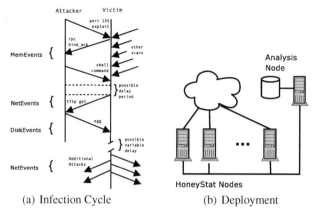

(a) Infection Cycle   (b) Deployment

Fig. 1. a) A time line of a Blaster worm attack. Because of modular worm architectures, victims are first overflowed with a simple RPC exploit, and instructed to obtain a separate worm "egg", which contains the full worm. The network activity between the initial overflow and download of the "egg" constitutes a single observation. Multiple observations allow one to filter out other scans arriving at the same time. b) HoneyStat nodes interact with malware on the Internet. Alerts are forwarded through a secure channel to an analysis node for correlation.

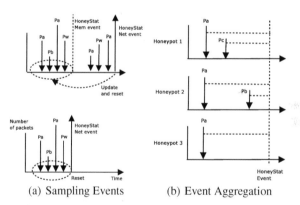

(a) Sampling Events   (b) Event Aggregation

Fig. 2. a) In the top diagram, a HoneyStat `MemEvent` occurs, and the honeypot is allowed to continue, in hopes of capturing an egg or payload. (The event is immediately analyzed, however, without delay.) If a subsequent `NetEvent` occurs, we update the previous `MemoryEvent` event and reset. In the bottom diagram, we see a `NetEvent` without any prior `MemoryEvent`, indicating our host-based IDS did not spot any anomaly. We immediately reset, and analyze the circled traffic segment. b) Aggregating multiple honeypot events can help spot a pattern. In all three diagrams, activity P_a is observed, even though others (P_b, P_c) appear closer in time to the event.

HoneyStat events are placed in a work queue and analyzed by worker threads. We can prioritize certain types of events, such as when outgoing connections attempt to reach many different IPs (i.e., it looks like a worm scanning.) These events are obviously more important than others, since they suggest an automated spread mechanism instead of a single connection back to the attacker's IP. This idea borrows from the work of researchers who observed the importance of tracking distinct destination IPs in worm detection systems [JPBB04,WVGK04]. Future work will explore queue processing and other prioritizations.

Several actions are taken when a HoneyStat event is analyzed.

1. First, we check if the event corresponds to a honeypot that has already been recorded as "awake" or active. If the event is a continuation of an ongoing infection, we simply annotate the previous event with the current event type. For example, if we first witness a MemoryEvent, and then see a DiskEvent for the same honeypot, we update the MemoryEvent to include additional information, such as the DiskEvent and all subsequent network work activity. The intuition here is that MemoryEvents are usually followed by something interesting, and it is worth keeping the honeypot active to track this.

2. Second, if the event involved NetworkEvents (e.g., either downloading an egg or initiating outgoing scans), the honeypot reporting the event is reset. The idea here is two-fold. In keeping with the principle of honeypot Data Control [LLO⁺03], we need to prevent the node from attacking other machines. Also, once network activity is initiated, we have enough attack behavior recorded to infer that the worm is now infective. If only DiskEvents or MemoryEvents are observed, the node is not reset.

   Since the honeypot is deployed using an emulator, resets are fast in practice. One merely has to kill and restart the emulator, using in round-robin style a fresh copy of the virtual disk. The disk image is kept in a suspended state, and no reboot of the guest OS is required. The reset delay is slight, often seconds or a minute, and always in practice completes before TCP timeouts occur. The effect of startup time on detection is considered in the analysis in Section 6.

3. Third, the analysis node examines basic properties of the event, and determines whether it needs to redeploy other honeypots to match the affected OS. The intuition here is that HoneyStat nodes are often deployed to cover a variety of operating systems: Linux, Windows, and with different patch levels. If one of the systems falls victim to a worm, it makes sense to redeploy most of the other nodes to run the vulnerable OS. This improves the probability that an array of HoneyStat nodes will capture similar events. Again, the delay this causes for detection is discussed in Section 7.

4. Finally, the HoneyStat event is correlated with other observed events. If a pattern emerges, this can indicate the presence of a worm or other automated attacks. Any reasonable correlation of events can be done. In the next section, we present a candidate analysis based on logistic regression.

As an example, in Figure 2(b), we see three different honeypots generating events. Prior input to the honeypots includes a variety of sources. For simplicity, the example in Figure 2(b) merely has three different active ports, P_a, P_b, P_c. Intuitively, we can use the time difference between the honeypot event and the individual port activity to infer what caused the honeypot to become active. But if all these events are from the same worm, then one would expect to see the same inputs to all three honeypots. In this case, only P_a is common to all three. A logistic regression presents a more flexible way of discovering the intersection of all inputs and provides a better explanation why a honeypot has become active.

4.1 Honeypot Evasion

As more honeypots are used in IDS settings, attackers may attempt to evade by having worms detect and avoid honeypot traps. Honeypot researchers have observed that a few assembly instructions behave slightly differently in various (often incomplete) emulators, and that emulated hardware may have predictable signatures (e.g., BIOS Strings, MAC address ranges for network cards) [Cor04,Sei02]. One can prevent trivial honeypot detection by patching emulated VMs [Kor04], and removing any obvious indicators like registry keys.

Hand crafted assembly instructions designed to detect VMWare present a different problem. Since Intel chips don't support multiple zero ring contexts, some instructions will elicit a VM monitor error, allowing attackers to evade the honeypot trap. This can be countered by filtering incoming traffic to identify the limited instruction set designed to detect VMWare. Failing this (e.g., if the emulator detection code is polymorphic), one can always just treat the crashed emulator as a HoneyStat memory event. This yields a more limited alert (e.g., you miss disk events), but allows HoneyStat to correlate what caused the error.

Attackers might also attempt to make machine observations, e.g., the time needed to perform lengthy calculations. This potentially benefits defenders, since worms may have a slower propagation rate, allowing for human intervention and earlier detection. Ultimately, we believe the honeypot evasion problem may devolve into a classic cat-and-mouse game, not unlike virus detection. In this case, however, the tables are turned, and it is the attacker who must perform reliable detection in a changing environment.

5   Logistic Analysis of HoneyStat Events

Our key objective is the detection of *zero-day* worms, or those without a known signature. Without the ability to perform pattern matching, our task is analogous to *anomaly detection*. We therefore use a statistical analysis of the events to identify worm behavior. Statistical techniques, e.g., [MHL94,AFV95,PN97,QVWW98], have been widely applied in anomaly detection, . In our prior work, we applied time series-based statistical analysis to alert correlation [QL03].

Our preference was for a technique that can effectively correlate variables collected in a *short* observation window with a short computation time. Time series-based analysis is good for a relatively long observation and requires a series of statistical tests in order to accurately correlate variables. It is also often not suitable for real-time analysis because of its computationally intensive nature. Therefore, in this work, we instead apply logistic analysis [HL00] to analyze port correlation.

Logistic regression is a non-linear transformation of the traditional linear regression model. Instead of correlating two continuous variables, logistic regression considers (in the simplest case) a dichotomous variable and continuous variables. That is, the dependent variable is a boolean "dummy" variable coded as 0 or 1, which corresponds to a state or category we wish to explain. In our case, we treat the honeypot event as a dichotomous variable, i.e., the honeypot is either awake (1) or quiescent (0). Logit analysis then seeks to explain what continuous variables explain the changes in the honeypot state, from asleep to awake.

We settled on using a logit analysis only after considering other, more restrictive analysis techniques. A simple linear regression, for example, would compare continuous-to-continuous variables. In the case of honeypots, this would require either measuring rates of outgoing packets, or identifying some other continuous measurement in the memory, network and disk events. Since it only takes one packet to be infected or cause an infection to spread, a simple linear regression approach would not clearly identify "sleeper worms" (a false negative scenario) and worms on busy networks (a false positive potential). Additionally, measuring outgoing packet rates would also include a significant amount of noise, since honeypots routinely complete TCP handshakes for the services they offer (e.g., normal, non-harmful webservice, mail service, ftp connections without successful login, etc.). Using continuous variables based on outgoing rates may only be slightly better than using incoming scan rates.

The basic form of the model expresses a binary expectation of the honeypot state, $E(Y)$ (asleep or awake) for k events, as seen in Eq. (1).

$$E(Y) = \frac{1}{1 + e^{-Z}}, \quad \text{where } Z = \beta_0 + \epsilon + \sum_{j=1}^{k} \sum_{i=1}^{n_j} (\beta_{i,j} X_{i,j}) \tag{1}$$

In Eq. (1), j is a counter for each individual honeypot event, and i is a counter for each individual port traffic observation for a specific honeypot. Each $\beta_{i,j}$ is the regression coefficient corresponding to the $X_{i,j}$ variable, a continuous variable representing each individual port observation. We have one error term ϵ and one constant β_0 for the equation. To set values of $X_{i,j}$, we use the inverse of time between an event and the port activity. Thus, if a `MemoryEvent` (or honeypot event j) occurs at time t, and just prior to this, port i on that same honeypot experienced traffic at time $t - \delta_t$, the variable $X_{i,j}$ would represent the port in the equation, and would have the value of $\frac{1}{\delta_t}$. This biases towards network traffic closer in time to the event, consistent with our infection model discussed in Section 3.

An example shows how honeypot events are aggregated. Suppose one honeypot event is observed, with activity to ports $\{P_1, P_2, \ldots, P_n\}$. We calculate the inverse time difference between the port activity and the honeypot event, and store the values for $X_{1,1}, X_{2,1}, \ldots X_{n,1}$ in a table that solves for Y. Suppose then a second event is recorded, in the same class as the first. We add the second event's values of $X_{1,2}$, $X_{2,2}, \ldots, X_{n,2}$ to the equation. This process continues. After each new event is added, we resolve for Y, and calculate new values of β. After sufficient observations, the logit analysis can identify candidate ports that explain why the honeypots are becoming active.

The inverse time relation between event and prior traffic allows one to record arbitrary periods of traffic. Traffic that occurred too long ago will, in practice, have such a low value for $X_{i,j}$ that it cannot affect the outcome. As a convenience, we cut off prior traffic t_p at 5 minutes, but even this arbitrary limit is generous. Future work will explore use of other time treatments, such as $\frac{1}{\delta_t^2}$, and $\frac{1}{\sqrt{\delta_t}}$, as a means of further biasing toward more recent network events. Note that this assumption prevents HoneyStat from tracking worms that sleep for a lengthy period of time before spreading. These worms are presumably self-crippling, and have a slow enough spread rate to allow for human intervention.

A key variable in this analysis includes the *Wald statistic*, which lets us test whether a variable's coefficient is zero. The Wald statistic is merely the ratio of the coefficient to its standard error, with a single degree of freedom [HL00]. The Wald statistic can be used to reject certain variables, and exclude them from a model. For example, if ports $P_0, P_1, \ldots P_n$ were observed prior to a honeypot event, we might exclude some of these ports based on the ratio of their coefficient $\beta_{i,j}$, and their standard error. Thus, the Wald statistic essentially poses a null hypothesis for each variable, and lets us exclude variables with zero coefficients. (After all, a variable with a zero β value does not contribute to solving Eq. 1). This analysis is helpful since it reduces noise in our model. However, since it uses a simple ratio, when the standard error is large, it can lead one to not reject certain variables. Thus, the Wald statistic can be used to remove unlikely variables, but might not always remove variables that have no affect.

Applying logistic analysis involves the following steps. First, for a particular honeypot event j, we estimate the coefficients, i.e., $\beta_{0,j}, \beta_{1,j} \ldots \beta_{n,j}$, using *maximum likelihood evaluation* [HL00] (MLE). In this step, we try to find a set of coefficients that minimize the prediction error. Stated another way, MLE assigns values that will maximize the probability of obtaining the observed set of data. (This is similar to the least squares method under simple regression analysis.) Second, we use the Wald statistic to evaluate each variable, and remove those below a user-selected threshold of significance level, say, 5%. The intuition of this step is that we try to evaluate whether the "causal" variable in the model is *significantly* related to the outcome. In other words we essentially ask the question: Is activity on port x significantly related to the honeypot activity or was it merely random?

If the analysis results in a single variable explaining changes in the honeypot, then we report the result as an alert. If the results are not conclusive, the event data is stored until additional events are observed, triggering a renewed analysis. Of course, since the events involve breakins to honeypots, users may also wish to receive informational alerts about these events.

6   HoneyStat in Practice

To evaluate HoneyStat's potential as a local worm detection system, we tested two key aspects of the algorithm: (a) does it properly identify worm outbreaks, and (b) what false positive rate does it produce? Testing showed that HoneyStat could identify worm outbreaks, with a low false positive rate. Our testing with available data showed the false positive rate of zero. This result is encouraging, given the enormous data set used. Nonetheless, a zero false positive rate may be due to properties of the data set and we will continue to run more experiments.

6.1   Worm Detection

In [QDG+], we used data from six honeypots that became active during the Blaster worm outbreak in August 2003. The trace data used for the analysis also included network traffic from some 100/24 darknet IPs. Figure 3 shows an aggregate view of traffic to all the honeypots on August 9 and 11, as well as background traffic to the darknets.

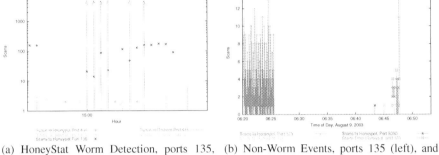

(a) HoneyStat Worm Detection, ports 135, 139, 445

(b) Non-Worm Events, ports 135 (left), and 80, 8080 (right)

Fig. 3. a) *HoneyStat worm detection for Blaster.* The Blaster attack on August 11, 2003, is detected by the honeypots. Upward arrows, not drawn to scale, indicate the presence of outgoing traffic from the HoneyStat nodes. Traffic prior to the honeypot activity is analyzed, using the inverse of time difference, so that more recent activities more likely explain the change in the honeypot. A logit analysis shows that prior scans to port 135 explains these episodes–effectively identifying the blaster worm. b) *Avoiding false positives.* Here, we see a trojaned honeypot node becoming active days prior to the Blaster worm outbreak. However, since this event is seen only in isolation (one honeypot), it does not trigger a worm alert. Traffic to ports 80 and 8080 does not bias the later analysis.

If we mark the honeypot activity as `NetEvents`, we can examine the previous network activity to find whether a worm is present. As shown in Table 1, a logit analysis of the honeypot data shows that of all the variables, port 135 explains the tendency of honeypots to become active. (In our particular example, one can even visually confirm in Figure 3(a) that honeypot activity took place right after port 135 traffic arrived.) The standard error reports the error for the estimated β, and the significance column reports the chance that the variable's influence was merely chance. The Wald statistic indicates whether the β statistic significantly differs from zero. The significance column is the most critical for our analysis, since it indicates whether the variable's estimated β is zero. The lower the score, the less chance the variable had no influence on the value of Y. Thus, we eliminate any variable with a significance above a threshold (5%). From this, the observations for ports 80, 8080, and 3128 can be discounted as not a significant explanation for changes in Y.

In this case, the logit analysis performs two useful tasks. First, we use the significance column to rule out variables above a certain threshold, leaving only ports 135, 139 and 445. Second, the analysis lets us rank the remaining variables by significance.

The logit analysis did not pick one individual port as explaining the value of Y. The alert that issues therefore identifies three possible causes of the honeypot activity. As it turns out, this was a very accurate diagnosis of the Blaster outbreak. Recall that just

Table 1. Logit Analysis of Multiple HoneyStat Events.

Variable	β	Standard Error	Wald	Significance
port_80	-17463.185	2696276.445	.000	.995
port_135	3.114	.967	10.377	.001
port_139	1869.151	303.517	37.925	.000
port_445	-1495.040	281.165	28.274	.000
port_3128	-18727.568	9859594.820	.000	.998
port_8080	10907.922	10907.922	6919861.448	.999
constant	.068	1.568	.210	1.089

prior to Blaster's outbreak on port 135, there were numerous scans being directed at ports 139 and 445. The port 135 exploit eventually became more popular, since only a few machines were vulnerable on 445 and 139. We are aware of no statistical test that could focus on port 135 alone, given the high rate of probing being conducted on ports 139 and 445. This required human insight and domain knowledge to sort out.

One complicating factor occurs when two zero-day worms attack at the same time, using different ports. For example, consider in the example what would happen if traffic to port 80 were a worm after all. In such a case, more data observations will be required to separate out which events support a leading theory of causation. The logit analysis will eventually select a pattern for one of the worms, and with the removal of those observations, the second worm can be identified. (Recall that once identified, the "explained" data is removed from the analysis queue.) Future work will explore the use of Best Subsets logistic regression models[HL00], to avoid the linear identification of multiple worms.

The number of observations required for logistic regression appears to be a matter of some recent investigation. In [HL00], the authors (eminent in the field) note "there has been surprisingly little work on sample size for logistic regression". Some rough estimates have been supplied. They note that at least one study show a minimum of 10 events per parameter are needed to avoid over/under estimations of variables [HL00]. Since each honeypot activity observation is paired with a corresponding inactivity observation, HoneyStat would need to generate five HoneyStat events to meet this requirement. Section 7 notes how waiting for this many observations potentially affects worm detection time.

Since each event involves an actual compromise of a system, one could also report alerts with a lower confidence level. While we might want more samples and certainty, we can at the very least rank likely ports in an alert.

6.2   Benefits of HoneyStat

HoneyStat provides the following benefits to local networks: (a) It provides a very accurate data stream for analysis. Every event is the result of a successful attack. This significantly reduces the amount of data that must be processed, compared to Kalman filter, and other traditional scan-based algorithms. (b) Since HoneyStat uses complete operating systems, it detects zero day worms, for which there is no known signature. (c) HoneyStat is agnostic about the incoming and outgoing ports for attack packets, as well as their origin. In this way, it can detect worms that enter on port P_a, and exit on port P_b.

Thus, HoneyStat reports *an explanation* of worm activation, and not merely the *presence* of a worm. Other information, such as rate of scans, can be obtained from the traffic logs captured for the logit analysis. [Kre03] has already suggested a simple method of quickly extracting a binary signature, in a manner compatible with Honey-Stat.

6.3   False Positive Analysis

Analyzing the false positive rate for HoneyStat is subtle. Since honeypot events always involve breakins and successful exploits, it might seem that honeypot-based alert systems would produce no false positives. This is not the case. Although the underlying data stream consists of serious alerts (successful attacks on honeypots), we still need to analyze the potential for the logit analysis to generate a false positive. Two types of errors could occur. First, normal network traffic could be misidentified as the source of an attack. That is, a worm could be present, but the analysis may identify other, normal traffic as the cause. Second, repeated human breakins could be identified as a worm. We do not consider this second failure scenario, since in such a case, the manual breakins are robotic in nature, and (for all practical purposes) indistinguishable from, and *potentially just as dangerous* as any worm.

Model Failure. It is not feasible to test HoneyStat on the Internet. This would require waiting for the outbreak of worms, and dedicating a large IP space to a test project. We can instead perform an retrospective analysis of a tracefile to estimate the chance of a false positive.

Using a honeypot activity log, dating from July 2002 to March 2004, we used uniform random sampling to collect background traffic samples, and injected a worm attack. The intuition is this: we wish to see if a HoneyStat logit analysis were to cause a false positive. This could occur if normal non-malicious background traffic occurs in such a pattern that random sampling produces a candidate solution to the logistic regression.

The data we use for the background sampling came from the Georgia Tech Honeynet project. We have almost two years of network data captured from the Honeynet. The first year of data was captured on a Generation I Honeynet, which is distinguishable by the use of a reverse firewall serving as the gateway for all the Honeypots. The second year of data was captured from a Generation II Honeynet, which is distinguishable by the use of a packet filtering bridge between all of the Honeypots and their gateway. The data is available to other researchers in a sanitized form.

A random sampling of over 250 synthetic honeypot events did not produce a false positive. This certainly does not prove that HoneyStat is incapable of producing a false positive. Rather, this may reflect the limited range of the data. A much larger data set is required to fully explore the potential of logistic regression to misidentify variables. Even if false positives are found, it should be noted that these are not the usual false positives, or type I errors found in IDS. Instead, a false positive with a HoneyStat node is half right: there are breakins to honeypots, even if the algorithm were to misidentify the cause.

7 HoneyStat as an IDS Tool

The previous sections have shown that HoneyStat can detect worm attacks with a low false positive rate. This shows that it could be incorporated into a local intrusion detection system. A more important question is whether this strategy can detect worm outbreaks early. In this section, we present an analytical model.

A HoneyStat deployment can effectively detect worms that use random scan techniques. The work in [WPSC03] presents a complete taxonomy of worms. In [QDG+], we discussed how a detection algorithm with a suitably low false positive can protect local networks. Accordingly, we evaluate HoneyStat against worms that use only random scanning strategies [ZGGT03]. Since we are interested in local network protections, the results should apply to other types of scanning worms [QDG+]. Realistically we assume the vulnerable hosts are uniformly distributed in the real assigned IPv4 space (all potential victims are located in this space, denoted as $T = 10^9$), not the whole IPv4 space (denoted as $\Omega = 2^{32}$). Assume N is the total number of vulnerable machines on the Internet, n_i is the number of whole Internet victims at time tick i and s is the scan rate of worm (per time tick). So the scans entering space T at time tick $i + 1$ should be $k_{i+1} = sn_i\frac{T}{\Omega}$. Within this space, the chance of one host being hit is $1 - (1 - \frac{1}{T})^{k_{i+1}}$. Then we have worm propagation equation Eq. (2).

$$n_{i+1} = n_i + [N - n_i]\left(1 - (1 - \frac{1}{T})^{sn_i\frac{T}{\Omega}}\right) \qquad (2)$$

In fact because T and Ω are very big, $(1 - (1 - \frac{1}{T})^{sn_i\frac{T}{\Omega}} \doteq \frac{1}{T}sn_i\frac{T}{\Omega} = \frac{sn_i}{\Omega}$. So the spread rate is almost the same as seen in previous models (e.g., Analytical Active Worm Propagation (AAWP) model [CGK03], epidemic model [KW93,KCW93,SPN02] etc.) Now suppose we have a honeypot network with size D ($D \subseteq T$). The initial number of vulnerable hosts is u_0. Generally a network with size D has DN/T vulnerable hosts on average. But with HoneyStat, each network has its own mix of vulnerable OS distributions. Since most worms target Windows, we can intentionally let most of our honeypots run Windows so that we present a higher number of initially vulnerable hosts to the worm. Without loss of generality we suppose $u_0 = D\alpha$. We let α be the minimum ratio for vulnerable hosts. The number of local victims at time tick i is v_i and $v_0 = 0$ which means initially there is no victim in our honeypot network. The time for the first HoneyStat node to become active is t_1 (clearly t_1 is the first time tick i when $v_i \geq 1$). We have

$$v_{i+1} = u_0\left(1 - (1 - \frac{1}{T})^{\sum_{j=0}^{i} sn_j\frac{T}{\Omega}}\right) \text{ when } i + 1 < t_1 + t_r \qquad (3)$$

Here $u_0 = D\alpha$. We let t_r represent the time required to reconfigure most of the non-vulnerable honeypots to run the same OS and patch level as the first victim. (In other words, this is the time required, say, to convert most of the Linux honeypots to Windows, if Windows is first attacked.) Since we need more observations for the logit analysis to work, as noted in Section 5, we shift some of our honeypots to match the vulnerable OS. As noted above, restarting the suspended OS happens quickly, before any traffic times out. We nonetheless express this delay as response time t_r. After the delay, the number of new vulnerable hosts becomes $u_1 = D\gamma$. We let γ represent the maximum ratio for vulnerable hosts. Normally $\gamma < 1$ because we may not convert *all* of our HoneyStat nodes to the operating system that is attacked. We might keep a few to detect other worms. Now we have

$$v_{i+1} = 1 + u_1 \left(1 - (1 - \frac{1}{T})^{\sum_{j=t_1+t_r}^{i} sn_j \frac{T}{\Omega}} \right) \text{ when } i + 1 >= t_1 + t_r \qquad (4)$$

Here $u_1 = D\gamma$. We can calculate the time (in terms of the whole Internet infection percentage) when our first HoneyStat node is infected. Table 2 and Figure 5 use the effect of different α and D. For example, we can see that using $D = 2^{10}$ and $\alpha = 10\%$, the first victim is found when only 0.9786% Internet vulnerable hosts are infected.

Table 2. Time (infection percentage) when HoneyStat network has a first victim.

α	$D = 2^8$	$D = 2^9$	$D = 2^{10}$	$D = 2^{11}$	$D = 2^{12}$	$D = 2^{13}$	$D = 2^{14}$	$D = 2^{15}$	$D = 2^{16}$
10%	3.9141%	1.9558%	0.9786%	0.4895%	0.2448%	0.1223%	0.0613%	0.0307%	0.0155%
25%	1.5634%	0.7825%	0.3910%	0.1959%	0.0981%	0.0491%	0.0247%	0.0124%	0.0063%
50%	0.7825%	0.3910%	0.1959%	0.0981%	0.0491%	0.0247%	0.0124%	0.0063%	0.0033%
75%	0.5210%	0.2606%	0.1305%	0.0655%	0.0328%	0.0165%	0.0083%	0.0043%	0.0022%
100%	0.3910%	0.1959%	0.0981%	0.0491%	0.0247%	0.0124%	0.0063%	0.0033%	0.0017%

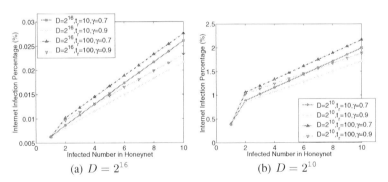

(a) $D = 2^{16}$ (b) $D = 2^{10}$

Fig. 4. Effect of HoneyStat network size, D, maximum percentage of vulnerable hosts,γ, and time to redeploy after first victim, t_r, on the victim count. These graphs, drawn with $\alpha = 0.25$; N=500,000; scanrate=20 per time tick; Hitlist=1, show that with a larger IP space monitored by HoneyStat, D, the detection time (as a precent of the infected Internet) improves greatly. Even with only 2^{10} IPs monitored, detection time is quick, requiring only a little more than 1% of the Internet to be infected.

When the first HoneyStat node becomes infected, the other nodes switch to the vulnerable OS. This takes time t_r, after which there will be $u_1 = D\gamma$ vulnerable hosts. After redeployment, the chance of getting the next victim improves. This is shown in Eq. (4). The effect of D, γ and t_r is shown in Figure 4. Here, we can see that after redeployment we will quickly get enough victims when the whole Internet has a low infection percentage. This occurs because we obtain more vulnerable honeypots after the HoneyStat array is switched to match the OS of the first victim. Therefore, we get higher chances of being hit by the worm. For example, if $\alpha = 0.25, D = 2^{16}, \gamma = 0.7, t_r = 10$, it is still very early to have 4 victims in the HoneyStat network, when only 0.013% Internet vulnerable hosts are infected. To have 10 victims, still only 0.0261% Internet vulnerable hosts are infected. And we can see that $t_r = 10$ or $t_r = 100, \gamma = 0.7$ or $\gamma = 0.9$ do not affect the outcome very much. Instead, the size of honeynet D is the most important factor. Thus, the delay in switching HoneyStat nodes does not play a critical role in overall worm detection time.

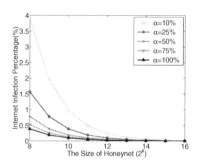

Fig. 5. Effect of α and D on Time (Infection Percentage) when HoneyStat network has a first victim. N=500,000, Scan rate=20 per time tick.

In section 4, we noted that machines can be massively multihomed, so that one piece of hardware can effectively handle hundreds of IP addresses in multiple virtual machines. From the discussion of D above, 2^{11} is already a reasonable number of IP addresses that can be used in our local early worm detection. Assuming we had a few computers sufficient to allow $D = 2^{11}$ and $\alpha = 0.25$, we can see from Table 2 that the first victim appears when on average 0.1959% of Internet vulnerable hosts are infected. Suppose $\gamma = 0.75, t_r = 10$, then to have 5 victims in our honeynet (or enough to have a minimal number of data points suggested in Section 6), it is still very early when only 0.4794% of the Internet's vulnerable hosts are infected. When one IP is infected, we reset the OS so that it can be infected again. This kind of "replacement" policy makes the whole honeynet work as we have discussed above although there are only, say, 64 virtual machines running on every GSX server.

8   Conclusion

Local detection systems deserve further exploration. We have suggested that in addition to increasing the *quantity* of data used by alert systems, the *quality* can be improved as well. It has been said that if intrusion detection is like finding a needle in a haystack, then a honeypot is like a stack of needles. Literally every event from a honeypot is noteworthy. Honeypots are therefore used to create a highly accurate alert stream.

Using logistic regression, we have shown how a honeypot alert stream can detect worm outbreaks. We define three classes of events to capture memory, disk and network activities of worms. The logit analysis can eliminate noise sampled during these events, and identify a likely list of causes. Using extensive data traces of previous worm events, we have demonstrated that HoneyStat can identify worm activity. An analytical model suggests that, with enough multihomed honeypots, this provides an effective way to detect worms early.

While participation in global monitoring efforts has value, we believe local network strategies require exploration as well. Further work could include identification of additional logistic models to sort through large sets of data, coordination of shared honeypot events, integration with other intrusion detection techniques, and response.

Acknowledgments

We thank Christian Kreibich at the University of Cambridge for his helpful comments. This work is supported in part by NSF grants CCR-0133629 and CCR-0208655 and Army Research Office contract DAAD19-01-1-0610. The contents of this work are solely the responsibility of the authors and do not necessarily represent the official views of NSF and the U.S. Army.

References

[AFV95]   D. Anderson, T. Frivold, and A. Valdes. Next-generation intrusion detection expert system (NIDES): A summary. Technical Report SRI-CSL-95-07, Computer Science Laboratory, SRI International, Menlo Park, California, May 1995.

[BGB03]   V.H. Berk, R.S. Gray, and G. Bakos. Using sensor networks and data fusion for early detection of active worms. In *Proceedings of the SPIE AeroSense*, 2003.

[CGK03]   Z. Chen, L. Gao, and K. Kwiat. Modeling the spread of active worms. In *Proceedings of the IEEE INFOCOM 2003*, March 2003.

[CLF03]   S. Cheung, U. Lindqvist, and M. W. Fong. Modeling multistep cyber attacks for scenario recognition. In *Proceedings of the Third DARPA Information Survivability Conference and Exposition (DISCEX III)*, Washington, D.C., April 2003.

[CM02]   F. Cuppens and A. Miège. Alert correlation in a cooperative intrusion detection framework. In *Proceedings of the 2002 IEEE Symposium on Security and Privacy*, pages 202–215, Oakland, CA, May 2002.

[Cor04]   Joseph Corey. Advanced honey pot identification and exploitation. (fake) Phrack, No. 63, 2004.

[DW01]   H. Debar and A. Wespi. The intrusion-detection console correlation mechanism. In *4th International Symposium on Recent Advances in Intrusion Detection (RAID)*, October 2001.

[GHH01]   R.P. Goldman, W. Heimerdinger, and S. A. Harp. Information modling for intrusion report aggregation. In *DARPA Information Survivability Conference and Exposition (DISCEX II)*, June 2001.

[GSQ+ 04] Guofei Gu, Monirul Sharif, Xinzhou Qin, David Dagon, Wenke Lee, and George Riley. Worm detection, early warning and response based on local victim information. Submitted for review, 2004.

[HL00]   D.W. Hosmer and S. Lemeshow. *Applied Logistic Regression*. Wiley-Interscience, 2000.

[Inc03]   Immunix Inc. Stackguard. http://www.immunix.org/stackguard.html, 2003.

[Ins]   SANS Institute. http://www.sans.org.

[JPBB04]   Jaeyeon Jung, Vern Paxson, Arthur W. Berger, and Hari Balakrishnan. Fast portscan detection using sequential hypothesis testing. In *2004 IEEE Symposium on Security and Privacy*, 2004.

[JX04]   Xuxian Jiang and Dongyan Xu. Collapsar: A vm-based architecture for network attack detention center. http://www.cs.purdue.edu/homes/jiangx/collapsar/, 2004.

[Kal60]   R.E. Kalman. A new approach to linear filtering and prediction problems. *Transaction of the ASME–Journal of Basic Engineering*, March, 1960.

[KCW93]   J.O. Kephart, D.M. Chess, and S.R. White. Computers and epidemiology. 1993.

[Kor04]   Kostya Kortchinsky. Vmware fingerprinting counter measures. The French Honeynet Project, 2004.

[Kre03]   Christian Kreibich. Honeycomb automated ids signature creation using honeypots. http://www.cl.cam.ac.uk/ cpk25/honeycomb/, 2003.

[KW93]   J.O. Kephart and S.R. White. Measuring and modeling computer virus prevalence. In *Proceedings of IEEE Symposium on Security and Privacy*, 1993.

[Lem01]   Jonathan Lemon. Kqueue: A generic and scalable event notification facility. pages 141–154, 2001.

[LLO+ 03]   John Levine, Richard LaBella, Henry Owen, Didier Contis, and Brian Culver. The use of honeynets to detect exploited systems across large enterprise networks. In *Proceedings of the 2003 IEEE Workshop on Information Assurance*, 2003.

[LUR03]   LURHQ. Msblast case study. http://www.lurhq.com/blaster.html, 2003.

[LUR04]   LURHQ. Witty worm analysis. http://www.lurhq.com/witty.html, 2004.

[MHL94]   B. Mukherjee, L. T. Heberlein, and K. N. Levitt. Network intrusion detection. *IEEE Network*, May/June 1994.

[MMDD02]   B. Morin, L. Mé, H. Debar, and M. Ducassé. M2d2: A formal data model for ids alert correlation. In *Proceedings of the 5th International Symposium on Recent Advances in Intrusion Detection (RAID)*, October 2002.

[Moo02a]   D. Moore. Code-red: A case study on the spread and victims of an internet worm. http://www.icir.org/vern/imw-2002/imw2002-papers/209.ps.gz, 2002.

[Moo02b]   D. Moore. Network telescopes: Observing small or distant security events. http://www.caida.org/outreach/presentations/2002/usenix_sec/, 2002.

[MSVS03]   D. Moore, C. Shannon, G. M. Voelker, and S. Savage. Internet quarantine: Requirements for containing self-propagating code. In *Proceedings of the IEEE INFOCOM 2003*, March 2003.

[NCR02]   P. Ning, Y. Cui, and D.S. Reeves. Constructing attack scenarios through correlation of intrusion alerts. In *9th ACM Conference on Computer and Communications Security*, November 2002.

[Par04]   Janak J Parekh. Columbia ids worminator project. http://worminator.cs.columbia.edu/, 2004.

[PN97]   P. A. Porras and P. G. Neumann. EMERALD: Event monitoring enabling responses to anomalous live disturbances. In *National Information Systems Security Conference*, Baltimore MD, October 1997.

[Pro03]   Niels Provos. A virtual honeypot framework. http://www.citi.umich.edu/techreports/reports/citi-tr-03-1.pdf, 2003.

[QDG+]   X. Qin, D. Dagon, G. Gu, W. Lee, M. Warfield, and P. Allor. Technical report.

[QL03]   X. Qin and W. Lee. Statistical causality analysis of infosec alert data. In *Proceedings of the 6th International Symposium on Recent Advances in Intrusion Detection (RAID 2003)*, Pittsburgh, PA, September 2003.

[QVWW98] D. Qu, B. Vetter, F. Wang, and S.F. Wu. Statistical-based intrusion detection for OSPF routing protocol. In *Proceedings of the 6th IEEE International Conference on Network Protocols*, Austin, TX, October 1998.

[Sei02]   Kurt Seifried. Honeypotting with vmware - basics. 2002.

[Sko02]   E. Skoudis. *Counter Hack*. Upper Saddle River, NJ: Prentice Hall PTR, 2002.

[Spi03]   Lance Spitzner. *Honeypots: Tracking Hackers*. Addison Wesley, 2003.

[SPN02]   S. Staniford, V. Paxson, and N.Weaver. How to Own the Internet in Your Spare Time. In *Proceedings of 2002 Usenix Security Symposium*, 2002.

[Sta01]   S. Staniford. Code red analysis pages: July infestation analysis. http://www.silicondefense.com/cr/july.html, 2001.

[VMW04]   Inc. VMWare. Gsx server 3. http://www.vmware.com/products/server, 2004.

[VS01]   A. Valdes and K. Skinner. Probabilistic alert correlation. In *Proceedings of the 4th International Symposium on Recent Advances in Intrusion Detection (RAID)*, October 2001.

[Wil02]   Matthew M. Williamson. Throttling viruses: Restricting propagation to defeat malicious mobile code. Technical report, 2002. HPL-2002-172.

[WL03]   Matthew M. Williamson and Jasmin Léveillé. An epidemiological model of virus spread and cleanup. Technical report, 2003. HPL-2003-30.

[WPSC03] N. Weaver, V. Paxson, S. Staniford, and R. Cunningham. A taxonomy of computer worms. In *2003 ACM Workshop on Rapid Malcode (WORM'03)*. ACM SIGSAC, October 2003.

[WVGK04] J. Wu, S. Vangala, L. Gao, and K. Kwiat. An efficient architecture and algorithm for detecting worms with various scan techniques. In *Proceedings of the 11th Annual Network and Distributed System Security Symposium (NDSS'04)*, February 2004. to appear.

[YBJ04]   Vinod Yegneswaran, Paul Barford, and Somesh Jha. Global intrusion detection in the domino overlay system. In *Proceedings of NDSS*, 2004.

[ZGGT03] C. C. Zou, L. Gao, W. Gong, and D. Towsley. Monitoring and early warning for internet worms. In *Proceedings of 10th ACM Conference on Computer and Communications Security (CCS'03)*, October 2003.

[ZGT02]   C. C. Zou, W. Gong, and D. Towsley. Code red worm propagation modeling and analysis. In *Proceedings of 9th ACM Conference on Computer and Communications Security (CCS'02)*, October 2002.

Fast Detection of Scanning Worm Infections

Stuart E. Schechter[1], Jaeyeon Jung[2], and Arthur W. Berger[2]

[1] Harvard DEAS,
33 Oxford Street, Cambridge MA 02138, USA
stuart@eecs.harvard.edu
[2] MIT CSAIL,
32 Vassar Street, Cambridge MA 02139, USA
{jyjung,awberger}@csail.mit.edu

Abstract. Worm detection and response systems must act quickly to identify and quarantine scanning worms, as when left unchecked such worms have been able to infect the majority of vulnerable hosts on the Internet in a matter of minutes [9]. We present a hybrid approach to detecting scanning worms that integrates significant improvements we have made to two existing techniques: sequential hypothesis testing and connection rate limiting. Our results show that this two-pronged approach successfully restricts the number of scans that a worm can complete, is highly effective, and has a low false alarm rate.

1 Introduction

Human reaction times are inadequate for detecting and responding to fast scanning worms, such as `Slammer`, which can infect the majority of vulnerable systems in a matter of minutes [18, 9]. Thus, today's worm response proposals focus on *automated* responses to worms, such as quarantining infected machines [10], automatic generation and installation of patches [14, 15], and reducing the rate at which worms can issue connection requests so that a more carefully constructed response can be crafted [22, 27].

Even an automated response will be of little use if it fails to be triggered quickly after a host is infected. Infected hosts with high-bandwidth network connections can initiate thousands of connection requests per second, each of which has the potential to spread the infection. On the other hand, an automated response that triggers too easily will erroneously identify hosts as infected, interfering with these hosts' reliable performance and causing significant damage.

Many scan detection mechanisms rely upon the observation that only a small fraction of addresses are likely to respond to a connection request at any given port. Many IPv4 addresses are dead ends as they are not assigned to active hosts. Others are assigned to hosts behind firewalls that block the port addressed by the scanner. When connection requests do reach active hosts, many will be rejected as not all hosts will be running the targeted service. Thus, scanners are likely to have a low rate of successful connections, whereas benign hosts, which only issue connection requests when there is reason to believe that addressees will respond, will have a much greater rate of success.

E. Jonsson et al. (Eds.): RAID 2004, LNCS 3224, pp. 59–81, 2004.

Existing methods for detecting scanning worms within a local network use fixed thresholds for the number of allowable failed connections over a time period [16] or limit the rate at which a host can initiate contact with additional hosts [27]. However, these threshold based approaches may fail to detect low-rate scanning. They may also require an excessive number of connection observations to detect an infection or lead to an unnecessary number of false alarms.

To detect inbound scans initiated by hosts outside the local network, previous work on which we collaborated [7] used an approach based on sequential hypothesis testing. This approach automatically adjusts the number of observations required to detect a scan with the strength of the evidence supporting the hypothesis that the observed host is, in fact, scanning. The advantage of this approach is that it can reduce the number of connection requests that must be observed to detect that a remote host is scanning while maintaining an acceptable false alarm rate.

While this approach shows promise for quickly detecting scanning by hosts inside a local network soon after they have been infected by a worm, there are significant hurdles to overcome. For one, to determine whether a request to connect to a remote host will fail, one must often wait to see whether a successful connection response will be returned. Until enough connection requests can be established to be failures, a sequential hypothesis test will lack the observations required to conclude that the system is infected. By the time the decision to quarantine the host is made, a worm with a high scan rate may have already targeted thousands of other hosts.

This earlier work used a single sequential hypothesis test per host and did not re-evaluate benign hosts over time. Unlike an intrusion detection system observing remote hosts, a worm detection system is likely to observe benign traffic originating from an infected host before it is infected. It is therefore necessary to adapt this method to continuously monitor hosts for indications of scanning.

We introduce an innovative approach that enables a Worm Detection System (WDS) to continuously monitor a set of *local* hosts for infection, requiring a small number of observations to be collected after an infection to detect that the host is scanning (Figure 1).

To detect infected hosts, the WDS need only process a small fraction of network events; a subset of connection request observations that we call *first-*

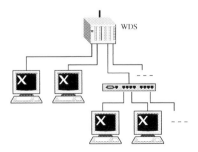

Fig. 1. A Worm Detection System (WDS) is located to monitor a local network

contact connection requests and the responses to these requests that complete the connections. A first-contact connection request is a packet (TCP or UDP) addressed to a host with which the sender has not previously communicated. These events are monitored because scans are mostly composed of first-contact connection requests.

In Section 2, we introduce a scan detection algorithm that we call a reverse sequential hypothesis test ($\overleftarrow{HT}$), and show how it can reduce the number of first-contact connections that must be observed to detect scanning[1]. Unlike previous methods, the number of observations $\overleftarrow{HT}$ requires to detect hosts' scanning behavior is not affected by the presence of benign network activity that may be observed before scanning begins.

In Section 3, we introduce a new credit-based algorithm for limiting the rate at which a host may issue the first-contact connections that are indicative of scanning activity. This credit-based connection rate limiting (CBCRL) algorithm results in significantly fewer false positives (unnecessary rate limiting) than existing approaches.

When combined, this two-pronged approach is effective because these two algorithms are complementary. Without credit-based connection rate limiting, a worm could rapidly issue thousands of connection requests before enough connection failures have been observed by Reverse Sequential Hypothesis Testing so that it can report the worm's presence. Because Reverse Sequential Hypothesis Testing processes connection success and failure events in the order that connection requests are issued, false alarms are less likely to occur than if we used an approach purely based on credit-based connection rate limiting, for which first-contact connections attempts are assumed to fail until the evidence proves otherwise.

We demonstrate the utility of these combined algorithms with trace-driven simulations, described in Section 4, with results presented in Section 5. The limitations of our approach, including strategies that worms could attempt to avoid detection, are presented in Section 6. We discuss related work, including previous approaches to the scanning worm detection problem, in Section 7. Our plans for future work are presented in Section 8, and we conclude in Section 9.

2 Detecting Scanning Worms by Using Reverse Sequential Hypothesis Testing

A worm is a form of malware that spreads from host to host without human intervention. A scanning worm locates vulnerable hosts by generating a list of addresses to probe and then contacting them. This address list may be generated sequentially or pseudo-randomly. Local addresses are often preferentially selected [25] as communication between neighboring hosts will likely encounter fewer defenses. Scans may take the form of TCP connection requests (SYN packets) or UDP packets. In the case of the connectionless UDP protocol, it is possible

---

[1] The letters in this abbreviation, $\overleftarrow{HT}$, stand for Hypothesis Testing and the arrow indicates the reverse sequential order in which observations are processed.

for the scanning packet to also contain the body of the worm as was the case with the `Slammer` worm [9].

In this section, we present an on-line algorithm for detecting the presence of scanners within a local network by observing network traffic. We use a sequential hypothesis test for its ability to adjust the number of observations required to make a decision to match the strength of the evidence it is presented with.

2.1   Sequential Hypothesis Testing

As with existing approaches to scan detection [7, 17, 22, 27], we rely upon the observation that only a small fraction of addresses are likely to respond to a connection request at any given port. Benign hosts, which only contact systems when they have reason to believe that this connection request will be accepted, are more likely to receive a response to a connection request.

Recall that a first-contact connection request is a packet (TCP or UDP) addressed to a host with which the sender has not previously communicated. When a local host l initiates a first-contact connection request to a destination address, d, we classify the outcome as either a "success" or a "failure". If the request was a TCP SYN packet, the connection is said to succeed if a SYN-ACK is received from d before a timeout expires. If the request is a UDP packet, any UDP packet from d received before the timeout will do. We let Y_i be a random (indicator) variable that represents the outcome of the ith first-contact connection request by l, where

$$Y_i = \begin{cases} 0 & \text{if the connection succeeds} \\ 1 & \text{if the connection fails} \end{cases}$$

Detecting scanning by local hosts is a problem that is well suited for the method of *sequential hypothesis testing* first developed by Wald [24], and used in our earlier work to detect remote scanners [7].

We call H_1 the hypothesis that host l is engaged in scanning (indicating infection by a worm) and H_0 the null hypothesis that the host is not scanning. We assume that, conditional on the hypothesis H_j, the random variables $Y_i|H_j$ $i = 1, 2, \ldots$ are independent and identically distributed (i.i.d.). That is, conditional on the hypothesis, any two connection attempts will have the same likelihood of succeeding, and their chances of success are unrelated to each other. We can express the distribution of the Bernoulli random variable Y_i as:

$$\Pr[Y_i = 0|H_0] = \theta_0, \quad \Pr[Y_i = 1|H_0] = 1 - \theta_0$$
$$\Pr[Y_i = 0|H_1] = \theta_1, \quad \Pr[Y_i = 1|H_1] = 1 - \theta_1$$

Given that connections originating at benign hosts are more likely to succeed than those initiated by a scanner, $\theta_0 > \theta_1$.

Sequential hypothesis testing chooses between two hypotheses by comparing the likelihoods that the model would generate the observed sequence of events, $\mathbf{Y}_n \equiv (Y_1, \ldots, Y_n)$, under each hypothesis. It does this by maintaining the ratio

$\Lambda(\mathbf{Y}_n)$, the numerator of which is the likelihood that the model would generate the sequence of events $\mathbf{Y}_n$ under hypothesis H_1, and the denominator under hypothesis H_0.

$$\Lambda(\mathbf{Y}_n) \equiv \frac{\Pr[\mathbf{Y}_n | H_1]}{\Pr[\mathbf{Y}_n | H_0]} \tag{1}$$

The i.i.d. assumption in the model enables us to state this ratio in terms of the likelihoods of the individual events.

$$\Lambda(\mathbf{Y}_n) \equiv \prod_{i=1}^{n} \frac{\Pr[Y_i | H_1]}{\Pr[Y_i | H_0]} \tag{2}$$

We can write the change to $\Lambda(\mathbf{Y}_n)$ as a result of the ith observation as $\phi(Y_i)$:

$$\phi(Y_i) \equiv \frac{\Pr[Y_i | H_1]}{\Pr[Y_i | H_0]} = \begin{cases} \frac{\theta_1}{\theta_0} & \text{if } Y_i = 0 \text{ (success)} \\[2mm] \frac{1-\theta_1}{1-\theta_0} & \text{if } Y_i = 1 \text{ (failure)} \end{cases}$$

This enables us to rewrite $\Lambda(\mathbf{Y}_n)$ inductively, such that $\Lambda(\mathbf{Y}_0) = 1$, and $\Lambda(\mathbf{Y}_n)$ may be calculated iteratively as each observation arrives.

$$\Lambda(\mathbf{Y}_n) = \prod_{i=1}^{n} \phi(Y_i) = \Lambda(\mathbf{Y}_{n-1})\phi(Y_n)$$

One compares the likelihood ratio $\Lambda(\mathbf{Y}_n)$ to an upper threshold, η_1, above which we accept hypothesis H_1, and a lower threshold, η_0, below which we accept hypothesis H_0. If $\eta_0 < \Lambda(\mathbf{Y}_n) < \eta_1$ then the result will remain inconclusive until more events in the sequence can be evaluated. This is illustrated in Figure 2.

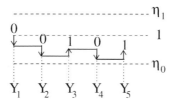

Fig. 2. A log scale graph of $\Lambda(\mathbf{Y})$ as each observation, Y_i, is added to the sequence. Each success (0) observation decreases $\Lambda(\mathbf{Y})$, moving it closer to the benign conclusion threshold η_0, whereas each failure (1) observation increases $\Lambda(\mathbf{Y})$, moving it closer to the infection conclusion threshold η_1

Writing the probability of correctly reporting detection (declaring host is infected when indeed it is) as P_D and the probability of a false positive (declaring host is infected when in fact it is not) as P_F, we can define our performance requirements as bounds α and β on these probabilities.

$$\alpha \geq P_F \quad \text{and} \quad \beta \leq P_D$$

Because every false positive can decrease productivity of both the users of a host and the security staff who need to inspect it, one would expect to use α values that are small fractions of a percentage point. Since scanners generate enough traffic to clearly differentiate their behavior from that of benign systems, a β of greater than 0.99 should be an achievable requirement.

Wald [24] showed that η_1 and η_0 can be bounded in terms of P_D and P_F.

$$\eta_1 \leq \frac{P_D}{P_F} \tag{3}$$

$$\frac{1 - P_D}{1 - P_F} \leq \eta_0 \tag{4}$$

Given our requirement parameters α and β, we assign the following values to our thresholds, η_0 and η_1:

$$\eta_1 \leftarrow \frac{\beta}{\alpha} \tag{5}$$

$$\eta_0 \leftarrow \frac{1 - \beta}{1 - \alpha} \tag{6}$$

From Equations (3) and (5), we can bound P_F in terms of α and β. Since $0 < P_D < 1$, we can replace P_D with 1 in Equation (3) to yield:

$$\eta_1 \leq \frac{P_D}{P_F} < \frac{1}{P_F} \tag{7}$$

It follows that:

$$P_F < \frac{1}{\eta_1} = \frac{\alpha}{\beta} \tag{8}$$

Likewise, using Equation (4) and given that $1 - P_D < (1 - P_D)/(1 - P_F)$, we can bound $1 - P_D$:

$$1 - P_D < \eta_0 = \frac{1 - \beta}{1 - \alpha} \tag{9}$$

While η_1 may result in a false positive rate above our desired bound by a factor of $\frac{1}{\beta}$, this difference is negligible given our use of β values in the range of 0.99 and above. Similarly, while our miss rate, $1 - P_D$ may be off by as much as a factor of $\frac{1}{1-\alpha}$, this too will have negligible effect given our requirements for very small values of α.

2.2   Detecting Infection Events

In our earlier work, it was assumed that each *remote* host was either a scanner or benign for the duration of the observed period. When a host was determined to be benign it would no longer be observed. In contrast, in this paper we are concerned with detecting infection events, in which a *local* host transitions from a benign state to an infected state. Should a host become infected while a hypothesis test is already running, the set of outcomes observed by the sequential hypothesis test may include those from both the benign and infected states, as shown in Figure 3. Even if we continue to observe the host and start a new hypothesis test each time a benign conclusion is reached, the test may take longer than necessary to conclude that an infection has occurred.

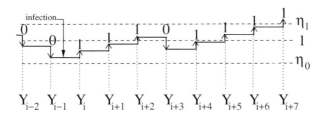

Fig. 3. A log scale graph tracing the value of $\Lambda(\mathbf{Y})$ as it is updated for a series of observations that includes first-contact connection requests before (Y_{i-1} and Y_{i-2}) and after (Y_i and beyond) the host was infected

The solution to this problem is to run a new sequential hypothesis test as each connection outcome is observed, evaluating these outcomes in reverse chronological order, as illustrated in Figure 4. To detect a host that was infected before it issued first-contact connection i (event Y_i), but after it had issued first-contact connection $i - 1$, a reverse sequential hypothesis test ($\overleftarrow{HT}$) would require the same number of observations to detect the infection as would a forward sequential hypothesis that had started observing the sequence at observation i. Because the most recent observations are processed first, the reverse test will terminate before reaching the observations that were collected before infection.

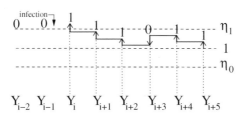

Fig. 4. A log scale graph tracing the value of $\Lambda(Y_{i+5}, Y_{i+4}, \ldots)$, in which the observations in $\mathbf{Y}$ are processed in *reverse* sequential order. The most recent, or rightmost, observation is the first one processed

When we used sequential hypothesis testing in our prior work to detect scanning of a local network by remote hosts, the intrusion detection system could know *a priori* whether a connection would fail given its knowledge of the network topology and services [7]. Thus, the outcome of a connection request from host i could immediately be classified as a success or failure observation (Y_i) and $\Lambda(\mathbf{Y}_n)$ could be evaluated without delay.

When a *local* host initiates first-contact connection requests to remote hosts, such as those shown in Figure 5, the worm detection system cannot immediately determine if the connection will succeed or fail. While some connection failures will result in a TCP RST packet or an ICMP packet [1, 3], empirical evidence has shown that most do not [2]. The remaining connection attempts can be classified as failures only after a timeout expires.

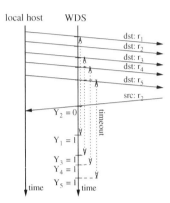

Fig. 5. The success of first-contact connection requests by a local host to remote hosts cannot be established by the Worm Detection System (WDS) until a response is observed or a timeout expires

While a sequential hypothesis test waits for unsuccessful connections to time out, a worm may send thousands of additional connection requests with which to infect other systems. To limit the number of outgoing first-contact connections, a sequential hypothesis testing approach can be paired with a credit-based connection rate limiter as described in Section 3.

2.3   Algorithmic Implementation

A naïve implementation of repeated reverse sequential hypothesis testing requires that we store an arbitrarily large sequence of first-contact connection observations. A naïve implementation must also step through a portion of this sequence each time a new observation is received in order to run a new test starting at that observation.

Fortunately, there exists an iterative function:

$$\bar{A}(\mathbf{Y}_n) = \max\left(1, \ \bar{A}(\mathbf{Y}_{n-1})\phi(Y_n)\right)$$

with state variable $\bar{A}(\mathbf{Y}_n)$, that can be calculated in the sequence in which events are observed, and that has the property that its value will exceed η_1 if and only if a reverse sequential hypothesis test would conclude from this sequence that the host was infected. This is proved in Appendix A.

Updating $\bar{A}$ for each observation requires only a single multiplication and two comparison operations[2]. Because $\bar{A}$ is updated in sequence, observations can be discarded immediately after they are used to update the value of $\bar{A}$.

---

[2] In fact, addition and subtraction operations are adequate as the iterative function is equivalent to $\Theta(\mathbf{Y}_n) = \max\left(0, \ \Theta(\mathbf{Y}_{n-1}) + \ \ln \phi(Y_n)\right)$ where $\Theta(\mathbf{Y}_n) \equiv \ln \bar{A}(\mathbf{Y}_n)$.

```
enum status {PENDING, SUCCESS, FAILURE};
struct FCC_Queue_Entry {
  ip4_addr DestAddr;
  time     WhenInitiated;
  status   Status;
}
```

Fig. 6. The structure of entries in the First-Contact Connection (FCC) queue

When running this algorithm in a worm detection system, we must maintain separate state information for each host being monitored. Thus, a state variable $\bar{\Lambda}_l$ is maintained for each local host l.

It is also necessary to track which hosts have been previously contacted by l. We track the set of Previously Contacted Hosts, or PCH set, for each local host.

Finally, each local host l has an associated queue of the first-contact connection attempts that l has issued but that have not yet been processed as observations. The structure of the records that are pushed on this FCC queue are shown in Figure 6. The choice of a queue for this data structure ensures that first-contact connection attempts are processed in the order in which they are issued, not in the order in which their status is determined.

The algorithm itself is quite simple and is triggered upon one of three events.

1. When the worm detection system observes a packet (TCP SYN or UDP) sent by local host l, it checks to see if the destination address d is in l's previously contacted host (PCH) set. If it isn't, it adds d to the PCH set and adds a new entry to the end of the FCC queue with d as the destination address and status PENDING.
2. When an incoming packet arrives addressed to local host l and the source address is also the destination address (DestAddr) of a record in l's FCC queue, the packet is interpreted as a response to the first-contact connection request and the status of the FCC record is updated. The status of the FCC record is set to SUCCESS unless the packet is a TCP RST packet, which indicates a rejected connection.
3. Whenever the entry on the front of the FCC queue has status PENDING and has been in the queue longer than the connection timeout period, a timeout occurs and the entry is assigned the status of FAILURE.

When any of the above events causes the entry at the front of the FCC queue to have status other than PENDING, it is dequeued and $\bar{\Lambda}_l$ is updated and compared to η_1. If $\bar{\Lambda}_l \geq \eta_1$, we halt testing for host l and immediately conclude that l is infected. Dequeuing continues so long as $\bar{\Lambda}_l < \eta_1$, the front entry of the FCC queue has status other than PENDING, and the queue is not empty.

3   Slowing Worm Propagation by Using Credit-Based Connection Rate Limiting

It is necessary to limit the rate at which first-contact connections can be initiated in order to ensure that worms cannot propagate rapidly between the moment scanning begins and the time at which the scan's first-contact connections have timed out and been observed by our reverse sequential hypothesis test ($\overleftarrow{HT}$).

Twycross and Williamson [27, 22] use a technique they call a virus throttle to limit outgoing first-contact connections. When observing a given host, their algorithm maintains a working set of up to five hosts previously contacted by the host they are observing. For the purpose of their work, a first-contact connection is a connection to a host not in this working set. First-contact connections issued when the working set is full are not sent out, but instead added to a queue. Once per second the least recently used entry in the working set is removed and, if the pending queue of first-contact connection requests is not empty, a request is pulled off the queue, delivered, and its destination address is added to the working set. All requests in the queue with the same destination address are also removed from the queue and delivered.

Virus throttling is likely to interfere with HTTP connection requests for inlined images, as many Web pages contain ten or more inlined images each of which is located on a distinct peering server. While a slow but bursty stream of requests from a Web browser will eventually be released by the throttle, mail servers, Web crawlers, and other legitimate services that issue first-contact connections at a rate greater than once per second will overflow the queue. In this case, the virus throttling algorithm quarantines the host and allows no further first-contact connections.

To achieve rate limiting with a better false positive rate we once again present a solution inspired by sequential hypothesis testing and that relies on the observation that benign first-contact connections are likely to succeed whereas those issued by scanners are likely to fail. This credit-based approach, however, is unlike $\overleftarrow{HT}$ in that it assumes that a connection will fail until evidence proves otherwise. Because it does not wait for a timeouts to act, it can react immediately to a burst of connections and halt the flow so that $\overleftarrow{HT}$ can then make a more informed decision as to whether the host is infected. As it does not force connections to be evaluated in order, CBCRL can also immediately process evidence of connection successes. This will enable it to quickly increase the allowed first-contact connection rate when these requests are benign.

Credit-based connection rate limiting, as summarized in Figure 7, works by allocating to each local host, l, a starting balance of ten credits ($C_l \leftarrow 10$) which can be used for issuing first-contact connection requests. Whenever a first-contact connection request is observed, a credit is subtracted from the sending host's balance ($C_l \leftarrow C_l - 1$). If the successful acknowledgment of a first-contact connection is observed, the host that initiated the request is issued two additional credits ($C_l \leftarrow C_l + 2$). No action is taken when connections fail, as the cost of issuing a first-contact connection has already been deducted from the issuing host's balance. Finally, first-contact connection requests are blocked if the host does not have any credit available ($C_l = 0$)[3].

---

[3] In Section 8, we discuss the alternative of allowing all TCP requests to be transmitted and queueing responses until credits are available.

Event	Change to C_l
Starting balance	$C_l \leftarrow 10$
FCC issued by l	$C_l \leftarrow C_l - 1$
FCC succeeds	$C_l \leftarrow C_l + 2$
Every second	$C_l \leftarrow \max(10, \frac{2}{3}C_l)$ if $C_l > 10$
Allowance	$C_l \leftarrow 1$ if $C_l = 0$ for 4 seconds

Fig. 7. The underlying equations behind credit-based connection rate limiting. Changes to a host's balance are triggered by the first-contact connections (FCCs) it initiates and by the passing of time

If a first-contact connection succeeds with probability θ, its expected payoff from issuing that connection is its expected success credit minus its cost, or $2\theta - 1$. This payoff is positive for $\theta > \frac{1}{2}$ and negative otherwise. Hosts that scan with a low rate of successful connections will quickly consume their credits whereas benign hosts that issue first-contact connections with high rates of success will nearly double their credits each time they invest them.

As described so far, the algorithm could result in two undesirable states. First, a host could acquire a large number of credits while performing a benign activity (e.g. Web crawling) which could be used later by a scanning worm. Second, a network outage could cause a benign host to use all of its credits after which it would starve for a lack of first-contact connection successes.

These problems are addressed by providing each host with a small allowance and by putting in place a high rate of inflation. If a host has been without credits for four seconds, we issue the host a single credit ($C_l \leftarrow 1$ if $C_l \leq 0$). This not only ensures that the host does not starve, but enables us to collect another observation to feed into our hypothesis test ($\overleftarrow{HT}$). Because $\overleftarrow{HT}$, as configured in Section 4, observes all first-contact connection requests as successes or failures within three seconds, providing a starving process with a credit allowance only after more than three seconds have passed ensures that $\overleftarrow{HT}$ will have been executed on all previously issued first-contact connection requests. If $\overleftarrow{HT}$ has already concluded that the host is a worm, it is expected that the system will be quarantined and so no requests will reach their destination regardless of the credit balance.

For each second that passes, a host that has acquired more than 10 credits will be forced to surrender up to a third of them, but not so many as to take its balance below 10 ($C_l \leftarrow \max(10, \frac{2}{3}C_l)$ if $C_l > 10$). A host that is subject to the maximum inflation rate, with a first-contact connection rate r, success rate $\theta > 0$, and credit balance $C_{l,t}$ at time t, will see this balance reach an equilibrium state $\hat{C}$ when $\hat{C} = C_{l,t} = C_{l,t+1}$.

$$C_{l,t+1} = \frac{2}{3}(C_{l,t} + r \cdot (2\theta - 1))$$

$$\hat{C} = \frac{2}{3}(\hat{C} + r \cdot (2\theta - 1))$$

$$\hat{C} = \frac{2}{3}\hat{C} + \frac{2}{3} \cdot r \cdot (2\theta - 1)$$

$$\frac{1}{3}\hat{C} = \frac{2}{3} \cdot r \cdot (2\theta - 1)$$

$$\hat{C} = 2 \cdot r \cdot (2\theta - 1)$$

One can now see that we chose the inflation constant $\frac{2}{3}$ to ensure that, in the upcoming second, a host that has a perfect first-contact connection success rate ($\theta = 1$) will have twice as many credits as it could have needed in the previous second. Also note that the maximum inflation rate, which seems quite steep, is only fully applied when $\hat{C} \geq 15$, which in turn occurs only when the first-contact connection rate r is greater than 7.5 requests per second. Twycross and Williamson's virus throttle, on the other hand, can only assume that any host with a first-contact connection rate consistently greater than one request per second is a worm.

The constant of 10 was chosen for the starting credit balance (and for the equilibrium minimum credit balance for benign hosts with first-contact connection rates below 5 requests/second) in order to match the requirements of our sequential hypothesis test ($\overleftarrow{HT}$) as currently configured (see parameters in Section 4), which itself requires a minimum of 10 observations in order to conclude that a host is engaged in scanning. Slowing the rate at which the first 10 observations can be obtained will only delay the time required by $\overleftarrow{HT}$ to conclude that a host is engaged in scanning. Should the parameters of $\overleftarrow{HT}$ be reconfigured and the minimum number of observations required to conclude a host is a scanner change, the starting credit balance for rate-limiting can be changed to match it.

4   Experimental Setup

We evaluated our algorithms using two traces collected at the peering link of a medium sized ISP; one collected in April 2003 (isp-03) containing 404 active hosts and the other in January 2004 (isp-04) containing 451 active hosts. These traces, summarized in Table 1, were collected using tcpdump.

Obtaining usable traces was quite difficult. Due to privacy concerns, network administrators are particularly loathe to share traces, let alone those that contain payload data in addition to headers. Yet, we required the payload data in order to manually determine which, if any, worm was present on a host that was flagged as infected.

To best simulate use of our algorithm in a worm detection system that is used to quarantine hosts, we only tested local hosts for infection. Remote hosts were not tested.

In configuring our reverse sequential hypothesis test ($\overleftarrow{HT}$), first-contact connection requests were interpreted as failures if they were not acknowledged within a three second grace period. First-contact connection requests for which TCP RST packets were received in response were immediately reported as failure observations. Connection success probability estimates were chosen to be:

$$\theta_0 = 0.7 \qquad \theta_1 = 0.1$$

Table 1. Summary of network traces

	isp-03	isp-04
Date	2003/04/10	2004/01/28
Duration	627 minutes	66 minutes
Total outbound connection attempts	1,402,178	178,518
Total active local host	404	451

Confidence requirements were set to:

$$\alpha = 0.00005 \qquad \beta = 0.99$$

Note that these confidence requirements are for each reverse sequential hypothesis test, and that a test is performed for each first-contact connection that is observed. Therefore, the false positive rate is chosen to be particularly low as testing will occur many times for each host.

For each local host we maintained a Previously Contacted Host (PCH) set of only the last 64 destination addresses that each local host had communicated with (LRU replacement). For the sake of the experiment, a first-contact connection request was any TCP SYN packet or UDP packet addressed to a host that was not in the local host's PCH set. While using a fixed sized PCH set demonstrates the efficacy of our test under the memory constraints that are likely to occur when observing large (e.g. class B) networks, this fixed memory usage comes at a cost. As described in Section 6, it is possible for a worm to exploit limitations in the PCH set size in order to avoid having its scans detected.

For sake of comparison, we also implemented Twycross and Williamson's 'virus throttle' as described in [22]. Since our traces contain only those packets seen at the peering point, our results may differ from a virus throttle implemented at each local host as Twycross and Williamson recommend. However, because observing connections farther from the host results in a reduction in the number of connections observed, it should only act to reduce the reported number of false positives in which benign behavior is throttled.

All algorithms were implemented in Perl, and used traces that had been pre-processed by the Bro Network Intrusion Detection System [13, 12].

We did not observe FTP-DATA, finger, and IDENT connections as these connections are the result of local hosts responding to remote hosts, and are not likely to be accepted by a host that has not issued a request for such a connection. These connections are thus unlikely to be useful for worm propagation.

5   Results

Our reverse sequential hypothesis test detected two hosts infected with CodeRed II [4, 20] from the April, 2003 trace (isp-03). Our test detected one host infected with Blaster/Lovsan [5], three hosts infected with MyDoom/Novarg [11, 21], and one host infected with Minmail.j [6] from the January, 2004 trace (isp-04).

Table 2. Alarms reported by reverse sequential hypothesis testing combined with credit-based rate limiting. The cause of each alarm was later identified manually by comparing observed traffic to signature behaviors described at online virus libraries

	isp-03	isp-04
Worms/Scanners detected		
CodeRed II	2	0
Blaster	0	1
MyDoom	0	3
Minmail.j	0	1
HTTP (other)	3	1
Total	5	6
False alarms		
HTTP	0	3
SMTP	0	3
Total	0	6
P2P detected	6	11
Total identified	11	23

Table 3. Alarms reported by virus throttling

	isp-03	isp-04
Worms/Scanners detected		
CodeRed II	2	0
MyDoom	0	1
HTTP (other)	1	1
Total	3	2
False alarms	0	0
P2P detected	2	3
Total identified	5	5

The worms were conclusively identified by painstakingly comparing the logged traffic with the cited worm descriptions at various online virus/worm information libraries. Our test also identified four additional hosts that we classify as HTTP scanners because each sent SYN packets to port 80 of at least 290 addresses within a single class B network. These results are summarized in Table 2.

While peer-to-peer applications are not necessarily malicious, many network administrators would be loathe to classify them as benign. Peer-to-peer file sharing applications also exhibit ambiguous network behavior, as they attempt to contact a large number of transient peers that are often unwilling or unavailable to respond to connection requests. While peer-to-peer clients are deemed undesirable on most of the corporate networks that we envision our approach being used to protect, it would be unfair to classify these hosts as infected. For this reason we place hosts that we detect running peer-to-peer applications into their own category. Even if detections of these hosts are classified as false alarms, the number of alarms is manageable.

Table 4. Composite results for both traces. A total of 7 HTTP scanning worms and 5 email worms were present

	Alarms	Detection	Efficiency	Effectiveness
$\overleftarrow{HT}$	34	11	0.324	0.917
virus-throttling	10	5	0.500	0.417

Table 5. Comparison of rate limiting by credit-based connection rate limiting (CBCRL) vs. a virus throttle. Unnecessary rate limiting means that CBCRL dropped at least one packet from a host. For virus throttling, we only classify a host as rate limited if the delay queue reaches a length greater than five

	CBCRL		Virus Throttling	
	isp-03	isp-04	isp-03	isp-04
Worms/Scanners	5	1	3	4
P2P	4	8	3	7
Unnecessary rate limiting	0	0	84	59

Three additional false alarms were reported for three of the 60 (isp-04) total hosts transmitting SMTP traffic. We suspect the false alarms are the result of bulk retransmission of those emails that have previously failed when the recipients' mail servers were unreachable. We suggest that organizations may want to white-list their SMTP servers, or significantly increase the detection thresholds for this protocol.

The remaining three false alarms are specific to the isp-04 trace, and resulted from HTTP traffic. It appears that these false alarms were raised because of a temporary outage at a destination network at which multiple remote hosts became unresponsive. These may have included servers used to serve inlined images.

Upon discovering these failures, we came to realize that it would be possible for an adversary to create Web sites that served pages with large numbers of inlined image tags linked to non-responsive addresses. If embedded with scripts, these sites might even be designed to perform scanning of the client's network from the server. Regardless, any client visiting such a site would appear to be engaged in HTTP scanning. To prevent such denial of service attacks from rendering a worm detection system unusable, we require a mechanism for enabling users to deactivate quarantines triggered by HTTP requests. We propose that HTTP requests from such hosts be redirected to a site that uses a CAPTCHA (Completely Automated Public Turing Test to Tell Computers and Humans Apart [23]), to confirm that a user is present and was using a Web browser at the time of quarantine.

Results for our implementation of Twycross and Williamson's virus throttle [22] are summarized in Table 3. Their algorithm blocked both instances of CodeRed II, but failed to detect Blaster, three instances of MyDoom (which is admittedly an email worm and not an IP scanning worm), and two low rate HTTP scanners. It did, however, detect one host infected with MyDoom that $\overleftarrow{HT}$ failed to detect. The virus throttle also detected fewer hosts running peer-to-peer

Table 6. The number of first-contact connections permitted before hosts were reported as infected. The value pairs represent individual results for two different `CodeRed II` infections and two different HTTP scanners

	$\overleftarrow{HT}$ with CBCRL	Virus Throttling
`CodeRed II`	10,10	6,7
Other HTTP scanners	10,10	102,526

applications, which for fairness we classify as a reduction in false alarms in virus throttling's favor in our composite results summarized in Table 4.

These composite results for both traces report the number of hosts that resulted in alarms and the number of those alarms that were detections of the 12 worms located in our traces. We also include the *efficiency*, which is the number of detections over the total number of alarms, and the *effectiveness*, which is the total number of detections over the total number of infected hosts we have found in these traces. While $\overleftarrow{HT}$ is somewhat less efficient than virus throttling, the more than two-fold increase in effectiveness is well worth the trade-off. In addition, corporate networks that forbid peer-to-peer file sharing applications will see a two-fold increase in efficiency.

Table 5 shows the number of hosts that had connection requests blocked by our credit-based algorithm and the number of hosts that were rate limited by Twycross and Williamson's algorithm. For credit-based connection rate limiting, we say that a machine has been rate limited if a single packet is dropped. For the virus throttle, we say that a machine has been rate limited if the outgoing delay queue length is greater than five, giving Twycross and Williamson the benefit of the doubt that users won't notice unless connections are severely throttled. Our credit-based algorithm only limited the rates of hosts that our reverse sequential hypothesis test reported as infected. In contrast, even given our generous definition, more than 10% of the hosts in both traces were rate limited by Twycross and Williamson's algorithm.

Table 6 reports the number of first-contact connections permitted by the two approaches for those scanners that both detected. `CodeRed II` is a fast scanner, and so virus throttling excels in blocking it after 6 to 7 connection requests. This speed is expected to come at the price of detecting any service, malicious or benign, that issues high-rate first-contact connections.

Reverse Sequential Hypothesis Testing with credit-based connection rate limiting detects worms after a somewhat higher number of first-contact connections are permitted (10), but does so regardless of the scanning rate. Whereas our approach detects a slow HTTP scanner after 10 first-contact connection requests, the virus throttle requires as many as 526.

6   Limitations

Credit-based connection rate limiting is resilient to network uplink outages as hosts starved for credits will receive an allowance credit seconds after the network is repaired. Unfortunately, this will be of little consolation as Reverse Sequential Hypothesis Testing($\overleftarrow{HT}$) may have already concluded that all hosts are scanners.

This may not be a problem if network administrators are given the power to invalidate observations made during the outage period, and to automatically reverse any quarantining decisions that would not have been taken without these invalid observations.

Of greater concern is that both Reverse Sequential Hypothesis Testing and credit-based connection rate limiting rely exclusively on the observation that hosts engaged in scanning will have lower first-contact connection success rates than benign hosts. New hypotheses and tests are required to detect worms for which this statistical relationship does not hold.

In particular, our approach is not likely to detect a *topological* worm, which scans for new victim hosts by generating a list of addresses that the infected host has already contacted. Nor is our approach likely to detect flash worms, which contain hit-lists of susceptible host addresses identified by earlier scans.

Also problematic is that two instances of a worm on different networks could collaborate to ensure that none of their first-contact connections will appear to fail. For example, if worm A does not receive a response to a first-contact connection request after half the timeout period, it could send a message to worm B asking it to forge a connection response. This *forged response attack* prevents our system from detecting connection failures. To thwart this attack for TCP connections, a worm detection system implemented on a router can modify the TCP sequence numbers of traffic as it enters and leaves the network. For example, the result of a hash function $h(\text{IP}_{\text{local}}, \text{IP}_{\text{remote}}, \text{salt})$ may be added to all sequence numbers on outgoing traffic and subtracted from all incoming sequence numbers. The use of the secret salt prevents the infected hosts from calculating the sequence number used to respond to a connection request which they have sent, but not received. By storing the correct sequence number in the FCC queue, responses can then be validated by the worm detection system.

Another concern is the possibility that a worm could arrive at its target already in possession of a list of known repliers – hosts that are known to reply to connection requests at a given port. This *known-replier attack* could employ lists that are programmed into the worm at creation, or accumulated by the worm as it spreads through the network. First-contact connections to these known-repliers will be very likely to succeed and can be interleaved with scans to raise the first-contact connection success rate. A one to one interleaving is likely to ensure that more than half of all connections succeed. This success rate would enable the scanner to bypass credit-based connection rate limiting, and delay detection by Reverse Sequential Hypothesis Testing until the scanner had contacted all of its known-repliers. What's worse, a worm could avoid detection altogether if the detection system defines a first-contact connection with respect to a fixed sized previously contact host (PCH) set. If the PCH set tracks only the n previously visited hosts, the scanner can cycle through $(n/2) + 1$ known-repliers, interleaved with as many new addresses, and *never* be detected[4]. To prevent a worm from scanning your local network by interleaving connections to known-

---

[4] For detecting such a worm, a random replacement policy will be superior to an LRU replacement policy, but will still not be effective enough for long known-replier lists.

repliers outside of your network, Weaver *et al.* [26] propose that one hypothesis test be run for local connections (i.e. those within the same IP block) and another for connections to remote hosts. If hosts in your local network are widely and randomly dispersed through a large IP space[5], then a worm will have a low probability of finding another host to infect before being quarantined.

A worm might also avoid detection by interleaving scanning with other apparently benign behavior, such as Web crawling. A subset of these *benign interleaving attacks* can be prevented by detecting scanners based on the destination port they target in addition to the source IP of the local host. While it is still fairly easy to create benign looking traffic for ports such as HTTP, for which one connection can lead to information about other active hosts receptive to new connections, this is not the case for ports such as those used by SSH. Running separate scan detection tests for each destination port that a local host addresses can ensure that connections to one service aren't used to mask scans to other services.

Finally, if an infected host can impersonate other hosts, the host could escape quarantine and cause other (benign) hosts to be quarantined. To address these *address impersonation attacks*, it is important that a complete system for network quarantining include strong methods for preventing IP masquerading by its local hosts, such as switch level egress filtering. Host quarantining should also be enforced as close to the host as is possible without relying on the host to quarantine itself. If these boundaries cannot be enforced between each host, one must assume that when one machine is infected, all of the machines within the same boundary will also be infected.

7   Related Work

We were motivated by the work of Moore *et al.* [10], who model attempts at containing worms using quarantining. They perform theoretical simulations, many of which use parameters principally from the `CodeRed II` [4, 20] outbreak. They argue that it is impossible to prevent systems from being vulnerable to worms and that treatment cannot be performed fast enough to prevent worms from spreading, leaving containment (quarantining) as the most viable way to prevent worm outbreaks from becoming epidemics.

Early work on containment includes Staniford *et al.*'s work on the GrIDS Intrusion Detection System [19], which advocates the detection of worms and viruses by tracing their paths through the departments of an organization. More recently, Staniford [16] has worked to generalize these concepts by extending models for the spread of infinite-speed, random scanning worms through homogenous networks divided up into 'cells'. Simulating networks with 2^{17} hosts (two class B networks), Staniford limits the number of first-contact connections that a local host initiates to a given destination port to a threshold, T. While he claims that for most ports, a threshold of $T = 10$ is achievable in practice,

---

[5] Randomly dispersing local hosts through a large IP space can be achieved by using a network address translation (NAT) switch.

HTTP and KaZaA are exceptions. In comparison, reverse sequential hypothesis testing reliably identifies HTTP scanning in as few as 10 observations.

The TRAFEN [2, 3] system also observed failed connections for the purpose of identifying worms. The system was able to observe larger networks, without access to end-points, by inferring connection failures from ICMP messages. One problem with acting on information at this level is that an attacker could spoof source IP addresses to cause other hosts to be quarantined.

Our use of rate limiting in order to buy time to observe worm behavior was inspired by the virus throttle presented by Twycross and Williamson [22], which we described in detail in Section 3. Worms can evade a throttle by scanning at rates below one connection per second, allowing epidemics to double in size as quickly as once every two seconds.

An approach quite similar to our own has been simultaneously developed by Weaver, Staniford, and Paxson [26]. Their approach combines the rate limiting and hypothesis testing steps by using a reverse sequential hypothesis test that (like our CBCRL algorithm) assumes that connections fail until they are proven to succeed. As with CBCRL, out-of-order processing could cause a slight increase in detection delay, as the successes of connections sent before an infection event may be processed after connections are initiated after the infection event. In the context of their work, in which the high-performance required to monitor large networks is a key goal, the performance benefits are likely to outweigh the slight cost in detection speed.

For a history and recent trends in worm evolution, we recommend the work of Kienzle and Elder [8]. For a taxonomy of worms and a review of worm terminology, see Weaver *et al.* [25].

8   Future Work

As worm authors become aware of the limitations discussed in Section 6, it will be necessary to revise our algorithms to detect scanning at the resolution of the local host (source address) and targeted service (destination port), rather than looking at the source host alone. Solutions for managing the added memory requirements imposed by this approach have been explored by Weaver, Staniford, and Paxson [26].

The intrusiveness of credit-based connection rate limiting, which currently drops outgoing connection requests when credit balances reach zero, can be further reduced. Instead of halting outgoing TCP first-contact connection requests from hosts that do not maintain a positive credit balance, the requests can be sent immediately and the responses held until a positive credit balance is achieved. This improvement has the combined benefits of reducing the delays caused by false rate limiting while simultaneously ensuring that fewer connections are allowed to complete when a high-speed scanning worm issues a burst of connection requests. As a result, the remaining gap in response speed between credit-based connection rate limiting and Twycross and Williamson's virus throttle can be closed while further decreasing the risk of acting on false positives.

Finally, we would like to employ additional indicators of infection to further reduce the number of first-contact connection observations required to detect a worm. For example, it is reasonable to conclude that, when a host is deemed to be infected, those hosts to which it has most recently initiated successful connections are themselves more likely to be infected (as was the premise behind GrIDS [19]). We propose that this be accomplished by adding an event type, the report of an infection of a host that has recently contacted the current host, to our existing hypothesis test.

9   Conclusion

When combined, credit-based connection rate limiting and reverse sequential hypothesis testing ensure that worms are quickly identified with an attractively low false alarm rate. While no system can detect all possible worms, our new approach is a significant improvement over prior methods, which detect a smaller range of scanners and unnecessarily delay network traffic. What's more, the techniques introduced in this paper lend themselves to efficient implementation, as they need only be activated to observe a small subset of network events and require little calculation for the common case that traffic is benign.

Acknowledgments

This paper could not have been completed without the continued support of Vern Paxson and Hari Balakrishnan. We are indebted to Dave Andersen and Noah Case for the network logs used for our analysis. We would also like to thank the anonymous reviewers as well as Nick Feamster, David Molnar, Rodrigo Miragaia Rodrigues, David Savitt, Matt Williamson, and especially Glenn Holloway for taking the time to review and comment on earlier drafts of this paper. Stuart Schechter would like to thank the National Science Foundation for support under grant CCR-0310877.

References

1. George Bakos and Vincent Berk. Early detection of internet worm activity by metering ICMP destination unreachable messages. In *Proceedings of the SPIE Aerosense*, 2002.
2. Vincent Berk, George Bakos, and Robert Morris. Designing a framework for active worm detection on global networks. In *Proceedings of the IEEE International Workshop on Information Assurance*, March 2003.
3. Vincent H. Berk, Robert S. Gray, and George Bakos. Using sensor networks and data fusion for early detection of active worms. In *Proceedings of the SPIE Aerosense Conference*, April 2003.
4. CERT. "Code Red II:" another worm exploiting buffer overflow in IIS indexing service DLL. http://tinyurl.com/2lzgb.
5. F-Secure. Computer virus information pages: Lovsan. http://tinyurl.com/ojd1.
6. F-Secure. Computer virus information pages: Mimail.J. http://tinyurl.com/3ybsp.
7. Jaeyeon Jung, Vern Paxson, Arthur W. Berger, and Hari Balakrishnan. Fast portscan detection using sequential hypothesis testing. In *Proceedings of the IEEE Symposium on Security and Privacy*, May 9–12, 2004.

8. Darrell M. Kienzle and Matthew C. Elder. Recent worms: a survey and trends. In *Proceedings of the 2003 ACM Workshop on Rapid Malcode*, pages 1–10. ACM Press, October 27, 2003.

9. David Moore, Vern Paxson, Stefan Savage, Colleen Shannon, Stuart Staniford, and Nicholas Weaver. Inside the Slammer worm. *IEEE Security and Privacy*, 1:33–39, July 2003.

10. David Moore, Colleen Shannon, Geoffrey M. Voelker, and Stefan Savage. Internet quarantine: Requirements for containing self-propagating code. In *Proceedings of IEEE INFOCOM*, April 1–3, 2003.

11. Network Associates Inc. Security threat report for W32/MydoomMM. http://tinyurl.com/2asgc.

12. Vern Paxson. Bro: A system for detecting network intruders in real-time. http://www.icir.org/vern/bro-info.html.

13. Vern Paxson. Bro: a system for detecting network intruders in real-time. *Computer Networks*, 31(23–24):2435–2463, 1999.

14. Stelios Sidiroglou and Angelos D. Keromytis. Countering network worms through automatic patch generation. Technical Report CUCS-029-03, 2003.

15. Stelios Sidiroglou and Angelos D. Keromytis. A network worm vaccine architecture. In *Proceedings of the IEEE International Workshops on Enabling Technologies: Infrastructure for Collaborative Enterprises (WETICE), Workshop on Enterprise Security*, June 2003.

16. Stuart Staniford. Containment of scanning worms in enterprise networks. *Journal of Computer Security*, Forthcoming.

17. Stuart Staniford, James Hoagland, and Joseph McAlerney. Practical automated detection of stealthy portscans. *Journal of Computer Security*, 10(1):105–136, 2002.

18. Stuart Staniford, Vern Paxson, and Nicholas Weaver. How to 0wn the Internet in your spare time. In *Proceedings of the 11th USENIX Security Symposium*, August 7–9, 2002.

19. S. Staniford-Chen, S. Cheung, R. Crawford, M. Dilger, J. Frank, J. Hoagland, K. Levitt, C. Wee, R. Yip, and D. Zerkle. GrIDS – A graph-based intrusion detection system for large networks. In *Proceedings of the 19th National Information Systems Security Conference*, volume 1, pages 361–370, October 1996.

20. Symantec. Security response – CodeRed II. http://tinyurl.com/89t0.

21. Symantec. Security response – W32.Novarg.Amm. http://tinyurl.com/2lv95.

22. Jamie Twycross and Matthew M. Williamson. Implementing and testing a virus throttle. In *Proceedings of the 12th USENIX Security Symposium*, August 4–8, 2003.

23. Luis von Ahn, Manuel Blum, and John Langford. Telling humans and computers apart (automatically) or how lazy cryptographers do AI. Technical Report CMU-CS-02-117, February 2002.

24. Abraham Wald. *Sequential Analysis*. J. Wiley & Sons, New York, 1947.

25. Nicholas Weaver, Vern Paxson, Stuart Staniford, and Robert Cunningham. A taxonomy of computer worms. In *Proceedings of the 2003 ACM Workshop on Rapid Malcode*, pages 11–18. ACM Press, October 27, 2003.

26. Nicholas Weaver, Stuart Staniford, and Vern Paxson. Very fast containment of scanning worms. In *Proceedings of the 13th USENIX Security Symposium*, August 9–13, 2004.

27. Matthew M. Williamson. Throttling viruses: Restricting propagation to defeat malicious mobile code. In *Proceedings of The 18th Annual Computer Security Applications Conference (ACSAC 2002)*, December 9–13, 2002.

A   Optimizing the Computation of Repeated Reverse Sequential Hypothesis Tests

It is unnecessarily expensive to repeatedly recompute Λ in reverse sequence each time a new first-contact connection is observed. A significant optimization requires that we maintain single state variable $\bar{\Lambda}$, calculated iteratively in the order in which events are observed.

$$\bar{\Lambda}(\mathbf{Y}_n) \;=\; \max\left(1,\ \bar{\Lambda}(\mathbf{Y}_{n-1})\phi(Y_n)\right) \quad \bar{\Lambda}(\mathbf{Y}_0) \;\equiv\; 1. \tag{1}$$

We will prove that $\bar{\Lambda}(\mathbf{Y}_n) > \eta_1$ if and only if a reverse sequential hypothesis test starting backward from observation n would lead us to conclude that the host was infected.

We first prove the following lemma stating that if a reverse sequential hypothesis test reports an infection, our optimized algorithm will also report an infection.

Lemma 1. *For $\eta_1 > 1$ and for mutually independent random variables Y_i,*

$$\forall m \in [1,n] : \Lambda(Y_n, Y_{n-1}, \ldots, Y_m) \geq \eta_1 \Rightarrow \bar{\Lambda}(\mathbf{Y}_n) \geq \eta_1 \tag{2}$$

Proof. We begin by replacing the Λ term with its equivalent expression in terms of ϕ:

$$\eta_1 \leq \Lambda(Y_n, Y_{n-1}, \ldots, Y_m) \tag{3}$$

$$\leq \prod_{i=m}^{n} \phi(Y_i) \tag{4}$$

We can place a lower bound on the value of $\bar{\Lambda}(Y_n)$ by exploiting the fact that, in any iteration, $\bar{\Lambda}$ cannot return a value less than 1.

$$\begin{aligned}
\bar{\Lambda}(\mathbf{Y}_n) &= \bar{\Lambda}(Y_1, Y_2, \ldots, Y_n) \\
&\geq 1 \cdot \bar{\Lambda}(Y_m, Y_{m+1}, \ldots, Y_n) \\
&\geq \prod_{i=m}^{n} \phi(Y_i) \geq \eta_1
\end{aligned}$$

where the last inequality follows the steps taken in Equations (3) and (4).
Thus, $\Lambda(Y_n, Y_{n-1}, \ldots, Y_m) \geq \eta_1 \Rightarrow \bar{\Lambda}(\mathbf{Y}_n) \geq \eta_1$.

We must also prove that our optimized algorithm will only report an infection when a reverse sequential hypothesis test would also report an infection. Recall that a reverse sequential hypothesis test will only report an infection if Λ exceeds η_1 before falling below η_0.

Lemma 2. *For thresholds $\eta_0 < 1 < \eta_1$ and for mutually independent random variables Y_i, if $\bar{\Lambda}(\mathbf{Y}_i) \geq \eta_1$ for some $i = n$, but $\bar{\Lambda}(\mathbf{Y}_i) < \eta_1$ for all $i \in [1, n-1]$, then there exists a subsequence of observations starting at observation n and moving backward to observation $m \in [1,n]$ for which $\Lambda(Y_n, Y_{n-1}, \ldots, Y_m) \geq \eta_1$ and such that there exists no k in $[m,n]$ such that $\Lambda(Y_n, Y_{n-1}, \ldots, Y_k) \leq \eta_0$.*

Proof. Choose m as the largest observation index for which it held that:

$$\bar{\Lambda}(\mathbf{Y}_{m-2})\phi(Y_{m-1}) < 1$$

We know that $m < n$ because $\bar{\Lambda}(\mathbf{Y}_{n-1})\phi(Y_n)$ is greater than η_1 which is in turn greater than 1. Let $m = 1$ if the above relation does not hold for any observation with index greater than 1. It follows that $\bar{\Lambda}(\mathbf{Y}_{m-1}) = 1$ and thus:

$$\bar{\Lambda}(\mathbf{Y}_m) = \phi(Y_m)$$

Because we chose m such that $\bar{\Lambda}(\mathbf{Y}_{j-2})\phi(Y_{j-1}) \geq 1$ for all $j > m$:

$$\bar{\Lambda}(\mathbf{Y}_n) = \prod_{j=m}^{n} \phi(Y_j)$$
$$= \Lambda(Y_n, Y_{n-1}, \ldots, Y_m)$$

Thus, $\bar{\Lambda}(\mathbf{Y}_n) \geq \eta_1 \Rightarrow \Lambda(Y_n, Y_{n-1}, \ldots, Y_m) \geq \eta_1$.

To prove that there exists no k in $[m, n]$ such that $\Lambda(Y_n, Y_{n-1}, \ldots, Y_k) \leq \eta_0$, suppose that such a k exists. It follows that:

$$\prod_{j=k}^{n} \phi(Y_j) \leq \eta_0 < 1 \tag{5}$$

Recall that we chose m to ensure that:

$$\eta_1 \leq \prod_{j=m}^{n} \phi(Y_j) \tag{6}$$

The product on the right hand side can be separated into factors from before and after observation k.

$$\eta_1 \leq \prod_{j=m}^{k-1} \phi(Y_j) \cdot \prod_{j=k}^{n} \phi(Y_j). \tag{7}$$

We then use Equation (5) to substitute an upper bound of 1 on the latter product.

$$\eta_1 \leq \prod_{j=m}^{k-1} \phi(Y_j)$$
$$\eta_1 \leq \bar{\Lambda}(\mathbf{Y}_{k-1})$$

This contradicts the hypothesis that $\bar{\Lambda}(\mathbf{Y}_i) < \eta_1$ for all $i \in [1, n-1]$.

If we were concerned with being notified when the test came to the 'benign' conclusion we could create an analogous function $\underline{\Lambda}$:

$$\underline{\Lambda}(\mathbf{Y}_n) = \min\left(1, \ \underline{\Lambda}(\mathbf{Y}_{n-1})\phi(Y_n)\right)$$

The lemmas required to show equivalence and proof are also analogous.

Detecting Unknown Massive Mailing Viruses Using Proactive Methods

Ruiqi Hu and Aloysius K. Mok

Department of Computer Sciences,
University of Texas at Austin, Austin, Texas 78712, USA
{hurq,mok}@cs.utexas.edu

Abstract. The detection of unknown viruses is beyond the capability of many existing virus detection approaches. In this paper, we show how proactive customization of system behaviors can be used to improve the detection rate of unknown malicious executables. Two general proactive methods, behavior skewing and cordoning, and their application in BESIDES, a prototype system that detects unknown massive mailing viruses, are presented.

Keywords: virus detection; malicious executable detection; intrusion detection.

1 Introduction

Two major approaches employed by intrusion detection systems (IDSs) are misuse-based detection and anomaly-based detection. Because misuse-based detection relies on known signatures of intrusions, misuse-based IDSs cannot in general provide protection against new types of intrusions whose signatures are not yet cataloged. On the other hand, because anomaly-based IDSs rely on identifying deviations from the "normal" profile of the protected system's behavior, they are prone to reporting false-positives unless the normal profile of the protected system is well characterized.

In either case, detection must be performed as soon as an intrusion occurs and certainly before the intruder can cause harm and/or hide its own tracks. In this paper, we present the paradigm of PAIDS (ProActive Intrusion Detection System) and describe an application of PAIDS that can detect some classes of intrusions without knowing *a priori* their signatures and does so with very small false positives. PAIDS also provides a way to dynamically trade off the time it takes to detect an intrusion and the damage that an intruder can cause, and can therefore tolerate intrusions to an extent. To achieve these advantages, PAIDS exploits two general techniques: *behavior skewing* and *cordoning*.

Traditionally, the security of a computer system is captured by a set of security policies. A complete security policy should classify each behavior of a system as either legal or illegal. In practice, however, specifications of security policies often fail to scale [1] and are likely to be incomplete. Given a security policy, we can instead partition the set of all behaviors of a system into three subsets: (S1) Legal behaviors, (S2) Illegal behaviors and (S3) Unspecified behaviors, corresponding to whether a behavior is consistent, inconsistent or independent of

E. Jonsson et al. (Eds.): RAID 2004, LNCS 3224, pp. 82–101, 2004.
© Springer-Verlag Berlin Heidelberg 2004

the security policy. (Alternatively, think of a security policy as the axioms of a theory for establishing the legality of system behaviors.) In this context, behavior skewing refers to the modification of a security policy P into P' such that the subset of legal behaviors remains unchanged under P', but some of the behaviors that are in the subset (S3) under P are illegal under P'. By implementing detectors that can recognize the enlarged subset (S2), behavior skewing can catch intruders that would otherwise be unnoticed under the unmodified policy P. The speed of detection depends on the length of the prefix of the illegal behavior that distinguishes it from the legal behaviors. To contain the damage caused by an intrusion, we seek ways to isolate the system components that are engaged in the illegal behavior, hopefully until we can distinguish it from the legal behaviors. By virtualizing the environment external to the system components that are engaged in the illegal behavior, cordoning prevents the system from permanent damage until the illegal behavior can be recognized.

In this paper, we illustrate an application of the PAIDS paradigm by BESIDES, a tool for detecting massive mailing viruses. We have applied behavior skewing and cordoning techniques to the NT-based Windows operating systems (Windows 2000 and Windows XP). Inasmuch as behavior skewing and cordoning are general techniques, we specialize them to certain types of system behaviors for efficient implementation. Specifically, we use behavior skewing to customize the security policy upon the use of certain information items on the protected system. An *information item* can be any logical entity that carries information, e.g., a filename, an email address, or a binary file. Behavior skewing is accomplished by customizing the access control mechanism that governs the access to the information items. In a similar vein, cordoning is applied to critical system resources whose integrity must be ensured to maintain system operability. Specifically, we provide mechanisms for dynamically isolating the interactions between a malicious process and a system resource so that any future interaction between them will not affect other legal processes' interaction with the resource. This is achieved by replacing the original resource with a virtual resource the first time a process accesses a system resource. The cordoning mechanism guarantees for each legal process that its updates to critical system resources are eventually committed to the actual system resources, If a malicious executable is detected, an execution environment (a cordon) consisting of virtual system resources is dynamically created for the malicious executable and its victims. Their previous updates to the actual system resources can be undone by performing recovery operations on those resources, while their future activities can be monitored and audited. Depending on the nature of the system resources, cordoning can be achieved through methods such as cordoning-in-time and cordoning-in-space.

The rest of this paper is organized as follows: Section 2 is a brief discussion of related works. Section 3 gives the details of how behavior skewing and cordoning work. Section 4 discusses the implementation of BESIDES, a prototype system we have implemented for detecting massive-mailing viruses. Section 5 presents the experiments we have performed with BESIDES and the analysis of the experimental results. Section 6 discusses some future directions.

2   Related Work

Virus detection is closely related to the more general topic of malicious executable detection [2, 3]. Traditional malicious executable detection solutions use signature-based methods, where signatures from known malicious executables are used to recognize attacks from them [4]. Security products such as virus scanners are examples of such applications. One of the focuses in signature-based methods research is the automatic generation of high quality signatures. Along this line of work, Kephart and Arnold developed a statistical method to extract virus signatures automatically [5]. Heuristic classifiers capable of generating signatures from a group of known viruses were studied in [6]. Recently, Schultz et al. examined how data mining methods can be applied to signature generation [7] and built a binary filter that can be integrated with email servers [8]. Although proved to be highly effective in detecting known malicious executables, signature-based methods are unable to detect unknown malicious executables. PAIDS explores the possibility of addressing the latter with a different set of methods, the proactive methods. In PAIDS, signatures of malicious behaviors are implicitly generated during the behavior skewing stage and they are later used in the behavior monitoring stage to detect malicious executables that perform such behaviors.

Static analysis techniques that verify programs for compliance with security properties have also been proposed for malicious executable detection. Some of them focus on the detection of suspicious symptoms: Biship and Dilger showed how file access race conditions can be detected dynamically [9]. Tesauro et al. used neural networks to detect boot sector viruses [10]. Another approach is to verify whether safe programming practices are followed. Lo et al. proposed to use "tell-tale signs" and "program slicing" for detecting malicious code [11]. These approaches are mainly used as preventive mechanisms and the approach used in PAIDS focuses more on the detection and tolerance of malicious executables.

Dynamic monitoring techniques such as sandboxes represent another approach that contributes to malicious executable detection. They essentially implement alternative reference monitoring mechanisms that observe software execution and enforce additional security policies when they detect violations [12]. The range of security policies that are enforcible through monitoring were studied in [13–15] and more general discussion on the use of security policies can be found in [1]. The behavior monitor mechanism used in PAIDS adopts a similar approach. Sandboxing is a general mechanism that enforces a security policy by executing processes in virtual environments (e.g., Tron [16], Janus [17], Consh [18], Mapbox [19], SubDomain [20], and Systrace [21]). Cordoning is similar to a light-weight sandboxing mechanism whose coverage and time parameters are customizable. However, cordoning emphasizes the virtualization of individual system resources, while traditional sandboxing mechanisms focus on the virtualization of the entire execution environment (e.g., memory space) of individual processes. More importantly, sandboxing usually provides little tolerance toward intrusions, while cordoning can tolerate misuse of critical system resources as explained in Section 3.2.

Deception tools have long been used as an effective way of defeating malicious intruders. Among them, Honeypot (and later Honeynet) is a vulnerable system (or network) intentionally deployed to lure intruders' attentions. They are useful for studying the intruders' techniques and for assessing the efficacy of system security settings [22, 23]. Traditional Honeypots are dedicated systems that are configured the same way as (or less secure than, depending on how they are used) production systems so that the intruders have no direct way to tell the difference between the two. In the context of the Honeypot, no modification is ever performed on production systems. The latest advances such as virtual Honeypots [24, 25] that simulate physical Honeypots at the network level still remain the same in this regard. Recently, the concept of Honeypots was generalized to Honeytokens – "an information system resource whose value lies in unauthorized or illicit use of that resource" [26]. So far, few implementation or experimental results have been reported (among them, a Linux patch that implements Honeytoken files was made available early 2004 [27]). The Honeytoken concept comes the closest to PAIDS. However, the proactive methods that PAIDS explores, such as behavior skewing and cordoning, are more comprehensive and systematic than Honeytokens. We note that the implementation of our IDS tool BESIDES was well on its way when the Honeytoken concept first appeared in 2003.

System behavior modifications are gaining more and more interest recently. Somayaji and Forrest applied "benign responses" to abnormal system call sequences [28]. The intrusion prevention tool LaBrea is able to trap known intruders by delaying their communication attempts [29]. The virus throttles built by Williamson et al. [30–32] utilized the temporal locality found in normal email traffics and were able to slow down and identify massive mailing viruses as they made massive connection attempts. Their success in both intrusion prevention and toleration confirms the effectiveness of behavior modification based methods. However, the modifications performed in all these methods do not attempt to modify possibly legal behaviors since that may incur false positives, while the behavior skewing method in PAIDS takes a further step and converts some of the legal but irrelevant behaviors into illegal behaviors. No false positives are induced in this context.

Intrusion detection is a research area that has a long history [33, 34]. Traditionally, IDSs have been classified into following categories: Misuse-based IDSs look for signatures of known intrusions, such as a known operation sequence that allows unauthorized users to acquire administrator privileges [35, 36]. This is very similar to the signature-based methods discussed earlier in this section. Anomaly-based IDSs detect intrusions by identifying deviations from normal profiles in system and network activities. These normal profiles can be studied from historical auditing data that are collected during legitimate system executions [34, 37–39]. Specification-based IDSs look for signatures of known legitimate activities that are derived from system specifications [40]. These IDSs differ from misused-based IDSs in that activities that do not match any signature are treated as intrusions in the former, but are regarded as legitimate ones in the latter. Hybrid IDSs integrate different types of IDSs as subsystems [41]. The limitations of different subsystems can be compensated and a better overall quality can be improved.

Many techniques devised in IDSs are applicable to malicious executable detection and vice versa. For example, in an effort to apply the specification-based approach to malicious executable detection, Giffin et al. showed how malicious manipulations that originated from mobile code can be detected [42]. Christodorescu and Jha proposed an architecture that detects malicious binary executables even in the presence of obfuscations [43]. One common goal of all IDSs (anomaly-based IDSs in particular) is to generate a profile using either explicit or implicit properties of the system that can effectively differentiate intrusive behaviors from normal behaviors. A wide variety of system properties, ranging from low-level networking traffic statistics and system call characteristics to high-level web access patterns and system resource usages, have been studied in literature. McHugh and Gates reported a rich set of localities observed in web traffic and pointed out such localities can be used to distinguish abnormal behaviors from normal behaviors [44]. None of them considers the possibility of modifying system security settings for intrusion detection purposes, which is explored in PAIDS. The proactive methods proposed in PAIDS modify the definition of normal behaviors through skewing the security policy in anticipation of the likely behavior of intruders. By doing so, PAIDS implicitly generates profiles that have small false positive rates, are easy to understand and configure, and are highly extensive.

3   Methodology

3.1   Behavior Skewing

As illustrated in Fig.1, behaviors are high-level abstractions of system activities that specify their intentions and effects, but ignore many of the implementation details of the actual operations they perform. We refer to the part of security assignments of behaviors that are explicitly specified to be legal (or illegal) as the *legal behavior set* (LBS) (or the *illegal behavior set* (IBS)). The security assignments of behaviors that are not explicitly specified either intentionally or unintentionally are denoted as the *unspecified behavior set* (UBS). The UBS consists of behaviors that either 1) the user considers to be irrelevant to her system's security or 2) the user is unaware of and unintentionally fails to specify their security assignments; the default security policy will apply to the behaviors in the set UBS. *Behavior skewing* refers to the manipulation of the security policy that customizes the security assignments of the behaviors in the set UBS that are implicitly assigned to be legal by default. The goal of behavior skewing is to create enough differences in the legal behaviors among homogeneous systems so that malicious executables are made prone to detection.

Specifically, behavior skewing customizes a security policy regarding the use of certain information items in a system. Behavior skewing creates its own access control mechanism that describes the use of information items since many

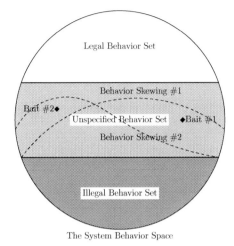

The System Behavior Space

Fig. 1. System States and Behavior Skewing

of the information items are not system resources and are thus not protected by native security mechanisms. The customization is performed on *information domains*, which are sets of information items that are syntactically equivalent but semantically different. For example, all text files in a target system form an information domain of text files. Specifically, behavior skewing reduces the access rights to existing items that are specified by the default access rights and creates new information items in an information domain with reduced access rights.

Figure 1 shows two possible behavior skewing instances. We emphasize that although different skewing mechanisms produce different security settings, they all preserve the same LBS. The modified security policy generated by a behavior skewing is called the *skewed security policy* (or *skewed policy* in short). The default security policy is transparent to the user and cannot be relied upon by the user to specify her intentions. Otherwise, additional conflict resolution mechanisms may be required.

After behavior skewing is completed, the usage of information items is monitored by a *behavior monitoring* mechanism that detects violations of the skewed policy. Any violation of the skewed policy triggers an intrusion alert. It should be noted that the monitoring mechanism does not enforce the skewed policy, instead it simply reports violations of the skewed policy to a higher-level entity (e.g., the user or an IDS) that is responsible for handling the reported violations.

3.2   Cordoning

Although behavior skewing and monitoring make malicious executables more prone to detection, actual detection cannot happen before the malicious executables have their chance to misbehave. Hence, there is a need for additional protection mechanisms to cope with any damage the malicious executables may incur before they are eventually detected. Among them, the recovery of system states is an obvious concern. In this section, we illustrate another proactive method, *cordoning*, that can be used to recover states of selected system resources. Existing system recovery solutions, such as restoring from backup media or from revertible file systems, usually perform bulk recovery operations, where the latest updates to individual system resources containing the most recent work of a user may get lost after the recovery. Cordoning addresses this problem by performing the recovery operation individually.

In general, cordoning is a mechanism that allows dynamic partial virtualization of execution environments for processes in a system. It is performed on *critical system resources* (CSRs), objects in the system whose safety are deemed critical to the system's integrity and availability (e.g., executables, network services, and data files, etc.). The cordoning mechanism converts a CSR (also called an *actual* CSR) to a *recoverable* CSR (or a *cordoned* CSR) that can be recovered to a known safe state by dynamically creating a virtual CSR (called the *current* CSR), and granting it to processes that intend to interact with the actual CSR. The current CSR provides the same interface as the actual CSR. The underlying cordoning mechanism ensures all updates to the current CSR are eventually applied to the actual CSR during normal system execution.

When a malicious executable is detected by the behavior monitor, its updates to all cordoned CSRs can be recovered by performing the corresponding *recover* operations on the cordoned CSRs that restore the actual CSRs to known secure states (called *recovered* CSRs). The malicious executable and its *victims* – its children, as well as processes accessing system resources that have been updated by the malicious executable[1] – continue to interact with the *current CSRs*, the same set of CSRs they are using at the time of detection. However, their future updates to this set of current CSRs will not be applied to the actual CSRs and are instead subject to audition and other intrusion investigation mechanisms. *Unaffected processes* – existing processes other than the malicious executable and its victims, and all newly started processes – will use the recovered CSRs in their future interactions. The malicious executable and its victims are thus *cordoned* by a dynamically created execution environment (called a *cordon*) that consists of these current CSRs. The operations performed by the malicious executable and its victims on CSRs are thus isolated from those performed by the unaffected processes.

CSRs can be classified as revertible CSRs, delayable CSRs, and substitutable CSRs based on their nature. Two cordoning mechanism: cordoning-in-time and cordoning-in-space can be applied to these CSRs as described below:

A *revertible* CSR is a CSR whose updates can be revoked. For example, a file in a journaling file system can be restored to a previous secure state if it is found corrupted during a virus infection. Cordoning of a revertible CSR can be

---

[1] We note that an accurate identification of victims can be as difficult as the identification of covert channels. The simple criteria we use here is a reasonable approximation although more accurate algorithms can be devised.

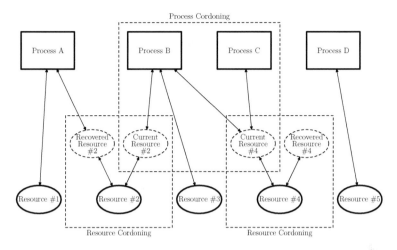

Fig. 2. A Cordoning Example

achieved by generating a *revocation list* consisting of revocation operations of all committed updates. The recovery of a revertible resource can be performed by carrying the revocation operations in the revocation list that leads to a secure state of the CSR.

Cordoning-in-time buffers operational requests on a CSR and delay their commitments until a secure state of the resource can be reached. It is thus also referred to as *delayed commitment*. Cordoning-in-time can be applied to *delayable* CSRs – CSRs that can tolerate certain delays when being accessed. For example, the network resource that serves a network transaction is delayable if the transaction is not a real-time transaction (e.g., a SMTP server). The delays on the requests can be made arbitrarily long unless it exceeds some transaction-specific time-out value. Time-outs constraint the maximum length of delays. Such a constraint, as well as others (e.g., constraints due to resource availability) may render a delayable CSR a *partially recoverable* CSR; the latter can only be recovered within a limited time interval. The recovery of a delayable resource can be performed by discarding buffered requests up to a secure state. If no such secure state can be found after exhausting all buffered requests, the CSR may not be securely recovered unless it is also revertible.

Cordoning-in-space is applied to a *substitutable* CSR – a CSR that can be replaced by another CSR (called its *substitute*) of the same type transparently. For example, a file is a substitutable CSR because any operation performed on a file can be redirected to a copy of that file. Cordoning-in-space redirects operational requests from a process toward a substitutable CSR to its substitute. The actual CSR is kept in secure states during the system execution and is updated by copying the content of its substitute only when the latter is in secure states. A substitutable CSR can be recovered by replacing it with a copy of the actual CSR saved when it is in a secure state. Where multiple substitutes exist for a CSR (e.g., multiple writer processes), further conflict resolution is required but

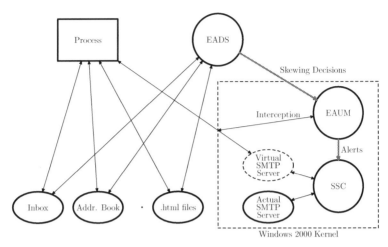

Fig. 3. The BESIDES Architecture

will not be covered in this paper. We note here that the cordoning and recovery of CSRs are independent mechanisms that can be separately performed.

Figure 2 shows an example of cordoning on two CSRs: Resource #2 and Resource #4. Process B and Process C are identified as victims of a virus infection. They are placed in a cordon consisting of the Current Resource #2 and the Current Resource #4. The cordoning mechanism performs the recovery operations, where the Recovered Resource #2 and the Recovered Resource #4 are created. Unaffected processes that shares CSRs with the victims, e.g., Process A, continue to use Recovered Resource #2. New processes such as Process D will be given the Recovered Resource #4 when it requests to access Resource #4 in the future. The remaining system resources, such as Resource #1, #3, and #5, are not cordoned.

4   Implementation

BESIDES is a prototype system that uses behavior skewing, behavior monitoring, and cordoning to detect unknown massive mailing viruses. As illustrated in Figure 3, BESIDES consists of an *email address domain skewer (EADS)*, an *email address usage monitor (EAUM)* and a *SMTP Server Cordoner (SSC)*. The EADS is a user-mode application and the EAUM and the SSC are encapsulated in a kernel-mode driver. BESIDES is implemented on Windows 2000 and also runs on Windows XP. The main reason we choose to build a Windows based system is that Windows is one of the most attacked systems and virus attacks in particular are frequently seen there. Developing and experimenting BESIDES on Windows allows us to illustrate our approach and to show that it can be implemented on commercial operating systems.

4.1   The Email Address Domain Skewer

After BESIDES is installed, the user needs to use the EADS to skew the behavior of the email address domain, an information domain that is actively exploited by malicious executables such as massive mailing viruses. The skewing is performed by modifying the usage policy of email addresses. A typical Windows system does not restrict the use of email addresses. In particular, all email addresses can be used as email senders or recipients. The EADS changes this default usage policy by making certain email addresses unusable in any locally composed email. The affected email addresses are referred to as *baiting addresses*, or simply *baits*. The existing email addresses are not skewed unless the user is able to determine which of them is skewable. By default, the EADS grants all subjects full usage (i.e., "allow all") of any email address except the baits. It deems any use of baits a violation of the skewed email address usage policy (i.e., "deny all") The EAUM will issue an intrusion alert whenever it detects the use of a bait in any email messages sent locally. In addition, the EADS sets access rights to certain email domains (e.g., `foo.com` in `alice@foo.com`) in baits to "deny all" as well. This makes the skewing more versatile so that even viruses manipulating email addresses before using them (e.g., Bugbear) can also be detected.

The skewing of email address domain requires the creation of enough unpredictability in the domain so that viruses are not likely to figure out whether an email address is legitimate by simply looking at the email address itself. The EADS uses both heuristic methods and randomization methods in its skewing procedure, i.e., it generates the baiting addresses either based on a set of baits the user specifies or in random.

Specifically, the EADS creates email baits in following file types: email boxes, e.g. `.eml` files; text-based files, e.g. `.HTM`, `.TXT`, and `.ASP` files, etc.; and binary files, e.g., `.MP3`, `.JPG`, and `.PDF` files, etc. Email boxes are skewed by importing baiting email messages that use baiting addresses as senders. Text-based files are skewed with newly created syntactically valid files that contain baits. Binary files are skewed with the same text files as in text-based file skewing but with modified extensions. Such baiting binary files have invalid format and cannot be processed by legitimate applications that operate on these files. This does not pose a problem because these baits are not supposed to be used by them in the first place. Many massive mailing viruses, however, are still able to discover the baits within these files because they usually access them by "brute-force" and neglect their formats, e.g., by searching for email addresses with straightforward string matching algorithms. By default, all these baits are placed in commonly accessed system directories such as "C:\", and "My Documents". The user is allowed to pick additional directories she prefers.

4.2   The Email Address Usage Monitor

BESIDES uses system call interposition to implement the EAUM (and the SSC as well). System call interposition is a general technique that allows interception of system call invocations and has been widely used in many places [45, 46, 20, 47, 19, 17, 48]. Windows 2000 has two sets of system calls [49]: The *Win32* application programming interfaces (APIs), the standard API for Windows applications, are implemented as user-mode dynamically linked libraries (DLLs). The *native APIs* (or *native system calls*) are implemented in kernel and are

exported to user-mode modules through dummy user-mode function thunks in
ntdll.dll. User-mode system DLLs use native APIs to implement Win32 APIs.
A Win32 API is either implemented within user-mode DLLs or mapped to one
(or a series of) native API(s). Windows 2000 implements the TCP/IP protocol stack inside the kernel [50]. At the native system call interface, application
level protocol behaviors are directly observable and can thus be efficiently monitored. Transport level protocol specific data (e.g., TCP/UDP headers) are not
present at this interface. This saves the additional time needed to parse them,
analyze them, and then reconstruct protocol data flow states that is unavoidable
in typical network based interceptors.

The EAUM runs in kernel mode and monitors the use of email addresses in
SMTP sessions. An *SMTP session* consists of all SMTP traffic between a process
and an SMTP server. It starts with a "HELO"(or "EHLO") command and usually
ends with a "QUIT" command. The EAUM registers a set of system call filters to
the system call interposition module (also referred to as the *BESIDES engine*)
during BESIDES initialization when the system boots up. It uses an SMTP automaton derived from the SMTP protocol [51] to simulate the progresses in both
the local SMTP client and the remote SMTP server. The SMTP automaton in
BESIDES is shared among all SMTP sessions. The BESIDES engine intercepts
native system calls that transmit network data and invokes the system call filters registered by the EAUM. These filters extract SMTP data from network
traffic, parse them to generate SMTP tokens, and then perform state transitions in the SMTP automaton that monitors the corresponding SMTP session.
Each SMTP session is represented in the EAUM by a SMTP context, which is
passed to the SMTP automaton as a parameter each time that particular SMTP
session makes progress. The use of email addresses in a SMTP session can be
monitored when the SMTP automaton enters corresponding states. Specifically,
the EAUM looks for SMTP commands that explicitly uses email addresses (i.e.,
"MAIL FROM:" and "RCPT TO:") and validates these usage against the skewed
email address usage policy specified by the EADS. If any violation is detected,
the EAUM notifies the SSC with an intrusion alert because none of the baiting
addresses should be used as either a recipient or sender. The use of legitimate
email addresses does not trigger any alert because their usage is allowed by the
EADS. One advantage of this monitoring approach is that viruses that carry
their own SMTP clients are subject to detection, while interpositions at higher
levels (e.g., Win32 API wrappers) are bypassable. Misuse detection mechanisms
in the form of wrappers around SMTP servers are not used since viruses may
choose open SMTP relays that are not locally administrated.

4.3   The SMTP Server Cordoner

In addition to detecting massive mailing viruses, BESIDES also attempts to
protect CSRs (here, SMTP servers) from possible abuses from them. A SMTP
server is a delayable CSR since emails are not considered a real-time communication mechanism and email users can tolerate certain amount of delays. It
is also weakly revertible (by this we mean the damage of a delivered message

containing a virus can be mollified by sending a follow-up warning message to the recipient when the virus is later detected). Whenever a SMTP session is started by a process, the SSC identifies the SMTP server it requests and assigns it the corresponding virtual SMTP server (the current SMTP server). Delayed-commitment is then used to buffer the SMTP messages the process send to the virtual SMTP server. The SSC also runs in kernel-mode and shares the same SMTP automaton with the EAUM.

Specifically, the SSC intercepts SMTP commands and buffers them internally. It then composes a positive reply and has the BESIDES engine forward it to the SMTP client indicating the success of the command. After receiving such a reply, the SMTP client will consider the previous command successful and proceeds with the next SMTP command. The SSC essentially creates a virtual SMTP server for the process to interact with. The maximum time a SMTP message can be delayed is determined by the cordoning period – a user specified time-out value that is smaller than the average user tolerable delays, as well as the user specified threshold on the maximum number of delayed messages. A SMTP message is delivered (committed) to the actual SMTP server when either it is delayed more than the cordoning period or the number of delayed messages exceeds the message number threshold. After delivering a SMTP message, the SSC creates a corresponding log entry (a revocation record) in the SMTP server specific log containing the time, subject, and the recipient of the delivered message. When informed of an intrusion alert, the SSC identifies the process that is performing the malicious activity be the malicious executable. It then determines the set of victims based on the CSR access history and process hierarchy, i.e, all processes that access CSRs updated by this process and all its child processes are labeled as victims. After this, the SSC initiates the recovery operations on all cordoned CSRs they have updated. If the process that owns a SMTP session is one of the victims or the malicious executable itself, no buffered messages from that SMTP session is committed; instead they are all quarantined. All messages that are previously committed are regarded as suspicious and the SSC sends a warning message for their recipients as a weak recovery mechanism using the information saved in the delivery log entries. Since the SMTP messages sent to a SMTP server are independent, the order they are received does not affect the correct operation of the SMTP server [52]. Thus the actual SMTP server can be kept in a secure state even if some of the messages are dropped during the recovery operation. In the mean time, the unaffected processes are unaware of this recovery and can proceed as if no intrusion has occurred.

5   Experimental Results

We performed a series of experiments on BESIDES with viruses we collected in the wild. These experiments are performed on a closed local area network (LAN) consisting of two machines: a server and a client. BESIDES is installed on the client and its EADS is set up the same way in all experiments. The server simulates a typical network environment to the client by providing essential net-

Table 1. Effectiveness of BESIDES (The BESIDES SSC is configured to intercept at most 10 total SMTP messages and for at most 60 seconds for each SMTP message during these experiments. The Outlook Express book is manually skewed)

Virus		BugBear	Haptime	Klez	MyDoom
Client	Detected?	Yes	Yes	Yes	Yes
	Baits Used at Detection	Addr. Book	.htm	.html	.htm
	Delayed Message Quarantined?	Yes	Yes	Yes	Yes
Server	Detected?(by anti-virus software)	Yes	No	Yes	No
	SMTP Message Received?	Yes	No	No	No

work services, such as DNS, Routing, SMTP, POP3, and Remote Access Service (RAS). The server is also equipped with anti-virus software (i.e., Symantec Antivirus) and network forensic tools (e.g., Ethereal, TcpDump, etc.). Evidences of virus propagation can be gathered from output of these tools as well as service logs.

Two sets of experimental results are presented in the remainder of this section. First we present the outcome when BESIDES is experimented with several actual viruses. These results demonstrate the effectiveness of behavior skewing and cordoning when they are applied in a real-world setting. The second set of results presents the performance overheads observed during normal system execution for normal system applications, including delays observed at the native system call interfaces, and those at the command-line interface. As we have expected, the overheads are within a reasonable range even though we have not perform any optimization in BESIDES.

5.1 Effectiveness Experiments

The results of our experiments with four actual viruses – BugBear [53], Haptime [54], Klez [55], and MyDoom [56] – are shown in Table 1. In all the experiments, BESIDES were able to detect the viruses being experimented. Although all these viruses attempted to collect email addresses on the client machine, their methods were different and the actual baiting addresses they were using when BESIDES detected them also differed from each other. In all experiments, the BESIDES SSC intercepted multiple SMTP messages sent by viruses and successfully quarantined them. However, some of the virus carrying messages were found delivered before the virus was detected during the experiment with Bugbear. From the email messages received by the SMTP server from Bugbear, we found Bugbear actually manipulated either the sender or the recipient addresses before sending them. Specifically, it forms a new email address by combining the user field of one email address and the domain field of another email address. BESIDES was initially unable to detect these messages since it only considers the matches of both the user name field and the domain field as an acceptable match to a bait. It then committed these messages to the SMTP server[2]. With

---

[2] This loophole is later fixed by creating additional email usage policy on email domains and creating baiting domains in the EADS. See Section 4.1 for details.

our experimental setups, an average two out of ten such messages were found committed to the SMTP server. We note that the actual numbers varies with the skewing manipulations. In one of our experiments, two such messages were thus committed before BESIDES detected the virus. The anti-virus software on the server detected Bugbear and Klez because they also spread over network shares, a mechanism that is not cordoned by BESIDES in all these experiments.

We observed significant hard disk accesses from Haptime when it tried to infect local files and collecting email addresses from them. All these happened before the virus start to perform massive mailing operations. This suggested that Haptime can be detected faster if BESIDES skews file access rights as well.

The outbreak of Mydoom was later than the version of BESIDES used in the experiments was completed. Thus BESIDES had no knowledge of the virus when it was experimented with it. BESIDES successfully detected the virus when it tried to send messages using baiting email addresses placed in .htm files. This demonstrated BESIDES's capability in detecting unknown viruses.

As some of the viruses use probabilistic methods, (e.g., Klez,) their behavior in different experiments can be different. The result shown here is thus only one possible behavior. Also, as some of the viruses use local time to decide whether particular operations are (or are not) to be performed (e.g., MyDoom does not perform massive mailing if it performs DDoS attacks, which is dependent on the system time.), we manually changed the client's system time to hasten the activation of massive mailing by the virus. We emphasize that this is done to speed up our experiments and that system time manipulation is not needed to effect detection in production.

5.2   Performance Experiments

Overall System Overheads. Table 2 shows statistical results of the system call overheads observed at three native system call interface during normal system executions. Two interceptors, the pre-interceptor and the post-interceptor, are used to perform interception operations before and after the actual system call is executed. The three native system calls shown in the table are representatives of three cordoning session phases.

NtCreateFile() is invoked to create or open a file (including a socket) [49]. BESIDES intercepts it so that SMTP sessions can be recognized and their corresponding SMTP contexts can be created. It is the *setup phase* of a SMTP session. The post-interceptor is used to perform these operations. As can be seen from Tab.2, the overhead is a fraction of actual system call.

NtDeviceIoControlFile() performs an I/O control operation on a file object that represents a device [49]. Network packets are also transmitted using this system call. BESIDES intercepts this system call so that it can inspect SMTP session control and data messages. This is the *inspection phase* of a SMTP session. During the interception, SMTP data are parsed, SMTP tokens are generated, and the BESIDES EAUM SMTP automaton's state is updated. The pre-interceptor and the post-interceptor processes sent data and received data, respectively. The overhead observed is only a small percentage of the ac-

Table 2. BESIDES system call overheads observed at native system call interface. All numbers are calculated from CPU performance counter values directly retrieved from the client machine (Pentium III 730MHz CPU with 128MB memory)

Native System Call	NtClose()	NtCreateFile()	NtDeviceIoControlFile()
Total Execution Time	283076	1997247	16110683
Pre-Interceptor Time	108520	24033	21748
Actual System Call Time	32960	1471367	15791127
Post-Interceptor Time	23588	371826	156350
System Call Interposition Time	118008	130021	141457
Overhead (in %)	758.85%	35.74%	2.02%

tual system call because the actual system call incurs expensive hardware I/O operations.

NtClose() is invoked by a user-mode process to close a handle to an object [49]. BESIDES intercepts it to terminate a SMTP session. This is called the *termination phase* of that SMTP session. The pre-interceptor releases system resources that are used to monitor this SMTP session. The actual system call is a lightweight system call and it takes much less time than the other two. The overhead observed dominates the actual system call. However, as both setup and termination phases are only performed once during a SMTP session's lifespan, their relatively high cost can be amortized by the much faster inspection phase.

Finally, it should be noted that a different type of overhead, the system call interposition overhead, exists in all system call interceptions. This overhead accounts for the mandatory overhead each intercepted system call has to pay, including extra system call lookup time, and kernel-stack setup time, etc. However, for those system calls that are not intercepted, optimized shortcuts are created in interception routines so that as little overhead as possible is generated.

Application Specific Overheads. We also measured the time overhead for several applications on the client machine where BESIDES is installed. Figure 4 shows the overheads (average values of 10 separate runs) observed on a series of applications that compile the postscript version of a draft of this paper from its .tex source files. The applications executed include delete (cleaning up the directory), dir (listing the directory content), mpost (building graphic .eps files), latex #1 (The first run of latex), bibtex (preparing bibliography items), latex #2 (The second run of latex), latex #3 (The third run of latex), and dvips (converting the .dvi file to the postscript file). Both CPU intensive and I/O intensive applications are present and this series can be regarded as a representative of applications that require no network access. These applications are only affected by the native system call interposition overhead induced by the BESIDES engine. The average time overhead observed in these experiments is around 8%. The highest increases (around 13%) occur in latex #1 and latex #2, both of which perform significant I/O operations. The lowest increases (around 1.5% and 3.3%) occur in dir and delete respectively. These are shell commands

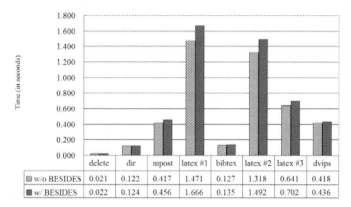

Fig. 4. Time overhead for the latex application series

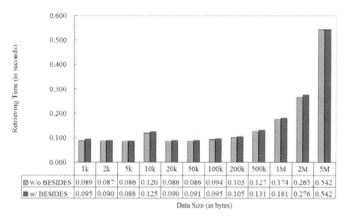

Fig. 5. Time overhead for the command-line web client

that perform simple tasks that require few system calls. We note that CPU intensive applications, e.g., dvips, suffer much smaller overheads (e.g., 4.3% for dvips). These results indicate that I/O intensive applications are likely to endure more overhead than CPU intensive applications. They conform to our expectation as essentially all I/O operations are carried out by native system calls and are thus subject to interception, while CPU intensive operations contain higher percentage of user-mode code that makes few system calls.

Figure 5 shows the overheads observed for a command-line based web client when it retrieves data files from the local web server. The sizes of data files used in this experiment range from 1kB to 5MB. Although the web client retrieves these data files using HTTP, its network traffic is still subject to inspection of the SMTP filters in BESIDES. The system call interposition overhead is relatively small since the web client performs few other system calls during the whole process. The two largest overheads observed are around 6.3% and 5% (at 1kB and 50kB, respectively). The two smallest overheads are 0% and 1.8% (at 5MB and 100kB, respectively). The average overhead is around 3.4%, which is close to 2.02%, the overhead observed at the NtDeviceIoControlFile() interface. This confirms our previous speculation that the seemingly high increase in the session setup phase and the session termination phase can be amortized by the low overhead of the session inspection phase.

6   Conclusions

This paper presents a general paradigm, PAIDS for intrusion detection and tolerance by proactive methods. We present our work on behavior skewing and cordoning, two proactive methods that can be used to create unpredictability in a system so that unknown malicious executables are more prone to be detected. This approach differs from existing ones in that such a proactive system anticipates the attacks from malicious executables and prepares itself for them in advance by modifying the security policy of a system.

PAIDS enjoys the advantage that it can detect intruders that have not been seen yet in the raw and yet PAIDS has a very low false-positive rate of detection. BESIDES is a proof-of-concept prototype using the PAIDS approach, and it can be enhanced in many directions. Obvious enhancements include skewers and cordoners for additional information domains (e.g., file access skewer) and system resources (e.g., file system cordoner). The BESIDES SSC can be augmented with more versatile handling and recovery schemes to cope with general malicious executables. We are also interested in devising more proactive methods. In general, we want to investigate to what extent we can systematically cordon off parts or even all of a system by cordoning all the protocols they use to interact with the external environment.

Finally, we would like to point out that the proactive methods we have studied are only part of the solution to the general problem of detecting unknown malicious executables. A system that is equipped with only proactive techniques are still vulnerable to new types of malicious executables that do not misuse any of the skewed information domains or abuse the system in more subtle ways such as stealing CPU cycles from legitimate applications. PAIDS is not a cure-all in that it works only for viruses' whose route of spreading infection or damage-causing mechanism is well characterized. A comprehensive solution that consists of techniques from different areas is obviously more effective because the weaknesses of each individual technique can be compensated by the strength of others. We would like to explore how proactive methods can be integrated with such hybrid solutions.

References

1. Blakley, B.: The Emperor's Old Armor. In: Proceedings of the ACM New Security Paradigms Workshop, Lake Arrowhead, California (1996)
2. Cohen, F.: Computer Viruses: Theory and Experiments. Computers and Security 6 (1987) 22–35
3. Chess, D.M., White, S.R.: An Undetectable Computer Virus. In: Proceedings of the 2000 Virus Bulletin International Conference, Orlando, Florida (2000)

4. Gryaznov, D.: Scanners of the Year 2000: Heuristics. In: Proceedings of the 5th Virus Bulletin International Conference, Boston, Massachusetts (1999) 225–234

5. Kephart, J.O., Arnold, W.C.: Automatic Extraction of Computer Virus Signatures. In: Proceedings of the 4th Virus Bulletin International Conference, Abingdon, England (1994) 178–184

6. Arnold, W., Tesauro, G.: Automatically Generated Win32 Heuristic Virus Detection. In: Proceedings of the 2000 Virus Bulletin International Conference, Orlando, Florida (2000)

7. Schultz, M.G., Eskin, E., Zadok, E., Stolfo, S.J.: Data Mining Methods for Detection of New Malicious Executables. In: Proceedings of the 2001 IEEE Symposium on Security and Privacy, Oakland, California (2001) 38–49

8. Schultz, M.G., Eskin, E., Zadok, E., Bhattacharyya, M., Stolfo, S.J.: MEF: Malicious Email Filter — A UNIX Mail Filter that Detects Malicious Windows Executables. In: Proceedings of the Annual USENIX Technical Conference, FREENIX Track, Boston, Massachusetts (2001) 245–252

9. Bishop, M., Dilger, M.: Checking for Race Conditions in File Accesses. Computing Systems 9 (1996) 131–152

10. Tesauro, G., Kephart, J., Sorkin, G.: Neural Networks for Computer Virus Recognition. IEEE Expert 11 (1996) 5–6

11. Lo, R.W., Levitt, K.N., Olsson, R.A.: MCF: A Malicious Code Filter. Computers and Security 14 (1995) 541–566

12. Anderson, J.P.: Computer Security Technology Planning Study. Technical report, ESD-TR-73-51, U.S. Air Force Electronic Systems Division, Deputy for Command and Management Systems, HQ Electronic Systems Division (AFSC), Bedford, Massachusetts (1972)

13. Viswanathan, M.: Foundations for the Run-time Analysis of Software Systems. PhD thesis, University of Pennsylvania (2000)

14. Hamlen, K.W., Morrisett, G., Schneider, F.B.: Computability Classes for Enforcement Mechanisms. Technical report, TR 2003-1908, Cornell University, Dept. of Computer Science (2003)

15. Bauer, L., Ligatti, J., Walker, D.: More Enforceable Security Policies. In: Foundations of Computer Security, Copenhagen, Denmark (2002)

16. Berman, A., Bourassa, V., Selberg, E.: TRON: Process-Specific File Protection for the UNIX Operating System. In: Proceedings of the 1995 Annual USENIX Technical Conference, New Orleans, Lousianna (1995) 165–175

17. Goldberg, I., Wagner, D., Thomas, R., Brewer, E.A.: A Secure Environment for Untrusted Helper Applications. In: Proceedings of the 6th USENIX Security Symposium, San Jose, California (1996)

18. Alexandrov, A., Kmiec, P., Schauser, K.: Consh: A Confined Execution Environment for Internet Computations. In: Proceedinges of the Annual USENIX Technical Conference, New Orleans, Louisianna (1998)

19. Acharya, A., Raje, M.: MAPbox: Using Parameterized Behavior Classes to Confine Untrusted Application. In: Proceedings of the 9th USENIX Security Symposium, Denver, Colorado (2000)

20. Cowan, C., Beattie, S., Kroah-Hartman, G., Pu, C., Wagle, P., Gligor, V.: Subdomain: Parsimonious Server Security. In: Proceedings of the 14th Systems Administration Conference, New Orleans, Louisianna (2000)

21. Provos, N.: Improving Host Security with System Call Policies. In: Proceedings of the 12th USENIX Security Symposium, Washington, DC (2003) 257–272

22. Honeypots, Intrusion Detection, Incident Response: http://www.honeypots.net/.

23. The Honeynet Project: http://project.honeynet.org/.
24. Provos, N.: A Virtual Honeypot Framework. In: Proceedings of the 13th USENIX Security Symposium, San Diego, California (2004)
25. Jiang, X., Xu, D.: Collapsar: A VM-Based Architecture for Network Attack Detention Center. In: Proceedings of the 13th USENIX Security Symposium, San Diego, California (2004)
26. Spitzner, L.: Honeytokens: The Other Honeypot (2003) http://www.securityfocus.com/infocus/1713.
27. Pontz, B.: Honeytoken. CERT Honeypot Archive (2004) http://cert.uni-stuttgart.de/archive/honeypots/2004/01/msg00059.html.
28. Somayaji, A., Forrest, S.: Automated Response Using System-Call Delays. In: Proceedings of the 9th USENIX Security Symposium, Denver, Colorado (2000)
29. LaBrea Sentry IPS: Next Generation Intrusion Prevention System: http://www.labreatechnologies.com/.
30. Williamson, M.M.: Throttling Viruses: Restricting propagation to defeat malicious mobile code. In: Proceedings of the 18th Annual Computer Security Applications Conference, Las Vegas, Nevada (2002)
31. Twycross, J., Williamson, M.M.: Implementing and Testing a Virus Throttle. In: Proceedings of the 12th USENIX Security Symposium, Washington, DC (2003)
32. Williamson, M.M.: Design, Implementation and Test of an Email Virus Throttle. In: Proceedings of the 19th Annual Computer Security Applications Conference, Las Vegas, Nevada (2003)
33. Anderson, J.P.: Computer Security Threat Monitoring and Surveillance. Technical report, James P. Anderson Company, Fort Washington, Pennsylvania (1980)
34. Denning, D.E.: An Intrusion–Detection Model. In: IEEE Transactions on Software Engineering. Volume SE-13:(2). (1987) 222–232
35. Porras, P.A., Kemmerer, R.A.: Penetration State Transition Analysis – A Rule-Based Intrusion Detection Approach. In: 8th Annual Computer Security Applications Conference, San Antonio, Texas (1992) 220–229
36. Kumar, S.: Classification and Detection of Computer Intrusions. PhD thesis, Purdue University (1995)
37. Lunt, T.F.: Detecting Intruders in Computer Systems. In: Proceedings of the Conference on Auditing and Computer Technology. (1993)
38. Javitz, H.S., Valdes, A.: The NIDES Statistical Component: Description and Justification. Technical report, SRI International, Computer Science Laboratory, Menlo Park, California (1993)
39. Anderson, D., Lunt, T.F., Javitz, H., Tamaru, A., Valdes, A.: Detecting Unusual Program Behavior Using the Statistical Components of NIDES. Technical report, SRI-CSL-95-06, SRI International, Computer Science Laboratory, Menlo Park, California (1995)
40. Wagner, D., Dean, D.: Intrusion Detection via Static Analysis. In: Proceedings of the 2001 IEEE Symposium on Security and Privacy, Oakland, California (2001) 156–169
41. Neumann, P.G., Porras, P.A.: Experience with EMERALD to Date. In: Proceedings of the 1st USENIX Workshop on Intrusion Detection and Network Monitoring, Santa Clara, California (1999) 73–80
42. Giffin, J.T., Jha, S., Miller, B.P.: Detecting Manipulated Remote Call Streams. In: Proceedings of the 11th USENIX Security Symposium, San Francisco, California (2002)

43. Christodorescu, M., Jha, S.: Static Analysis of Executables to Detect Malicious Patterns. In: Proceedings of the 12th USENIX Security Symposium, Washington, DC (2003)
44. McHugh, J., Gates, C.: Locality: A New Paradigm for Thinking about Normal Behavior and Outsider Threat. In: Proceedings of the ACM New Security Paradigms Workshop, Ascona, Switzerland (2003)
45. Jain, K., Sekar, R.: User-Level Infrastructure for System Call Interposition: A Platform for Intrusion Detection and Confinement. In: Proceedings of the Network and Distributed System Security Symposium, San Diego, California (2000) 19–34
46. Ghormley, D.P., Petrou, D., Rodrigues, S.H., Anderson, T.E.: SLIC: An Extensibility System for Commodity Operating Systems. In: Proceedinges of the Annual USENIX Technical Conference, New Orleans, Louisianna (1998) 39–52
47. Fraser, T., Badger, L., Feldman, M.: Hardening COTS Software with Generic Software Wrappers. In: Proceedings of the IEEE Symposium on Security and Privacy, Oakland, California (1999) 2–16
48. Ko, C., Fraser, T., Badger, L., Kilpatrick, D.: Detecting and Countering System Intrusions Using Software Wrappers. In: Proceedings of the 9th USENIX Security Symposium, Denver, Colorado (2000)
49. Nebbett, G.: Windows NT/2000 Native API Reference. 1st edn. MacMillan Technical Publishing (2000)
50. Solomon, D.A., Russinovich, M.E.: Inside Microsoft Windows 2000. 3rd edn. Microsoft Press (2000)
51. Postel, J.B.: Simple Mail Transfer Protocol (1982)
    http://www.ietf.org/rfc/rfc0821.txt.
52. Russell, D.L.: State Restoration in Systems of Communicating Processes. IEEE Transactions on Software Engineering **SE6** (1980) 133–144
53. Liu, Y., Sevcenco, S.: W32.bugbear@mm. Symantec Security Response (2003)
    http://securityresponse.symantec.com/avcenter/venc/data/
    w32.bugbear@mm.html.
54. Sevcenco, S.: Vbs.haptime.a@mm. Symantec Security Response (2004)
    http://securityresponse.symantec.com/avcenter/venc/data/
    vbs.haptime.a@mm.html.
55. Gudmundsson, A., Chien, E.: W32.klez.e@mm. Symantec Security Response (2003)
    http://securityresponse.symantec.com/avcenter/venc/data/
    w32.klez.e@mm.html.
56. Ferrie, P., Lee, T.: W32.mydoom.a@mm. Symantec Security Response (2004)
    http://securityresponse.symantec.com/avcenter/venc/data/
    w32.novarg.a@mm.html.

Using Adaptive Alert Classification
to Reduce False Positives in Intrusion Detection

Tadeusz Pietraszek

IBM Zurich Research Laboratory
Säumerstrasse 4, CH-8803 Rüschlikon, Switzerland
pie@zurich.ibm.com

Abstract. Intrusion Detection Systems (IDSs) are used to monitor computer systems for signs of security violations. Having detected such signs, IDSs trigger alerts to report them. These alerts are presented to a human analyst, who evaluates them and initiates an adequate response.

In practice, IDSs have been observed to trigger thousands of alerts per day, most of which are false positives (i.e., alerts mistakenly triggered by benign events). This makes it extremely difficult for the analyst to correctly identify the true positives (i.e., alerts related to attacks).

In this paper we describe ALAC, the Adaptive Learner for Alert Classification, which is a novel system for reducing false positives in intrusion detection. The system supports the human analyst by classifying alerts into true positives and false positives. The knowledge of how to classify alerts is learned adaptively by observing the analyst. Moreover, ALAC can be configured to process autonomously alerts that have been classified with high confidence. For example, ALAC may discard alerts that were classified with high confidence as false positive. That way, ALAC effectively reduces the analyst's workload.

We describe a prototype implementation of ALAC and the choice of a suitable machine learning technique. Moreover, we experimentally validate ALAC and show how it facilitates the analyst's work.

Keywords: Intrusion detection, false positives, alert classification, machine learning

1 Introduction

The explosive increase in the number of networked machines and the widespread use of the Internet in organizations has led to an increase in the number of unauthorized activities, not only by external attackers but also by internal sources, such as fraudulent employees or people abusing their privileges for personal gain. As a result, intrusion detection systems (IDSs), as originally introduced by Anderson [1] and later formalized by Denning [8], have received increasing attention in recent years.

On the other hand, with the massive deployment of IDSs, their operational limits and problems have become apparent [2, 3, 15, 23]. False positives, i.e., alerts that mistakenly indicate security issues and require attention from the intrusion

E. Jonsson et al. (Eds.): RAID 2004, LNCS 3224, pp. 102–124, 2004.

detection analyst, are one of the most important problems faced by intrusion detection today [28]. In fact, it has been estimated that up to 99% of alerts reported by IDSs are not related to security issues [2, 3, 15].

In this paper we address the problem of false positives in intrusion detection by building an alert classifier that tells true from false positives. We define *alert classification* as attaching a label from a fixed set of user-defined labels to an alert. In the simplest case, alerts are classified into false and true positives, but the classification can be extended to indicate the category of an attack, the causes of a false positive or anything else.

Alerts are classified by a so-called *alert classifier* (or *classifier* for short). Alert classifiers can be built automatically using machine learning techniques or they can be built manually by human experts. The Adaptive Learner for Alert Classification (ALAC) introduced in this paper uses the former approach. Moreover, ALAC learns alert classifiers whose classification logic is explicit so that a human expert can inspect it and verify its correctness. In that way, the analyst can gain confidence in ALAC by understanding how it works.

ALAC classifies alerts into true positives and false positives and presents these classifications to the intrusion detection analyst, as shown in Fig. 1 on page 106. Based on the analyst's feedback, the system generates training examples, which are used by machine learning techniques to initially build and subsequently update the classifier. The classifier is then used to classify new alerts. This process is continuously repeated to improve the alert classification. At any time the analyst can review the classifier.

Note that this approach hinges on the analyst's ability to classify alerts correctly. This assumption is justified because the analyst must be an expert in intrusion detection to perform incident analysis and initiate appropriate responses. This raises the question of why analysts do not write alert classification rules themselves or do not write them more frequently. An explanation of these issues can be based on the following facts:

Analysts' knowledge is implicit: Analysts find it hard to generalize, i.e., to formulate more general rules, based on individual alert classifications. For example, an analyst might be able to individually classify some alerts as false positives, but may not be able to write a general rule that characterizes the whole set of these alerts.

Environments are dynamic: In real-world environments the characteristics of alerts change, e.g., different alerts occur as new computers and services are installed or as certain worms or attacks gain and lose popularity. The classification of alerts may also change. As a result, rules need to be maintained and managed. This process is labor-intensive and error-prone.

As stated above, we use machine learning techniques to build an alert classifier that tells true from false positives. Viewed as a machine learning problem, alert classification poses several challenges.

First, the distribution of classes (true positives vs. false positives) is often skewed, i.e., false positives are more frequent than true positives. Second, it is also common that the cost of misclassifying alerts is most often asymmetrical i.e., misclassifying true positives as false positives is usually more costly than the other way round. Third, ALAC classifies alerts in real-time and updates its classifier as new alerts become available. The learning technique should be efficient enough to perform in real-time and work incrementally, i.e., to be able to modify its logic as new data becomes available. Fourth, we require the machine learning technique to use background knowledge, i.e., additional information such as network topology, alert database, alert context, etc., which is not contained in alerts, but allows us to build more accurate classifiers (e.g., classifiers using generalized concepts). In fact, research in machine learning has shown that the use of background knowledge frequently leads to more natural and concise rules [16]. However, the use of background knowledge increases the complexity of a learning task and only some machine learning techniques support it.

We revisit these challenges in Sect. 2.2, where we discuss them and present a suitable learning technique. The point made here is that we are facing a highly challenging machine learning problem that requires great care to solve properly.

1.1   Related Work

To the best of our knowledge, machine learning has not previously been used to incrementally build alert classifiers that take background knowledge into account. However, some of the concepts we apply here have been successfully used in intrusion detection and related domains.

Building IDSs. In intrusion detection, machine learning has been used primarily to build systems that classify network connections (e.g., 1999 KDD CUP [13]) or system call sequences (e.g., [22]) into one of several predefined classes.

This task proved to be very difficult because it aimed at building IDSs only from training examples. Lee [17] developed a methodology to construct additional features using data mining. He also showed the importance of domain-specific knowledge in constructing such IDSs. The key differences of our work is the real-time use of analyst feedback and that we classify alerts generated by IDSs, whereas other researchers used machine learning to build a new IDS.

Fan [10] performed a comprehensive study of cost-sensitive learning using classifier ensembles with RIPPER, therefore his work is particularly relevant to ours. The work differs from ours in design goals: we developed a system to assist human users to classify alerts generated by an IDS, whereas Fan built an IDS using machine learning techniques. We also used a simplified cost model, in order to reduce the number of variable parameters in the system. Finally, the type of learning methods used is also different: ensemble-based learning methods vs. a single classifier in our case.

Alert Classification. The methods used to classify alerts can be divided into two categories: first, methods that identify true positives and second, methods that identify false positives.

Methods that identify true positives have been studied particularly well and can be summarized as follows:

- In environments with multiple IDSs, some methods enhance the confidence of alerts generated by more than one IDS (based on the assumption that the real attack will be noticed by multiple IDSs, whereas false positives tend to be more random) [28],
- Couple sensor alerts with background knowledge to determine whether the attacked system is vulnerable [20, 28],
- Create groups of alerts and use heuristics to evaluate whether an alert is a false positive [6, 35]. The work by Dain and Cunningham [6] is particularly relevant to us as it uses machine learning techniques: neural networks and decision trees to build a classifier grouping alerts into so-called scenarios. They also discuss domain-specific background knowledge used to discover scenarios. In contrast, our work focuses on alert classification, uses different background knowledge and different machine-learning algorithms.

The second category of alert classification methods identifies false positives and can be based on data mining and include root cause analysis [15], or on statistical profiling [23]. For example, Julisch [15] shows that the bulk of alerts triggered by an IDS can be attributed to a small number of root causes. He also proposes a data mining technique to discover and understand these root causes. Knowing the root causes of alerts, one can easily design filters to remove alerts originating from benign root causes. Our work differs from the above in that we use real-time machine learning techniques that take advantage of background knowledge.

1.2   Paper Overview

The remainder of this paper is organized as follows. In Section 2 we present the design of our system and analyze machine learning techniques and their limitations with regard to the learning problem we are facing. Section 3 describes the prototype implementation of the system and shows results obtained with synthetic and real intrusion detection data. In Section 4 we present conclusions and future work.

2   ALAC – An Adaptive Learner for Alert Classification

In this section we describe the architecture of the system and contrast it to a conventional setup. We introduce two modes in which the system can operate, namely recommender mode and agent mode. We then focus on machine learning techniques and discuss how suitable they are for alert classification.

2.1   ALAC Architecture

In a conventional setup, alerts generated by IDSs are passed to a human analyst. The analyst uses his or her knowledge to distinguish between false and true positives and to understand the severity of the alerts. Note that conventional systems may use manual knowledge engineering to build an alert classifier or may use no alert classifier at all. In any case, the conventional setup does not take advantage of the fact that the analyst is analyzing the alerts in real-time: the manual knowledge engineering is separated from analyzing alerts.

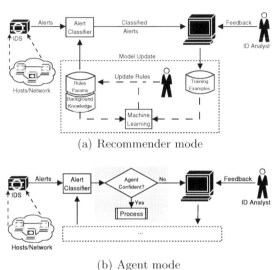

(a) Recommender mode

(b) Agent mode

Fig. 1. Architecture of ALAC in agent and recommender mode.

As shown in Fig. 1, our system classifies alerts and passes them to the analyst. It also assigns a *classification confidence* (or *confidence* for short), to alerts, which shows the likelihood of alerts belonging to their assigned classes. The analyst reviews this classification and reclassifies alerts, if necessary. This process is recorded and used as training by the machine learning component to build an improved alert classifier.

Currently we use a simple human-computer interaction model, where the analyst *explicitly* classifies alerts into true and false positives. More sophisticated interaction techniques are possible and will be investigated as part of our future work. In addition to the training examples, we use background knowledge to learn improved classification rules. These rules are then used by ALAC to classify alerts. The analyst can inspect the rules to make sure they are correct.

The architecture presented above describes the operation of the system in *recommender mode*. The second mode, *agent mode*, introduces autonomous processing to reduce the operator's workload.

In recommender mode (Fig. 1(a)), ALAC classifies alerts and passes all of them to the console to be verified by the analyst. In other words, the system assists the analyst suggesting the correct classification. The advantage for the analyst is that each alert is already preclassified and that the analyst has only to verify its correctness. The analyst can prioritize his or her work, e.g., by dealing with alerts classified as true positives first or sorting the alerts by classification confidence. It is important to emphasize that at the end, the analyst will review all classifications made by the system.

In agent mode (Fig. 1(b)), ALAC autonomously processes some of the alerts based on criteria defined by the analyst (i.e., classification assigned by ALAC and classification confidence). By processing alerts we mean that ALAC executes user-defined actions associated with the class labels and classification confidence values. For example, attacks classified as false positives can be automatically removed, thus reducing the analyst's workload. In contrast, alerts classified as true positives and successful attacks can initiate an automated response, such as reconfiguring a router or firewall. It is important to emphasize that such actions should be executed only for alerts classified with high confidence, whereas the other alerts should still be reviewed by the analyst.

Note that autonomous alert processing may change the behavior of the system and negatively impact its classification accuracy. To illustrate this with an example, suppose the system classifies alerts into true and false positives and it is configured to autonomously discard the latter if the classification confidence is higher than a given threshold value. Suppose the system learned a good classifier and classifies alerts with high confidence. In this case, if the system starts classifying all alerts as false positives then these alerts would be autonomously discarded and would never be seen by the analyst. These alerts would not become training examples and would never be used to improve the classifier.

Another problem is that alerts classified and processed autonomously cannot be added to the list of training examples as the analyst has not reviewed them. If alerts of a certain class are processed autonomously more frequently than alerts belonging to other classes (as in the above example), we effectively change the class distribution in the training examples. This has important implications as machine learning techniques are sensitive to class distribution in training examples. In the optimal case, the distribution of classes in training and testing examples should be identical.

To alleviate these problems, we propose a technique called *random sampling*. In this technique we randomly select a fraction k of alerts which would normally be processed autonomously and instead forward them to the analyst. This ensures the stability of the system. The value of k is a tradeoff between how many alerts will be processed autonomously and how much risk of misclassification is acceptable.

Background Knowledge Representation. Recall that we use machine learning techniques to build the classifier. In machine learning, if the learner has no prior knowledge about the learning problem, it learns exclusively from examples. However, difficult learning problems typically require a substantial body of prior knowledge [16], which makes it possible to express the learned concept in a more natural and concise manner. In the field of machine learning such knowledge is referred to as *background knowledge*, whereas in the field of intrusion detection it is quite often called *context information* (e.g., [32]).

The use of background knowledge is also very important in intrusion detection [28]. Examples of background knowledge include:

Network Topology. Network topology contains information about the structure of the network, assigned IP addresses, etc. It can be used to better understand the function and role of computers in the network. In the context of machine learning, network topology can be used to learn rules that make use of generalized concepts such as `Subnet1, Intranet, DMZ, HTTPServer`.

Alert Context. Alert context, i.e., other alerts *related* to a given one, is in the case of some alerts (e.g., portscans, password guessing, repetitive exploits attempts) crucial to their classification. In intrusion detection various definitions of alert context are used. Typically, the alert context has been defined to include all alerts similar to it, however the definition of similarity varies greatly [6, 5, 34].

Alert Semantics and Installed Software. By alert semantics we mean how an alert is interpreted by the analyst. For example, the analyst knows what type of intrusion the alert refers to (e.g., scan, local attack, remote attack) and the type of system affected (e.g., Linux 2.4.20, Internet Explorer 6.0). Typically the alert semantics is correlated with the software installed (or the device type, e.g., `Cisco PIX`) to determine whether the system is vulnerable to the reported attack [20]. The result of this process can be used as additional background knowledge used to classify alerts.

Note that the information about the installed software and alert semantics can be used even when alert correlation is not performed, as it allows us to learn rules that make use of generalized concepts such as `OS Linux, OS Windows`, etc.

2.2   Machine Learning Techniques

Until now we have been focusing on the general system architecture and issues specific to intrusion detection. In this section we focus on the machine learning component in our system. Based on the discussion in Sect. 1 and the proposed system architecture, we can formulate the following requirements for the machine learning technique:

1. Learn from training examples (alert classification given by the analyst).
2. Build the classifier whose logic can be interpreted by a human analyst, so its correctness can be verified.
3. Be able to incorporate the background knowledge required.
4. Be efficient enough to perform real-time learning.
5. Be able to assess the confidence of classifications. Confidence is a numerical value attached to the classification, representing how likely it is to be correct.
6. Support cost-sensitive classification and skewed class distributions.
7. Learn incrementally.

Learning an Interpretable Classifier from Examples. The first requirement yields *supervised* machine learning techniques, that is techniques that can learn from training examples. The requirement for an understandable classifier further limits the range of techniques to *symbolic* learning techniques, that is techniques that present the learned concept in a human readable form (e.g., predictive rules, decision trees, Prolog clauses) [22].

Background Knowledge and Efficiency. The ability to incorporate background knowledge differentiates two big groups of symbolic learners: inductive logic programming and symbolic attribute-value learners. In general, inductive logic programming provides the framework for the use of background knowledge, represented in the form of logic predicates and first-order rules, whereas attribute-value learners exclusively learn from training examples. Moreover, training examples for attribute-value learners are limited to a fixed number of attributes.

The inductive logic programming framework can easily handle the background knowledge introduced in Sect. 2.1, including alert context as well as arbitrary Prolog clauses. As the search space is much bigger than in other machine learning techniques, such as rule and decision tree learners, the size of problems that can be solved efficiently by inductive logic programming is smaller and these learners are much less efficient. This may make such a system unsuitable for real-time learning.

On the other hand, attribute-value learners can use a limited form of background knowledge using so-called *feature construction* (also known as propositionalization [16]) by creating additional attributes based on values of existing attributes or existing background knowledge.

Given that most background knowledge for intrusion detection can be converted to additional features using feature construction, and considering the runtime requirement, symbolic attribute-value learners seem to be a good choice for alert classification.

Confidence of Classification. Symbolic attribute-value learners are decision tree learners (e.g., C4.5 [30]) and rule learners (e.g., AQ [26], C4.5rules [30], RIPPER [4]). Both of these techniques can estimate the confidence of a classification based on its performance on training examples. However, it has been shown that rules are much more comprehensible to humans than decision trees [27, 30]. Hence, rule learners are particularly advantageous in our context.

We analyzed the characteristics of available rule learners, as well as published results from applications in intrusion detection and related domains. We have not found a good and publicly available rule learner that fulfills all our requirements, in particular cost-sensitivity and incremental learning.

Of the techniques that best fulfill the remaining requirements, we chose RIPPER [4] – a fast and effective rule learner. It has been successfully used in intrusion detection (e.g., on system call sequences and network connection data [17, 18]) as well as related domains and it has proved to produce concise and intuitive rules. As reported by Lee [17], RIPPER rules have two very desirable conditions for intrusion detection: a good generalization accuracy and concise conditions. Another advantage of RIPPER is its efficiency with noisy data sets.

RIPPER has been well documented in the literature and its description is beyond the scope of this paper. However, for the sake of a better understanding of the system we will briefly explain what kind of rules RIPPER builds.

Given a set of training examples labeled with a class label (in our case false and true alerts), RIPPER builds a set of rules discriminating between classes.

Each rule consists of conjunctions of attribute value comparisons followed by a class label and if the rule evaluates to *true* a prediction is made.

RIPPER can produce *ordered* and *unordered* rule sets. Very briefly, for a two class problem, an unordered rule set contains rules for both classes (for both false and true alerts), whereas an ordered rule set contains rules for one class only, assuming that all other alerts fall into another class (so-called default rule). Both ordered and unordered rule sets have advantages and disadvantages. We decided to use ordered rule sets because they are more compact and easier to interpret. We will discuss this issue further in Sect. 3.6.

Unfortunately, the standard RIPPER algorithm is not cost-sensitive and does not support incremental learning. We used the following methods to circumvent these limitations.

Cost-Sensitive Classification and Skewed Class Distribution. Among the various methods of making a classification technique cost-sensitive, we focused on those that are not specific to a particular machine learning technique: Weighting [33] and MetaCost [9]. By changing costs appropriately, these methods can also be used to address the problem of skewed class distribution. These methods produce comparable results, although this can be data dependent [9, 24]. Experiments not documented here showed that in our context Weighting gives better run-time performance. Therefore we chose Weighting for our system.

Weighting resamples the training set so that a standard cost-insensitive learning algorithm builds a classifier that optimizes the misclassification cost. The input parameter for Weighting is a cost matrix, which defines the costs of misclassifications for individual class pairs. For a binary classification problem, the cost matrix has only one degree of freedom – the so-called cost ratio. These parameters will be formally defined in Sect. 3.

Incremental Learning. Ours is an incremental learning task which is best solved with an incremental learning technique, but can also be solved with a batch learner [12]. As we did not have a working implementation of a purely incremental rule learner (e.g., AQ11 [26], AQ11-PM [22]) we decided to use a "batch-incremental" approach.

In this approach we add subsequent training examples to the training set and build the classifier using the entire training set as new examples become available. It would not be feasible to rebuild the classifier after each new training example, therefore we handle training examples in batches. The size of such batches can be either constant or dependent on the current performance of the classifier. In our case we focused on the second approach. We evaluate the current classification accuracy and, if it drops below a user-defined threshold, we rebuild the classifier using the entire training set. Note that the weighted accuracy is more suitable than the accuracy measure for cost-sensitive learning. Hence, the parameter controlling "batch-incremental" learning is called the *threshold weighted accuracy*. It will be formally defined in Sect. 3.

The disadvantage of this technique is that the size of the training set grows infinitely during a system's lifetime. A future work item of ours will be to limit the number of training examples to a certain time window and use a technique called partial memory [22] to reduce the number of training examples.

Summary. To summarize, we have not found a publicly available machine learning technique that addresses all our requirements, in particular cost-sensitivity and incremental learning. Considering the remaining requirements the most suitable techniques are rule learners. Based on desirable properties and successful applications in similar domains, we decided to use RIPPER as our rule-learner. To circumvent its limitations with regard to our requirements, we used a technique called Weighting to implement cost-sensitivity and adjust for skewed class distribution. We also implemented incremental learning as a "batch-incremental", approach, whose batch size dependent on the current classification accuracy.

3   Experimental Validation

We have built a prototype implementation of ALAC in recommender and agent mode using the Weka framework [36]. The prototype has been validated with synthetic and real intrusion detection data and we summarize the results obtained in this section.

Similar to the examples used throughout this paper, our prototype focuses on binary classification only, that is on classifying alerts into true and false positives. This does not affect the generality of the system, which can be used in multi-class classification. However, it simplifies the analysis of a system's performance. We have not evaluated the classification performance in a multi-class classification.

So far we have referred to alerts related to attacks as *true positives* and alerts mistakenly triggered by benign events as *false positives*. To avoid confusion with the terms used to evaluate our system, we henceforth refer to true positives as *true alerts* and false positives as *false alerts*, respectively. This allows us to use the terms true and false positives for measuring the quality of the alert classification.

More formally, we introduce a *confusion matrix* C to evaluate the performance of our system. Rows in C represent actual class labels and columns represent class labels assigned by the system. Element $C[i, j]$ represents the number of instances of class i classified as class j by the system. For a binary classification problem, the elements of the matrix are called true positives (tp), false negatives (fn), false positives (fp) and true negatives (tn) as shown in Table 1(a).

For cost-sensitive classification we introduce a *cost matrix* Co with identical meaning of rows and columns. The value of $Co[i, j]$ represents the cost of assigning a class j to an example belonging to class i. Most often the cost of correct classification is zero, i.e., $Co[i, i] = 0$. In such cases, for binary classifications (Table 1(b)), there are only two values in the matrix: c_{21} (cost of misclassifying a false alert as a real one) and c_{12} (cost of misclassifying a true alert as a false one).

In the remainder of the paper we use the following measures defined on cost and confusion matrices: true positive rate (TP), false positive rate (FP), false

Table 1. Confusion and cost matrices for alert classification. The positive class $(+)$ denotes true alerts and the negative class $(-)$ denotes false alerts. The columns represent classes assigned given by the system; the rows represent actual classes.

(a) Confusion matrix C

actual \ classified	+	−
+	tp	fn
−	fp	tn

(b) Cost matrix Co

actual \ classified	+	−
+	0	c_{12}
−	c_{21}	0

negative rate (FN). We also use cost ratio (CR), which represents the ratio of the misclassification cost of false positives to false negatives, and its inverse – inverse cost ratio (ICR), which we found more intuitive for intrusion detection. For cost-sensitive classification we used a commonly used evaluation measure – so-called weighted accuracy (WA). Weighted accuracy expresses the accuracy of the classification with misclassifications weighted by their misclassification cost.

$$TP = \frac{tp}{tp + fn}, \quad FP = \frac{fp}{fp + tn}, \quad FN = \frac{fn}{tp + fn}$$

$$CR = \frac{c_{21}}{c_{12}}, \quad ICR = \frac{1}{CR}, \quad WA = \frac{CR \cdot tn + tp}{CR \cdot (tn + fp) + tp + fn}$$

3.1   Data Sources

We used Snort [31] – an open-source network–based IDS – to detect attacks and generate alerts. We purposely used the basic out-of-the box configuration and rule set to demonstrate the performance of ALAC in reducing the amount of false positives and therefore reducing time-consuming IDS tuning.

Snort was run on two data sources: a synthetic one known as DARPA 1999 [19], and a real-world one – namely the traffic observed in a medium-sized corporate network (called *Data Set B*). Alerts are represented as tuples of attribute values, with the following seven attributes: signature name, source and destination IP addresses, a flag indicating whether an alert is a scan, number of scanned hosts and ports and the scan time.

DARPA 1999 Data Set is a synthetic data set collected from a simulated medium-sized computer network in a fictitious military base. The network was connected to the outside world by a router. The router was set to open policy, i.e., not blocking any connections. The simulation was run for 5 weeks which yielded three weeks of training data and two weeks of testing data. Attack truth tables describing the attacks that took place exist for both periods. DARPA 1999 data consists of: two sets of network traffic (files with tcpdump [14] data) both inside and outside the router, BSM and NT audit data, and directory listings.

In our experiments we ran Snort in batch mode using traffic collected from outside the router for both training and testing periods. Note that Snort missed some of the attacks in this dataset. Some of them could only be detected using host-based intrusion detection, whereas for others Snort simply did not have the signature. It is important to note that our goal was not to evaluate the detection rate of Snort on this data, but to validate our system in a realistic environment.

The DARPA 1999 data set has many well-known weaknesses (e.g., [21, 25]) and we want to make sure that using it we get representative results for how ALAC performs in real-world environments. To make this point we analyze how the weaknesses identified by McHugh [25], namely the generation of attack and background traffic, the amount of training data for anomaly based systems, attack taxonomy and the use of ROC analysis; can affect ALAC.

With respect to the training and test data, we use both training and test data for the incremental learning of ALAC, so that we have sufficient data to train the system. With respect to attack taxonomy, we are not using the scoring used in the original evaluation, and therefore attack taxonomy is of less significance. Finally, we use ROC analysis correctly.

The problem of the simulation artifacts is more thoroughly analyzed by Mahoney and Chan [21] thus we use their work to understand how these artifacts can affect ALAC. These artifacts manifest themselves in various fields, such as the TCP and IP headers and higher protocol data. Snort, as a signature based system, does not take advantage of these artifacts and ALAC sees only a small subset of them, namely the source IP address. We verified that the rules learned by ALAC seldom contain a source IP address and therefore the system does not take advantage of simulation artifacts present in source IP addresses. On the other hand, we cannot easily estimate how these regularities affect aggregates used in the background knowledge. This is still an open issue.

We think that the proper analysis of these issues is beyond the scope of our work, and would also require comparing multiple real-world data sets. DARPA 1999 data set is nonetheless valuable for evaluation of our research prototype.

Data Set B is a real-world data set collected over the period of one month in a medium-sized corporate network. The network connects to the Internet through firewalls and to the rest of the corporate intranet and does not contain any externally accessible machines. Our Snort sensor recorded information exchanged between the Internet and the intranet. Owing to privacy issues this data set cannot be shared with third parties. We do not claim that it is representative for all real-world data sets, but it is an example of a real data set on which our system could be used. Hence, we are using this data set as a second validation of our system.

3.2   Alert Labeling

Our system assumes that alerts are labeled by the analyst. In this section we explain how we labeled alerts used to evaluate the system (the statistics for both datasets are shown in Table 2).

DARPA 1999 Data Set. In a first step we generated alerts using Snort running in batch mode and writing alerts into a relational database. In the second step we used automatic labeling of IDS alerts using the provided attack truth tables.

Table 2. Statistics generated by the Snort sensor with DARPA 1999 data set and Data set B.

	DARPA 1999	Data Set B
Duration of experiment:	5 weeks	1 month
Number of IDS alerts:	59812	47099
False alerts:	48103	33220
True alerts:	11709	13383
Unidentified:	–	496

For labeling, we used an automatic approach which can be easily reproduced by researchers in other environments, even with different IDS sensors. We consider all alerts meeting the following criteria related to an attack: (i) matching source IP address, (ii) matching destination IP address and (iii) alert time stamp in the time window in which the attack has occurred. We masked all remaining alerts as false alerts. While manually reviewing the alerts we found that, in many cases, the classification is ambiguous (e.g., a benign PING alert can be as well classified as malicious if it is sent to the host being attacked). This may introduce an error in class labels.

Note that different attacks triggered a different number of alerts (e.g., wide network scans triggered thousands of alerts). For the evaluation of our system we discarded the information regarding which alerts belong to which attack and labeled all these alerts as true alerts.

Data Set B. We generated these alerts in real-time using Snort. As opposed to the first data set we did not have information concerning attacks. The alerts have been classified based on the author's expertise in intrusion detection into groups indicating possible type and cause of the alert. There was also a certain number of alerts that could not be classified into true or false positives. Similarly to the first data set we used only binary classification to evaluate the system, and labeled the unidentified alerts as true positives.

Note that this data set was collected in a well maintained and well protected network with no direct Internet access. We observed a low number of attacks in this network, but many alerts were generated. We observed that large groups of alerts can be explained by events such as a single worm infection and unauthorized network scans. The problem of removing such redundancy can be solved by so-called *alert correlation systems* [5, 7, 34], where a group of alerts can be replaced by a meta-alert representative of the alerts in the group, prior to classification. The topic of alert correlation is beyond the scope of this paper and will be addressed as a future work item.

Another issue is that the classification of alerts was done by only one analyst and therefore may contain errors. This raises the question of how such classification errors affect the performance of ALAC. To address this issue, one can ask multiple analysts to classify the dataset independently. Then the results can be compared using interrater reliability analysis.

3.3   Background Knowledge

We decided to focus on the first two types of background knowledge presented in Sect. 2.1, namely network topology and alert context. Owing to a lack of required information concerning installed software, we decided not to implement matching alert semantics with installed software. This would also be a repetition of the experiments by Lippmann et al. [20].

As discussed in Sect. 3.1, we used an attribute-value representation of alarms with the background knowledge represented as additional attributes. Specifically, the background knowledge resulted in 19 attributes, which are calculated as follows:

Classification of IP addresses resulted in an additional attribute for both source and destination IP classifying machines according to their known subnets (e.g., Internet, intranet, DMZ).

Classification of hosts resulted in additional attributes indicating the operating system and the host type for known IP addresses.

Aggregates1 resulted in additional attributes with the number of alerts in the following categories (we calculated these aggregates for alerts in a time window of 1 minute):
  - alerts with the same source IP address,
  - alerts with the same destination IP address,
  - alerts with the same source or destination IP address,
  - alerts with the same signature,
  - alerts classified as intrusions.

Aggregates2,3 were calculated similarly to the first set of attributes, but in time windows of 5 and 30 minutes, respectively.

This choice of background knowledge, which was motivated by heuristics used in alert correlation systems, is necessarily a bit *ad-hoc* and reflects the author's expertise in classifying IDS attacks. As this background knowledge is not especially tailored to training data, it is natural to ask how useful it is for alert classification. We discuss the answer to this question in the following sections.

3.4   Results Obtained with DARPA 1999 Data Set

Our experiments were conducted in two stages. In the first stage we evaluated the performance of the classifier and the influence of adding background knowledge to alerts on the accuracy of classification. The results presented here allowed us to set some parameters in ALAC. In the second stage we evaluated the performance of ALAC in recommender and agent mode.

Background Knowledge and Setting ALAC Parameters. Here we describe the results of experiments conducted to evaluate background knowledge and to set ALAC parameters. Note that in the experiments we used only the machine

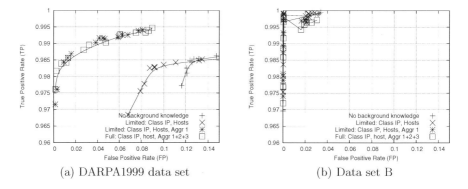

Fig. 2. ROC curves for classifier used with different types of background knowledge.

learning component of ALAC, namely a RIPPER module, to build classifiers for the entire data set. Hereafter we refer to these results as *batch classification*.

Since the behavior of classifiers depends on the assigned costs, we used ROC (Receiver Operating Characteristic) analysis [29] to evaluate the performance of our classifier for different misclassification costs. Figure 2(a) shows the performance of the classifier using data with different amounts of background knowledge. Each curve was plotted by varying the cost ratio for the classifier. Each point in the curve represents results obtained from 10-fold cross validation for a given misclassification cost and type of background knowledge.

As we expected, the classifier with no background knowledge (plus series) performs worse than the classifier with simple classifications of IP addresses and operating systems running on the machines (cross series) in terms of false positives. Using the background knowledge consisting of the classifications above and aggregates introduced in Sect. 3.3 significantly reduces the false positive rate and increases the true positive rate (star series). Full background knowledge (having additional aggregates in multiple time windows) performs comparably to the reduced one (star vs. box series). In our experiments with ALAC we decided to use full background knowledge.

ROC curves show the performance of the system under different misclassification costs, but they do not show how the curve was built. Recall from Sect. 2.2 that we use the inverse cost ratio in Weighting to make RIPPER cost sensitive and varied this parameter to obtain a multiple points on the curve. We used this curve to select good parameters of our model.

ALAC is controlled by a number of parameters, which we had to set in order to evaluate its performance. To evaluate the performance of ALAC as an incremental classifier we first selected the parameters of its base classifier.

The performance of the base classifier at various costs and class distributions is depicted by the ROC curve and it is possible to select an optimal classifier for a certain cost and class distribution [11]. As these values are not defined for our task, we could not select an optimal classifier using the above method. Therefore we arbitrarily selected a base classifier that gives a good tradeoff between false positives and false negatives, for $ICR = 50$.

The second parameter is the threshold weighted accuracy (WA) for rebuilding the classifier (see Sect. 2.2). The value of threshold weighted accuracy should be chosen carefully as it represents a tradeoff between classification accuracy and how frequently the machine learning algorithm is run. We chose the value equal to the accuracy of a classifier in batch mode. Experiments not documented here showed that using higher values increases the learning frequency with no significant improvement in classification accuracy.

We assumed that in real-life scenarios the system would work with an initial model and only use new training examples to modify its model. To simulate this we used 30% of input data to build the initial classifier and the remaining 70% to evaluate the system.

ALAC in Recommender Mode. In recommender mode the analyst reviews each alert and corrects ALAC misclassifications. We plotted the number of misclassifications: false positives (Fig. 3(a)) and false negatives (Fig. 3(b)) as a function of processed alerts.

The resulting overall false negative rate ($FN = 0.024$) is much higher than the false negative rate for the batch classification on the entire data set ($FN = 0.0076$) as shown in Fig. 2(a). At the same time, the overall false positive rate ($FP = 0.025$) is less than half of the false positive rate for batch classification ($FP = 0.06$). These differences are expected due to different learning and evaluation methods used, i.e., batch incremental learning vs. 10-fold cross validation. Note that both ALAC and a batch classifier have a very good classification accuracy and yield comparable results in terms of accuracy.

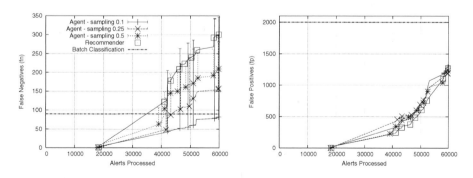

Fig. 3. False negatives and false positives for ALAC in agent and recommender modes (DARPA1999 data set, ICR=50).

ALAC in Agent Mode. In agent mode ALAC processes alerts autonomously based on criteria defined by the analyst, described in Sect. 2.1. We configured the system to forward all alerts classified as true alerts and false alerts classified

with low confidence ($confidence < c_{th}$) to the analyst. The system discarded all
other alerts, i.e., false alerts classified with high confidence, except for a fraction
k of randomly chosen alerts, which were also forwarded to the analyst.

Similarly to the recommender mode, we calculated the number of misclassifications made by the system. We experimented with different values of c_{th} and
sampling rates k. We then chose $c_{th} = 90\%$ and three sampling rates k: 0.1,
0.25 and 0.5. Our experiments show that the sampling rates below 0.1 make the
agent misclassify too many alerts and significantly changes the class distribution
in the training examples. On the other hand, with sampling rates much higher
than 0.5, the system works similarly to recommender mode and is less useful for
the analyst.

Notice that there are two types of false negatives in agent mode – the ones
corrected by the analyst and the ones the analyst is not aware of because the
alerts have been discarded. We plotted the second type of misclassification as an
error bar in Fig. 3(a). Intuitively with lower sampling rates, the agent will have
fewer false negatives of the first type, in fact missing more alerts. As expected
the total number of false negatives is lower with higher sampling rates.

We were surprised to observe that the recommender and the agent have similar false positive rates ($FP = 0.025$ for both cases) and similar false negative
rates, even with low sampling rates ($FN = 0.026$ for $k = 0.25$ vs. $FN = 0.025$).
This seemingly counterintuitive result can be explained if we note that automatic processing of alerts classified as false positives effectively changes the class
distribution in training examples in favor of true alerts. As a result the agent
performs comparably to the recommender.

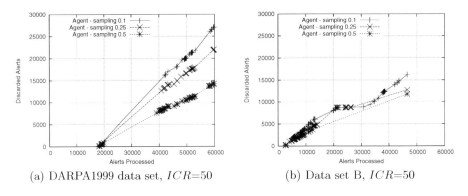

(a) DARPA1999 data set, $ICR{=}50$ (b) Data set B, $ICR{=}50$

Fig. 4. Number of alerts processed autonomously by ALAC in agent mode.

As shown in Fig. 4(a), with the sampling rate of 0.25, more than 45% of false
alerts were processed and discarded by ALAC. At the same time the number
of unnoticed false negatives is half the number of mistakes for recommender
mode. Our experiments show that the system is useful for intrusion detection

analysts as it significantly reduces number of false positives, without making many mistakes.

3.5   Results Obtained with Data Set B

We used the second dataset as an independent validation of the system. To avoid "fitting the model to the data" we used the same set of parameters as for the first data set. However, a ROC curve in Fig. 2(b) shows that the classifier achieves much higher true positive rate and much lower false negative rate than for the first data set, which means that Data Set B is easier to classify. The likely explanation of this fact is that Data Set B contains fewer intrusions and more redundancy than the first data set.

Notice that the ROC curve consists of two distinct parts. An analysis shows that the left part corresponds to RIPPER run for small ICRs, where it learns the rules describing true alerts. The right part of the curve corresponds to high ICRs, where RIPPER learns the rules describing false alerts. Better performance in the first case can be explained by the fact that the intrusions in this data set are more structured and therefore easier to learn. On the other hand, false alerts are more difficult to describe and hence the performance is poorer.

Background Knowledge and Setting ALAC Parameters. Results with ROC analysis (Fig. 2(b)) show that the classifier correctly classifies most of the examples, and adding background knowledge has little effect on classification. To have the same conditions as with the first data set, we nonetheless decided to use the full background knowledge. We also noticed that $ICR = 50$ is not the optimal value for this dataset as it results in a high false positive rate ($FN = 0.002, FP = 0.05$).

We observed that ALAC, when run with 30% of the alerts as an initial classifier, classified the remaining alerts with very few learning runs. Therefore, to demonstrate its incremental learning capabilities, we decided to lower the initial amount of training data from 30% to 5% of all the alerts.

ALAC in Recommender Mode. Figure 5 shows that in recommender mode the system has a much lower overall false negative rate ($FN = 0.0045$) and a higher overall false positive rate ($FP = 0.10$) than for DARPA 1999 data set, which is comparable to the results of the classification in batch mode. We also observed that the learning only took place for approximately the first 30% of the entire data set and the classifier classified the remaining alerts with no additional learning. This phenomena can also be explained by the fact that Data Set B contains more regularities and the classifier is easier to build.

This is different in the case of the DARPA1999 data set, where the classifier was frequently rebuilt in the last 30% of the data. For DARPA1999 data set the behavior of ALAC is explained by the fact that most of the intrusions actually took place in the last two weeks of the experiment.

ALAC in Agent Mode. In agent mode we obtained results similar to those in recommender mode, with a great number of alerts being processed autonomously by the system ($FN = 0.0065, FP = 0.13$). As shown in Fig. 4(b), with the sampling rate of 0.25, more than 27% of all alerts were processed by the agent. At the same time the actual number of unnoticed false negatives is one third smaller than the number of false negatives in recommender mode. This confirms the usefulness of the system tested with an independent data set.

Similarly to observation in Sect. 3.4 with lower sampling rates, the agent will have seemingly fewer false negatives, in fact missing more alerts. As expected the total number of false negatives is lower with higher sampling rates. This effect is not as clearly visible as with DARPA1999 data set.

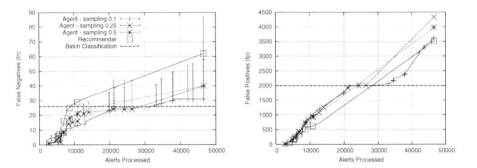

Fig. 5. False negatives and false positives for ALAC in agent and recommender modes (Data set B, $ICR=50$).

3.6   Understanding the Rules

One requirement of our system was that the rules can be reviewed by the analyst and their correctness can be verified. The rules built by RIPPER are generally human interpretable and thus can be reviewed by the analyst. Here is a representative example of two rules used by ALAC:

```
(cnt_intr_w1 <= 0) and (cnt_sign_w3 >= 1) and (cnt_sign_w1 >= 1)
        and (cnt_dstIP_w1 >= 1) => class=FALSE
(cnt_srcIP_w3 <= 6) and (cnt_int_w2 <= 0) and (cnt_ip_w2 >= 2)
        and (sign = ICMP PING NMAP) => class=FALSE
```

The first rule reads as follows: If a number of alerts classified as intrusions in the last minute (window `w1`) equals zero and there have been other alerts triggered by a given signature and targeted at the same IP address as the current alert, then the alert should be classified as false positive. The second rule says that, if the number of `NMAP PING` alerts originating from the same IP address is less than six in the last 30 minutes (window `w3`), there have been no intrusions in the last 5 minutes (window `w2`) and there has been at least 1 alert with identical source or destination IP address, then the current alert is false positive.

These rules are intuitively appealing: If there have been similar alerts recently and they were all false alerts, then the current alert is also a false alert. The second rule says that if the number of NMAP PING alerts is small and there has not been any intrusions recently, then the alert is a false alert.

We observed that the comprehensibility of rules depends on several factors including the background knowledge and the cost ratio. With less background knowledge RIPPER learns more specific and difficult to understand rules. The effect of varying cost ratio is particularly apparent for rules produced while constructing the ROC curve, where RIPPER induces rules for either true or false alerts. This is due to the use of RIPPER running in ordered rule set mode.

4   Conclusions and Future Work

We presented a novel concept of building an adaptive alert classifier based on an intrusion detection analyst's feedback using machine learning techniques. We discussed the issues of human feedback and background knowledge, and reviewed machine learning techniques suitable for alert classification. Finally, we presented a prototype implementation and evaluated its performance on synthetic as well as real intrusion data.

We showed that background knowledge is useful for alert classification. The results were particularly clear for the DARPA 1999 data set. For the real-world dataset, adding background knowledge had little impact on the classification accuracy. The second set was much easier to classify, even with no background knowledge. Hence, we did not expect improvement from background knowledge in this case. We also showed that the system is useful in recommender mode, where it adaptively learns the classification from the analyst. For both datasets we obtained false negative and false positive rates comparable to batch classification. Note that in recommender mode all system misclassifications would have been corrected by the analyst.

In addition, we found that our system is useful in agent mode, where some alerts are autonomously processed (e.g., false positives classified with high confidence are discarded). More importantly, for both data sets the false negative rate of our system is comparable to that in the recommender mode. At the same time, the number of false positives has been reduced by approximately 30%.

The system has a few numeric parameters that influence its performance and should be adjusted depending on the input data. In the future, we intend to investigate how the value of these parameters can be automatically determined. We are also aware of the limitations of the data sets used. We aim to evaluate the performance of the system on the basis of more realistic intrusion detection data and to integrate an alert correlation system to reduce redundancy in alerts. Our system uses RIPPER, a noise-tolerant algorithm, but the extent to which ALAC can tolerate errors in the data, is currently unknown. We will address this issue by introducing an artificial error and observing how it affects the system.

The topic of learning comprehensible rules is very interesting and we plan to investigate it further. We are currently looking at learning multiple classifiers for each signature and using RIPPER in unordered rule set mode.

In the machine learning part we intend to focus on the development of incremental machine learning technique suitable for learning a classifier for intrusion detection. Initially we want to perform experiments with partial memory technique and batch classifiers. Later we will focus on truly incremental techniques. It is important that such techniques be able to incorporate the required background knowledge.

Acknowledgments

Many thanks to Klaus Julisch and Anderas Wespi for their contribution to the system and valuable comments. Thanks also goes to other members of the Global Security Analysis Laboratory and anonymous reviewers for their insightful remarks.

References

1. Anderson, J.P.: Computer security threat monitoring and surveillance. Technical report, James P. Anderson Co (1980).
2. Axelsson, S.: The base-rate fallacy and its implications for the intrusion detection. In: Proceedings of the 6th ACM conference on Computer and Communications Security, Kent Ridge Digital Labs, Singapore (1999) 1–7.
3. Bloedorn, E., Hill, B., Christiansen, A., Skorupka, C., Talbot, L., Tivel, J.: Data Mining for Improving Intrusion Detection. Technical report, MITRE (2000).
4. Cohen, W.W.: Fast effective rule induction. In Prieditis, A., Russell, S., eds.: Proceedings of the 12th International Conference on Machine Learning, Tahoe City, CA, Morgan Kaufmann (1995) 115–123.
5. Cuppens, F.: Managing alerts in multi-intrusion detection environment. In: Proceedings 17th Annual Computer Security Applications Conference, New Orleans (2001) 22–31.
6. Dain, O., Cunningham, R.K.: Fusing a heterogeneous alert stream into scenarios. In: Proc. of the 2001 ACM Workshop on Data Mining for Security Application, Philadelphia, PA (2001) 1–13.
7. Debar, H., Wespi, A.: Aggregation and correlation of intrusion-detection alerts. In: Recent Advances in Intrusion Detection (RAID2001). Volume 2212 of Lecture Notes in Computer Science., Springer-Verlag (2001) 85–103.
8. Denning, D.E.: An intrusion detection model. IEEE Transactions on Software Engineering **SE-13** (1987) 222–232.
9. Domingos, P.: Metacost: A General Method for Making Classifiers Cost-Sensitive. In: Proceedings of the Fifth ACM SIGKDD International Conference on Knowledge Discovery and Data Mining, San Diego, California (1999) 155–164.
10. Fan, W.: Cost-Sensitive, Scalable and Adaptive Learning Using Ensemble-based Methods. PhD thesis, Columbia University (2001).
11. Fawcett, T.: ROC graphs: Note and practical considerations for researchers (HPL-2003-4). Technical report, HP Laboratories (2003).
12. Giraud-Carrier, C.: A Note on the Utility of Incremental Learning. AI Communications **13** (2000) 215–223.
13. Hettich, S., Bay, S.D.: The UCI KDD Archive. Web page at `http://kdd.ics.uci.edu` (1999).

14. Jacobson, V., Leres, C., McCanne, S.: TCPDUMP public repository. Web page at http://www.tcpdump.org/ (2003).
15. Julisch, K.: Using Root Cause Analysis to Handle Intrusion Detection Alarms. PhD thesis, University of Dortmund (2003).
16. Lavrač, N., Džeroski, S.: Inductive Logic Programming: Techniques and Applications. Ellis Horwood (1994).
17. Lee, W.: A Data Mining Framework for Constructing Features and Models for Intrusion Detection Systems. PhD thesis, Columbia University (1999).
18. Lee, W., Fan, W., Miller, M., Stolfo, S.J., Zadok, E.: Toward cost-sensitive modeling for intrusion detection and response. Journal of Computer Security **10** (2002) 5–22.
19. Lippmann, R., Haines, J.W., Fried, D.J., Korba, J., Das, K.: The 1999 DARPA Off-Line Intrusion Detection Evaluation. Computer Networks: The International Journal of Computer and Telecommunications Networking **34** (2000) 579–595.
20. Lippmann, R., Webster, S., Stetson, D.: The effect of identifying vulnerabilities and patching software on the utility of network intrusion detection. In: Recent Advances in Intrusion Detection (RAID2002). Volume 2516 of Lecture Notes in Computer Science., Springer-Verlag (2002) 307–326.
21. Mahoney, M.V., Chan, P.K.: An Analysis of the 1999 DARPA/Lincoln Laboratory Evaluation Data for Network Anomaly Detection. In: Recent Advances in Intrusion Detection (RAID2003). Volume 2820 of Lecture Notes in Computer Science., Springer-Verlag (2003) 220–237.
22. Maloof, M.A., Michalski, R.S.: Incremental learning with partial instance memory. In: Proceedings of Foundations of Intelligent Systems: 13th International Symposium, ISMIS 2002. Volume 2366 of Lecture Notes in Artificial Intelligence., Springer-Verlag (2002) 16–27.
23. Manganaris, S., Christensen, M., Zerkle, D., Hermiz, K.: A Data Mining Analysis of RTID Alarms. Computer Networks: The International Journal of Computer and Telecommunications Networking **34** (2000) 571–577.
24. María, J., Hidalgo, G.: Evaluating cost-sensitive unsolicited bulk email categorization. In: Proceedings of the 2002 ACM Symposium on Applied Computing, Springer-Verlag (2002) 615–620.
25. McHugh, J.: The 1998 Lincoln Laboratory IDS Evaluation. A critique. In: Recent Advances in Intrusion Detection (RAID2000). Volume 1907 of Lecture Notes in Computer Science., Springer-Verlag (2000) 145–161.
26. Michalski, R.: On the quasi-minimal solution of the general covering problem. In: Proceedings of the V International Symposium on Information Processing (FCIP 69)(Switching Circuits). Volume A3., Yugoslavia, Bled (1969) 125–128.
27. Mitchel, T.M.: Machine Learning. Mc Graw Hill (1997).
28. Morin, B., Mé, L., Debar, H., Ducasse, M.: M2D2: A formal data model for IDS alert correlation. In: Recent Advances in Intrusion Detection (RAID2002). Volume 2516 of Lecture Notes in Computer Science., Springer-Verlag (2002) 115–137.
29. Provost, F., Fawcett, T.: Robust classification for impresice environments. Machine Learning Journal **42** (2001) 203–231.
30. Quinlan, R.: C4.5: Programs for Machine Learning. Morgan Kaufman (1993).
31. Roesch, M.: SNORT. The Open Source Network Intrusion System. Web page at http://www.snort.org (1998–2003).
32. Sommer, R., Paxson, V.: Enhancing Byte-Level Network Intrusion Detection Signatures with Context. In: Proceedings of the 10th ACM conference on Computer and Communication Security, Washington, DC (2003) 262–271.

33. Ting, K.: Inducing cost-sensitive trees via instance weighting. In: Proceedings of The Second European Symposium on Principles of Data Mining and Knowledge Discovery. Volume 1510 of Lecture Notes in AI., Springer-Verlag (1998) 139–147.

34. Valdes, A., Skinner, K.: Probabilistic alert correlation. In: Recent Advances in Intrusion Detection (RAID2001). Volume 2212 of Lecture Notes in Computer Science., Springer-Verlag (2001) 54–68.

35. Wang, J., Lee, I.: Measuring false-positive by automated real-time correlated hacking behavior analysis. In: Information Security 4th International Conference. Volume 2200 of Lecture Notes in Computer Science., Springer-Verlag (2001) 512–.

36. Witten, I.H., Frank, E.: Data Mining: Practical machine learning tools with Java implementations. Morgan Kaufmann, San Francisco (2000).

Attack Analysis and Detection
for Ad Hoc Routing Protocols

Yi-an Huang and Wenke Lee

College of Computing
Georgia Institute of Technology
801 Atlantic Dr.
Atlanta, GA, USA 30332
{yian,wenke}@cc.gatech.edu

Abstract. Attack analysis is a challenging problem, especially in emerging environments where there are few known attack cases. One such new environment is the Mobile Ad hoc Network (MANET). In this paper, we present a systematic approach to analyze attacks. We introduce the concept of basic events. An attack can be decomposed into certain combinations of basic events. We then define a taxonomy of anomalous basic events by analyzing the basic security goals.

Attack analysis provides a basis for designing detection models. We use both specification-based and statistical-based approaches. First, normal basic events of the protocol can be modeled by an extended finite state automaton (EFSA) according to the protocol specifications. The EFSA can detect anomalous basic events that are direct violations of the specifications. Statistical learning algorithms, with statistical features, i.e., statistics on the states and transitions of the EFSA, can train an effective detection model to detect those anomalous basic events that are temporal and statistical in nature.

We use the AODV routing protocol as a case study to validate our research. Our experiments on the MobiEmu wireless emulation platform show that our specification-based and statistical-based models cover most of the anomalous basic events in our taxonomy.

Keywords: MANET, Attack Analysis, Intrusion Detection, Routing Security, AODV

1   Introduction

Network protocol design and implementation have become increasingly complex. Consequently, securing network protocols requires detailed analysis of normal protocol operations and vulnerabilities. The process is tedious and error-prone. Traditional attack analysis categorizes attacks based on knowledge of known incidents. Therefore, such analysis cannot be applied to new (unknown) attacks. The problem is even more serious in new environments where there are very few known attacks. Mobile ad hoc networking (MANET) is such an example. An ad hoc network consists of a group of autonomous mobile nodes with no infrastructure support. Recently, many MANET applications have emerged, such as

E. Jonsson et al. (Eds.): RAID 2004, LNCS 3224, pp. 125–145, 2004.

battlefield operations, personal digital assistant (PDA) communication, among others. MANET and its applications are very different from traditional network and applications. They are also more vulnerable due to their unique characteristics, such as open physical medium, dynamic topology, de-centralized computing environment, and lack of a clear line of defense. Recent research efforts, such as [Zap01,HPJ02] attempt to apply cryptography techniques to secure MANET routing protocols. However, existing experience in wired security has already taught us the necessity of defense-in-depth because there are always human errors and design flaws that enable attackers to exploit software vulnerability. Therefore, it is also necessary to develop *detection* and *response* techniques for MANET.

Designing an effective intrusion detection system (IDS), as well as other security mechanisms, requires a deep understanding of threat models and adversaries' attack capabilities. We note that since MANET uses a TCP/IP stack, many well-known attacks can be applied to MANET but existing security measures in wired networks can address these attacks. On the other hand, some protocols, especially routing protocols, are MANET specific. Very few attack instances of these protocols have been well studied. It follows that traditional attack analysis cannot work effectively. In this paper, we propose a new attack analysis approach by decomposing a complicated attack into a number of basic components called *basic events*. Every basic event consists of casually related protocol behavior and uses resources solely within a single node. It is easier to study the protocol behavior more accurately from the point of view of a single node. Specifically, we study the basic routing behavior in MANET. We propose a taxonomy of anomalous basic events for MANET, which is based on potential targets that attackers can compromise and the security goals that attackers attempt to compromise for each target.

Based on the taxonomy, we build a prototype IDS for MANET routing protocols. We choose one of the most popular MANET routing protocols, AODV, as a case study. We develop specifications in the form of an extended finite state automaton (EFSA) from AODV IETF Draft [PBRD03] . We apply two detection approaches which use the EFSA in different ways. First, we can detect violations of the specification directly, which is often referred to as a **specification-based approach**. Second, we can also detect statistical anomalies by constructing statistical features from the specification and apply machine learning methods. This **statistical-based approach** is more suitable for attacks that are temporal and statistical in nature.

In short, our main contribution is the concept of basic events and its use in attack taxonomy analysis. We also show how to use protocol specifications to model normal basic events and derive features from the specification to design an intrusion detection system.

We use MobiEmu [ZL02] as our evaluation platform for related experiments. MobiEmu is an experimental testbed that emulates MANET in a wired network. It shows that our approach involves a much smaller set of features in order to capture the same set of attacks, compared with our previous work in developing

IDS for MANET [HFLY02] that attempted an exhaustive search of features without the help of taxonomy and protocol specification. As the feature set is smaller and derived directly from the protocol specification, it has the additional advantage that domain experts can review it. This further improves accuracy.

The rest of the paper is organized as follows. Section 2 discusses related concepts of basic events and presents a taxonomy of anomalous basic events in MANET. Section 3 presents an AODV EFSA specification. Section 4 describes the design of a MANET IDS, experiments and results. Finally, related work and conclusions are discussed in Sections 5 and 6.

2   Taxonomy of Anomalous Basic Events

2.1   Concepts

Anomalies or attacks can be categorized using different criteria. Since there is no well-established taxonomy yet in MANET, we describe a systematic approach to study MANET attacks based on the concept of **anomalous basic events**. We use MANET routing as the subject of our study.

A **routing process** in MANET involves causally related, cooperative operations from a number of nodes. For example, the *Route Discovery* process, frequently appeared in on-demand routing protocols [JMB01,PBRD03], consists of chained actions from the source node to the destination node (or an intermediate node who knows a route to the destination) and back to the source node. Such process can be decomposed into a series of basic routing events. A **basic routing event** is defined as an indivisible local segment of a routing process. More precisely, it is the smallest set of causally related routing operations on a single node. We will use the term **basic event** for short. Therefore, the *Route Discovery process* can be decomposed into the following basic events: 1) The source node delivers an initial *Route Request*; 2) Each node (except for the source node and the node that has a route to the destination) in the forward path receives a *Route Request* from the previous node and forwards it; 3) The replying node receives the *Route Request* and replies with a *Route Reply* message; 4) An intermediate node in the reverse path receives a *Route Reply* message and forwards it; 5) Finally, the source node receives the *Route Reply* message and establishes a route to the destination.

Note that a basic (routing) event may contain one or more operations, such as receiving a packet, modify a routing parameter, or delivering a packet. However, the integrity of routing logic requires every basic event be conducted in a transaction fashion. That is, it is considered successful (or normal) if and only if it performs all of its operations in the specified order. We assume that certain **system specification** exists which specifies normal protocol behavior. As we will show later in the paper, system specification can be represented in the form of an extended finite state machine; a (normal) basic event maps to a single transition in a given extended finite state machine. We further note that to define a basic event, operations are restricted to the scope of a single MANET node because only local data source can be fully trusted by the intrusion detection agent on the same node.

On the other hand, an **anomalous basic event** is a basic event that does not follow the system specification. Obviously, it is useful to study anomalous basic events in order to capture the characteristics of basic attack components. Nevertheless, we note that it is possible that some attacks do not trigger any anomalous basic events. For example, an attack may involve elements from a different layer that the system specification does not describe, or it may involve knowledge beyond a single node. A Wormhole attack [HPJ01] is an example of the first case, where two wireless nodes can create a hidden tunnel through wires or wireless links with stronger transmission power. A network scan on known (vulnerable) ports is an example of the latter case because each single node observes only legitimate uses. To deal with these issues, we plan to work on a multiple layer and global intrusion detection system.

2.2   Taxonomy of Anomalous Basic Events in MANET Routing Protocols

We identify an anomalous basic event by two components, its **target** and **operation**. A protocol agent running on a single node has different elements to operate on, with different semantics. The routing behavior of MANET typically involves three elements or targets: *routing messages*, *data packets* and *routing table (or routing cache) entries*. Furthermore, we need to study what are the possible attack operations on these targets. Individual security requirements can be identified by examining the following well-known security goals: *Confidentiality*, *Integrity* and *Availability*. We summarize possible combinations of routing targets and operations in Table 1. In this table, we list three basic operations for *Integrity* compromise: add, delete and change. The exact meanings of these operations need to be interpreted properly in the context of individual targets.

Conceptually, we can characterize a normal basic event in a similar way, i.e., its target and its operation type. Nevertheless, many different normal operations can be applied and it is hard to find a universal taxonomy of normal operations for all system specification. Thus, a more logical way is to represent normal basic events with a different structure, such as the extended state machine approach we introduce in Section 3.

In MANET routing security, cryptography addresses many problems, especially those involving confidentiality and integrity issues on data packets. Intrusion detection techniques are more suitable for other security requirements. *Availability* issue, for example, is difficult for protection techniques because attack packets appear indistinguishable from normal user packets. Some *integrity* problems also require non-cryptographic solutions for efficiency reasons. For example, an attacker can compromise the routing table in a local node and change the cost of any specific route entry. It may change the sequence number or a hop count so that some specific route appears more attractive than other valid routes. Encrypting every access operation on routing entries could be too expensive. Intrusion detection solutions can better address these issues, based on existing experience in the wired networks. We identify a number of anomalous basic events that are more suitable for intrusion detection systems in bold face in Table 1.

There are two types of anomalous basic events marked by asterisks in the table, *Fabrication of Routing Messages* and *Modification of Routing Messages*. There are cryptographic solutions for these types of problems, but they are not very efficient and sometimes require an expensive key establishment phase. We want to study them in our IDS work because they are related to the routing logic and we can see later that some attacks in these categories can be detected easily.

Table 1. Taxonomy of Anomalous Basic Events

Compromises to Security Goals		Events by Targets		
		Routing Messages	Data Packets	Routing Table Entries
Confidentiality		Location Disclosure	Data Disclosure	N/A
Integrity	Add	**Fabrication***	Fabrication	**Add Route**
	Delete	**Interruption**	**Interruption**	**Delete Route**
	Change	**Modification***	Modification	**Change Route Cost**
		Rushing		
Availability		**Flooding**	**Flooding**	Routing Table Overflow

We examine a number of basic MANET routing attacks noted in the literature [HFLY02,NS03,TBK+03]. By comparing them (shown in Table 2) with taxonomy in Table 1, we find they match very well with the definitions of anomalous basic events. We refer to each attack with a unique name and optionally a suffix letter. For example, "Route Flooding (S)" is a flooding attack of routing messages that uses a unique source address.

In addition, we consider a number of more complex attack scenarios that contains a sequence of anomalous basic events. We use some examples studied by Ning and Sun [NS03]. These attack scenarios are summarized in Table 3.

As a case study, we analyze AODV [PBRD03], a popular MANET routing protocol. We analyze its designed behavior using an extended finite state automaton approach. This is inspired by the work on TCP/IP protocols in [SGF+02].

3   A Specification of the AODV Protocol

3.1   An Overview of Extended Finite State Automaton (EFSA)

Specification-based approach provides a model to analyze attacks based on protocol specifications. Similar to the work by Sekar et al. for TCP/IP protocols [SGF+02], we also propose to model the AODV protocol with an EFSA approach.

An *extended finite state automaton (EFSA)* is similar to a finite-state machine except that transitions and states can carry a finite set of parameters.

Table 2. Basic MANET Attacks, where suffix letters stand for different attack variations. R, S, D stand for randomness, source only and destination only, respectively. Other letters include M (maximal value), F (failure), Y (reply), I (invalid) and N (new)

Attacks	Attack Description	Corresponding Anomalous Basic Events
Active Reply	A *Route Reply* is actively forged with no related incoming *Route Request* messages.	Fabrication of Routing Messages
False Reply	A *Route Reply* is forged for a *Route Request* message even though the node is not supposed to reply.	
Route Drop (R)	Drop routing packets. (R) denotes a random selection of source and destination addresses.	Interruption of Routing Messages
Route Drop (S)	A fixed percentage of routing packets with a specific source address are dropped. (S) stands for source address.	
Route Drop (D)	A fixed percentage of routing packets with a specific destination address are dropped. (D) stands for destination address.	
Modify Sequence (R)	Modify the destination's sequence number randomly. (R) stands for randomness.	Modification of Routing Messages
Modify Sequence (M)	Increase the destination's sequence number to the largest allowed number. (M) stands for the maximal value.	
Modify Hop	Change the hop count to a smaller value.	
Rushing (F)	Shorten the waiting time for *Route Replies* when a route is unavailable. (F) stands for failure.	Rushing of Routing Messages
Rushing (Y)	Shorten the waiting time to send a *Route Reply* after a *Route Request* is received. (Y) stands for reply.	
Route Flooding (R)	Flood with both source and destination addresses randomized.	Flooding of Routing Messages
Route Flooding (S)	Flood with the same source address and random destination addresses.	
Route Flooding (D)	Flood to a single destination with random source addresses.	
Data Drop (R | S | D)	Similar to Route Drop (R), Route Drop (S), or Route Drop (D), but using data packets.	Interruption of Data Packets
Data Flooding (R | S | D)	Similar to Route Flooding (R), Route Flooding (S), or Route Flooding (D), but using data packets.	Flooding of Data Packets
Add Route (I)	An invalid route entry is randomly selected and validated. (I) stands for invalid.	Add Route of Routing Table Entries
Add Route (N)	A route entry is added directly with random destination address. (N) stands for new.	
Delete Route	A random valid route is invalidated.	Delete Route of Routing Table Entries
Change Sequence (R | M)	Similar to Modify Sequence attacks but the sequence number is changed directly on the routing table.	Change Route Cost of Routing Table Entries
Change Hop	Similar to Modify Hop, but the hop count is changed directly on the routing table.	
Overflow Table	Add excessive routes to overflow the routing table.	Routing Table Overflow of Routing Table Entries

Conventionally, we call them transition *parameters* and state *variables*. We can derive EFSA from documentation, implementations, RFCs or other materials.

Furthermore, we distinguish two types of transitions: input and output transitions. Input transitions include packet-receiving events and output transitions

Table 3. More Complex MANET Attacks

Attacks	Attack Description	Corresponding Anomalous Basic Events
Route Invasion	Inject a node in an active route.	Fabrication of Routing Messages (two RREQs)
Route Loop	Create a route loop.	Fabrication of Routing Messages (two RREPs)
Partition	Separate a network into two partitions.	Fabrication of Routing Messages (RREP) Interruption of Data Packets

include packet-delivery events. If there are no packet communication events involved in a transition (which can take place with a timeout, for example), it is also treated as an input transition.

According to the original definition in [SGF+02], input and output transitions are separate transitions because only one event can be specified in a transition. Here we relax the definition of a transition by allowing a transition to have both a packet-receiving event and a packet-delivery event (either of them can still be optional). The relaxed definition of a transition δ is: $\delta = \{$S_old $\rightarrow$ S_new, input_cond $\rightarrow$ output_action$\}$, where the old and new states are specified in S_old and S_new. The new definition assumes the following semantics. The output action, if defined, must be performed immediately after the input condition is met, and before the new state is reached. Unless the output action has accomplished, no other transitions are allowed.

An **input condition** (input_cond) can specify timeouts or predicates and at most one packet-receiving event. It uses a C-like expression syntax where operators like &&, || etc., can be used. State variables (of the original state) and transition parameters can be accessed in input conditions. To distinguish, state variables start with lower case letters and transition parameters start with capitalized letters. **Packet-receiving events**, predicates and **timeouts** can be used as Boolean functions in input conditions. A packet-receiving event or a predicate has its own parameters, which must be matched with provided values, unless the value is a dash (-), which specifies that the corresponding parameter can match any value. An **output action** (output_action) can specify state variable modifications, tasks and at most one packet-delivery event. Predicates and tasks refer to functionalities that we plan to implement later. An output action is a list of operations, which can be **packet-delivery events**, **state variable assignments**, or tasks. Either input_cond or output_action can be optional but at least one must be present.

In addition, a number of **auxiliary functions** can be used in either input conditions or output actions. They are actually evaluated by IDS. We use auxiliary functions simply to improve readability.

Protocol state machines are in general non-deterministic, as one incoming packet can lead to multiple states. We solve non-determinism by introducing a set of finite state automata, which start from the same state, but fork into different paths when a state can have multiple transitions based on an incoming event. For instance, in TCP, every extended finite state automaton corresponds to the state of a unique connection. In AODV, operations on a particular route entry to a single destination can be defined in an extended finite state automaton. For example, an incoming *Route Reply* message can add new routes to both the destination node and the previous hop node, thus the EFSAs for both nodes need to process this message. In addition, the *Route Reply* message may also be forwarded to the originator, which is conducted by a third EFSA corresponding to the originator.

Clearly, the number of state machines can increase up to the number of possible nodes in the system if their lifetime is unbounded. Thus, we should remove unnecessary state machines to reduce memory usage. In AODV, a route entry is removed after it has been invalidated for a certain period. In other words, we can identify a final state from which no further progress could be made. Therefore, state machines reaching the final state can be deleted from the state machine repository safely.

We construct an AODV EFSA by following the AODV Internet draft version 13 [PBRD03]. AODV uses hop-by-hop routing similar to distant vector based protocols such as RIP [Mal94]. Nevertheless, there are no periodical route advertisements. Instead, a route is created only if it is demanded by data traffic with no available routes [PBRD03].

3.2   The AODV EFSA Specification

Our AODV EFSA is based on the AODV state machine from Bhargavan et al.'s work [BGK$^+$02]. It is shown in Figures 1 and 2.

Each EFSA contains two sub graphs. The second sub graph (Figure 2) is only in use within a certain period after a node has rebooted. After all other nodes have updated their routing entries accordingly, normal routing operations resume and the other graph (the normal sub graph, Figure 1) is used. The two sub graphs are shown separately for a better layout.

Note that we only capture major AODV functionalities in the EFSA. Some specified protocol behavior relies on information from other layers, which we cannot model for now.

The routing behavior in AODV is defined for every single route entry or destination. In other words, there is a unique EFSA for each destination host. We use the abbreviation *ob* to specify the destination, which stands for an **ob**served node. We define EFSA(*ob*) as the corresponding EFSA of *ob*. In addition, there is a special EFSA, EFSA(**cur**), where **cur** is a global variable that defines the node's IP address. We create this special EFSA specifically to reply *Route Requests* for the current node. Thus, for each node, we have a total of $n+1$ EFSAs where n is the number of entries in the node's routing table. That is, n instances of EFSA(*ob*), one for each destination, and one instance of EFSA(**cur**).

Timeouts, predicates, packet-receiving events, packet-delivery events, tasks and auxiliary functions are further explained below. Note that a predicate or a packet-receiving event ends with '?', while a packet-delivery event ends with '!'.

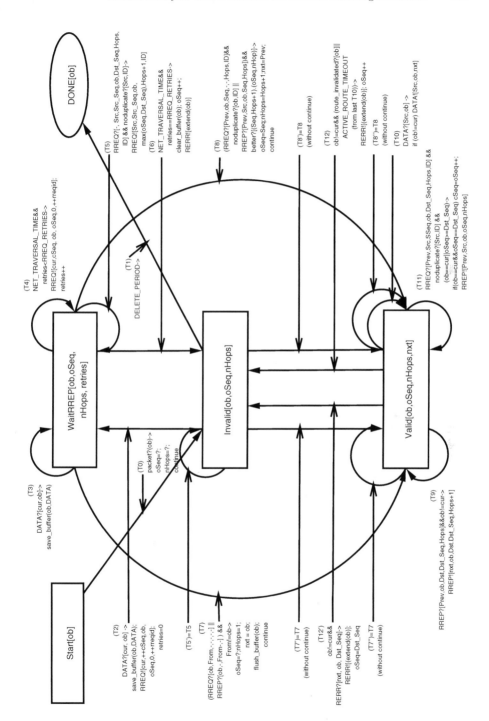

Fig. 1. AODV Extended Finite State machine (*ob*): In Normal Use

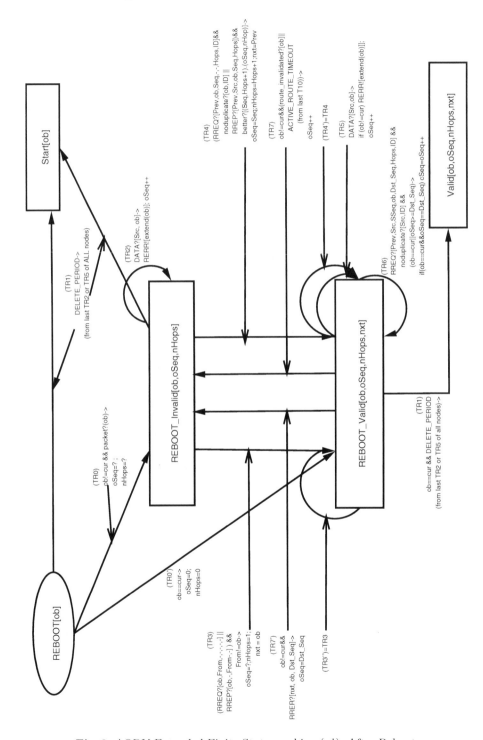

Fig. 2. AODV Extended Finite State machine (*ob*): After Reboot

- Timeouts:
  1. **DELETE_PERIOD**: specify how long an invalidated route should remain in memory.
  2. **ACTIVE_ROUTE_TIMEOUT**: specify how long before a valid route should be invalidated due to inactivity.
  3. **NET_TRAVERSAL_TIME**: specify the maximal round trip time after a RREQ has been sent and before the corresponding RREP is received.
- Predicates (the expected behavior):
  1. **noduplicate?[Src, ID]**: return true if RREQ from *Src* with RREQ ID is not seen before. The pair is then cached and can be used for comparison in later calls.
  2. **route_invalidated?[Dst]**: return true if a route to *Dst* has been invalidated due to link loss or incoming RERR, etc.
- Packet-receiving events:
  1. **DATA?[Src, Dst]**: return true if there is an incoming data packet that was originated from *Src*, and is destined to *Dst*.
  2. **RREQ?[Prev, Src, Src_Seq, Dst, Dst_Seq, Hops, ID]**: return true if a RREQ message has been received and it contains the following fields. The originator is *Src* with sequence number *Src_Seq* and a unique RREQ *ID*. The destination is *Dst* with sequence number *Dst_Seq*. The number of hops from *Src* is *Hops*. Finally, the *Prev* field specifies the address of the previous hop. Although not shown in the outgoing RREQ! event, this field can be found in the incoming packet's IP header.
  3. **RREP?[Prev, Src, Dst, Dst_Seq, Hops]**: return true if there is an incoming RREP and named fields match the specified parameters (similar to RREQ?, except that *Hops* here represents the hops to *Dst*).
  4. **RERR?[Src, Dst, Dst_Seq]**: return true if an incoming RERR message was sent by *Src*, and includes *Dst* in its unreachable destination list, with sequence number *Dst_Seq*.
- Packet-delivery events:
  1. **DATA![Src, Dst, Next]**: forward a data packet that was originated from *Src* and is destined to *Dst*, to the next hop *Next*.
  2. **RREQ![Src, Src_Seq, Dst, Dst_Seq, Hops, ID]**: broadcast RREQ with supplied fields.
  3. **RREP![Next, Src, Dst, Dst_Seq, Hops]**: deliver RREP. We explicitly specify *Next* here since RREP, different from RREQ, is not broadcast.
  4. **RERR![Dsts]**: deliver RERR with the list of unreachable destinations in *Dsts*. Corresponding sequence numbers of these destinations are also included in *Dsts*.
- Tasks (the expected behavior):
  1. **save_buffer(Dst, DATA)**: buffer the data with destination *Dst*.
  2. **flush_buffer(Dst, Next)**: deliver all packets in the data buffer with destination *Dst* through *Next*, and removes them from the data buffer.

3. **clear_buffer(Dst)**: remove all data with destination *Dst* from the data buffer.

– Auxiliary functions:

1. **packet?(Dst)**: return true if there is an incoming packet destined to *Dst*. It is a shorthand of DATA?[-,Dst] || RREQ?[-,-,-,Dst,-,-,-] || RREP?[-,-,Dst,-,-] || RERR?[Dsts] && Dst ∈ Dsts.

2. **better?([seq1, hop1],[seq2, hop2])**: return true if (seq1 > seq2 || seq1==seq2 && hop1 < hop2 || seq2 is unknown).

3. **extend(Dst)**: return a list of unreachable destinations (with their sequence numbers) due to a broken link to *Dst*. Routes to these destinations include *Dst* as their next hop. Obviously, $Dst \in extend(Dst)$.

4. **continue**: do not stop in the new state after a transition. Instead, attempt to make another state transition from the new state.

4 Design of an Intrusion Detection System for AODV

Before we analyze design issues of an Intrusion Detection System (IDS) for AODV, we make the following assumptions: 1) IDS should have access to internal routing elements, such as routing table entries. Currently, we modify the AODV implementation in our testbed to store routing table entries in a shared memory block, so that other processes can access them. In the future, hardware assistance may be necessary to achieve this; 2) IDS should also have the capability of intercepting incoming and outgoing packets, including data and routing messages.

Statistical-based detection technique, equipped with machine learning tools, can be used to detect abnormal patterns. It has the potential advantage of detecting unknown attacks. But it usually comes with a high false alarm rate. Its detection performance heavily depends on selected features.

In contrast, specification-based techniques use specifications to model legitimate system behavior and do not produce false alarms. However, developing specification is time consuming. Furthermore, many complex attacks do not violate the specification directly and cannot be detected using this approach.

Our detection approach combines the advantages of both techniques. Consequently, we separate anomalous basic events into two sets, events that directly violate the semantics of EFSAs, and events that require statistical measures.

4.1 Detection of Specification Violations

Some anomalous basic events can be directly translated into violations of EFSAs. We identify three types of violations: **Invalid State Violation**, **Incorrect Transition Violation** and **Unexpected Action Violation**.

Invalid State Violation involves a state that does not appear to be valid in the specification. In our specification, an invalid state means the combination of state variables in the current state is invalid according to the specification. For example, a state with a negative hop count is considered an invalid state. In our implementation, we keep a copy of state variables every five seconds. Thus, we can track invalid changes in state variables.

Incorrect Transition Violations occur if invalid transitions are detected. We verify the proper transition by comparing possible input conditions on all transitions from the current state. If a state change occurs while no input conditions can be met, this type of violation is detected. In addition, there are self-looping transitions that do not change the current state. For these transitions, we examine output actions. If some of these output actions (which include packet delivery events and state variable modifications) are detected while corresponding input conditions do not match, we also identify this type of violation. Our implementation monitors incoming and outgoing traffic to determine if input conditions and output actions are properly handled.

Unexpected Action Violation corresponds to the situation when the input condition during a transition matches and the new state is as expected, but the output action is not correctly or fully performed.

We show that the specification-based approach can detect the following anomalous basic events:

Interruption of Data Packets: We monitor the transition T10, where data is forwarded when a valid route is available. An attacker interrupts data packets by receiving but not forwarding data. It is observed as a type of *Unexpected Action Violation* in the transition.

Interruption of Routing Messages: An attacker may choose to interrupt certain types of routing messages by conducting the corresponding transition but not actually sending the routing packets. For more details, *Route Request* messages are delivered in transition T4, T5, or T5'; *Route Reply* messages are delivered in T9 or T11; *Route Error* messages are delivered in TR2, TR5, T6, T12 or T12'. They can always be identified as *Unexpected Action Violations* in the corresponding transition.

Add Route of Routing Table Entries: We monitor state change to the state when a route to *ob* becomes available (state **Valid**) from other states. If it does not go through legitimate transitions (which include T7, T8, T7' and T8'), it implies that a new route is created bypassing the normal route creation path. It is an *Incorrect Transition Violation* in these transitions.

Delete Route of Routing Table Entries: Similarly, we monitor state change in a reverse direction, i.e., from a valid state (state **Valid**) to a state when a route becomes unavailable (state **Invalid**). If it does not go through legitimate transitions (T12 and T12'), it is detected as an *Incorrect Transition Violation* of these transitions.

Change Route Cost of Routing Table Entries: We can identify changes in sequence numbers or hop counts to the routing table using the memorized state variable copy, when a valid route is available (state **Valid**). They are examples of *Invalid State Violations*.

Fabrication of Routing Messages: Currently, our approach can identify a special type of *Fabrication of Routing Messages*, namely, *Route Reply Fabrication*. We examine the transitions that deliver *Route Reply* messages (transitions

T9 and T11). If the output actions are found but the input conditions do not match, we will identify an *Incorrect Transition Violation* in these transitions, which is an indication that outgoing routing messages are in fact fabricated.

To summarize, we define a violation detection matrix. It maps violation information (the violated transition(s) or state and the violation type) to an anomalous basic event. The matrix is shown in Table 4. It can be used to detect attacks that directly violate the AODV specification where we can identify the corresponding types of anomalous basic events. Detection results are summarized in Section 4.3.

Table 4. Violation Detection Matrix in AODV

State or Transition(s)	Invalid State Violation	Incorrect Transition Violation	Unexpected Action Violation
TR2, TR5, T6			Interruption of Route Errors
T4, T5, T5'			Interruption of Route Requests
T7, T8, T7', T8'		Add Route	
T9, T11		Fabrication of Route Replies	Interruption of Route Replies
T10			Interruption of Data Packets
T12, T12'		Delete Route	Interruption of Route Errors
Valid	Change Route Cost		

4.2   Detection of Statistical Deviations

For anomalous events that are temporal and statistical in nature, statistical features can be constructed and applied to build a machine learning model that distinguishes normal and anomalous events. RIPPER [Coh95], a well-known rule based classifier, is used in our experiments.

We first determine a set of statistical features based on activities from anomalous basic events that cannot be effectively detected using the specification-based approach. Features are computed periodically based on the specified statistics from **all** running EFSAs, and stored in audit logs for further inspection. To build a detection model, we use a number of off-line audit logs (known as training data) which contain attacks matching these anomalous basic events. Furthermore, each record is pre-labeled with the type of the corresponding anomalous basic event (or normal if the record is not associated with any attacks) because we know which attacks are used. They are processed by RIPPER and a detection model is generated. The model is a set of detection rules. The model is then used to detect attacks in the test data.

Using the taxonomy of anomalous basic events in Table 1, we identify the following anomalous basic events that remain to be addressed, because they cannot be detected in the specification-based approach. For each type of anomalous basic event, we discuss what features are needed to capture its behavior. All features are defined within a sampling window. We use a sampling window of five seconds in all cases. In addition, features are normalized in a scale of 0 to 50.

Flooding of Data Packets: In order to capture this anomalous event, we need to capture the volume of incoming data packets. In AODV, data packets can be accepted under three different situations: when a valid route is available (which is transition T10), when a route is unavailable and no route request has been sent yet (transition T2) or when a route is unavailable and a route request has been sent to solicit a route for the destination (transition T3). Accordingly, we should monitor frequencies of all these data packet receiving transitions. We define three statistical features, *Data1*, *Data2*, and *Data3*, for each transition (T10, T2 and T3) respectively.

Flooding of Routing Messages: Similarly, we need to monitor the frequencies of transitions where routing messages are received. However, a larger set of transitions need to be observed because we need to take into account of every type of routing messages (which include 15 transitions, T5, T5', T7, T8, T7', T8', T7", T8", T9, T11, TR3, TR4, TR3', TR4', and TR6). In order not to introduce too many features, we use an aggregated feature *Routing* which denotes the frequency of all these transitions. Note that it is not the same as monitoring the rate of incoming routing messages. An incoming routing message may not be processed by any EFSA in a node. We need only to consider messages that are being processed.

Modification of Routing Messages: Currently, we consider only modifications to the sequence number field. We define *Seq* as the highest destination sequence number in routing messages during transitions where they are received (see above for the transitions involved in routing messages).

Rushing of Routing Messages: We monitor two features where some typical routing process may be rushed. *Rushing1* is the frequency of the transition where a route discovery process fails because the number of *Route Requests* sent has exceeded a threshold (RREQ_RETRIES) or certain timeout has elapsed (NET_TRAVERSAL_TIME in transition T6). *Rushing2* is the frequency of the transition where a *Route Request* message was received and it is replied by delivering a *Route Reply* message (transition T11).

4.3 Experiments and Results

Environment: We use MobiEmu [ZL02] as the evaluation platform. MobiEmu is an experimental testbed that emulates MANET environment with a local wired network. Mobile topology is emulated through Linux's packet filtering mechanism. Different from many simulation tools, MobiEmu provides a scalable application-level emulation platform, which is critical for us to evaluate the intrusion detection framework efficiently on a reasonably large network. We use the AODV-UIUC implementation [KZG03], which is designed specifically to work with the MobiEmu platform.

Experiment Parameters: The following parameters are used throughout our experiments. Mobility scenarios are generated using a random way-point model with 50 nodes moving in an area of 1000m by 1000m. The pause time between movements is 10s and the maximum movement speed is 20.0m/s. Randomized TCP and UDP/CBR (Constant Bit Rate) traffic are used but the maximum number of connections is set to 20; and the average traffic rate is 4 packets per second. These parameters define a typical MANET scenario with modest traffic load and mobility. They are similar to the parameters used in other MANET experiments, such as [PRDM01,MBJJ99,MGLB00]. Nevertheless, we have not systematically explored all possible scenarios (for instance, with high mobility or under high traffic load). We plan to address this issue in our future work.

We test our framework with multiple independent runs. A normal run contains only normal background traffic. An attack run, in addition, contains multiple attack instances which are randomly generated from attacks specified in Tables 2 and 3 or a subset according to certain criteria.

We use ten attack runs and two normal runs as the test data, each of which runs 100,000 seconds (or 20,000 records since we use a sampling window of five seconds). In each attack run, different types of attacks are generated randomly with equal probability. Attack instances are also generated with random time lengths, but we guarantee that 80% of total records are normal. It is a relatively practical setting considering that normal events should be the majority in a real network environment. We use normal data in normal runs and attack runs to evaluate false alarm rates.

Detection of Specification Violations: The following attacks are detected in the test data as direct violations of the EFSA, which verifies our previous analysis that these attacks match anomalous basic events that can be directly detected by verifying the specification. For complex attacks, a different network size may be used if appropriate. Note that detection rates are 100% and false alarm rates are 0% for attacks when the specification-based approach is used.

Data Drop (R | S | D): detected as *Interruption of Data Packets.*
Route Drop (R | S | D): detected as *Interruption of Routing Messages.*
Add Route (I | N): detected as *Add Route of Routing Table Entries.*
Delete Route: detected as *Delete Route of Routing Table Entries.*
Change Sequence (R | M); Change Hop: detected as *Change Route Cost of Routing Table Entries.*
Active Reply; False Reply: detected as *Route Reply Fabrication.*
Route Invasion; Route Loop: They are detected since they use fabricated routing messages similar to what the **Active Reply** attack does. In particular, *Route Invasion* uses *Route Request* messages, and *Route Loop* uses *Route Reply* messages. With the same set of transitions in **Route Drop**, we can detect them as *Incorrect Transition Violations* in *Route Request* or *Route Reply* delivery transitions.
Partition: This attack can be detected since it uses a fabricated routing message (*Route Reply*) and interrupts data packets. Therefore, monitoring the transitions related to *Route Reply* (as in **Route Drop**), and the transition related

to data packet forwarding (T10, as described in **Data Drop**), we can detect this attack with the following violations identified: *Incorrect Transition Violation* in *Route Reply* delivery transitions and *Unexpected Action Violation* in the data forwarding transition.

Detection of Statistical Deviations: Some attacks are temporal and statistical in nature and should be detected using the statistical approach. The following are four representative examples of such attacks: **Data Flooding (S | D | R); Route Flooding (S | D | R); Modify sequence (R | M); Rushing (F | Y)**.

Four attacks data sets, each of which contains an attack run of 25,000 seconds (or 5,000 records), are used to train the detection model. Each data set contains attacks that match to one type of anomalous basic event. Attack instances are generated in such a way that the number of abnormal records accounts for roughly 50% of total records, instead of 80% in the case of test data. It helps improve detection accuracy by using approximately the same amount of normal and abnormal data. We train separately with each training data set. The same test data set is used to evaluate the learned model.

Table 5. Detection and False Alarm Rates of the Statistical-based Approach

(a) Attack Detection Rates

Attack	Detection rate
Data Flooding (S)	93±3%
Data Flooding (D)	91±4%
Data Flooding (R)	92±4%
Route Flooding (S)	89±3%
Route Flooding (D)	91±2%
Route Flooding (R)	89±3%
Modify sequence (R)	59±19%
Modify sequence (M)	100±0%
Rushing (F)	91±3%
Rushing (Y)	85±4%

(b) Detection and False Alarm Rates of Anomalous Basic Events

Anomalous Basic Event	Detection Rate	False Alarm Rate
Flooding of Data Packets	92±3%	5±1%
Flooding of Routing Messages	91±3%	9±4%
Modification of Routing Messages	79±10%	32±8%
Rushing of Routing Messages	88±4%	14±2%

The detailed detection results are shown in Table 5. We show the detection rates of tested attacks (in Table 5(a)). We consider a successful detection of an attack record if and only if the corresponding anomalous basic event is correctly identified. We also show the detection and false alarm rates (in Table 5(b)) directly against anomalous basic events. We analyze these results for each type of anomalous basic event below.

Flooding of Data Packets and Routing Messages: We implement flooding as traffic over 20 packets per second. For flooding of data packets, 92% can be detected. They are detected by observing abnormally high volume on at least one of related statistics, *Data1*, *Data2*, or *Data3*. Similar results are also observed for flooding of routing messages.

Modification of Routing Messages: The corresponding detection result is not very satisfactory. It shows high variations in both the detection and false alarm rates. In fact, the corresponding detection rule assumes that this anomalous basic event can be predicted when at least some incoming packet has a sequence number larger than certain threshold. It is not a rule that can be generally applied. Randomly generated sequence numbers may only be partially detected as attacks. We further discuss problem in the end of this section. In contrast, for a special type of sequence modification (*Modify Sequence (M)*), the detection rate is perfect. Because we know that it is very rare for the largest sequence number to appear in the sequence number field of routing messages.

Rushing of Routing Messages: Detection performance varies significantly on different rushing attacks, namely, *Rushing (F)* and *Rushing (Y)*. In *Rushing (F)*, the attacker tries to shorten the waiting time for a *Route Reply* message even if a route is not available yet. Because more requests to the same destination may follow if route discovery was prematurely interrupted, the attack results in abnormally high frequency where the route discovery process is terminated (*Rushing1*). In *Rushing (Y)*, the attacker expedites *Route Reply* delivery when a *Route Request* message has been received. It can be captured because the corresponding transition (T11) now occurs more frequently than a computed threshold (*Rushing2*). Nevertheless, we also observe significant false alarms in detecting these attacks. It results from irregularity of route topology change due to MANET's dynamic nature. Some normal nodes may temporarily suffer a high route request volume that exceeds these thresholds.

Discussion: Comparing with the taxonomy of anomalous basic events in Table 1, we realize that a few of them cannot be detected effectively yet. First, we cannot detect **Route Message Modification with incoming packets** in which the modification patterns are not known in advance. We identify the problem as it requires knowledge beyond a local node. However, these attacks can usually be detected using other security mechanisms or by other nodes. If the message comes from external sources, it may be successfully prevented by a cryptographic authentication scheme. Otherwise (i.e., it was delivered by the routing agent from another legitimate node), the IDS agent running on that node may have detected the attack. In addition, **Rushing** attacks cannot be detected very effectively, especially when features beyond the routing protocol, such as delays in the MAC layer, are involved. Our system can be improved if we were able to extend our detection architecture across multiple network layers. It is part of our future work.

5   Related Work

Many cryptographic schemes have been proposed to secure ad hoc routing protocols. Zapata [Zap01] proposed a secure AODV protocol using asymmetric cryptography. Hu et al. [HPJ02] proposed an alternative authentication scheme based on symmetric keys to secure the DSR protocol [JMB01], because public key computation appears too expensive for MANET nodes with limited power and computation capabilities. As we have demonstrated, protection approaches are suitable for a certain class of security problems. Intrusion detection approaches may be more suitable to address other problems.

Vigna and Kemmerer [VK98] proposed a misuse intrusion detection system, NetSTAT, which extends the original state transition analysis technique (STAT) [IKP95]. It models an attack as a sequence of states and transitions in a finite state machine. Whereas in our work, finite state machines are modeled for normal events. Specification-based intrusion detection was proposed by Ko et al. [KRL97] and Sekar et al. [SGF+02]. Specification-based approaches reduce false alarms by using manually developed specifications. Nevertheless, many attacks do not directly violate specifications and thus, specification-based approaches cannot detect them effectively. In our work, we apply both specification-based and statistical-based approaches to provide better detection accuracy and performance.

Bhargavan et al. [BGK+02] analyzed simulations of AODV protocols. Their work included a prototype AODV state machine. Our AODV EFSA is based on their work but has been heavily extended. Ning and Sun [NS03] also studied the AODV protocol and used the definition of atomic misuses, which is similar to our definition of basic events. However, our definition is more general because we have a systematic study of taxonomy of anomalous basic events in MANET routing protocols.

Recently, Tseng et al. [TBK+03] proposed a different specification-based detection approach. They assume the availability of a cooperative network monitor architecture, which can verify routing request-reply flows and identify many attacks. Nevertheless, there are security issues as well in the network monitor architecture which were not clearly addressed.

6   Conclusion and Future Work

We proposed a new systematic approach to categorize attacks. Our approach decomposes an attack into a number of basic events. We showed its use in attack taxonomy analysis. In addition, protocol specifications can be used to model normal protocol behavior and can be used by intrusion detection systems. By applying both specification-based and statistical-based detection approaches, we have the advantages of both. Specification-based approach has no false alarm, statistical-based approach can detect attacks that are statistical or temporal in nature.

We proposed a taxonomy of anomalous basic events in MANET routing protocols and presented a case study of the AODV protocol. We constructed an AODV extended finite state automaton specification. By examining direct violations of the specification, and by constructing statistical features from the specification and applying machine learning tools, we showed that most anomalous basic events were detected in our experiments.

Future Work: We plan to enhance our framework by automatically extracting useful features for detection of unknown attacks. We also plan to design an intrusion detection system across multiple network layers to detect more sophisticated attacks.

Acknowledgment

This work is supported in part by NSF grants CCR-0133629 and CCR-0311024 and Army Research Office contract DAAD19-01-1-0610. The contents of this work are solely the responsibility of the authors and do not necessarily represent the official views of NSF and the U.S. Army.

References

[BGK⁺02] K. Bhargavan, C. A. Gunter, M. Kim, I. Lee, D. Obradovic, O. Sokolsky, and M. Viswanathan. Verisim: Formal analysis of network simulations. *IEEE Transactions on Software Engineering*, 2002.

[Coh95] W. W. Cohen. Fast effective rule induction. In *Proceedings of the International Conference on Machine Learning*, pages 115–123, 1995.

[HFLY02] Y. Huang, W. Fan, W. Lee, and P. S. Yu. Cross-feature analysis for detecting ad-hoc routing anomalies. In *Proceedings of the 23rd International Conference on Distributed Computing Systems*, May 2002.

[HPJ01] Y.-C. Hu, A. Perrig, and D. B. Johnson. Wormhole detection in wireless ad hoc networks. Technical Report TR01-384, Department of Computer Science, Rice University, December 2001.

[HPJ02] Y.-C. Hu, A. Perrig, and D. B. Johnson. Ariadne: A secure on-demand routing protocol for ad hoc networks. In *Proceedings of the Eighth Annual International Conference on Mobile Computing and Networking (MobiCom'02)*, September 2002.

[IKP95] K. Ilgun, R. A. Kemmerer, and P. A. Porras. State transition analysis: A rule-based intrusion detection approach. *Software Engineering*, 21(3):181–199, 1995.

[JMB01] D. B. Johnson, D. A. Maltz, and J. Broch. DSR: The dynamic source routing protocol for multi-hop wireless ad hoc networks. In C. E. Perkins, editor, *Ad Hoc Networking*, chapter 5, pages 139–172. Addison-Wesley, 2001.

[KRL97] C. Ko, M. Ruschitzka, and K. N. Levitt. Execution monitoring of security-critical programs in distributed systems: A specification-based approach. In *Proceedings of the 1997 IEEE Symposium on Security and Privacy*, pages 134–144, 1997.

[KZG03] V. Kawadia, Y. Zhang, and B. Gupta. System services for ad-hoc routing: Architecture, implementation and experiences. In *First International Conference on Mobile Systems, Applications, and Services (MobiSys'03)*, San Francisco, CA, May 2003.

[Mal94] G. Malkin. RIP version 2 - carrying additional information. RFC 1723, Internet Engineering Task Force, November 1994.

[MBJJ99]   D. A. Maltz, J. Broch, J. G. Jetcheva, and D. B. Johnson. The effects of on-demand behavior in routing protocols for multi-hop wireless ad hoc networks. *IEEE Journal on Selected Areas in Communications*, August 1999.

[MGLB00]   S. Marti, T. J. Giuli, K. Lai, and M. Baker. Mitigating routing misbehavior in mobile ad hoc networks. In *Mobile Computing and Networking*, pages 255–265, 2000.

[NS03]   P. Ning and K. Sun. How to misuse AODV: A case study of insider attacks against mobile ad-hoc routing protocols. In *Proceedings of the 4th Annual IEEE Information Assurance Workshop*, pages 60–67, June 2003.

[PBRD03]   C. E. Perkins, E. M. Belding-Royer, and S. R. Das. Ad hoc on-demand distance vector (AODV) routing. Internet draft draft-ietf-manet-aodv-13.txt, Internet Engineering Task Force, February 2003. expired 2003.

[PRDM01]   C. E. Perkins, E. M. Royer, S. R. Das, and M. K. Marina. Performance comparison of two on-demand routing protocols for ad hoc networks. *IEEE Personal Communications Magazine special issue on Ad hoc Networking*, pages 16–28, February 2001.

[SGF⁺02]   R. Sekar, A. Gupta, J. Frullo, T. Shanbhag, A. Tiwari, H. Yang, and S. Zhou. Specification-based anomaly detection: A new approach for detecting network intrusions. In *Proceedings of the ACM Computer and Communication Security Conference (CCS'02)*, 2002.

[TBK⁺03]   C.-Y. Tseng, P. Balasubramanyam, C. Ko, R. Limprasittiporn, J. Rowe, and K. N. Levitt. A specification-based intrusion detection system for AODV. In *ACM Workshop on Security of Ad Hoc and Sensor Networks (SASN'03)*, George W. Johnson Center at George Mason University, Fairfax, VA, October 2003.

[VK98]   G. Vigna and R. A. Kemmerer. NetSTAT: A network-based intrusion detection approach. In *Proceedings of the 14th Annual Computer Security Applications Conference*, 1998.

[Zap01]   M. G. Zapata. Secure ad hoc on-demand distance vector (SAODV) routing. Internet draft draft-guerrero-manet-saodv-00.txt, Internet Engineering Task Force, August 2001. expired 2002.

[ZL02]   Y. Zhang and W. Li. An integrated environment for testing mobile ad-hoc networks. In *Proceedings of the Third ACM International Symposium on Mobile Ad Hoc Networking and Computing (MobiHoc'02)*, Lausanne, Switzerland, June 2002.

On the Design and Use of Internet Sinks
for Network Abuse Monitoring

Vinod Yegneswaran[1], Paul Barford[1], and Dave Plonka[2]

[1] Dept. of Computer Science, University of Wisconsin, Madison
[2] Dept. of Information Technology, University of Wisconsin, Madison

Abstract. Monitoring *unused* or *dark* IP addresses offers opportunities to significantly improve and expand knowledge of abuse activity without many of the problems associated with typical network intrusion detection and firewall systems. In this paper, we address the problem of designing and deploying a system for monitoring large unused address spaces such as class A telescopes with 16M IP addresses. We describe the architecture and implementation of the Internet Sink (iSink) system which measures packet traffic on unused IP addresses in an efficient, extensible and scalable fashion. In contrast to traditional intrusion detection systems or firewalls, iSink includes an *active* component that generates response packets to incoming traffic. This gives the iSink an important advantage in discriminating between different types of attacks (through examination of the response payloads). The key feature of iSink's design that distinguishes it from other unused address space monitors is that its active response component is *stateless* and thus highly scalable. We report performance results of our iSink implementation in both controlled laboratory experiments and from a case study of a live deployment. Our results demonstrate the efficiency and scalability of our implementation as well as the important perspective on abuse activity that is afforded by its use.

Keywords: Intrusion Detection; Honeypots; Deception Systems

1 Introduction

Network abuse in the form of intrusions by port scanning or self propagating worms is a significant, on-going threat in the Internet. Clever new scanning methods are constantly being developed to thwart identification by standard firewalls and network intrusion detection systems (NIDS). Work by Staniford *et al.* [27] and by Moore *et al.* [18] project and evaluate the magnitude of the threat of new classes of worms and the difficulty of containing such worms. The conclusions of both papers is that addressing these threats presents the research and operational communities with serious challenges. An important step in protecting networks from malicious intrusions is to improve measurement and detection capabilities.

One means for improving the perspective and effectiveness of detection tools is to monitor both used *and* unused address space in a given network. Monitoring the unused addresses is not typically done since packets destined for those addresses are often dropped by a network's gateway or border router. However, tracking packets sent to unused addresses offers two important advantages. First, other than misconfigurations, packets destined to unused addresses are almost always malicious, thus false positives

E. Jonsson et al. (Eds.): RAID 2004, LNCS 3224, pp. 146–165, 2004.

– a significant problem in NIDS – are minimized. Second, unlike NIDS that monitor traffic passively, a detection tool that monitors unused addresses can actively respond to connection requests, thus enabling the capture of data packets with attack-specific information. The possibility for unused address space monitoring is perhaps most significant in class A and class B networks where the number of unused addresses is often substantial. The idea of monitoring unused address space has been adopted in a number of different studies and on-going projects including the DOMINO project [31], the Honeynet project [29], LaBrea tarpits [14] and in the backscatter analysis conducted by Moore *et al.* in [19].

This paper makes two contributions. The first is our description of a new system architecture and implementation for measuring IP traffic. An *Internet Sink* or iSink, is a system we developed for monitoring abuse traffic by both active and passive means. The key design requirements of an iSink are extensibility of features and scalability of performance since it is meant to be used to monitor potentially large amounts of IP address space.

Our design of an iSink includes capabilities to trace packets, to actively respond to connection requests, to masquerade as several different application types, to fingerprint source hosts and to sample packets for increased scalability. The passive component of our implementation (which we call Passive Monitor) is based on Argus [3] – a freely available IP flow measurement tool. The active component of our implementation (which we call Active Sink) is based on the Click modular router platform [12]. Click is an open-source toolkit for building high performance network systems on commodity hardware. The focus of Active Sink's development was to build a set of *stateless responder elements* which generate the appropriate series of application level response packets for connections that target different network services including HTTP, NetBIOS/SMB and DCERPC (Windows RPC Service).

The second contribution of this paper is a measurement and evaluation case study of our iSink implementation. We use the results from the case study to demonstrate the scale and diversity of traffic characteristics exposed by iSink-based monitoring. These results provide validation of our architectural requirements and rationale for subsequent evaluation criteria. We also deployed the iSink *in situ* to monitor four class B address spaces within our campus network for a period of 4 months and one entire class A address space to which we have access. From these data sets we report results that demonstrate the iSink's capabilities and the unique information that can be extracted from this measurement tool. One example is that since the traffic characteristics from our class B monitor are substantially different from those on the class A monitor, we conclude that the location of the iSink in IP address space is important. Another example is that we see strong evidence of periodic probing in our class A monitor which we were able to isolate to the LovGate worm [2]. We also uncovered an SMTP hot-spot within the class A network that has been unreported prior to our study. We were able to attribute that anomaly to misconfigured wireless routers from a major vendor. Finally, we assess basic performance of the iSink in controlled laboratory experiments and show that our implementation has highly scalable response capability.

These results demonstrate that our iSink architecture is able to support a range of capabilities while providing scalable performance. The results also demonstrate that

Active iSinks are a simple and very useful way to extend basic intrusion monitoring capabilities in individual networks or in the Internet as a whole.

2   Related Work

The notion of monitoring unused IP addresses as a source of information on intrusions has been in use in various forms for some time. While we coin the terms "Internet Sink" and "iSink", these monitors have variously been referred to as "Internet Sink-holes" [8], "Blackhole Routers" [9] and "Network Telescopes" [15]. Traditional *Honeypots* are defined as systems with no authorized activity that are deployed with the sole purpose of monitoring intrusions. *Honeynets* are network of honeypots (typically set up as VMware hosts). Their deployment is often associated with significant management and scalability challenges [29]. In [15], Moore raises the challenges of deploying honeypots in a class A network telescope. The systems that are perhaps most similar to the Active Sink have been developed in the Honeyd [10] and Labrea Tarpit projects [14]. Active Sink's design differs in significant ways from these two systems. Much like the Active Sink, Honeyd is designed to simulate virtual honeypots over unused IP addresses, with the potential for a diverse set of interactive response capabilities. However, Honeyd's stateful active responder design has significant scalability constraints that make it inappropriate for monitoring large IP address ranges which is one of iSinks primary objectives. LaBrea's primary design objective is to slow the propagation of Internet worms (*i.e.*, a sticky honeypot), and as such, it lacks the richness of interaction capabilities that is required to gather important response information. In addition to a richer response set, our Active Sink's performance greatly exceeds that of LaBrea as will be seen in Section 5.

There are a number of empirical studies of intrusion and attack activity that motivate and inform our work. In [33], the authors explore the statistical characteristics of Internet intrusion activity from a global perspective. That study is based on the use of intrusion logs from NIDS and firewalls located broadly across the Internet. Moore *et al.* examined the global prevalence of denial-of-service attacks using backscatter analysis in [19]. That work was conducted by gathering packet traces from a relatively quiescent class A network. Characteristics of the Code Red worm have been analyzed in a number of studies. In [17] the authors investigate the details of the Code Red outbreak and provide important perspective on the speed of worm propagation. Moore *et al.* provide further insights on the speed at which countermeasures would have to be installed to inhibit worms propagation [18]. While the prospects for successful containment are rather grim, it is clear that rapid detection will be a key component in any quarantine strategy.

Intrusion detection systems are a standard component in network security architectures. These tools typically monitor packet traffic at network ingress/egress points and identify potential intrusions using a variety of techniques. Standard methods for intrusion identification include misuse detection (*eg.* [21, 25]), statistical anomaly detection (*eg.* [26]), information retrieval (*eg.* [1]), data mining (*eg.* [13]), and inductive learning (*eg.* [28]). Our work is distinguished from general NIDS in that they operate on active IP addresses and must deal with the problem of identifying the nefarious traffic mixed in with all of the legitimate traffic. We expect iSinks and NIDS to complement each other in future operational environment.

High performance packet monitors have been used for collecting packet traces in the Internet for years. These systems relate directly to our iSink design in that they must scale to reliably log packets on very high speed links. Examples of these include systems that have been developed with a variety of commodity and special purpose hardware such as [4, 7, 11]. Our iSink differs significantly from these systems (as well as the NIDS mentioned above) in that it not only passively monitors and logs packets, but it also *actively responds* to incoming TCP connection requests and has application level response capability.

3   Internet Sink Architecture

In this section we describe the iSink requirements, architecture and implementation. The implementation is described within the context of deployments on two different sets of address spaces.

3.1   Design Requirements

The general requirements for an iSink system are that it possess scalable capability for both passive and active monitoring and that it be secure. We discuss the issues of security in more detail in [32].

Passive monitoring capability must be able to capture packet header and payload information accurately. While there are many standard tools and method for packet capture, if either these or new tools are employed, they should be flexible and efficient in the ways in which data is captured and logged.

Active response capability is included in iSink's design as a means to gather more detailed information on abuse activity. This capability is enabled by generating appropriate response packets (at both transport and application levels) to a wide range of intrusion traffic. While active responses also have the potential to interfere with malicious traffic in beneficial ways such as tarpitting, this is not a focus of iSink's design.

We expect Internet Sinks to measure abuse activity over potentially vast unused IP address spaces. For example, in our experimental setup, we needed the ability to scale to an entire class A network (16 million addresses). With the continued growth in malicious Internet traffic, and transition to IPv6, we expect the scalability needs to grow significantly for both the active and passive components of our system. Our basic approach to scalability is to maintain as little state as possible in our active responders. Another means for increasing scalability is through the use of sampling techniques in both active and passive components of the system. If sampling is employed, then the measurement results must not be substantially altered through their use.

Finally, our intent is to develop iSink as an open platform, thus any systems that are used as foundational components must be open source.

3.2   Active Response: The Design Space

In this section we explore the architectural alternatives for sink-hole response systems. The choices we consider are LaBrea, Honeyd, Honeynets and Active Sink (iSink's active response system) as shown in Table 1. We compare these systems based on the following characteristics.

Table 1. Design Space of Sink-Hole Responders

	Configurability	Modularity	Flexibility	Interactivity	Scalability
Active Sink	High	High	High	Low-Medium	High
Honeyd	High	Low-Medium	High	Low-Medium	Low-Medium
Honeynet	Low	Medium	Medium	High	Low-Medium
LaBrea	Low	Low	Low	Limited	High

1. **Configurability** describes the ability of the configuration language to define the layout and components of response networks. Honeyd's strengths are in fine-grained control of virtual network topologies and network protocol stacks. However Honeyd's language does not provide support for assigning large blocks of IP addresses to templates (except for the default template)[1]. Active Sink's configuration language (inherited from Click) uses a BPF like language and provides excellent support for both fine-grained and coarse-grained control of a virtual network topology. Active Sink's design is stateless and hence does not replicate network stack retransmission timers. LaBrea and Honeynets only allow for limited configurability.

2. **Flexibility** relates to the ability to mix and match services with operating systems. For example, the ability to define two types of Windows Servers: one with a telnet service and FTP service and another with NetBIOS Service and a Web server. The design of Honeyd and Active Sink both provide a high degree of flexibility. It is somewhat harder to do the same with Honeynets. LaBrea's flexibility in this regard is limited as it was designed with a different objective.

3. **Modularity** describes the ability to compose and layer services on top of one another. For example, layering Server Message Block (SMB) service over NetBIOS or layering Web services over SSL. Active Sink's design is inherently modular which directly facilitates service composition. In contrast, Honeyd's design is more monolithic and hence less straightforward to layer services.

4. **Interactivity** refers to the scope of response capability. The levels of interactivity of Honeyd and Active Sink are comparable. Obviously, Honeynets could provide more complete response capabilities. However, to mitigate the risk of Honeynets being used as a stepping-stone for additional attacks, data controls are required to be placed which limit interactivity. There are other practical configuration issues that also could limit interactivity. For example, Active Sink's NetBIOS responder grants session requests for all NetBIOS names and all user/password combinations, while a Honeynet Windows monitor would only allow NetBIOS session requests if it matches its list of valid names. Hence, the realized degree of interaction in Active Sinks are often higher than honeynets.

5. **Scalability** refers to the number of connections that can be handled in a given time period. In our monitoring environment we typically see hundreds of thousands of connection attempts per minute. Active Sink's stateless kernel module design provides high degree of scalability by eliminating unnecessary system calls and inter-

---

[1] This feature is particularly necessary for large network sinks.

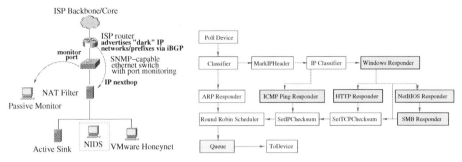

Fig. 1. Internet Sink Implementation. In our current implementation the NIDS is run offline

Fig. 2. Active Sink Configuration based on Click's modular design. Shaded elements are iSink extensions

rupt handling overheads[2]. LaBrea's stateless design also provides reasonable scaling properties, however its user level implementation makes it inferior to the Active Sink. A weakness of Honeyd's design is its inherent statefulness that limits its scalability[3]. Our experience suggests that Honeyd works well in environments that see tens of connection attempts per minute. The scalability of Honeynet systems vary from low to medium depending on the service and licensing issues.

3.3 Implementation

The objective of our monitoring infrastructure implementation was to create a highly scalable backplane with sufficient interactivity to filter out known worms, attacks and misconfiguration. To accomplish this, the iSink design includes a Passive Monitor, an Active Sink and a Honeynet component. Unsolicited traffic can be directed to each of these components which provide unique measurement capabilities. These components, in addition to MRTG [20] and FlowScan [23], were run on Linux-based commodity PCs. Details of our implementation as illustrated in Figure 1 and include:

1. **Passive Monitor** – This component is based on Argus which is a generic libpcap based IP network auditing tool. It allows for flow level monitoring of sink traffic and can be interfaced with FlowScan which is a flow level network traffic visualization tool.
2. **Active Sink** – The standard collection of elements provided with Click enabled many of the basic capabilities required for building active responses in iSink. Figure 2 illustrates iSink's configuration based on Click's modular design. Some of the fundamental elements include: (i) Poll Device which constantly polls the interface for new packets; (ii) IP Classifier which routes ARP packets to the ARP Responder, ICMP ping packets to the Ping Responder and TCP packets to the Windows

---

[2] Click also provides the flexibility to be run as a userlevel module which greatly simplifies debugging and development.

[3] Honeyd forks a process per connection attempt. A more recent version of Honeyd includes support for python threads. However, scalability improvements are limited by the overhead of the python interpreter.

Responder (all other packets are discarded); (iii) Windows Responder which responds to connection attempts on open ports and forwards HTTP requests to the Web Responder and SMB data packets to the NetBIOS Responder. The application responders developed specifically for iSink are shaded. As far as we know, we are the first non-commercial Honeypot system to provide emulation capabilities for Windows Networking(NetBIOS/SMB/CIFS) and DCERPC. The current suite of responders that are available also includes an HTTP responder, an SMTP responder, an IRC responder, Dameware responder and a responder for backdoor ports such as MyDoom and Beagle.

Stateless responders are enabled by the following two observations:

(a) It is almost always possible to concoct a suitable response just by looking at the contents of the request packet from the client – even for complex protocols like SMB. Knowledge of prior state is not compulsory.

(b) We need to continue the packet exchange only until the point where we can reliably identify the worm/virus.

3. **NAT Filter** – The motivation behind filtering is to reduce the volume of traffic generated by active responders. This module serves two purposes. It routes requests to appropriate responders (Active Sink or Honeynets) through network address translation. It also filters requests that attempt to exploit known vulnerabilities or misconfiguration. This makes mapping of iSinks more difficult and increases scalability of analysis daemons that have to process large volumes of data. We experimented with several filtering strategies:

For each source IP allow only:

(a) first N connections

(b) first N connections per <destination port>

(c) connections to first N destinations IPs targeted by the source

Of the three strategies, **option (c)** [N destination IPs per source IP] seemed the most attractive. The performance of options (a) and (c) were comparable. They both provided two orders of reduction in the volume of packets and bytes) and were significantly better than option(b). We chose **option (c)** because it has the additional advantage of providing a *consistent view* of the network to the scan sources thus allowing the iSink to appear as if it were a subnet with N live hosts[4].

4. **VMware Honeynets** – These are, quite simply, commodity operating systems running on VMware. Currently, we route packets of services for which we don't have complete responders to fully patched Windows systems.

5. **NIDS** – This system can be used to evaluate the packet logs collected at the filter. We plan to implement support for NIDS rules that can communicate with the filter and implement real time filtering decisions. For example, the decision to route packets or migrate connection to VMware Honeynet could be triggered upon the absence of a signature in the NIDS ruleset for the connection.

For this study, we built and deployed two separate iSinks: a "campus-enterprise" iSink and a "service-provider" iSink. These were used to assess our iSink design and demonstrate its capabilities.

---

[4] The set of N destination hosts varies with each source depending on the order in which the source scans the address space.

3.4   Deployment: Campus-Enterprise Sink

The campus iSink received unsolicited traffic destined for approximately 100,000 unused IPv4 addresses within 4 sparsely-to-moderately utilized class-B networks that are
in use at our campus. Essentially, these unused addresses are in the "holes" between
active subnets, each of which typically contains 128 to 1024 contiguous host addresses
(*i.e.*, 25 through 22-bit netmasks, respectively).

A so called "black-hole" intra-campus router was configured to also advertise the
class B aggregate /16 routes into the intra-campus OSPF. The result was that there were
persistent less-specific (16 bit netmask) routes for every campus address. Unsolicited
traffic, whether from campus or outside sources, destined for unused campus IP addresses always "falls through" to those less-specific /16 routes, and therefore is routed
to the iSink and measured. Furthermore, *occasionally* traffic destined for campus addresses that are normally in use can fall through to the iSink if its subnet's more specific
route disappears. Typically, this only happens during network outages, making the iSink
a potential warning system of problems because it can passively detect routing failures.
Whenever traffic that was destined for a campus IP address known to be in use reaches
the iSink instead, the operators know that there is a problem.

It was important in our environment that the iSink machine was not capable of
actively participating in the intra-campus routing, other than to respond via ARP as
the IP nexthop on its transit link. The iSink is not an OSPF router, but instead is the
destination of a static route. This limits the possible damage that could be caused if
ever the iSink system was compromised and was attempted to be used maliciously.

3.5   Deployment: Service-Provider Sink

The service-provider iSink received unsolicited traffic destined for 16 million IPv4 addresses in one class A network. An ISP router, located at our campus' service-provider,
served as the gateway for the service-provider iSink. The service-provider was responsible for advertising the class A network via BGP to our service provider's commercial
transit providers, Internet2's Abilene network, and to various other peers. SNMP-based
measurements at the Ethernet switch's ports were used to compute any packet loss by
the libpcap-based Argus software.

4   Experiences with Internet Sink

Investigating Unique Periodic Probes. The periodicity observed in the service
provider iSink data is an excellent example of the perspective on intrusion traffic afforded by iSink. The first step in our analysis of this periodicity was to understand the
services that contributed to this phenomenon. We found that most of the periodicity
observed in the TCP flows could be isolated to sources scanning two services (port 139
and 445) simultaneously. Port 139 is SMB (Server Message Block protocol) over Net-
BIOS and port 445 is direct SMB. However, this did not help us isolate the attack vector
because it is fairly common for NetBIOS scanners to probe for both these services. Passive logs provided three additional clues: 1) scans typically involve 256 successive IP

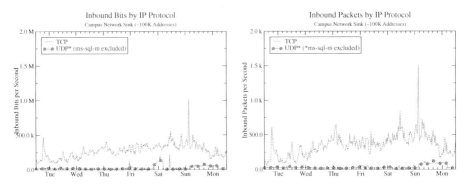

Fig. 3. Inbound Traffic for a Typical Week on Campus-Enterprise Sink (bits/pkts per second)

addresses that span a /24 boundary, 2) the probes had a period of roughly 2.5 hours, 3) the small timescale periodicity seemed to be super imposed over a diurnal periodic behavior at larger timescales.

Figure 6 shows the number of flows scanning both services in a week. To simplify our analysis we then focused on a single day's data and classified scanners on these services based on their scan footprints. We defined scanners that match our profile (between 250-256 successive IP addresses spanning a /24 boundary) as *type-1* sources. We also defined sources that scan five or more subnets simultaneously as *type-5* sources. This includes processes that pick destination IP addresses randomly and others that are highly aggressive. Figure 7 shows a time-volume graph of the *type-1* and *type-5* scanners. **The interesting aspect of this figure is that the number of sources in each peak (around 100) is more than an order of magnitude smaller than the total number of participants observed in a day (2,177).** We can also see that most of the diurnal behavior could be attributed to type *type-5* sources.

This mystery motivated our development of NetBIOS and SMB responders. By observing the packet logs generated by the active response system we concluded that the scanning process was the LovGate worm [2] which creates the file `NetServices.exe` among others.

This section demonstrates iSink's capabilities and illustrates the complementary roles of the Passive Monitor and the Active Sink using results from our two iSink deployments. We first discuss issues of perspective by comparing the passive-monitoring results observed in the campus-enterprise sink with that of the service-provider sink. We then demonstrate the utility of the Active Sink in investigating network phenomenon revealed by the Passive Monitor including periodic probing and SMTP hot-spots.

4.1 Campus Enterprise iSink Case Study

Because the campus iSink is located inside one autonomous system and advertised via the local interior routing protocol, this system sees traffic from local sources in addition to traffic from sources in remote networks. Traffic observed from local sources included:

– Enterprise network management traffic attempting to discover network topology and address utilization (such as ping sweeps and SNMP query attempts)

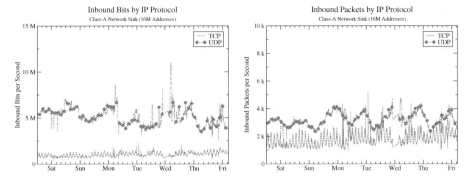

Fig. 4. Inbound Traffic for a Typical Week on Service Provider Sink (bits/pkts per second)

- Traffic from misconfigured hosts. For instance, a few hosts continually send domain queries to what is now an unused campus IP address. Presumably, an operational DNS server used to be at that address. We also see traffic from misconfigured AFS clients and NetBIOS name registration requests from local windows hosts with incorrect WINS address.
- Malicious probes and worm traffic that has an affinity for hosts within their classful network.

Figure 3 shows the traffic observed from only remote sources in a typical week at the campus-enterprise iSink. There are several notable features. The dominant protocol is TCP since the campus border routers filter scans to port 1434 (ms-sql-m) that was exploited by the SQL-Slammer worm [16]. The peak rate of traffic is about 1Mb/s and 1500 packets per second. There is no obvious periodicity in this dataset. Finally, because TCP is the dominant protocol, the packet sizes are relatively constant and the number of bytes and packets follow a predictable ratio. Hence, the graphs of bit and packet rate show very similar trends.

4.2 Service Provider iSink Case Study

The volume of unsolicited inbound traffic to the class A network varied between average rates of 5,000 packets-per-second (pps) when we brought the system on line to over 20,000pps six months later at the end of our study. One consequence that was relayed to us by experienced network operators is that it is not possible to effectively operate even this relatively quiescent class A network at the end of a 1.5 megabit-per-second T1 link because the link becomes completely saturated by this unsolicited traffic.

To operate the service-provider iSink continuously, we originally assumed that we could safely introduce the class A least-specific /16 route for the iSink and still allow operators to occasionally introduce more-specific routes to draw the network's traffic elsewhere in the Internet when need-be. While sound in theory (according to "CIDR and Classful Routing" [24]), it didn't work in practice. Because today's Internet is bifurcated into commercial/commodity networks and research/education networks (Internet2's Abilene), some institutions connected to both types employ creative routing policies. We found that some sites prefer less-specific routes over more-specific *when*

Table 2. Top Services (Service Provider Sink)

Service:	Inbound flows per second
udp_netbios-ns_dst	1932
udp_ms-sql-m_dst	1187
http_dst	197
netbios-ssn_dst	133
microsoft-ds_dst	115
smtp_dst	67
http_src	44
https_dst	11
ms-sql-s_dst	10
telnet_dst	2

Table 3. Backscatter sources (victims) in service provider sink (12 hrs – 5 min avg)

Type	Num IPs	% IPs
TCP_RST	295	38%
TCP_SYN_RST	105	14%
TCP_ACK	81	10%
TCP_ACK_RST	80	10%
ICMP_INTRANS_TIME_EXCEEDED	58	7%
ICMP_PORT_UNREACH	29	4%
ICMP_PKT_FILTERED_UNREACH	23	3%
TCP_SYN_ACK	10	1%
ICMP_HOST_UNREACH	6	1%
OTHER	87	11%

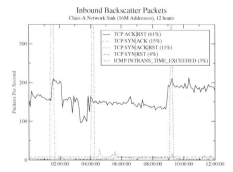

Fig. 5. Time-volume graph of backscatter packet types on service-provider sink over a typical 12 hour period

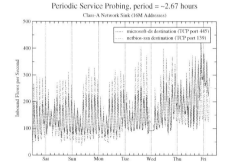

Fig. 6. Inbound flows (per second) observed at service-provider sink on ports 139 and 445 over a typical week

the less-specific route is seen on what is likely to be a higher-performance (or fixed cost) service such as Internet2.

Figure 4 depicts the traffic observed in a typical week at the service-provider iSink. Unlike the campus-enterprise network, the dominant protocol is UDP, most of which can be attribute to Windows NetBIOS scans on port 137 and the ms-sql-m traffic from worm attempting to exploit the vulnerable MS-SQL monitor. Since UDP traffic with payloads of varying sizes dominates, there is no strong correspondence between the graphs for bytes and packets. The most interesting feature is the striking periodic behavior of the TCP flows, discussed in more detail in the section 4. Table 2 provides a summary of the inbound per second flow rate of the top services.

Analysis of Backscatter Packets. Backscatter packets are responses to spoofed DoS attacks and have been effectively used to project Internet wide attack behavior [19]. Figure 5 provides a time series graph of the backscatter packet volume observed in our service-provider sink. Noteworthy features include the following:

1. TCP packets with ACK/RST dominate as might be expected. This would be the most common response to a SYN flood from forged sources.

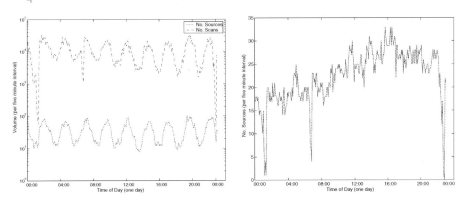

Fig. 7. Left: Volume/Count of *type-1* port 139 scanners: 24 hours, Dec 14, 2003, (no. sources per peak = 100, total sources = 2,177) Right: Volume of *type-5* port139 scanners

2. Vertical lines that correspond to less common short duration spikes of SYN/ACK and SYN/ACK/RST.
3. ICMP TTL exceeded packets could be attributed to either routing loops or DoS floods with a low initial TTL.

Table 3 provides a summary of the number of active sources of backscatter traffic, *i.e.*, the estimated count of the victims of spoofed source attacks. These numbers are an average during the 12 hours shown in Figure 5 of the number of sources in each 5 minute sample. In terms of the distribution of the volumes of Backscatter scan types, our results are consistent with those published in [19]. Backscatter made up a small percentage (under 5%) of the overall traffic seen on our service-provider sink.

We proceeded to setup a controlled experiment which began by trying to infect a Windows 2000 host running on VMware with LovGate. LovGate uses a dictionary attack, so we expected a machine with blank administrative password to be easily infected. However, the NetBIOS sessions were continually getting rejected due to Net-BIOS name mismatches. So we modified the lmhosts file to accept the name *SMB-SERVER enabling us to capture the worm.

We verified that LovGate's NetBIOS scanning process matched the profile of the *type-1* scanners[5]. To date, we have not been able to disassemble the binary as it is a compressed self-extracting executable. So we monitored the scans from the infected host. There were two relevant characteristics that provide insight into the periodicity: 1) The scanning process is deterministic, *i.e.*, after every reboot it repeats the same scanning order 2) During the course of a day there are several 5-10 minute intervals where it stops scanning. Our conjecture is that these gaps occur due to approximately synchronized clocks in the wide area thus producing the observed periodicity.

SMTP Hot-Spot. Analysis of SMTP (Simple Mail Transfer Protocol) scans in the service provider sink is another important demonstration of active sink's capabilities. From passive measurements, we identified an SMTP hot-spot *i.e.*, there was one IP

---

[5] Besides the NetBIOS scanning LovGate also sent SMTP probes to www.163.com.

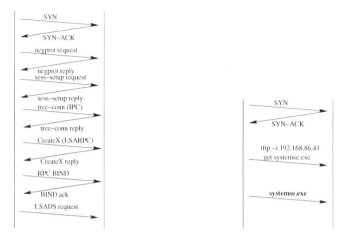

Fig. 8. RBOT.CC timeline of lsarpc ex-   **Fig. 9.** RBOT.CC follow-up commands(port
ploit(port 445)   44445)

address that was attracting a disproportionately large number of SMTP scans (20-50 scans per second). Hot-spots in unused address space are typically good indicators of misconfiguration. During a 10 day period in December we observed over 4.5 million scans from around 14,000 unique IP addresses all bound to one destination IP within our monitor. A cursory analysis suggested that these scans were all from cable-modem and DSL subscribers. Finally, the scans also seemed to have an uncommon TCP SYN fingerprint (win 8192, mss 1456).

The possibility of spam software as a source of this anomaly was ruled out due to the non-standard TCP fingerprint. We then hypothesized that this could be from a specific cable-modem or DSL device. We set up an SMTP responder on the target IP address and captured the incoming email. **This revealed the source of the email to be misconfigured wireless-router/firewall systems from a major vendor**[6]. The emails are actual firewall logs!

To better understand the reasons behind this SMTP hot-spot, we examined the firewall system's firmware. The `unarj` utility was used to extract the compressed binary. However, searching for the hot-spot IP address string in the binary proved fruitless. Examination of the firmware "application" revealed that there was an entry for SMTP server that was left blank by default. This led us to conjecture that the target IP address was the result of an uninitialized garbage value that was converted to a network ordered IP address. It also turns out that every byte in our hot-spot address is a printable ASCII character. So we searched for this four byte ASCII string and found a match *in almost all versions of firmware for this device*. The string occurred in both the extracted and compressed versions of the firmware. As a sanity check, we looked for other similar ASCII strings, but did not find them. These kind of hot-spots can have very serious ramifications in network operations. For example, one the authors discovered a similar problem with Netgear routers that inadvertently flood our campus NTP servers [22].

---

[6] We are in the process of notifying the manufacturer and plan to reveal the name of the vendor once this is completed.

Experiences with Recent Worms. Our iSink deployment has proved quite useful in detecting the advent of recent worms such as Sasser [5]. Without active response capability, such as that provided by the Active Sink, it would be impossible to distinguish existing worm traffic on the commonly exploited ports such as port 445 from new worm activity. Detection of such new worms is often possible without modifications to the responder, as was the case for the lsarpc exploit used by Sasser. Our active response system enabled accurate detection of not only Sasser, but also more fine-grained classification of several variants. Prior to the release of Sasser, we were also able to observe early exploits on the lsarpc service which could be attributed to certain strains of Agobot. Figures 8 and 9 illustrate the interaction of RBOT.CC [30], a more recent virus that also exploits the lsarpc vulnerability, with the Active Sink.

5   Basic Performance

One of the primary objectives of the iSink's design is scalability. We performed scalability tests on our Active Sink implementation using both TCP and UDP packet streams. The experimental setup involved four 2GHz Pentium 4 PCs connected in a common local area network. Three of the PCs were designated as load generators and the fourth was the iSink system that promiscuously responded to all ARP requests destined to any address within one class A network. Figures 10 demonstrates the scalability under of LaBrea[7] and Active Sink under TCP and UDP stress tests. The primary difference between the TCP and UDP tests is that the TCP connection requests cause the iSink machine to respond with acknowledgments, while the UDP packets do not elicit a response. Ideally, we would expect the number of outbound packets to equal the number of inbound packets. The Click-based Active Sink scales well to TCP load with virtually no loss up to about 20,000 packets (connection attempts) per second. LaBrea performance starts to degrade at about 2,000 packets. The UDP test used 300 byte UDP packets (much like the SQL-Slammer worm). In this case, both the LaBrea and Active Sink perform admirably well. LaBrea starts to experience a 2% loss rate at about 15,000 packets/sec.

6   Sampling

There are three reasons why *connection sampling* can greatly benefit an iSink architecture: *(i) reduced bandwidth requirements, (ii) improved scalability, (iii) simplified data management and analysis.* In our iSink architecture, we envision building packet-level sampling strategies in the Passive Monitor and source-level sampling in the NAT Filter.

   We considered two different resource constraint problems in the passive portion of the iSink and evaluated the use of sampling as a means for addressing these constraints. We first considered the problem of a fixed resource in the iSink itself. Estan and Varghese in [6] describe sampling methods aimed at monitoring "heavy hitters" in IP flows through routers with a limited amount of memory. We adapted one of these methods for use in iSink. Second, we considered the problem of bandwidth as the limited resource.

---

[7] We compare Active Sink with LaBrea because unlike LaBrea, Honeyd is stateful(forks a process per connection), and hence is much less scalable. Since Honeyd also relies on a packet filter LaBrea's scalability bounds affect Honeyd as well.

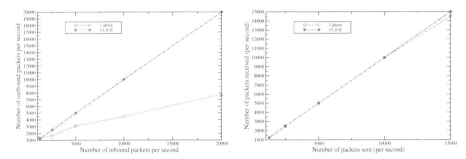

Fig. 10. Scalability of Click-based Internet Sink and LaBrea for TCP (left) and UDP (right) flows

In this case, the idea is to reduce the total amount of traffic routed to an iSink by selecting subnets within the total address space available for monitoring. These methods would be used in combination with the filtering methods described in Section 3.3.

Memory Constrained iSink Sampling. The method that forms the basis of our sampling approach with a memory constrained iSink is called *Sample and Hold* [6]. This method accurately identifies flows larger than a specified threshold (*i.e.*, heavy hitters). Sample and hold is based on simple random sampling in conjunction with a hash table that is used to maintain flow ID's and byte counts. Specifically, incoming packets are randomly sampled and entries in the hash table are created for each new flow. After an entry has been created, *all* subsequent packets belonging to that flow are counted. While this approach can result in both false positives and false negatives, its accuracy is shown to be high in workloads with varied characteristics. We apply sample and hold in iSink to the problem of identifying "heavy hitters", which are the worst offending source addresses based on the observed number of scans.

Adapting the sample and hold method to the iSink required us to define the size of the hash table that maintains the data, and the sampling rate based on empirical observation of traffic at the iSink. In [6], the objective is identifying accurately the flows that take over $T\%$ of a link's capacity. An oversampling factor O is then selected to reduce the possibility of false negatives in the results. These parameters result in allocating $HT_{len} = 1/T * O$ locations in each hash table. The packet sampling rate is then set to HT_{len}/C where C is the maximum packet transmission capacity of the incoming link over a specified measurement period t. At the end of each t, the hash table is sorted and results are produced.

Bandwidth Constrained iSink Sampling. In the bandwidth constrained scenario, the sampling design problem is to select a set of subnets from the total address space that is available for monitoring on the iSink. The selection of the number of subnets to monitor is based on the bandwidth constraints. In this case we assume that we know the mean and variance for traffic volume on a "typical" class B or class C address space. We then divide the available bandwidth by this value to get the number of these subnets that can be monitored. The next step is to select the specific subnets within the entire space that will minimize the error introduced in estimates of probe populations.

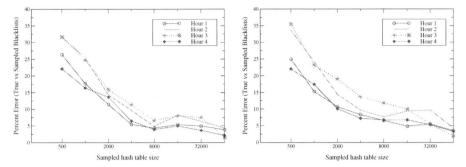

Fig. 11. Error rates for different hash table sizes (x-axis is log scale) using Sample and Hold method with rates of 1/100 (left) and 1/300 (right)

Our analysis in this paper is based on the use of random sampling as a means for subnet selection. Our rationale for this approach is based on the observation that overall traffic volumes across the service-provider class A address space that we monitor is quite uniform. The strengths of this approach are that it provides a simple method for subnet selection, it provides unbiased estimates and it lends itself directly to analysis. The drawback is that sampling designs that take advantage of additional information such as clustered or adaptive sampling could provide more accurate population estimates. We leave exploration of these and other sampling methods to future work.

After selecting the sampling design, our analysis focused on the problem of *detectability*. Specifically, we were interested in understanding the accuracy of estimates of total probe populations from randomly selected subsets. If we consider $\hat{\tau}$ is an unbiased estimator of a population total τ then the estimated variance of $\hat{\tau}$ is given by:

$$var(\hat{\tau}) = N^2 \left[\left(\frac{N-n}{N} \right) \frac{\sigma^2}{n} + \left(\frac{1-p}{p} \right) \frac{\mu}{n} \right]$$

where N is the total number of units (in our case, subnets), n is the sampled number of units, μ is the population mean (in our case, the mean number of occurrences of a specific type of probe), σ^2 is the population variance and p is the probability of detection for a particular type of probe. In the analysis presented in Section 6.1, we evaluate the error in population estimates over a range of detection probabilities for different size samples. The samples consider dividing the class A address space into its component class B's. The probabilities relate directly to detection of worst offenders (top sources of unsolicited traffic) as in the prior sampling analysis. The results provide a means for judging population estimation error rates as a function of network bandwidth consumption.

6.1 Sampling Evaluation

Our evaluation of the impact of sampling in an iSink was an *offline* analysis using traces gathered during one day selected at random from the service-provider iSink. Our objective was to empirically assess the accuracy of sampling under both memory constrained and bandwidth constrained conditions. In the memory constrained evaluation, we compare the ability to accurately generate the top 100 heavy hitter source list over four

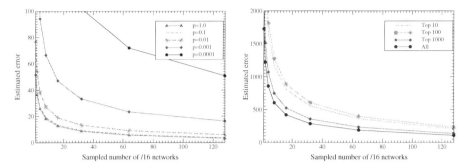

Fig. 12. Estimated error (σ/μ) for a given number of randomly selected /16's. Included are error estimates for total probes from worst offending source IP over a range of detection probabilities (left), estimates for total probes for worst offender lists of several sizes (right)

consecutive 1 hour periods using different hash table sizes and different sampling rates. For each hour in the data set, we compare the percentage difference in the number of scans generated by the "true" top 100 blacklist and sampled top 100 blacklist sources. In the bandwidth constrained evaluation, we consider accuracy along three dimensions: 1) estimating the worst offender population with partial visibility, 2) estimating black lists of different lengths, 3) estimating backscatter population.

Our memory constrained evaluation considers hash table sizes varying from 500 to 64K entries where each entry consists of a source IP and a access attempt count. Note that the hash table required to maintain the complete list from this data was on the order of 350K entries We consider two different arbitrarily chosen sampling rates – 1 in 100 and 1 in 300 with uniform probability. In each case, once a source IP address has been entered into the table, all subsequent packets from that IP are counted. If tables become full during a given hour then entries with the lowest counts are evicted to make room for new entries. At the end of each hour, the top 100 from the true and sampled lists are compared. New lists are started for each hour. The results are shown in Figure 11. These results indicate that even coarse sampling rates (1/300) and relatively small hash tables enable fairly accurate black lists (between 5%–10% error). The factor of improvement between sampling at 1/100 and 1/300 is about 1.5, and there is little benefit to increasing the hash table size from 5,000 to 20,000. Thus, from the perspective of heavy hitter analysis in a memory constrained system, sampling can be effectively employed in iSinks.

As discussed in the prior section in our bandwidth constrained evaluation we consider error introduced in population estimates when using simple random sampling over a portion of the available IP address space. We argue that simple random sampling is appropriate for some analysis given the uniform distribution of traffic over our class A monitor. The cumulative distribution of traffic over a one hour period for half of the /16 subnets in our class A monitor is shown in Figure 13(right). This figure shows that while traffic across all subnets is relatively uniform (at a rate of about 320 packets per minute per /16), specific traffic subpopulations – TCP backscatter as an example – can show significant non-uniformity which can have a significant impact on sampling.

We use the mean normalized standard deviation (σ/μ) as an estimate of error in our analysis. In each case, using the data collected in a typical hour on the /8, we empirically

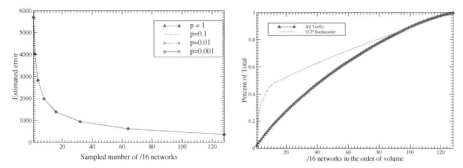

Fig. 13. Estimated error for TCP backscatter traffic (left). Cumulative distribution of all traffic and TCP backscatter traffic across half of the class A address space monitor over a one hour period. The average number of probes per /16 is 320 packets per minute (right)

assess the estimated error as a function of a randomly selected sample of /16 subnets. The results of this approach are shown in Figure 12. The graph on the left shows the ability to accurately estimate the number of probes from the single worst offending IP source over a range of detection probabilities (*i.e.*, the probability of detecting a source in a selected /16). This graph indicates that worst offenders are detectable even with a small sample size and error-prone or incomplete measurements. The graph on the right shows the ability to accurately estimate black lists from a selected sample of /16's. This graph indicates that it is easier to estimate larger rather than smaller black lists when sampling. We attribute this to the variability in black list ordering across the /16's. Finally, Figure 13(left) shows the ability to accurately estimate TCP backscatter traffic over a range of detection probabilities. The graph suggests that while backscatter estimates are robust in the face of error-prone or incomplete measurements, estimated error of total backscatter is quite high even with a reasonably large number of /16's. This can be attributed to the non-uniformity of backscatter traffic across the class A monitor shown in Figure 13(right) and suggests that alternative sampling methods for backscatter traffic should be explored. On a broader scale, this indicates that traditional backscatter methodologies that assumes uniformity could be error prone.

7   Summary and Future Work

In this paper we describe the architecture and implementation of an Internet Sink: a useful tool in a general network security architecture. iSinks have several general design objectives including scalability, the ability to passively monitor network traffic on unused IP addresses, and to actively respond to incoming connection requests. These features enable large scale monitoring of scanning activity as well as attack payload monitoring. The implementation of our iSink is based on a novel application of the Click modular router, NAT Filter and the Argus flow monitor. This platform provides an extensible, scalable foundation for our system and enables its deployment on commodity hardware. Our initial implementation includes basic monitoring and active response capability which we test in both laboratory and live environments.

We report results from our iSink's deployment in a live environment comprising four class B networks and one entire class A network. The objectives of these case studies were to evaluate iSink's design choices, to demonstrate the breadth of information available from an iSink, and to assess the differences of perspective based on iSink location in IP address space. We show that the amount of traffic delivered to these iSinks can be large and quite variable. We see clear evidence of the well documented worm traffic as well as other easily explained traffic, the aggregate of which can be considered Internet background noise. While we expected overall volumes of traffic in the class B monitors and class A monitor to differ, we also found that the overall characteristics of scans in these networks were quite different. We also demonstrate the capability of iSinks to provide insights on interesting network phenomenon like periodic probing and SMTP hot-spots, and their ability gather information on sources of abuse through sampling techniques. A discussion of operational issues, security, and passive fingerprinting techniques is provided in [32].

The evaluation of our iSink implementation demonstrates both its performance capabilities and expectations for live deployment. From laboratory tests, we show that iSinks based on commodity PC hardware have the ability to monitor and respond to over 20,000 connection requests per second, which is approximately the peak traffic volume we observed on our class A monitor. This also exceeds the current version of LaBrea's performance by over 100%. Furthermore, we show that sampling techniques can be used effectively in an iSink to reduce system overhead while still providing accurate data on scanning activity.

We intend to pursue future work in a number of directions. First, we plan to expand the amount of IP address space we monitor by deploying iSinks in other networks. Next, we intend to supplement iSink by developing tools for datamining and automatic signature generation.

Acknowledgements

The authors would like to thank Jeff Bartig, Geoff Horne, Bill Jensen and Jim Martin for all of their help. Exploration of the filtering techniques grew out of fruitful discussions during Vinod's internship with Vern Paxson. We would also like to acknowledge contributions of Ruoming Pang in the development of the DCERPC responder. Finally, we would like to thank the anonymous reviewers for their insightful comments and Diego Zamboni for his excellent shepherding.

References

1. R. Anderson and A. Khattak. The Use of Information Retrieval Techniques for Intrusion Detection. In *Proceedings of RAID*, September 1998.
2. Network Associates. LovGate Virus Summary. http://vil.nai.com/vil/content/Print100183.htm, 2002.
3. C. Bullard. Argus Open Project. http://www.qosient.com/argus/.
4. C. Cranor, Y. Gao, T. Johnson, V. Shkapenyuk, and O. Spatscheck. Gigascope: High Performance Network Monitoring with an SQL Interface.
5. E-eye. Analysis: Sasser Worm.
   http://www.eeye.com/html/Research/Advisories/AD20040501.html.

6. C. Estan and G. Varghese. New Directions in Traffic Measurement and Accounting. In *Proceedings of ACM SIGCOMM '02*, Pittsburgh, PA, August 2002.
7. A. Feldmann, A. Greenberg, C. Lund, N. Reingold, and J. Rexford. NetScope: Traffic Engineering for IP Networks. IEEE Network Magazine, Special Issue on Internet Traffic Engineering, 2000.
8. B. Greene. BGPv4 Security Risk Assessment, June 2002.
9. B. Greene. Remote Triggering Black Hole Filtering, August 2002.
10. Honeyd: Network Rhapsody for You. http://www.citi.umich.edu/u/provos/honeyd.
11. G. Iannaccone, C. Diot, I. Graham, and N. McKeown. Monitoring very high speed links. In *SIGCOMM Internet Measurement Workshop*, November 2001.
12. E. Kohler, R. Morris, B. Chen, J. Jannotti, and F. Kaashoek. The click modular router. *ACM Transactions on Computer Systems*, August 2000.
13. W. Lee, S.J. Stolfo, and K.W. Mok. A Data Mining Framework for Building Intrusion Detection Models. In *IEEE Symposium on Security and Privacy*, 1999.
14. T. Liston. The Labrea Tarpit Homepage. http://www.hackbusters.net/LaBrea/.
15. D. Moore. Network Telescopes.
http://www.caida.org/outreach/presentations/2003/dimacs0309/.
16. D. Moore, V. Paxson, S. Savage, C. Shannon, S. Staniford, and N. Weaver. The Spread of the Sapphire/Slammer Worm. Technical report, CAIDA, 2003.
17. D. Moore, C. Shannon, and K. Claffy. Code Red: A Case Study on the Spread and Victims of an Internet Worm. In *Proceedings of ACM SIGCOMM Internet Measurement Workshop*, Marseilles, France, November 2002.
18. D. Moore, C. Shannon, G. Voelker, and S. Savage. Internet Quarantine: Requirements for Containing Self-Propagating Code. In *Proceedings of IEEE INFOCOM*, April 2003.
19. D. Moore, G. Voelker, and S. Savage. Inferring Internet Denial of Service Activity. In *Proceedings of the 2001 USENIX Security Symposium*, Washington D.C., August 2001.
20. T. Oetiker. The multi router traffic grapher. In *Proceedings of the USENIX Twelvth System Administration Conference LISA XII*, December 1998.
21. V. Paxson. BRO: A System for Detecting Network Intruders in Real Time. In *Proceedings of the 7th USENIX Security Symposium*, 1998.
22. D. Plonka. Flawed Routers Flood University of Wisconsin Internet Time Server. http://www.cs.wisc.edu/ plonka/netgear-sntp.
23. D. Plonka. Flowscan: A network traffic flow reporting and visualization tool. In *Proceedings of the USENIX Fourteenth System Administration Conference LISA XIV*, December 2000.
24. Y. Rekhter. RFC 1817: CIDR and Classful Routing, August 1995.
25. M. Roesch. The SNORT Network Intrusion Detection System. http://www.snort.org.
26. S. Staniford, J. Hoagland, and J. McAlerney. Practical Automated Detection of Stealthy Portscans. In *Proceedings of the ACM CCS IDS Workshop*, November 2000.
27. S. Staniford, V. Paxson, and N. Weaver. How to Own the Internet in Your Spare Time. In *Proceedings of the 11th USENIX Security Symposium*, San Francisco, CA, August 2002.
28. H.S. Teng, K. Chen, and S. C-Y Lu. Adaptive Real-Time Anomaly Detection Using Inductively Generated Sequential Patterns. In *IEEE Symposium on Security and Privacy*, 1999.
29. The Honeynet Project. http://project.honeynet.org.
30. Trend Micro. WORM_RBOT.CC. http://uk.trendmicro-europe.com/enterprise/security_info/-ve_detail.php?Vname=WORM_RBOT.CC.
31. V. Yegneswaran, P. Barford, and S. Jha. Global Intrusion Detection in the DOMINO Overlay System. In *Proceedings of NDSS*, San Diego, CA, 2004.
32. V. Yegneswaran, P. Barford, and D. Plonka. On the Design and Use of Internet Sinks for Network Abuse Monitoring. University of Wisconsin Technical Report #1497, 2004.
33. V. Yegneswaran, P. Barford, and J. Ullrich. Internet Intrusions: Global Characteristics and Prevalence. In *Proceedings of ACM SIGMETRICS*, San Diego, CA, June 2003.

Monitoring IDS Background Noise Using EWMA Control Charts and Alert Information

Jouni Viinikka and Hervé Debar

France Télécom R&D, Caen, France
{jouni.viinikka,herve.debar}@francetelecom.com

Abstract. Intrusion detection systems typically create large amounts of alerts, processing of which is a time consuming task for the user. This paper describes an application of exponentially weighted moving average (EWMA) control charts used to help the operator in alert processing. Depending on his objectives, some alerts are individually insignificant, but when aggregated they can provide important information on the monitored system's state. Thus it is not always the best solution to discard those alerts, for instance, by means of filtering, correlation, or by simply removing the signature. We deploy a widely used EWMA control chart for extracting trends and highlighting anomalies from alert information provided by sensors performing pattern matching. The aim is to make output of verbose signatures more tolerable for the operator and yet allow him to obtain the useful information available. The applied method is described and experimentation along its results with real world data are presented. A test metric is proposed to evaluate the results.

Keywords: IDS background noise, alert volume reduction, EWMA

1 Introduction

Perfectly secure systems have been shown to be extremely difficult to design and implement, thus practically all systems are vulnerable to various exploits or at least to legitimate users' privilege abuse. Systems used to discover these attacks are called Intrusion Detection Systems (IDSes).

The work in intrusion detection begun from the need to automate audit trail processing [1] and nowadays IDSes themselves can generate enormous amounts of alerts. Just one sensor can create thousands of alerts each day, and a large majority of these can be irrelevant [2], partly because the diagnostic capabilities of current, fielded intrusion detection systems are rather weak [3] [4]. This alert flood can easily overwhelm the human operating the system and the interesting alerts become buried under the noise.

1.1 Alert Overflow and Correlation

The need to automate alert processing and to reduce the amount of alerts displayed to the operator by the system is a widely recognized issue and the research community has proposed as one solution to correlate related alerts to facilitate the diagnostics by the operator [5].

E. Jonsson et al. (Eds.): RAID 2004, LNCS 3224, pp. 166–187, 2004.

Alert correlation has three principal objectives with regard to information displayed to the operator:

Volume reduction: Group or suppress alerts, according to common properties. E.g. several individual alerts from a scan should be grouped as one
meta alert.

Content improvement: Add to the information carried by individual alert.
E.g. the use of topology and vulnerability information of monitored system
to verify or evaluate the severity of the attack.

Activity tracking: Follow multi-alert intrusions evolving as time passes. E.g.
if attacker first scans a host, then gains remote-to-local access, and finally
obtains root access, individual alerts from these steps should be grouped
together.

We perform volume reduction eliminating redundant information by aggregating alerts that are not strictly symptoms of compromise and appear in high
volumes. Only changes in the behavior of the aggregate flow are reported to the
user. Correlation techniques capable of detecting unknown, novel relationships
in data are said to be *implicit* and techniques involving some sort of definition of
searched relationships are called *explicit*. As the aggregation criteria is manually
selected, this is an explicit correlation method. Overall, we aim to save operator
resources by freeing the majority of time units that manually processing the
background noise would require and thus to enable him to focus on more relevant alerts. Even though this manual processing is likely to be periodic skimming
through the accumulated noise, if there are several sources with omnipresent activity, the total time used can be significant. Next we discuss why despite the
large amounts of alerts background noise monitoring can be useful.

1.2   The Need for Other Type of Processing

Also according to our experience (see Sect. 2.3) a relatively large portion of alerts
generated by a sensor can be considered as background noise of the operational
system. However, the division to true and false positives is not always so black
and white. The origins of problem can be coarsely divided to three. 1) Regardless
of audit source, the audit data usually does not contain all required technical
information, such as the topology and the vulnerability status for the monitored
system for correct diagnosis. 2) The non-technical contextual factors, such as operator's task and the mission of the monitored system, have an effect on which
types of alerts are of high priority and relevant. 3) Depending on the context of
the event, it can be malicious or not, and part of this information can not be acquired by automated tools or inferred from the isolated events. For the first case,
think of a Snort sensor that does not know if the attack destination is running
a vulnerable version of certain OS or server and consequently can not diagnose
whether it should issue an alert with very precise prerequisites for success. An
example of the second is a comparison of on-line business and military base. At
the former the operator is likely to assign high priority on the availability of the

company web server, and he might easily discard port scans as minor nuisance. At the latter the operator may have only minor interest towards the availability of the base web server hosting some PR material, but reconnaissance done by scanning can be considered as activity warranting user notification. Instead of high priority attacks, the third case involves action considered only as potentially harmful activity, such as ICMP and SNMP messages that indicate information gathering or network problems, malicious as well as innocuous as part of normal operation of the network. Here the context of the event makes the difference, one event alone is not interesting, but having a thousand or ten events instead of the normal average of a hundred in a time interval can be an interesting change and this difference can not be encoded into signature used by pattern matching sensor.

This kind of activity can be see to be on the gray area, and the resulting alerts somewhere between false and true positive. Typically the operator can not afford to monitor it as such because of the sheer amount of events. The current work on correlation is largely focusing on how to pick out the attacks having an impact on monitored system and show all related events in one attack report to the operator. Depending on the approach, the rest of the alerts are assigned such a low priority that they do not reach the alert console [3], or they can be filtered out before entering the correlation process [6, 4]. However, if the signature reacting to gray area events is turned on, the operator has some interest towards them. Therefore it is not always the best solution to only dismiss these less important alerts albeit their large number. Monitoring aggregated flows can provide information about the monitored system's state not available in individual alerts, and with a smaller load on operator. Our work focuses on providing this type of contextual information to the user.

1.3   Objectives

We want to examine the possibility to track the behavior of alert flows and the goals for this work are following:

1. **Highlight abnormalities.** The primary interest was to detect interesting artifacts from high volume alert flows. Even though traffic considered only harmful is so commonplace that operators can not usually afford to monitor it as such, by focusing on abnormal changes, the burden would be smaller.
2. **Reduce the number of alerts handled by the operator while retaining the information source.** We would also like to point out *only* the interesting artifacts. Given the first objective, a significant alert reduction would be required. If achieved, it would be feasible to keep these signatures activated in the system, providing the operator the desired information through the aggregates. A sufficiently low artifact output would also allow the use of this method in parallel with other correlation components for additional information, regardless how the correlation engine considers the alerts.

3. **Measure the reduction.** We do not know what we do not measure. To see the effect of the techniques some metrics are needed. This goal is essentially linked to the next one, the determination of the applicability. It is also important for the operator to know how much is being suppressed for better situation understanding.
4. **Determine the applicability of the approach with different alert flows.** The applicability of the method for processing high volume alert flows, and more specifically with different types of alert flows, needs to be defined.
5. **Trend visualization.** The power of human visual processing capability has been found useful also in intrusion detection, especially to detect anomalies or patterns difficult to handle for an AI [7]. To improve operator's view of current system state and the nature of anomalies, alert flow and trend ought to be visualized.

A variation of the EWMA control charts is proposed to achieve these goals. This control chart was designed and has been used to process alerts created and logged by sensors deployed in a production system at France Télécom.

The rest of the paper describes our findings, Sect. 2 presents the EWMA control charts and our variation. Section 3 describes practical experimentation and proposes a new metric for evaluating our approach. Related work is viewed in Sect. 4 and we offer our conclusions in Sect. 5.

2   EWMA Control Charts

In this section we present shortly mathematical backgrounds of EWMA, its use for control chart procedure, and then our variation for noise monitoring.

2.1   Backgrounds in Statistical Process Control

EWMA control charts were originally developed for statistical process control (SPC) by Roberts [8], who used the term geometric moving averages instead of EWMA, and since then the chart and especially the exponentially weighted moving average have been used in various contexts, such as economic applications and intrusion detection [9–11]. More details are available in Sect. 4.

In SPC a manufacturing process is seen as a measurable entity with a distribution. The over-all quality of the product resulting from the process is considered dependent on the process mean, which is to be kept at the fixed level and the variations as small as possible. An EWMA control chart can be used to monitor the process mean by maintaining an *exponentially moving average* of the process value. The average is compared to preset *control limits*, defining the acceptable range of values. Next we describe this procedure in more detail.

The exponentially weighted moving average is defined as

$$z_i = (1 - \lambda)z_{i-1} + \lambda x_i \ , \tag{1}$$

where $0 < \lambda < 1$. Here z_i is the current value of exponentially smoothed average, z_{i-1} the previous smoothed value, and x_i is the current value of monitored statistic. The name exponential smoothing is also used for this type of averaging.

This recursive formulation distinguishes EWMA from the basic moving averages, such as simple moving average or weighted moving average. Exponential smoothing takes all past data into account with significance decaying exponentially as a function of time. However, at the same time only the previous smoothed value and current measure are required to compute the new smoothed value. The decay is controlled by the factor λ and $(1 - \lambda)$ is called the *smoothing factor*. The name becomes more apparent by rewriting (1) as

$$z_i = \lambda x_i + \lambda(1 - \lambda)^1 x_{i-1} + \lambda(1 - \lambda)^2 x_{i-2} + \dots \tag{2}$$
$$\dots + \lambda(1 - \lambda)^{i-2} x_2 + \lambda(1 - \lambda)^{i-1} x_1 + (1 - \lambda)^i x_0 \ ,$$

where $i \geq 0$. Now it can be seen that the current data from time instant i receives weight λ and old data from instant $i - j$ receives weight $\lambda(1 - \lambda)^j$. If the interest is in the long-term trend, large smoothing factors should be used and vice versa.

As the monitored statistic in (1) is process mean, x_i is the average of subgroup of n samples taken at time instant i. The standard deviation for z can be obtained with equation

$$\sigma_z = \sqrt{\frac{\lambda}{2 - \lambda}} \sigma_{\bar{x}} \ . \tag{3}$$

Since x_i is an average of n samples $\sigma_{\bar{x}}$ is $\sigma_x / \sqrt{n}$, where σ_x is the the standard deviation of x, supposed to be known a priori.

The upper and lower control limits (UCL, LCL) set as

$$x_0 \pm 3\sigma_z \tag{4}$$

define the interval for z where process is deemed to be under control. Here x_0 is the nominal average of the process, also supposed to be known a priori. For each new measurement, the current value of statistic z is calculated by using (1), and if the control limits are surpassed, instability is signaled.

Exponential smoothing can be approximated by a standard moving average with a window size n. According to Roberts [8], for a given λ a roughly equivalent window size n is determined from

$$n = \frac{2}{\lambda} - 1 \ . \tag{5}$$

With this equation the decay speed becomes more intuitive knowing the measurement interval length. We call the product of n and the sampling interval length for x the *memory* of the statistic, as events older than that have only little significance on current z. For example, smoothing factor 0.92 would translate to a window size 24, and for 0.80 corresponding n is 9. This shows also how larger smoothing factor corresponds to averaging over larger number of samples.

2.2   The Control Chart for Alert Flows

Our needs differ from those of Roberts' quite much, and also to a smaller degree from those of the related work in intrusion detection (Sect. 4). Below our variation of the technique is described, building largely on [11], and the rationale for changes and choices is provided.

The monitored measure is the alert intensity of a flow x, the number of alerts per time interval. One alert flow consists typically of alerts generated by one signature, but also other flows, such as alerts generated by a whole class of signatures, were used. Intensity x is used to form the EWMA statistic of (1). This statistic is called the *trend* at time i.

It is quite impossible to define a nominal average as the test baseline x_0 for (4), since these flows evolve significantly with time. Like Mahadik et al. [11], to accommodate the dynamic, non-stationary nature of the flows, the test baseline is allowed to adapt to changes in alert flow, and the control limits for time instant i are

$$z_{i-1} \pm n \cdot \sigma_{z_{i-1}} . \tag{6}$$

Here n is a factor expressing how large a deviation from trend is acceptable and σ_{z-1} is z's standard deviation at interval $i-1$. The control limits for interval i are thus calculated using trend statistics from interval $i-1$.

To obtain the standard deviation σ_z, another EWMA statistic

$$z_i^2 = (1 - \lambda)z_{i-1}^2 + \lambda x_i^2 \tag{7}$$

is maintained, where x_i is the current intensity as in trend calculation. The standard deviation is computed as

$$\sigma_{z_i} = \sqrt{z_i^2 - (z_i)^2 i} . \tag{8}$$

Now for each new interval and for each alert flow, 1) the alert intensity is measured, 2) the control limits are calculated, and 3) the decision whether the interval is abnormal or not is taken. Both [9] and [11] test smoothed event intensity against the control limits. They use a larger smoothing factor with (1) to obtain the baseline z_i from (6) and apply (1) with smaller smoothing factor to have smoothed event intensity that is tested against control limits. This is done to reduce the effect of wild values in the observations. However, in the case of alerts, these outliers are usually of interest for the operator and testing the raw intensity, or in other words using $(1 - \lambda) = 0$ to obtain the value that is tested against control limits, gave us better capability to capture small variations occurring in some extremely stable alert flows.

2.3 Learning Data

The tool was developed for an IDS consisting of Snort sensors logging alerts into a relational database. The sensors are deployed in a production network, one closer to Internet and two others in more protected zones. This adds to the difficulty of measuring and testing, since we do not know the true nature of traffic that was monitored. On the other hand, we expect the real world data to contain such background noise and operational issues that would not be easily incorporated to simulated traffic.

Table 1. Five most prolific signatures in the first data set

signature name	number of alerts	proportion
SNMP Request udp	176 009	30 %
ICMP PING WhatsupGold Windows	72 427	13 %
ICMP Destination Unreachable (Comm Adm Proh)	57 420	10 %
LOCAL-POLICY External connexion from HTTP server	51 674	9 %
ICMP PING Speedera	32 961	6 %
sum	**390 491**	**68 %**

The data set available to us in this phase contained over 500 K alerts accumulated during 42 days. Of the 315 activated signatures, only five were responsible for 68 % of alerts as indicated in Table 1 and we chose them for further scrutiny. To give an idea of the alert flow behavior, examples of alert generation intensities for four of these signatures are depicted in Fig. 1 and the fifth, ICMP PING WhatsupGold Windows, is visible in Figs. 2 and 3 (described with more details in Sect. 2.4). The relatively benign nature of these alerts and their high volume was one of the original inspirations for this work. These alerts are good examples of the problem three discussed in Sect. 1.2 and demonstrate the reason why we opt not just filter even the more deterministic components out. For example, the alert flow in Fig. 1(c) triggered by SNMP traffic over UDP had only few (source, destination) address pairs, and the constant component could be easily filtered out. However, this would deprive the operator being notified of behavior such as the large peak and shift in constant component around February 15th as well or the notches in the end of February and during March 15th. Not necessarily intrusions, but at least artifacts worth further investigation. On the other hand, we do not want to distract the operator with the alerts created during the hours that represent the stable situation with constant intensity. For the others, Fig. 1(a) shows alerts from a user defined signature reacting to external connections from an HTTP server. The alerts occur in bursts as large as several thousands during one hour and the intensity profile resembles impulse train. As custom made, the operator has likely some interest in this activity. In Figs. 1(b) and 1(d) we have alerts triggered by two different ICMP Echo messages, former being remarkably more regular than latter. In the system in question, deactivation of ICMP related signatures was not seen as an solution by the operator as they are useful for troubleshooting problems. Consequently, we had several high volume alert flows for which the suppression was not the first option.

2.4   Deploying the Control Chart

The behavior of the model defined in Sect. 2.2 was explored with five flows made up from these five signatures (Figs 1, 2, and 3) by varying several parameters. A combination that would 1) catch desired artifacts from the alert flow and 2) create as small amount of new alerts as possible, was searched. Not having

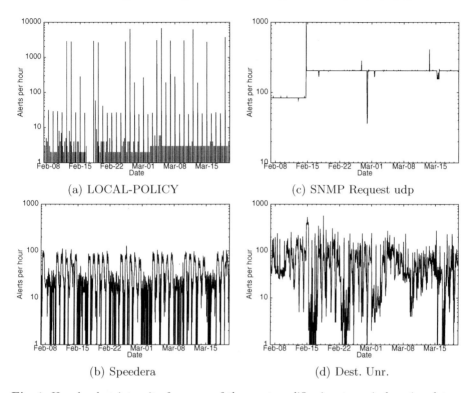

Fig. 1. Hourly alert intensity for some of the most prolific signatures in learning data. Horizontal axis is the time, and the vertical shows the number of alerts per hour

an exact definition for interesting artifacts from the real users, we had to look for behavior that seemed to us worth further investigation. In addition to the actual parameters, also different aggregation criteria and input preprocessing were used.

Setting chart parameters. The width of control limits in (6) was set to three standard deviations as already proposed by Roberts [8]. Values $\{1, 2, 3, 6\}$ were tried before making the choice. The memory of the chart depends on the smoothing factor and sampling interval length. Figures 2 and 3 depict the effect of memory length on the trend and control limits with sampling interval of one hour and $(1 - \lambda)$ with values 0.8 and 0.99407, respectively. The smaller smoothing factor results in trend and control limits following the current value closely. The difference between the trend and reality is nearly invisible in the Fig. 2, and the control limits tighten relatively fast after an abrupt shift in flow intensity. The model behavior with significantly larger smoothing factor in Fig. 3 shows how the recent values have relatively small effect on trend. The standard deviation reaches such large values that the control limits absorb all variations in the flow. For $(1 - \lambda)$ in $[0.2, 0.8]$ the flagging rate increased towards smaller smoothing factors, the steepness of increase varying from flow to flow.

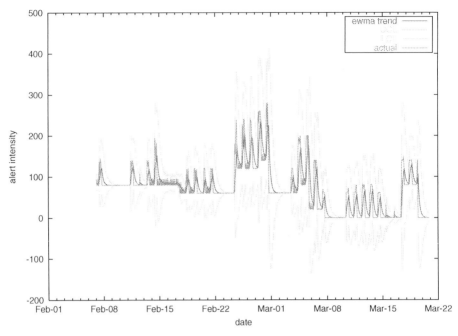

Fig. 2. The effect of small smoothing factor on trend and control limits

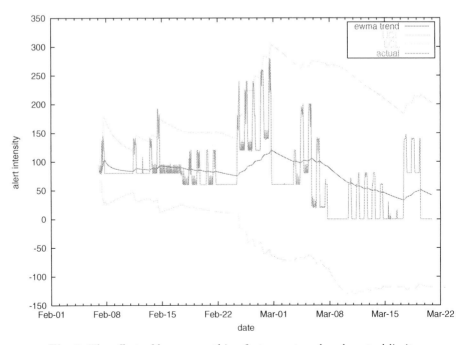

Fig. 3. The effect of large smoothing factor on trend and control limits

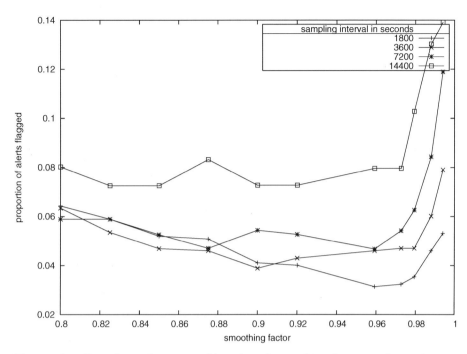

Fig. 4. The effect of sampling interval length and smoothing factor on alert reduction

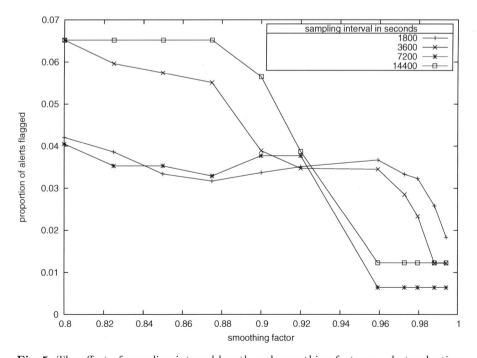

Fig. 5. The effect of sampling interval length and smoothing factor on alert reduction

However, the sampling interval length had surprisingly little effect on the proportion of both intervals and alerts deemed as anomalous. The same applies also for the smoothing interval apart from the very extreme values. Figures 4 and 5 show the proportion of anomalous alerts for two signatures triggered by ICMP Echo messages as the function of smoothing factor, where $(1 - \lambda) \in [\,0.8, 0.99407\,]$ and sampling intervals $\{0.5, 1, 2, 4\}$ hours. For both the proportion of alerts marked as anomalous is within range of four percentage units for except with the largest smoothing factors. In Fig. 4 alert flagging shoots up with largest smoothing factors, a phenomenon which was caused by the large difference in trend and current value due to lagging trend. In Fig. 5 there is a sharp drop in flagging as the smoothing factor increases. This inverse effect was usually related to wide control limits causing all flow behavior to be considered as normal. An example of this kind of situation is visible in the right half of Fig. 3.

Setting the sampling interval to one hour and using smoothing factors 0.8 and 0.92 allowed flagging those kinds of anomalies in alert flows considered interesting also by the visual exploration shown in Figs. 2 and 3. As stated above, the sampling interval length seemed have only a minor effect on the flagging rate. In addition, according to (5), this gives the model a memory of 9 and 24 hours, respectively. For the user this provides an intuitive association with workday and day, which is also an important aspect to consider. One hour from event to notification is a long time in terms of intrusion detection. However, instead of real time detection of compromise, the need was to heavily summarize the background noise and in addition our target IDS is not under constant surveillance by the operator. As such, the one hour sampling interval was considered suitable. Depending on the user's requirements, the sampling frequency could be increased.

To capture the time related behavior visible for some signatures, two other models were deployed in addition to the one monitoring the alert flow in continuous manner. The second model, later referred as *daily*, uses separate statistic for the intensity of each hour of the day. The third model, *weekday*, maintains separate statistics for weekday and weekend intensities.

The aggregation criteria. Combining different signatures as one flow was also tried. For example, Snort has several signatures for different ICMP Destination Unreachable messages and for web traffic that were used to form two aggregates, respectively. In learning data, 232 web related signatures were activated, and only those Destination Unreachable signatures reacting to Communication Administratively events (Snort SIDs 485, 486, 487) were present. These combinations did not seem to make sense, since there were few signatures dominating the sums that only reflected the behavior of alerts caused by them. Only separate signatures and signature classes were chosen for further examination. However, the aggregate flows could be formed in many different ways, refer to Sect. 5 for more on this.

Input processing. Instead of using the measured value of event intensity as x_i in (1), additional smoothing operation with small smoothing factor is done in [9]. We experimented with smoothing factors 0.2 and 0.3 for the trend input, but the effect on alert reduction was negligible. By feeding the raw intensity to trend calculations, σ_z reaches higher values more quickly. This means also that the control limits widen up rapidly, which helps to avoid flagging several intervals after an abrupt shift in intensity level. For example, in Fig. 1(c) as the intensity increases around February 15th, the trend line lags below the real value for a moment. If the control limits are not wide enough, several intervals become flagged instead of only the one containing the shift.

Mostly out of curiosity, cutoff values for x_i based on σ_z to limit trend updates were also used. This did not work well, and caused problems especially with stable flows. When σ_z approached zero the trend became too slow adapting to drastic changes. Again, the above mentioned example with SNMP Request udp applies.

In order to validate the choice of parameters and to see the suitability of our approach, experimentation with a larger data set was performed.

3 Practical Experimentation

For testing a more complete alert data base dump than the one used in learning phase was obtained. It contains nearly 2M alerts from 1836 signatures accumulated during 112 days from the same system. We use two statistics to measure the applicability of the EWMA monitoring to a particular alert flow. The statistics are the percentage of alerts flagged and proportion of anomalous intervals from intervals with non-zero activity, discussed in 3.1. For each flow these measurements are made with the three models, continuous, daily and weekday, and with two different smoothing factors, resulting to six statistics per flow. These results are presented in 3.2. Then the overall usefulness of our method for summarizing the alerts is evaluated with respect to number of applicable and non-applicable flows.

3.1 The Rationale for the Test Metric

As noted by Mell et al. [12] testing IDSes is no simple task and lacks rigorous methodology. The difficulty in our situation arises from the fact that we intend to signal the user when something odd is going on with the background noise and help him to cope with alert floods by reducing the number of alerts reported. As such we cannot make a strict separation between correct and false alarms, and using metrics like accuracy or completeness [13] is difficult. It is the user in the very end who decides whether the extracted information is useful or not.

However, we can describe the summarizing capabilities with the two above mentioned statistics, 1) the proportion of alerts flagged as anomalous, and 2) the proportion of busy time slots. As the control chart signals only the abnormality of an interval, we count all alerts from anomalous interval to be flagged, resulting to a rough approximation of the alert reduction in individual alerts. Since we intend to summarize background noise, it is unlikely that the operator would go through individual alerts even from an anomalous interval. Let us assume that he uses a time unit t to skim through the raw background noise generated by one flow during an interval T to detect that it seems normal, where T equals to sampling interval of EWMA monitoring. In our case T is one hour and it is likely that $t << T$. If the operator uses EWMA monitoring for the flow, he will be notified only when flow behaves in anomalous way. Now the time units t that would be used to manually detect normal behavior can be used for more useful tasks like treating the more severe alerts. Thus it is more interesting to look at the number of anomalous intervals after summarization with respect to intervals showing activity in the raw flow than just the alert reduction.

The proportion of busy time slots is obtained by dividing the number of anomalous intervals by the number of intervals showing non-zero activity for the flow. The proportion indicates how constantly the operator would be bothered by the flow with EWMA monitoring compared to manually checking the accumulated noise every T. Small values for a flow mean smaller nuisance to the user where as large values tell that EWMA monitoring is not capable to summarize the activity of this flow.

As an anomaly can be caused by an interval with zero alerts, the proportion could in theory be above unity. For example, imagine a flow with impulse train type profile, such as LOCAL-POLICY in Fig. 1(a), for which all active intervals plus some zero intensity intervals could be flagged. However, in practice we never saw this. For the daily and weekday models we combine the results of individual time slot statistics to obtain the overall performance. One drawback in these metrics is that there is no cost associated to them even though viewing only the flow anomaly alerts instead of individual alerts, some information is lost.

3.2   Results

As the interest is to monitor high volumed aggregates, we considered only signatures that had created more than 100 alerts. After this preselection we had 85 signatures left. This section first describes how the flow volume affected the summarization, and the identified reasons for poor efficiency. Secondly we analyze the alert types causing large numbers of alerts, the impact of time slot choice and larger aggregates for the flow behavior, and the stability of flow profiles.

Effect of flow volume. Judging from the busy interval reduction, the method is useful for alert flows that had created more than 10 K alerts, the effectiveness increasing with the flow volume. The busy interval reduction for flows below 10 K alerts is already more modest, and below 1 K alerts the reduction is relatively negligible. Tables 2 and 3 depict respectively the reduction as percentage from non-zero intervals and alerts flagged anomalous, due to space constraints only for flows of over 10 K alerts. Reduction is shown with smoothing factors 0.80 and 0.92 for each three model, continuous, hourly, and weekday. In Table 2 also the total number of active intervals, and in Table 3 the total number of alerts are shown for each flow.

Table 2. The proportion of flagged intervals from intervals showing activity for the flow with different models and smoothing factors

flow	int.	cont.		daily		weekd.	
		.80	.92	.80	.92	.80	.92
Known DDOS Stacheldraht infection	563	1.6	1.8	8.9	8.5	2.0	2.5
SNMP request udp	2311	4.3	2.9	5.8	4.6	4.2	3.0
ICMP PING WhatsupGold Windows	2069	5.1	3.3	5.8	2.6	5.1	3.2
DDOS Stacheldraht agent→handler (skillz)	512	1.2	1.6	12	16	1.8	2.1
ICMP Dst Unr (Comm Adm Proh)	2578	5.4	3.5	6.7	5.8	5.4	3.4
ICMP PING speedera	2456	3.3	1.7	4.2	2.9	3.3	0.9
WEB-IIS view source via translate header	2548	5.2	3.8	6.4	5.7	5.1	4.0
WEB-PHP content-disposition	2287	6.8	4.3	7.7	5.2	6.7	4.0
SQL Sapphire Worm (incoming)	1721	2.2	1.2	4.9	3.5	2.4	1.6
(spp_rpc_decode) Frag RPC Records	421	13	7.8	20	20	12	9.0
(spp_rpc_decode) Incompl RPC segment	276	21	13	27	27	22	13
BAD TRAFFIC bad frag bits	432	34	23	37	33	35	22
LOCAL-WEB-IIS Nimda.A attempt	537	24	16	30	25	24	16
LOCAL-WEB-IIS CodeRed II attempt	1229	6.3	4.6	14	14	6.9	5.3
DNS zone transfer	855	9.7	6.7	13	10	9.8	6.5
ICMP L3retriever Ping	107	29	26	71	70	28	23
WEB-MISC http directory traversal	708	12	9.3	15	13	12	9.5
(spp_stream4)STLTH ACT(SYN FIN scan)	29	65	58	82	79	62	62

Table 3. The percentage of flagged alerts with different models and smoothing factors

flow	alerts	cont.		daily		weekd.	
		.80	.92	.80	.92	.80	.92
Known DDOS Stacheldraht infection	308548	1.2	1.2	4.4	8.4	1.4	1.5
SNMP request udp	303201	4.4	3.0	4.9	4.4	4.2	3.2
ICMP PING WhatsupGold Windows	297437	5.4	4.0	4.5	2.9	5.2	3.1
DDOS Stacheldraht agent→handler (skillz)	280685	0.8	1.0	7.3	7.0	1.2	1.2
ICMP Dst Unr (Comm Adm Proh)	183020	32	28	39	37	32	28
ICMP PING speedera	95850	5.5	3.1	2.5	2.3	5.3	1.4
WEB-IIS view source via translate header	58600	25	21	12	11	24	22
WEB-PHP content-disposition	48423	18	14	15	13	18	14
SQL Sapphire Worm (incoming)	38905	3.0	1.9	11	9.1	3.1	2.5
(spp_rpc_decode) Frag RPC Records	38804	63	62	94	93	63	62
(spp_rpc_decode) Incompl RPC segment	28715	64	62	93	93	64	62
BAD TRAFFIC bad frag bits	27203	51	42	57	54	53	42
LOCAL-WEB-IIS Nimda.A attempt	25038	65	61	69	64	64	62
LOCAL-WEB-IIS CodeRed II attempt	20418	11	7.5	17	22	11	7.1
DNS zone transfer	15575	32	35	55	55	32	36
ICMP L3retriever Ping	12908	11	12	90	90	11	12
WEB-MISC http directory traversal	10620	41	38	46	45	41	38
(spp_stream4)STLTH ACT(SYN FIN scan)	10182	96	90	93	93	96	96

Table 4. All 85 flows grouped by the number of alerts created and the percentage level below which busy intervals or alerts were flagged

busy interval reduction					alert reduction				
alerts	5%	10%	50%	100%	alerts	5%	10%	50%	100%
> 100 K	5	0	0	0	> 100 K	4	0	1	0
> 10 K	5	3	4	1	> 10 K	2	1	6	4
> 1 K	0	4	19	7	> 1 K	0	1	15	14
> 100	0	1	12	24	> 100	0	0	8	29
sum	10	8	35	32	**sum**	6	2	30	47

Table 4 summarizes alert reduction results with continuous model and smoothing factor 0.92. All 85 flows are grouped to four classes according to both their output volume (over 100, 1 K, 10 K or 100 K alerts) and the achieved reduction in busy intervals and alerts (below 5 %, 10 %, 50 % or 100 % of original), respectively. These results show also the poorer performance for flows below the 10 K limit. The busy intervals show more consistent relation between the volume and reduction. On the right hand side of Table 4 in the class over 100 K alerts, ICMP Dest Unr (Comm Admin Proh) stands out with reduction significantly smaller than others in the same class. We found two explanations for this behavior. First, there was one large alert impulse of approximately 17 K alerts flagged in the test data. This makes up roughly 10 % of flagged alerts. Second, the flow nature is more random compared to others, this is visible in Fig. 1(d) for learning data and applies also for the larger data set. This randomness causes more alert flagging, but still the reduction in busy intervals is comparable to other flows in this volume class.

Reasons for poor summarization. There seems to be two main reasons for poorer performance. 1) Many flows had few huge alert peaks that increase the alert flagging significantly. 2) The intensity profile has the form of impulse train that has negative impact both on reduction of alerts and busy intervals. As the first cause does not increase remarkably the number of reported anomalous intervals i.e. the number of times the user is disturbed, this is smaller problem. However, the second cause renders our approach rather impractical for monitoring such a flow, as the operator is notified on most intervals showing activity. The flow (spp_stream4) on the last row of Tables 2 and 3 is a typical example, as its alert profile consisted only from impulses. In such situation a large majority of active intervals are flagged as anomalous. A closer look on alert impulses revealed that they were usually generated in such a short time interval that increasing the sampling frequency would not help much. Instead, other means should be considered to process them.

Represented alert types. Amongst the most prolific signatures, we can identify three main types of activity, *hostile*, *information gathering* and alerts that can be seen to reflect the *dynamics* of networks.

Hostile activity is represented by DDoS tool traffic and worms with five signatures. The two DDoS signatures are actually the same, different names were used by the operator for alert management reasons. If busy interval reduction below 5 % with continuous model and $(1 - \lambda) = 0.92$ is used to define EWMA monitoring applicable for a flow, then we have three fourths in feasible range for the hostile activity.

In the system in question, possible information gathering is the most common culprit for numerous alerts. This category can be further divided to information gathering on applications (web related signatures) and network architecture (ICMP, SNMP and DNS traffic). In both categories, there are both suitable and unsuitable flows for this type monitoring.

The ICMP Destination Unreachable (Communication Administratively Prohibited) message is an example of the activity that describes the dynamics of the network. It reflects the network state in terms of connectivity, and the origins and causes of these events are generally out of operators control.

Signatures firing on *protocol anomalies* can be considered as an orthogonal classification, since they can present any of the three types above. ((spp rpc decode), (spp stream4) and BAD TRAFFIC) were all poorly handled by the method. Another common factor is the smaller degree of presence in the data set in terms of non-zero intervals. As the (spp_stream4) means possible reconnaissance, and being present only on 29 intervals, it is less likely to be just background noise.

The nature of these alerts and their volumes in general support the claim that large proportion of generated alerts can be considered as noise. Even in the case of hostile activity the originating events warrant aggregation. This applies in our case, but the situation may vary with different operating environments.

Table 5 shows the signature flows ordered by their omnipresence giving the number of active intervals and the percentage this makes out of the whole testing interval. A rough division according to the 5 % watershed is made and type of signature according to above discussion is assigned. We can see that for all signatures showing activity on more than 45 % of the intervals the number of alerts issued to operator can be significantly reduced in this system.

It would seem that the omnipresence of alerts would be better criteria than the alert type for determining whether EWMA monitoring would be useful or not.

Impact of time slot choice. According to these metrics the usefulness of daily and weekday models was limited to a few exceptions, generally the continuous model was performing as well as the others. We just happened to have one of the exceptions that really profited from hourly approach in our early experimentations, and made the erroneous hypothesis of their commonness. The metrics are however limited for this kind of comparisons. It is especially difficult to say if the hourly approach just marks more intervals as anomalous or is it actually capturing interesting artifacts differently. On many occasions the smaller reduction was at least partly due to abrupt intensity shifts. As several different statistics making up the hourly model signal an anomaly whereas the

Table 5. The omnipresence of signatures and their types. Presence measured in active intervals

signature	type	< 5 %	active	present
ICMP Dst Unr (Comm Adm Proh)	network	ok	2578	95 %
WEB-IIS view source via translate header	info_web	ok	2548	93 %
ICMP PING speedera	info_net	ok	2456	90 %
SNMP request udp	info_net	ok	2311	85 %
WEB-PHP content-disposition	info_web	ok	2287	84 %
ICMP PING WhatsupGold Windows	info_net	ok	2069	76 %
SQL Sapphire Worm (incoming)	hostile	ok	1721	63 %
LOCAL-WEB-IIS CodeRed II attempt	hostile	ok	1229	45 %
DNS zone transfer	info_net	no	855	31 %
WEB-MISC http directory traversal	info_web	no	708	26 %
Known DDOS Stacheldraht infection	hostile	ok	563	20 %
LOCAL-WEB-IIS Nimda.A attempt	hostile	no	537	19 %
DDOS Stacheldraht agent-¿handler (skillz)	hostile	ok	512	18 %
BAD TRAFFIC bad frag bits	proto	no	432	15 %
(spp_rpc_decode) Frag RPC Records	proto	no	421	15 %
(spp_rpc_decode) Incompl RPC segment	proto	no	276	10 %
ICMP L3retriever Ping	info_net	no	107	3 %
(spp_stream4)STLTH ACT(SYN FIN scan)	proto	no	29	1 %

continuously updated statistic does this only once. The two DDoS flows had intensity profiles resembling a step function, which caused the hourly model to flag significantly more alerts than the continuous. Another factor encumbering the comparisons are the differences in efficient lengths of model memories. As the time slot statistics of hourly and weekday models are updated with only the corresponding intensity measures the values averaged have longer span in real time. For example the hourly model's statistics are affected by 8 or 24 *days* old measurements.

Class flows. Grouping signature classes together increased the flagging percentage. Table 6 shows obtained reductions with continuous model and $(1 - \lambda) = 0.92$ for class aggregates with more than 1000 alerts. In fact, almost every class contains one or more voluminous signatures that were problematic statistically already by themselves, and this affects the behavior of class aggregate. The increased flagging could also indicate that anomalies in signature based flows with smaller volume are detected to some degree. The levels of busy intervals are reduced relatively well and again generally the flagging increases as alert volume decreases. The aggregation by class might be used to gain even more abstraction and higher level summaries in alert saturated situations. However, there are likely to be better criteria for aggregation than than the alert classes.

Flow stability. To give an idea of the stability of flow profiles, Table 7 compares the alert and busy interval reduction obtained for four signatures used in

Table 6. The reduction in alerts and busy intervals when aggregating according to signature classes. Results for continuous model with $1 - \lambda = 0.92$

flow	raw		anomalous	
	int.	alerts	int.	alerts
misc-activity	2678	618273	1.9 %	8.9 %
class_none	1429	380568	4.8 %	18.3 %
attempted-recon	2635	360613	3.7 %	7.0 %
known-issue	563	308548	1.7 %	1.1 %
web-application-activity	2569	88554	3.3 %	16.3 %
bad-unknown	2559	65883	3.7 %	20.9 %
known-trojan	1511	46014	5.4 %	34.9 %
misc-attack	1727	39070	1.3 %	2.1 %
web-application-attack	1017	9587	9.1 %	40.5 %
attempted-user	272	3694	19.4 %	40.6 %
attempted-dos	361	2782	24.3 %	67.8 %
attempted-admin	444	1760	20.2 %	33.1 %

Table 7. A comparison of results obtained during learning and testing phases. $(1-\lambda) = 0.92$

flow	alerts		intervals	
	learn.	test	learn.	test
SNMP request udp	2.7	3.5	2.2	3.5
ICMP PING WhatsupGold Windows	4.6	3.6	2.9	3.6
ICMP Dst Unr (Comm Adm Proh)	12	36	3.2	3.7
ICMP PING speedera	2.8	3.2	1.3	2.0

the learning phase against the reduction in testing data. In general the flagging is slightly higher in the training data set, but for `ICMP Dest Unr (Comm Adm Proh)` significantly more alerts are marked anomalous in the test set. The large alert impulse in this flow, mentioned earlier, accounts for approximately 14 % units of this increase in test data. Even if those alerts were removed, the increase would be large. Still, the reduction in busy intervals is quite similar, suggesting higher peaks in the test set. The fifth signature enforcing a local policy, also viewed in the learning phase, did not exist anymore in the testing data set. This signature created alert impulses (see LOCAL-POLICY in Fig. 1(a)) and the alert reduction was marginal in learning data.

It seems like with the used parameters the reduction performance stays almost constant. This would suggest that after setting parameters meeting the operators needs, our approach is able to adapt to lesser changes in alert flow behavior without further adjustment. At least during this test period, none of the originally nicely-enough-behaving flows changed to more problematic impulse-like nor vice versa. Also signatures having a constant alert flow or more random process type behavior, both feasible for the method, kept to their original profile.

To wrap up the results, it seems possible to use this approach to summarize and monitor the levels of high volume background noise seen by an IDS. Up to 95 % of the one hour time slots showing activity from such an alert flow can be unburdened from the distraction. For the remaining intervals, instead of a barrage of alerts, only one alert would be outputted in the end of the interval. As both data sets came from the same system, the generality of these observations is rather limited, and more comprehensive testing would be required for further validation.

If the user is worried that aggregation at signature level loses too much data, it is possible to use additional criteria, such as source and destination addresses and/or ports to have more focused alert streams. The reduction in aggregation is likely to create more flagged intervals, and this is a tradeoff that the user needs to consider according to his needs and the operating environment. Determining if the summarization masked important events in the test set was not possible, as we do not possess records of actual detected intrusions and problems in the monitored system against which we could compare our results.

4   Related Work

The focus of this work was only on volume reduction and alert aggregation, not on content improvement nor activity tracking. In addition, the target is high volume background noise instead of high impact alerts, so we consider the approach to be different from other correlation efforts, such as presented by Valdes and Skinner [14] or Qin and Lee [15].

Manganaris et al. [16] use data mining to gain better understanding of alert data. Julisch and Dacier [2] take the approach further and report episode rules a labor intensive approach and develop conceptual clustering to construct filters for false positives. Instead of filtering, we propose to monitor the levels of background noise, if it is possible to significantly reduce the number of alerts displayed to the operator.

In addition to a plethora of other applications, the EWMA model has also been harnessed for intrusion detection. There are two relatively recent approaches, a non-named from Ye et al.[9] [10], and ArQoS[1] developed by Mahadik et al. [11].

Both of these IDSes are meant mainly to detect Denial of Service (DoS) attacks. Methods proposed by Ye et al. use host-based data source, the Solaris BSM audit event intensity, for attack detection. ArQoS monitors DiffServ network's Quality of Service (QoS) parameters, like bit rate, jitter and packet drop rate to detect attacks on QoS. So the latter can be said to be a network-based approach.

Ye et al. test different control charts, in [9] one meant for autocorrelated, another for uncorrelated data, and [10] adds still one for the standard deviation, to find out the suitability for intrusion detection. Their conclusion was that all dif-

---

[1] http://arqos.csc.ncsu.edu

ferent charts could be used for detecting attacks causing statistically significant changes in event intensity.

Mahadik et al. [11] rely on EWMA techniques only to analyze the more stationary flows. For the less stationary they deploy a χ^2 statistic. Their control chart differs from those used by Ye et al., and according to their tests the overall system is capable to quickly detect QoS degradation. The approach we propose differs from these two in the following ways: 1) A view on system state instead of detecting DoS attacks or intrusions in more general is provided. 2) The audit source is the alert database created by network based sensor instead of host based or network traffic information. So no access to host audit trail or routers is required. 3) The control chart is defined slightly differently.

5   Conclusions and Future Work

Alerts triggered by activity not considered as actual attacks but only harmful tend to create huge amounts of alerts. Typically this kind of raw intelligence outputted by sensors is insignificant and distracting for the operator, but the changes in the levels of this background noise can be of interest. If these alerts are removed by simply filtering or judging them as false by correlation engine, the operator will lose this information.

An alert processing method based on EWMA control charts to summarize the behavior of such alert flows was presented to meet the five objectives set in Sect. 1.3: anomaly highlighting, decreasing operator load, reduction measurement, determination of suitable flows for monitoring, and trend visualization.

According to the experience with the technique, it can be used to highlight anomalies in high volume alert flows showing sufficient degree of regularity. With this approach it is possible to make the high alert levels associated with these flows more sustainable without deactivating them. We believe that the method could be used as such, or in complement to other means of correlation, to monitor alerts considered as background noise of an operational system. The provided additional diagnostic capabilities may be modest, but more importantly via summarization the operator can save time for more relevant tasks as he is informed only of significant changes in the noise level. A metric based on the proportion of time units freed from manual processing when monitoring an aggregate instead of raw alert flow was proposed.

Alert flows creating less alerts or having strict requirements for the timeliness of detection are better to be treated with other means, since the sampling interval is scarce and the method is not able to find useful trends from small amount of alerts.

As the method applicability for a particular flow is determined from its visualization, this goal is not met, and requires the definition of explicit criteria and an automated process. Also the generation of meaningful alert summaries for the operator needs to be addressed for the the objective 'trend visualization' to be met.

For the moment, only the signatures and signature classes have been used as the aggregation criterion. The use of source and destination hosts or networks could be a step towards more specific flows, if required. We also intend to investigate different similarity measures for forming the monitored aggregates. For example similar packet payload is one such possibility.

Gathering user experience from the operators would be interesting, and for this the method is being integrated as part of alert console used internally at France Télécom.

References

1. James P. Anderson. Computer Security Threat Monitoring and Surveillance. Technical report, James P. Anderson Co., Fort Washington, Pa 19034, April 1980.
2. Klaus Julisch and Marc Dacier. Mining Intrusion Detection Alarms for Actionable Knowledge. In *Proceedings of Knowledge Discovery in Data and Data Mining (SIGKDD)*, 2002.
3. P. A. Porras, M. W. Fong, and A. Valdes. A Mission-Impact-Based Approach to INFOSEC Alarm Correlation. In Wespi et al. [17], pages 95–114.
4. B. Morin and H. Debar. Correlation of Intrusion Symptoms: an Application of Chronicles. In Vigna et al. [18], pages 94–112.
5. H. Debar and B. Morin. Evaluation of the Diagnostic Capabilities of Commercial Intrusion Detection Systems. In Wespi et al. [17].
6. Klaus Julisch. Mining Alarm Clusters to Improve Alarm Handling Efficiency. In *Proceedings of the 17th Annual Computer Security Applications Conference (ACSAC2001)*, December 2001.
7. Soon Tee Teoh, Kwan-Liu Ma, S. Felix Wu, and Xiaoliang Zhao. A Visual Technique for Internet Anomaly Detection. In *Proceedings of IASTED Computer Graphics and Imaging*. ACTA Press, 2002.
8. S. W. Roberts. Control Chart Tests Based On Geometric Moving Averages. *Technometrics*, 1(3):230–250, 1959.
9. Nong Ye, Sean Vilbert, and Qiang Chen. Computer Intrusion Detection Through EWMA for Autocorrelated and Uncorrelated Data. *IEEE Transactions on Reliability*, 52(1):75–82, March 2003.
10. Nong Ye, Connie Borror, and Yebin Chang. EWMA Techniques for Computer Intrusion Detection Through Anomalous Changes In Event Intensity. *Quality and Reliability Engineering International*, 18:443–451, 2002.
11. Vinay A. Mahadik, Xiaoyong Wu, and Douglas S. Reeves. Detection of Denial of QoS Attacks Based on χ^2 Statistic and EWMA Control Chart.
    URL: http://arqos.csc.ncsu.edu/papers.htm, February 2002.
12. Peter Mell, Vincent Hu, Richard Lippman, Joss Haines, and Marc Zissman. An Overview of Issues in Testing Intrusion Detection Systems. NIST IR 7007, NIST CSRC - National Institute of Standards and Technology, Computer Security Resource Center, June 2003.
13. Hervé Debar, Marc Dacier, and Andreas Wespi. A Revised Taxonomy of Intrusion-Detection Systems. Technical Report RZ 3176 (#93222), IBM Research, Zurich, October 1999.
14. A. Valdes and K. Skinner. Probabilistic Alert Correlation. In Wenke Lee, Ludovic Mé, and Andreas Wespi, editors, *Proceedings of the 4th International Symposium on Recent Advances in Intrusion Detection (RAID 2001)*, volume 2212 of *Lecture Notes in Computer Science*, Heidelberg, Germany, 2001. Springer–Verlag.

15. Xinzhou Qin and Wenke Lee. Statistical Causality Analysis of INFOSEC Alert Data. In Vigna et al. [18], pages 73–93.
16. Stefanos Manganaris, Marvin Christensen, Dan Zerkle, and Keith Hermiz. A Data Mining Analysis of RTID Alarms. 2nd International Symposium on Recent Advances in Intrusion Detection (RAID 1999), 1999. Available online: http://www.raid-symposium.org/raid99/PAPERS/Manganaris.pdf.
17. Andreas Wespi, Giovanni Vigna, and Luca Deri, editors. *Proceedings of the 5th International Symposium on Recent Advances in Intrusion Detection (RAID 2002)*, volume 2516 of *Lecture Notes in Computer Science*, Heidelberg, Germany, 2002. Springer–Verlag.
18. Giovanni Vigna, Erland Jonsson, and Christopher Kruegel, editors. *Proceedings of the 6th International Symposium on Recent Advances in Intrusion Detection (RAID 2003)*, volume 2820 of *Lecture Notes in Computer Science*, Heidelberg, Germany, 2003. Springer–Verlag.

Symantec Deception Server Experience with a Commercial Deception System

Brian Hernacki, Jeremy Bennett, and Thomas Lofgren

Symantec Corporation
Redwood City, CA
{brian_hernacki,jeremy_bennett,thomas_lofgren}@symantec.com

Abstract. This paper provides an examination of an emerging class of security mechanisms often referred to as *deception technologies* or *honeypots*. It is based on our experience over the last four years designing and building a high, end commercial deception system called ManTrap. The paper will provide an overview of the various technologies and techniques and will examine the strengths and weaknesses of each approach. It will discuss deployment criteria and strategies and will provide a summary of our experiences designing and constructing these systems. It also presents the results of work demonstrating the feasibility and utility of a deep deception honeypot.

Keywords: Deception, Honeypot, ManTrap.

1 Introduction

Over the past several years network systems have grown considerably in size, complexity, and susceptibility to attack. At the same time, the knowledge, tools, and techniques available to attackers have grown just as fast if not faster. Unfortunately defensive techniques have not grown as quickly. The current technologies are reaching their limitations and innovative solutions are required to deal with current and future classes of threats. Firewalls and intrusion detection/protection systems are valuable components of a security solution but they are limited in the information they can provide. While they can provide very broad protection for a large variety of services, they also provide very shallow protection. Even the solutions with the most complete "application protection" or "deep inspection" can determine very little about host-side effects, attacker capability, or attacker intent. In order to provide scalable detection for a wide variety of applications and systems, they cannot support the necessary environment in which to completely evaluate a potential threat. High bandwidth and network encryption also present barriers to such solutions. While host monitoring solutions (e.g. host intrusion detection systems, a.k.a. HIDS) do not suffer from all of these limitations, they are encumbered with their own. Using such host solutions poses significant management and scalability challenges and also places real assets at risk. Deception systems, also called "honeypots" present a valuable combination of these two approaches.

This paper presents the results of our experience designing and deploying honeypots for the last four years. It will first provide a basic overview of honeypot technology, including a classification system that we have developed and used. It will then examine deployment techniques and strategies we have used and observed. Finally, it

E. Jonsson et al. (Eds.): RAID 2004, LNCS 3224, pp. 188–202, 2004.
© Springer-Verlag Berlin Heidelberg 2004

will discuss our specific experiences designing and constructing our honeypot, called ManTrap [1]. It will provide a detailed look at some of the design challenges and existing problems yet to be solved.

2 Honeypot Basics

A honeypot appears to be an attractive target to an attacker. These targets can be real systems or some type of emulator designed to appear as servers, desktops, network devices, etc. When the attacker attempts to attack the network, they either stumble into or are led into the honeypot. The honeypot then records all of the attacker's actions as they assess and attempt to compromise it. Depending on the specific class of honeypot it may provide additional functionality such as automated alerting, triggered responses, data analysis, and summary reporting.

Using a honeypot has numerous advantages. First it wastes the attacker's time. Any time spent attacking a honeypot is time not spent attacking a real machine. Second, it provides extremely detailed information about what the attacker does and how they do it. Third it gives the attacker a false impression of the existing security measures. Thus the attacker spends time finding tools to exploit the honeypot that may not work on a real system. Fourth the existence of a honeypot decreases the likelihood that a random attack or probe will hit a real machine. Finally, a honeypot has no false positives. Any activity recorded is suspicious as a honeypot is not used for any other purpose.

Much like a pot of honey used to attract and trap insects, a honeypot ensnares an attacker by appearing to be an attractive target. Depending on the depth of the deception an attacker can spend large amounts of time attempting to exploit and then exploring the honeypot. Meanwhile all this activity is recorded and reported to the honeypot owner. The more time the attacker spends with the honeypot the more information about her means and motives is given to the owner. This information can be used to make other machines immune to the tools being used.

If an attacker does not know the weaknesses of a system he cannot exploit it. Honeypots give attackers a false sense of accomplishment. They spend time researching the vulnerabilities presented by the honeypot. They create or find tools to exploit those vulnerabilities. Finally, they spend time executing these exploits and demonstrating to the honeypot owner exactly how to thwart their attack should it be viable on other machines.

Many attackers scan large blocks of computers looking for victims. Even attackers targeting a specific organization will scan the publicly accessible machines owned by the organization looking for a machine to compromise as a starting point. Using honeypots decreases the chance an attacker will choose a valuable machine as a target. A honeypot will detect and record the initial scan as well as any subsequent attack.

Unlike other intrusion detection measures there are no false positives with a honeypot. All IDS systems produce false positives to varying degrees. This is because there is always a chance that valid traffic will match the characteristics the IDS uses to detect attacks. This is not the case with a honeypot. Any communication with a honeypot is suspect. This is because the honeypot is not used for any purpose other than detecting attacks. There is no valid traffic to produce false positives.

In this way a honeypot can detect more attacks than other IDS measures. New vulnerabilities can be found and analyzed because all actions an attacker takes are recorded. New attack tools can be detected based on their interaction with a honeypot. Since all communication is suspect, even new or unknown attacks which exhibit no signature or anomalous characteristics can be detected. These can include feeding false information into a service or database, using compromised credentials to gain unauthorized access, or exploiting some new application logic flaw. Finally, a honeypot can detect and record incidents that may last for months. These so-called 'slow scans' are difficult to detect using an IDS as the time involved makes them very difficult to differentiate from normal traffic without being false positive prone.

3   Classification of Honeypots

Honeypots are not a new idea. Researchers and security professionals have been using different forms of honeypots for many years [8][9][10]. In recent years however, there has been rapid innovation in the technology and significant increases in deployment. As honeypots become more mainstream, it is useful to discuss them in a slightly more formal sense.

Honeypots can be classified into three primary categories: facades, sacrificial lambs, and instrumented systems. A *facade* is the most lightweight form of a honeypot and usually consists of some type of simulation of an application service in order to provide the illusion of a victim system. A *sacrificial lamb* usually consists of an "off the shelf" or "stock" system placed in a vulnerable location and left as a victim. An *instrumented system* honeypot is a stock system with additional modification to provide more information, containment, or control.

Each class of honeypots has different strengths and weaknesses and is appropriate to different types of use according to these. The sections below explore each class with respect to implementation, strengths and weaknesses and typical uses.

Note that while these classifications are primarily our creation, we have been using them with others in the field for a number of years. Other classification systems do exist [12], however ours attempts to provide more information of the honeypot (form, capability, risk, etc) rather than just the degree of interaction.

3.1   Facades

A facade honeypot is a system which provides a false image of a target host. It is most often implemented as software emulation of a target service or application. This emulation acts like a vulnerable host or service. Some implementations can emulate large numbers of hosts, varieties of operating systems, and different applications or services. When the facade is probed or attacked, it gathers information about the attacker and provides a fictitious response. This is analogous to having a locked door with nothing behind it and watching to see who attempts to open it. The depth of the simulation varies depending on implementation. Some will provide only partial application level behavior (e.g. banner presentation). Other implementations will actually simulate the target service down as far as the network stack behavior. This is done in order to prevent remote signaturing by O/S fingerprinting. The value of a facade honeypot is defined primarily by what systems and applications it can simulate and how easy to deploy and administrator it is.

Facades offer simple, easy deployment as they often have very minimal installation or equipment requirements and are easy to administer. They can provide a large number of targets of considerable variety. Since they are not real systems, they do not have the vulnerabilities of real systems. They also present very little additional risk to your environment due to the nature of the emulation. While the system underneath is "real", the emulated services are not. They cannot be compromised on the same fashion as they "live" services they emulate. Thus the honeypot cannot be used as a jumping off point. While it is technically possible that someone could attempt to actually exploit the emulated service (knowing that it is a honeypot) this seems very unlikely. At worst it simply merits caution in deployment.

Their only significant limitation is that due to their limited depth, they provide only basic information about a potential threat. They may also fail to engage the attacker for long periods of time since there is not anything to compromise. This lack of depth can potentially create a signature which drives the attacker away from the honeypot. While this can be considered a limitation, by the time the attacker becomes suspicious, they have usually interacted with the honeypot enough to generate alerts, provide intelligence, etc.

Examples of this type of honeypot include NetFacade and Honeyd [2].

Sites that wish to deploy very simple deception as a form of early warning system should consider facade products given their simplicity to deploy and low administrative overhead. These are typically used by small to medium enterprises or by large enterprises in conjunction with other technology. While very little hard data exists to indicate the exact scale of this, our field experience supports this conclusion.

3.2 Sacrificial Lambs

A sacrificial lamb is a normal system left vulnerable to attack. They can be built from virtually any device (a Linux server, a Cisco router, etc). The typical implementation involves loading the operating system, configuring some applications and then leaving it on the network to see what happens. The administrator will examine the system periodically to determine if it has been compromised and if so what was done to it. In many cases, the only form of data collection used is a network sniffer deployed near the honeypot. While this provides a detailed trace of commands sent to the honeypot, it does not provide any data in terms of host effects. In other cases additional examination is done either by hand or using various third-party forensic tools. Also the systems themselves are "live" and thus present a possible jumping off point for an attacker. Additional deployment considerations must be made to isolate and control the honeypot by means of firewalls or other network control devices.

Sacrificial lambs provide real targets. All the results are exactly as they would be on a real system and there is no signature possible since there is nothing different about the system. These types of honeypots are also fairly simple to build locally since they only use off-the-shelf components. Sacrificial lambs provide a means to analyze a compromised system down to the last byte with no possible variation. However, this type of honeypot requires considerable administrative overhead. The installation and setup requires the administrator to load the operating system themselves and manually perform any application configuration or system hardening. The analysis is manual and often requires numerous third-party tools. They also do not provide integrated containment or control facilities, so will require additional network considerations (as mentioned above) to deploy in most environments.

There are no specific examples of sacrificial lambs since they can be constructed from virtually anything. However the Honeynet Project [3] provides good examples on constructing these.

Groups or individuals that are interested in doing vulnerability research should consider a sacrificial lamb honeypot. It will require dedicated expert security resources to support but will provide a great deal of information and flexibility.

3.3   Instrumented Systems

Instrumented systems provide a compromise between the low cost of a facade and the depth of detail of a sacrificial lamb. They are implemented by modifying a stock system to provide additional data collection, containment, control and administration.

Designed as an evolutionary step from earlier forms of deception, they provide easy to deploy and administer honeypots that are built on real systems. They are able to provide an exceptional level of detail (often more than a sacrificial lamb) while also providing integrated containment and control mechanisms. There are two important considerations when using instrumented systems. First is that building one can be very expensive and difficult to do correctly. It requires significant time, skill and knowledge to create even moderately good deception which is not detectable (e.g. a signature) or itself a security risk. Some administrators attempt to construct their own but often run into difficulty creating an effective deception, providing effective isolation, and providing sufficient management functionality. Sites interested in instrumented systems should consider one designed by a security professional with significant honeypot experience and which is provided as a real software product (including support).

An example of this type of honeypot would be Symantec's ManTrap product.

Sites interested in receiving more information than a facade provides but that cannot afford the large administrative overhead of a sacrificial lamb system should consider an instrumented system honeypot. These provide a richer integrated feature set and have taken into consideration scalability, deployment, reporting, and administration. These are typically used by medium to large enterprise.

3.4   Additional Considerations

While not specific to a particular class or form of honeypot, there are a number of additional features or functions which should be considered by an organization evaluating honeypots.

It is important to consider the nature and the cost of containment and control. Any system deployed in a network presents possible risk. Measures should be taken to mitigate that. Risk level, functionality, and restriction capability should be considered in any product that provides containment and control. If the product does not support any native containment and control, the cost and complexity of implementing it should be seriously considered.

While honeypots can provide an excellent source of data, it is important to remember that the data by itself does nothing. In order to be useful, the data must be analyzed. Some products provide integrated analysis, reporting and alerting. Others require the administrator to provide the data review and security expertise. How much analysis is offered and how the administration is done is an important consideration and has significant impact on the cost of using such a system.

Cluster or group administration functionality should be considered when deploying multiple deception devices. Systems which provide the ability to work in clusters and have single points of administration and reporting provide for a much more scalable solution than those that require manual operation of each node.

Maintenance of content and restoration of the honeypot should also be taken into consideration. These both contribute to the ongoing administrative cost of maintaining a deception system. Content on a deception device needs to be periodically updated so it appears valid and "live". Deception systems which have been attacked may also need to be periodically restored to a "clean" state. In both of these cases, solutions which provided automated capabilities for this can reduce administrative costs.

Finally, it is worth considering the relationship of honeypots to *host-based intrusion detection systems* (HIDS) [4] and *integrity monitoring systems*. HIDS are usually deployed on a production system and designed more as a burglar alarm. Running these on a production system really does not provide the same value as a honeypot. They are much more prone to false positives, force the administrator to deal with the difficulty of monitoring normal user activity, and generally do not provide containment or good administration functionality (for a honeypot approach). These can be used to create honeypots, but often produce very large signatures since they are not designed for stealth.

Integrity monitoring software has many of the same deficiencies as HIDS for honeypot use. It is designed for monitoring a production system for change, not user activity or security. It provides none of the additional functionality needed for a honeypot. As with a HIDS, these also create very large signatures (indications that this is not a normal system) that are not desirable for a honeypot.

4 Deployment Strategies

While many honeypot implementations may function well in single deployments with dedicated administrative efforts, larger deployments (a.k.a. "enterprise deployments") require additional functionality to be effective solutions. An organization that wishes to deploy honeypots should have an overall computer security policy that states what the threats are, what the main goals for an attacker might be where high-value systems are, and how potential targets will be protected. This security policy will dictate what the honeypot deployment strategy will be.

This section describes a few different deployment strategies. These strategies, or combinations of them, can be used together with firewalls and IDS to form a cohesive security infrastructure to protect an organization.

4.1 Minefield

In a minefield deployment, honeypots are installed among live machines, possibly mirroring some of the real data. The honeypots are placed among external servers in the DMZ, to capture attacks against the public servers, and/or in the internal network, to capture internal attacks (which either originated internally or external attacks that penetrated the firewall and now use internal machines as launching pads).

Attacks are rarely restricted to a single machine. Many manual and automated network attacks follow the same pattern: Assuming a successful attack has taken place on one machine in the network, that machine is then used to scan the network for other potential targets, which are subsequently attacked. For manual attacks, this takes some time, while worms will normally execute the scan just seconds after the first infection [11]. The scanning can be done in a way to specifically avoid setting off IDS systems (e.g., through "slow scans"), but honeypots in a minefield will be alerted.

For example, if a network has one honeypot for every four servers, then the chance of hitting a honeypot with a random, single-point attack is 20%. In reality, the chance is significantly better than that because in most cases an entire block of network addresses will be scanned. When this happens, it is practically guaranteed that the honeypot will detect the intrusion shortly after any machine on the network has been compromised.

Even though the intrusion detection aspect alone is important, another feature of using honeypots is to gain info on attack tools and purpose. With good security practices on the production machines, weaker security on the honeypots may increase the chance that they will be the first machines that are attacked. A well-designed honeypot will then have the information about what service was attacked, how that service was attacked, and – if the attack was successful – what the intruder did once inside. Having the honeypots configured exactly the same way as the regular servers, however, has other advantages. It increases their deception value slightly, and it also means that when a honeypot has detected a successful attack, that attack is likely to succeed on the production hosts.

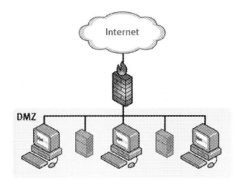

Fig. 1. A "minefield" deployment

4.2 Shield

In a shield deployment, each honeypot is paired with a server it is protecting. While regular traffic to and from the server is not affected, any suspicious traffic destined for the server is instead handled by the honeypot shield. This strategy requires that a firewall/router filters the network traffic based on destination port numbers, and redirects the traffic according to the shielding policy.

For instance, consider a web server deployed behind a firewall. Web server traffic will be directed to the web server IP address on TCP port 80. Any other traffic to the web server is considered suspicious, and can be directed to a honeypot.

The honeypot should be deployed in a DMZ, and to maximize the deception value, it may replicate some or all of the non-confidential content of the server it is shielding. In the example of the web server, this is merely a matter of mirroring some or the entire web content to the honeypot.

In conjunction with the firewall or router, honeypots deployed in this fashion provide actual intrusion prevention in addition to intrusion detection. Not only can potential attacks be detected, they can be prevented by having the honeypot respond in place of the actual target of the attack. It should be added that a honeypot shield cannot protect a mail server from SMTP exploits, nor a web server from HTTP exploits, since "regular" traffic must be able to reach its target. However, since live servers generally need very few open ports, it is reasonably easy to find the point of an attack – both for prevention and forensic purposes – and all other ports lead straight to the honeypot, where the attack can be analyzed in detail.

A shield deployment is an example of how honeypots can protect a high-value system, where attacks can be expected.

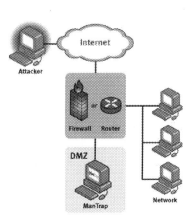

Fig. 2. A "shield" deployment

4.3 Honeynet

In a honeynet deployment, a network of honeypots imitates an actual or fictitious network. From an attacker's point of view, the honeynet appears to have both servers and desktop machines, many different types of applications, and several different platforms. Another term for this deployment is "zoo", as it captures the wild hacker in their natural environment.

In a sense, a honeynet is an extension of the honeypot concept, in that it takes multiple deception hosts (single honeypots), and turns them into an entire deception network. A typical honeynet may consist of many facades (because they are light-weight and reasonably easy to deploy), some instrumented systems for deep deception, and possibly some sacrificial lambs. In order to provide a reasonably realistic network environment, some sort of content generation is necessary. On a host basis, this involves simulating activity on each deep honeypot, as well as generating network traffic to and from the clients and servers, so that the network itself looks realistic from the outside.

In a small example of a DMZ that contains a web server and a mail server, consider two honeypots that act as shields to the servers. Any traffic to the web server that is not HTTP traffic will be directed to the web server's shield. Any traffic to the mail server that is not SMTP will be directed to the mail server's shield. By adding a few more honeypots, another dimension can be added to this deception; all traffic to unknown IP addresses can be directed to honeypots, not only traffic to known hosts. The strength of the honeynet shield is that it shields an entire network instead of a single host. Similarly, honeynet minefields represent the scenario where each mine is an entire network, as opposed to just a single honeypot. It is also possible to configure a honeypot so that any outbound traffic (e.g. the attacker trying to attack another system from the honeypot) can be directed only into an isolated honeynet. This provides both containment and the possibility of gathering additional and very useful information about the attacker's attempts.

Honeynets can be useful in a large enterprise environment, and offer a good early warning system for attacks. A honeynet may also provide an excellent way to figure out an intruder's intention, by looking at what kind of machines and services are attacked, and what is done to them. The Honeynet Project (http://project.honeynet.org) is an excellent example of a honeynet used as a research tool to gather information about attacks on computer infrastructure.

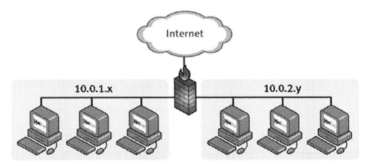

Fig. 3. A "honeynet" deployment

5   Experiences Constructing and Deploying an Instrumented System

ManTrap is a commercial honeypot product in the category of "instrumented systems". It was originally developed by Recourse Technologies and is now a Symantec product. The remainder of this paper discusses our experience with ManTrap. We will first present a brief overview of its design and functionality and then discuss some of the challenges we faced in constructing and deploying it. Finally we will present a number of existing problems that have not yet been solved.

We believe that these types of instrumented systems provide a useful, deployable tool for many organizations interested in using honeypots. Many of the design considerations made were intended to create a honeypot which was simple enough for most administrators to use, secure enough to deploy, and still deep enough to gather valuable information about potential attacks. Our goal was to provide a professional quality high interaction honeypot usable by a broad audience.

5.1 ManTrap Goals

ManTrap was designed to be a commercially usable honeypot. While there are many ways to implement and deploy honeypots, most require far too much administrative overhead, far too much technical expertise, or create far too much risk to be deployed in most commercial environments. ManTrap's goal was to create a honeypot which could be easily deployed and maintained by a standard enterprise IT/security staff and provide valuable security data which could not be easily obtained from other existing tools.

5.2 A Brief Overview

High Level Architecture

A ManTrap system consists of a single physical computer. ManTrap is installed on top of the operating system (Solaris) and provides operating system level virtualization of the system to implement its "honeypots". Each machine can provide up to four different honeypots – or "cages" – with each cage being completely isolated from the other cages as well as from the real host system. A user logged into a cage will not be able to see the processes, network traffic, and other system resources of the other cages, nor of the host system itself. To the attacker, each cage appears to be a separate machine. If a system file is deleted in one cage, it will still exist in the others.

If an attacker obtains access to a cage, whether by a stolen password, remote network exploit, or other means, the cage will provide a controlled environment where information is gathered about the activity, while at the same time containing the attacker, and stopping him from discovering that he is being monitored.

ManTrap also provides a mechanism to automatically create and maintain dynamic content. While it is possible to initially load the system with a set of static content (e.g. web pages for a web server), content which changes over time provides a much more convincing deception to an attacker. ManTrap provides a module that automatically generates email traffic to and from some of the users on the system. This provides an additional piece of deception, as an intruder may be fooled into thinking he is capturing actual email traffic. The generated email messages are instead created from templates provided by the ManTrap administrator.

The ManTrap system also includes an administration console application. This application, built in Java, allows the user to remotely administer the ManTrap machines. It is possible to administer multiple ManTrap hosts from a single console. A cluster of ManTraps in an enterprise can therefore be managed by a single administrator.

Audit

ManTrap keeps extensive audit logs of activities in its cages. Since all activity in a cage is suspicious (because no legitimate users belong there), as much information as possible is logged. Examples of the activities that a running ManTrap will log:

- All terminal input and output
- All files opened for writing
- All device accesses
- All processes that are started
- All network activity

The ManTrap logs are meant to provide an (almost) complete view of the activities inside the cage. ManTrap also allows the administrator to cryptographically verify that the logs have not been tampered with (see *Audit Reliability* below).

Response

When ManTrap detects cage activity, it is capable of alerting the administrator and/or responding automatically. The administrator can configure a response policy including:

- SMTP (E-mail) alerts
- SNMP traps (alerts to network management software)
- Integration with other commercial threat management solutions (e.g. NIDS)
- Custom responses: administrator-specified scripts or binaries to be run on a particular event

These responses can be used to alert administrators when a cage is accessed; to shutdown a cage once the attacker has achieved a certain level of access (e.g. gained root), etc.

Analysis

The log data that is collected inside a cage is used to provide different types of activity reports. Reports can be generated on-demand or on a scheduled, regular basis, and cover cage activities such as:

- File modifications
- Successful logins to the cage
- Responses triggered by the cage
- Attempted connections
- Outgoing connections
- TCP and/or UDP port activity on the cage

In addition, the ManTrap administration console allows a user to be able to monitor interactive sessions in a terminal window, either while the session is active, or after the fact. This gives the ManTrap administrator a unique and realistic view of what the intruder saw and did during the attack.

5.3   Construction Experience

General Technique

As mentioned above, ManTrap is an instrumented system. It is constructed primarily by means of a kernel module that intercepts systems calls and provides filtering and modification. This is backed by a virtualized file system and various coordination and supporting administration processes. For example, if a process in a cage attempts to call open() to open /etc/passwd, the ManTrap module intercepts this call and redirects it so that the cage copy of the file is opened instead.

Isolation

ManTraps foremost requirement is that the cages be isolated from the root system and from each other. A process within the cage is not allowed to access files, directories, or devices except those explicitly exposed to it. A process within the cage is not allowed to interact with a process outside the cage. However, this must all be accomplished without causing compatibility problems for applications running inside the cage. One important feature of ManTrap was that the users (administrators) are allowed to run existing applications inside the deception environment without any modification. This was quite a challenge. While we were not universally successful as some applications require raw device support, require conflicting kernel functionality, or present some unacceptable privilege risk, in general ManTrap is able to provide this isolation while still maintaining compatibility.

Stealth
One of the key requirements which differentiate ManTrap from many existing host virtualization techniques (VMware [5], Solaris zones [6], etc) is stealth. ManTrap required that processes running within the virtualized environment, the cage, not be able to determine that it was not the "real" system. This required that all traces of monitoring, virtualization and other instrumentation be hidden. It also required that all activity in other cages on the same host be hidden. This included local files, running process lists, network data and many other things. This also needed to be done without causing compatibility functions for applications running inside the cages and without doing anything that would tip off an attacker. As there are numerous such interfaces in the operating system, and many of them not well documented, this proved to be one of the most significant challenges. It is also one in which there exists an adversarial pressure. Attackers (and sometimes researchers) would actively attempt to find ways in which the cage could be differentiated from the real system. While several techniques were eventually discovered nearly all were easily addressed. The only remaining ones were those which required root access and relied on accessing some hard-to-emulate resources such as /dev/kmem (see below *Current Challenges*).

Audit Reliability
Since one of the values of something like ManTrap is its ability to collect detailed data for use in analysis or potentially as evidence, the reliability of the data is very important. While the prior isolation requirement should provide a guarantee that an attacker inside the cage not be able to access or influence the audit trail, ManTrap was designed with an additional integrity control in its audit system. ManTraps are deployed with a hardware crypto-token called an iButton [7]. One of the tasks the system uses the iButton for is log signing. Periodically, ManTrap will sign its log files using functionality embedded in the token. If an attacker later succeeds in accessing the log files, any modifications they make can be easily detected since the signature validation will later fail. At best, such an attacker could delete the logs or portions of them.

Cage Restoration
One of the key features added to later version of ManTrap was the ability to easily restore a pristine cage image. A problem encountered with early version of ManTrap (and other honeypots) is that once an attacker has "compromised" the honeypot and made modifications, the cage is tainted. While it may be useful to maintain it in a tainted state for some period of time (so an attacker can return to what they believe is a compromised system), eventually the administrator may wish to restore the system to a clean state and begin again. This would allow them for example to clearly differentiate between what one attacker did and what subsequent attackers may do. It is a

very difficult task for an administrator to "undo" modifications made by an attacker, even assuming sufficient audit trail exists to reliably perform this task. While it is always possible to completely reload the system and perform all customization and configuration again, this are very time consuming tasks. ManTrap added functionality to allow administrators to easily restore configurations post installation and customization. Thus restoring to a clean but configured and customized state is mostly a matter of clicking a button.

Automated Analysis

Since ManTrap is intended to be used by administrators with limited security and systems expertise, it attempts to provide some level of automated analysis of the data it collects. In some cases this is merely presentation or basic aggregation of lower level data. In other cases it is application of a basic knowledge of security impact of common events. In the former case, ManTrap is able to reconstruct data from keystroke traces into a session view of the attackers "terminal" for easy observation. In the latter case, it is able to make the determination that a root shell has been created from a non-root shell (without explicitly authenticating) and that it may possibly indicate use of a local privilege escalation exploit. While this is still a long ways from providing an "expert in a box", it does succeed in lowering the amount expertise required for use. Improvement in this area is discussed below.

5.4 Current Challenges

While we consider the ManTrap product a great success, there are still a number of open problems or challenges to be addressed to fully realize our original goals. We discuss four of the most significant below.

Once an attacker has succeeded in obtaining root access, even emulated, it becomes difficult to maintain some portions of our functionality; most notably stealth. While it is possible to prevent the "root" process in the cage from accessing external resources, in some cases this presents a significant signature. For example, consider the situation in which a root process attempts to access /dev/kmem directly. If the system disallows the access it presents a property which can be used as a signature. If access is allowed the system must virtualize this resource. Allowing access (e.g. via a pass-thru to the real /dev/kmem) would allow an intruder to see and possibly modify anything in memory, even things outside the cage. Unfortunately virtualizing some resources, like kernel memory, is quite difficult (maybe impossible) and not something we have accomplished yet.

Another difficulty we encountered in developing ManTrap is that, due to its design, it has a very high porting cost. Since many of the modifications performed to instrument the system are done using very platform specific interfaces and must emulate functionality which is very specific to a particular operating system, any port is almost a complete rewrite. While administrative components and general design can be reused, much of the hard work (and the research necessary to design it) must be done for each operating system supported. Additionally some operating systems (e.g. Windows) differ enough in their basic architecture that considerable redesign must be done.

One of the original goals was to reduce the expertise required to operate a honeypot to increase the size of the potential user base. While we think the functionality provided in ManTrap makes great progress in this area, there is still room for improvement. While basic maintenance tasks are well automated and data presentation is easy to use, the system cannot perform much automated *analysis*. There would be considerable value in a system which could automatically assess attacker intent and skill level. Functionality which could automatically assess the nature, risk, and purpose of new files transferred onto the system (e.g. exploit kits) would also be very valuable. Automated analysis in general is a large and open area for computer security research, but there are a number of very honeypot specific tasks in which we envision future progress.

6 Summary and Conclusions

Our experience developing ManTrap validated our initial concept that it was possible to build such a deep instrumented system honeypot. It was possible by modifying the operating system using existing access points to provide for the needed isolation, stealth, and audit functionality. It was also possible to automate enough of the administrative tasks to create a tool that was usable without considerable honeypot expertise. Our practical experience with the users revealed that most administrators capable of administering a Solaris system were also capable of administering a ManTrap. We did however discover that in many environments where it was desirable to deploy honeypots, even that level of expertise did not exist. We conclude that while we met our original design goals, this suggests there is a need to further reduce the administrative complexity.

Through numerous incidents, these honeypots proved to be valuable compliments to existing security infrastructure. They were able to detect attacks earlier than other systems, detect attacks other systems did not, and provide an extremely high level of data about the attackers, their methods and intent. We conclude that deception technologies or honeypots are an important, emerging security technology. They provide the defender with both the time and information needed to effectively respond to a wide variety of threats. They are cost effective to deploy and administer and are capable of detecting threats other detection technologies cannot. They provide a powerful defense mechanism that should be a component of any security solution.

References

1. "Symantec Enterprise Solutions. Symantec Corporation", Retrieved Mar. 2004, http://enterprisesecurity.symantec.com/products
2. "Honeyd – Network Rhapsody for You. Center for Information Technology Integration",Retrieved Mar 2004, http://www.citi.umich.edu/u/provos/honeyd/index.html
3. "The Honeynet Project",Retrieved Mar 2004, http://project.honeynet.org/misc/project.html
4. "Talisker Host Intrusion Detection System. Security Wizardry", Retrieved Feb. 2004, http://www.networkintrusion.co.uk/HIDS.htm
5. "Vmware", Retrieved Mar. 2004, http://www.vmware.com
6. "Solaris Zones. Sun Microsystems - BigAdmin", Retrieved Mar. 2004, http://www.sun.com/bigadmin/content/zones/index.html
7. "iButton Products: iButton Overview", Retrieved Mar. 2004, http://www.ibutton.com/ibuttons/index.html

8. C. Stoll, 2000, "Cuckoo's Egg: Tracking a Spy Through the Maze of Computer Espionage", Pocket Books

9. "SecurityFocus HOME Products: Cybercopy Sting", Retrieved Jun. 2004, http://www.securityfocus.com/products/515

10. B. Cheswick, "An Evening with Berferd In Which a Cracker is Lured, Endured and Studied", Proc. Winter USENIX Conference, 1992

11. D. Moore, V. Paxson, S. Savage, C. Shannon, S. Staniford, and N. Weaver, " The Spread of the Sapphire/Slammer Worm", 2003, http://www.caida.org/outreach/papers/2003/sapphire/sapphire.html

12. L. Spitzner, "Honeypots Definitions and Value of Honeypots", Retrieved Jun. 2004, http://www.tracking-hackers.com/papers/honeypots.html

Anomalous Payload-Based Network Intrusion Detection

Ke Wang and Salvatore J. Stolfo

Computer Science Department, Columbia University
500 West 120th Street, New York, NY, 10027
{kewang,sal}@cs.columbia.edu

Abstract. We present a payload-based anomaly detector, we call PAYL, for intrusion detection. PAYL models the normal application payload of network traffic in a fully automatic, unsupervised and very effecient fashion. We first compute during a training phase a profile byte frequency distribution and their standard deviation of the application payload flowing to a single host and port. We then use Mahalanobis distance during the detection phase to calculate the similarity of new data against the pre-computed profile. The detector compares this measure against a threshold and generates an alert when the distance of the new input exceeds this threshold. We demonstrate the surprising effectiveness of the method on the 1999 DARPA IDS dataset and a live dataset we collected on the Columbia CS department network. In once case nearly 100% accuracy is achieved with 0.1% false positive rate for port 80 traffic.

1 Introduction

There are many IDS systems available that are primarily signature-based detectors. Although these are effective at detecting known intrusion attempts and exploits, they fail to recognize new attacks and carefully crafted variants of old exploits. A new generation of systems is now appearing based upon anomaly detection. Anomaly Detection systems model normal or expected behavior in a system, and detect deviations of interest that may indicate a security breach or an attempted attack.

Some attacks exploit the vulnerabilities of a protocol, other attacks seek to survey a site by scanning and probing. These attacks can often be detected by analyzing the network packet headers, or monitoring the network traffic connection attempts and session behavior. Other attacks, such as worms, involve the delivery of bad payload (in an otherwise normal connection) to a vulnerable service or application. These may be detected by inspecting the packet payload (or the ill-effects of the worm payload execution on the server when it is too late after successful penetration). State of the art systems designed to detect and defend systems from these malicious and intrusive events depend upon "signatures" or "thumbprints" that are developed by human experts or by semi-automated means from known prior bad worms or viruses. They do not solve the "zero-day" worm problem, however; the first occurrence of a new unleashed worm or exploit.

E. Jonsson et al. (Eds.): RAID 2004, LNCS 3224, pp. 203–222, 2004.

Systems are protected after a worm has been detected, and a signature has been developed and distributed to signature-based detectors, such as a virus scanner or a firewall rule. Many well known examples of worms have been described that propagate at very high speeds on the internet. These are easy to notice by analyzing the rate of scanning and probing from external sources which would indicate a worm propagation is underway. Unfortunately, this approach detects the early onset of a propagation, but the worm has already successfully penetrated a number of victims, infected it and started its damage and its propagation. (It should be evident that slow and stealthy worm propagations may go unnoticed if one depends entirely on the detection of rapid or bursty changes in flows or probes.)

Our work aims to detect the first occurrences of a worm either at a network system gateway or within an internal network from a rogue device and to prevent its propagation. Although we cast the payload anomaly detection problem in terms of worms, the method is useful for a wide range of exploit attempts against many if not all services and ports.

In this paper, the method we propose is based upon analyzing and modeling normal payloads that are expected to be delivered to the network service or application. These normal payloads are specific to the site in which the detector is placed. The system first learns a model or profile of the expected payload delivered to a service during normal operation of a system. Each payload is analyzed to produce a *byte frequency distribution* of those payloads, which serves as a model for normal payloads. After this *centroid* model is computed during the learning phase, an anomaly detection phase begins. The anomaly detector captures incoming payloads and tests the payload for its consistency (or distance) from the centroid model. This is accomplished by comparing two statistical distributions. The distance metric used is the Mahalanobis distance metric, here applied to a finite discrete histogram of byte value (or character) frequencies computed in the training phase. Any new test payload found to be too distant from the normal expected payload is deemed anomalous and an alert is generated. The alert may then be *correlated* with other sensor data and a decision process may respond with several possible actions. Depending upon the security policy of the protected site, one may filter, reroute or otherwise trap the network connection from being allowed to send the poison payload to the service/application avoiding a worm infestation.

There are numerous engineering choices possible to implement the technique in a system and to integrate the detector with standard firewall technology to prevent the first occurrence of a worm from entering a secured network system. We do not address the correlation function and the mitigation strategies in this paper; rather we focus on the method of detection for anomalous payload.

This approach can be applied to any network system, service or port for that site to compute its own "site-specific" payload anomaly detector, rather than being dependent upon others deploying a specific signature for a newly detected worm or exploit that has already damaged other sites. As an added benefit of the approach described in this paper, the method may also be used to detect encrypted channels which may indicate an unofficial secure tunnel is operating against policy.

The rest of the paper is organized as follows. Section 2 discusses related work in network intrusion detection. In Section 3 we describe the model and the anomaly detection technique. Section 4 presents the results and evaluations of the method applied to different sets of data and it's run time performance. One of the datasets is publicly available for other researchers to verify our results. Section 5 concludes the paper.

2 Related Work

There are two types of systems that are called anomaly detectors: those based upon a specification (or a set of rules) of what is regarded as "good/normal" behavior, and others that learn the behavior of a system under normal operation. The first type relies upon human expertise and may be regarded as a straightforward extension of typical misuse detection IDS systems. In this paper we regard the latter type, where the behavior of a system is automatically learned, as a true anomaly detection system.

Rule-based network intrusion detection systems such as Snort and Bro use hand-crafted rules to identify known attacks, for example, virus signatures in the application payload, and requests to nonexistent services or hosts. Anomaly detection systems such as SPADE [5], NIDES [6], PHAD [13], ALAD [12] compute (statistical) models for normal network traffic and generate alarms when there is a large deviation from the normal model. These systems differ in the features extracted from available audit data and the particular algorithms they use to compute the normal models. Most use features extracted from the packet headers. SPADE, ALAD and NIDES model the distribution of the source and destination IP and port addresses and the TCP connection state. PHAD uses many more attributes, a total of 34, which are extracted from the packet header fields of Ethernet, IP, TCP, UDP and ICMP packets.

Some systems use some payload features but in a very limited way. NATE is similar to PHAD; it treats each of the first 48 bytes as a statistical feature starting from the IP header, which means it can include at most the first 8 bytes of the payload of each network packet. ALAD models the incoming TCP request and includes as a feature the first word or token of each input line out of the first 1000 application payloads, restricted only to the header part for some protocols like HTTP and SMTP.

The work of Kruegel et al [8] describes a service-specific intrusion detection system that is most similar to our work. They combine the type, length and payload distribution of the request as features in a statistical model to compute an anomaly score of a service request. However, they treat the payload in a very coarse way. They first sorted the 256 ASCII characters by frequency and aggregate them into 6 groups: 0, 1-3, 4-6, 7-11, 12-15, and 16-255, and compute one single uniform distribution model of these 6 segments for all requests to one service over all possible length payloads. They use a chi-square test against this model to calculate the anomaly score of new requests. In contrast, we model the full byte distribution conditioned on the length of payloads and use Mahalanobis distance as fully described in the following discussion. Furthermore, the modeling we introduce includes automatic clustering of centroids that is shown to increase accuracy and dramatically reduce resource consumption.

The method is fully general and does not require any parsing, discretization, aggregation or tokenizing of the input stream (eg, [14]).

Network intrusion detection systems can also be classified according to the semantic level of the data that is analyzed and modeled. Some of the systems reconstruct the network packets and extract features that describe the higher level interactions between end hosts like MADAMID [9], Bro [15], EMERALD [18], STAT [24], ALAD [13], etc. For example, session duration time, service type, bytes transferred, and so forth are regarded as higher level, temporally ordered features not discernible by inspecting only the packet content. Other systems are purely packet-based like PHAD [14], NATED [12], NATE [23]. They detect anomalies in network packets directly without reconstruction. This approach has the important advantage of being simple and fast to compute, and they are generally quite good at detecting those attacks that do not result in valid connections or sessions, for example, scanning and probing attacks.

3   Payload Modeling and Anomaly Detection

There are many design choices in modeling payload in network flows. The primary design criteria and operating objectives of any anomaly detection system entails:

- automatic "hands-free" deployment requiring little or no human intervention,
- generality for broad application to any service or system,
- incremental update to accommodate changing or drifting environments,
- accuracy in detecting truly anomalous events, here anomalous payload, with low (or controllable) false positive rates,
- resistance to mimicry attack and
- efficiency to operate in high bandwidth environments with little or no impact on throughput or latency.

These are difficult objectives to meet concurrently, yet they do suggest an approach that may balance these competing criteria for payload anomaly detection.

We chose to consider "language-independent" statistical modeling of sampled data streams best exemplified by well known n-gram analysis. Many have explored the use of n-grams in a variety of tasks. The method is well understood, efficient and effective. The simplest model one can compose is the 1-gram model. A 1-gram model is certainly efficient (requiring a linear time scan of the data stream and an update of a small 256-element histogram) but whether it is accurate requires analysis and experimentation. To our surprise, this technique has worked surprisingly well in our experiments as we shall describe in Section 4. Furthermore, the method is indeed resistant to mimicry attack. Mimicry attacks are possible if the attacker has access to the same information as the victim to replicate normal behavior. In the case of application payload, *attackers (including worms) would not know the distribution of the normal flow to their intended victim*. The attacker would need to sniff for a long period of time and analyze the traffic in the same fashion as the detector described herein, and would also then need to figure out how to pad their poison payload to mimic the normal model.

3.1 Length Conditioned n-Gram Payload Model

Network payload is just a stream of bytes. Unlike the network packet headers, payload doesn't have a fixed format, small set of keywords or expected tokens, or a limited range of values. Any character or byte value may appear at any position of the datagram stream. To model the payload, we need to divide the stream into smaller clusters or groups according to some criteria to associate similar streams for modeling. The port number and the length are two obvious choices. We may also condition the models on the direction of the stream, thus producing separate models for the inbound traffic and outbound responses.

Usually the standard network services have a fixed pre-assigned port number: 20 for FTP data transmission, 21 for FTP commands, 22 for SSH, 23 for Telnet, 25 for SMTP, 80 for Web, etc. Each such application has its own special protocol and thus has its own payload type. Each site running these services would have its own "typical payload" flowing over these services. Payload to port 22 should be encrypted and appear as uniform distribution of byte values, while the payload to port 21 should be primarily printable characters entered by a user and a keyboard.

Within one port, the payload length also varies over a large range. The most common TCP packets have payload lengths from 0 to 1460. Different length ranges have different types of payload. The larger payloads are more likely to have non-printable characters indicative of media formats and binary representations (pictures, video clips or executable files etc.). Thus, we compute a payload model for each different length range for each port and service and for each direction of payload flow. This produces a far more accurate characterization of the normal payload than would otherwise be possible by computing a single model for all traffic going to the host. However, many centroids might be computed for each possible length payload creating a detector with a large resource consumption.

To keep our model simple and quick to compute, we model the payload using n-gram analysis, and in particular the byte value distribution, exactly when n=1. An n-gram is the sequence of n adjacent bytes in a payload unit. A sliding window with width n is passed over the whole payload and the occurrence of each n-gram is counted. N-gram analysis was first introduced by [2] and exploited in many language analysis tasks, as well as security tasks. The seminal work of Forrest [3] on system call traces uses a form of n-gram analysis (without the frequency distribution and allowing for "wildcards" in the gram) to detect malware execution as uncharacteristic sequences of system calls.

For a payload, the feature vector is the relative frequency count of each n-gram which is calculated by dividing the number of occurrences of each n-gram by the total number of n-grams. The simplest case of a 1-gram computes the average frequency of each ASCII character 0-255. Some stable character frequencies and some very variant character frequencies can result in the same average frequency, but they should be characterized very differently in the model. Thus, we compute in addition to the mean value, the variance and standard deviation of each frequency as another characterizing feature.. So for the payload of a fixed length of some port, we treat each character's relative frequency as a variable and compute its <u>mean and standard deviation</u> as the payload model.

Figure 1 provides an example showing how the payload byte distributions vary from port to port, and from source and destination flows. Each plot represents the characteristic profile for that port and flow direction (inbound/outbound). Notice also that the distributions for ports 22 (inbound and outbound) show no discernible pattern, and hence the statistical distribution for such encrypted channels would entail a more uniform frequency distribution across all of the 256 byte values, each with low variance. Hence, encrypted channels are fairly easy to spot. Notice that this figure is actually generated from a dataset with only the first 96 bytes of payload in each packet, and there is already a very clear pattern with the truncated payload. Figure 2 displays the variability of the frequency distributions among different length payloads. The two plots characterize two different distributions from the incoming traffic to the same web server, port 80 for two different lengths, here payloads of 200 bytes, the other 1,460 bytes. Clearly, a single monolithic model for both length categories will not represent the distributions accurately.

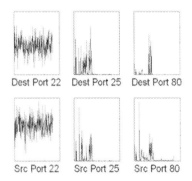

Fig. 1. Example byte distributions for different ports. For each plot, the X-axis is the ASCII byte 0-255, and the Y-axis is the average byte frequency

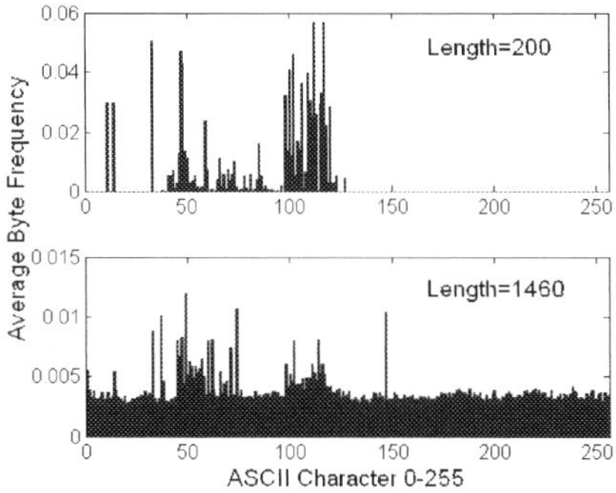

Fig. 2. Example byte distribution for different payload lengths for port 80 on the same host server

Given a training data set, we compute a set of models M_{ij}. For each specific observed length i of each port j, M_{ij} stores the average byte frequency and the standard deviation of each byte's frequency. The combination of the mean and variance of each byte's frequency can characterize the payload within some range of payload lengths. So if there are 5 ports, and each port's payload has 10 different lengths, there will be in total 50 centroid models computed after training. As an example, we show the model computed for the payload of length 185 for port 80 in figure 3, which is derived from a dataset described in Section 4. (We also provide an automated means of reducing the number of centroids via clustering as described in section 3.4.)

PAYL operates as follows. We first observe many exemplar payloads during a training phase and compute the mean and variance of the byte value distribution producing model M_{ij}. During detection, each incoming payload is scanned and its byte value distribution is computed. This new payload distribution is then compared against model M_{ij}; if the distribution of the new payload is significantly different from the norm, the detector flags the packet as anomalous and generates an alert.

The means to compare the two distributions, the model and the new payload, is described next.

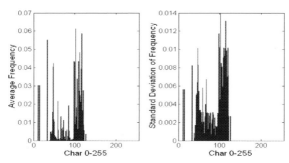

Fig. 3. The average relative frequency of each byte, and the standard deviation of the frequency of each byte, for payload length 185 of port 80

3.2 Simplified Mahalanobis Distance

Mahalanobis distance is a standard distance metric to compare two statistical distributions. It is a very useful way to measure the similarity between the (unknown) new payload sample and the previously computed model. Here we compute the distance between the byte distributions of the newly observed payload against the profile from the model computed for the corresponding length range. The higher the distance score, the more likely this payload is abnormal.

The formula for the Mahalanobis distance is:

$$d^2(x, \overline{y}) = (x - \overline{y})^T C^{-1} (x - \overline{y})$$

where x and $\overline{y}$ are two feature vectors, and each element of the vector is a variable. x is the feature vector of the new observation, and $\overline{y}$ is the averaged feature vector computed from the training examples, each of which is a vector. And C^{-1} is the inverse covariance matrix as $C_{ij} = Cov(y_i, y_j)$. y_i, y_j are the ith and jth elements of the training vector.

The advantage of Mahalanobis distance is that it takes into account not only the average value but also its variance and the covariance of the variables measured. Instead of simply computing the distance from the mean values, it weights each variable by its standard deviation and covariance, so the computed value gives a statistical measure of how well the new example matches (or is <u>consistent</u> with) the training samples.

In our problem, we use the "naïve" assumption that the bytes are statistically independent. Thus, the covariance matrix C becomes diagonal and the elements along the diagonal are just the variance of each byte.

Notice, when computing the Mahalanobis distance, we pay the price of having to compute multiplications and square roots after summing the differences across the byte value frequencies. To further speed up the computation, we derive the *simplified Mahalanobis distance*:

$$d(x, \overline{y}) = \sum_{i=0}^{n-1} (|x_i - \overline{y_i}| / \overline{\sigma_i})$$

where the variance is replaced by the *standard deviation*. Here n is fixed to 256 under the 1-gram model (since there are only 256 possible byte values). Thus, we avoid the time-consuming square and square-root computations (in favor of a single division operation) and now the whole computation time is linear in the length of the payload with a small constant to compute the measure. This produces an exceptionally fast detector (recall our objective to operate in high-bandwidth environments).

For the simplified Mahalanobis distance, there is the possibility that the standard deviation $\overline{\sigma_i}$ equals zero and the distance will become infinite. This will happen when a character or byte value never appears in the training samples or, oddly enough, it appears with exactly the same frequency in each sample. To avoid this situation, we give a smoothing factor α to the standard deviation similar to the prior observation:

$$d(x, \overline{y}) = \sum_{i=0}^{n-1} (|x_i - \overline{y_i}| / (\overline{\sigma_i} + \alpha))$$

The *smoothing factor* α reflects the statistical confidence of the sampled training data. The larger the value of α, the less the confidence the samples are truly representative of the actual distribution, and thus the byte distribution can be more variable. Over time, as more samples are observed in training, α may be decremented automatically.

The formula for the simplified Mahalanobis distance also suggests how to set the threshold to detect anomalies. If we set the threshold to 256, this means we allow each character to have a fluctuation range of one standard deviation from its mean. Thus, logically we may adjust the threshold to a value in increments of 128 or 256, which may be implemented as an automatic self-calibration process.

3.3 Incremental Learning

The 1-gram model with Mahalanobis distance is very easy to implement as an incremental version with only slightly more information stored in each model. An incremental version of this method is particularly useful for several reasons. A model may be computed on the fly in a "hands-free" automatic fashion. That model will improve in accuracy as time moves forward and more data is sampled. Furthermore, an incremental online version may also "age out" old data from the model keeping a more accurate view of the most recent payloads flowing to or from a service. This "drift in environment" can be solved via incremental or online learning [25].

To age out older examples used in training the model, we can specify a decay parameter of the older model and emphasize the frequency distributions appearing in the new samples. This provides the means of automatically updating the model to maintain an accurate view of normal payloads seen most recently.

To compute the incremental version of the Mahalanobis distance, we need to compute the mean and the standard deviation of each ASCII character seen for each new sample observed. For the mean frequency of a character, we compute $\overline{x} = \sum_{i=1}^{N} x_i / N$ from the training examples. If we also store the number of samples processed, N, we can update the mean as $\overline{x} = \dfrac{\overline{x} \times N + x_{N+1}}{N+1} = \overline{x} + \dfrac{x_{N+1} - \overline{x}}{N+1}$ when we see a new example x_{N+1}, a clever update technique described by Knuth [7].

Since the standard deviation is the square root of the variance, the variance computation can be rewritten using the expected value E as:

$$Var(X) = E(X - EX)^2 = E(X^2) - (EX)^2$$

We can update the standard deviation in a similar way if we also store the average of the x_i^2 in the model.

This requires maintaining only one more 256-element array in each model that stores the average of the x_i^2 and the total number of observations N. Thus, the n-gram byte distribution model can be implemented as an incremental learning system easily and very efficiently. Maintaining this extra information can also be used in clustering samples as described in the next section.

3.4 Reduced Model Size by Clustering

When we described our model, we said we compute one model M_{ij} for each observed length bin i of payloads sent to port j. Such fine-grained modeling might introduce several problems. First, the total size of the model can become very large. (The payload lengths are associated with media files that may be measured in gigabytes and many length bins may be defined causing a large number of centroids to be computed.) Further, the byte distribution for payloads of length bin i can be very similar to that of payloads of length bins $i-1$ and $i+1$; after all they vary by one byte. Storing a model for each length may therefore be obviously redundant and wasteful.

Another problem is that for some length bins, there may not be enough training samples. Sparseness implies the data will generate an empirical distribution that will be an inaccurate estimate of the true distribution leading to a faulty detector.

There are two possible solutions to these problems. One solution for the sparseness problem is relaxing the models by assigning a higher smoothing factor to the standard deviations which allows higher variability of the payloads. The other solution is to "borrow" data from neighboring bins to increase the number of samples; i.e. we use data from neighboring bins used to compute other "similar" models.

We compare two neighboring models using the simple Manhattan distance to measure the similarity of their average byte frequency distributions. If their distance is smaller than some threshold t, we merge those two models. This clustering technique is repeated it until no more neighboring models can be merged. This merging is easily computed using the incremental algorithm described in Section 3.3; we update the means and variances of the two models to produce a new updated distribution.

Now for a new observed test data with length i sent to port j, we use the model M_{ij}, or the model it was merged with. But there is still the possibility that the length of the test data is outside the range of all the computed models. For such test data, we use the model whose length range is nearest to that of the test data. In these cases, the mere fact that the payload has such an unusual length unobserved during training may itself be cause to generate an alert.

The reader should note that the modeling algorithm and the model merging process are each linear time computations, and hence the modeling technique is very fast and can be performed in real time. The online learning algorithm also assures us that models will improve over time, and their accuracy will be maintained even when services are changed and new payloads are observed.

3.5   Unsupervised Learning

Our model together with Mahalanobis distance can also be applied as an unsupervised learning algorithm. Thus, training the models is possible even if noise is present in the training data (for example, if training samples include payloads from past worm propagations still propagating on the internet.) This is based on the assumption that the anomalous payload is a minority of the training data and their payload distribution is different from the normal payload. These abnormal payloads can be identified in the training set and their distributions removed from the model. This is accomplished by applying the learned models to the training dataset to detect outliers. Those anomalous payloads will have a much larger distance to the profile than the "average" normal samples and thus will likely appear as statistical outliers. After identifying these anomalous training samples, we can either remove the outliers and retrain the models, or update the frequency distributions of the computed models by removing the counts of the byte frequencies appearing in the anomalous training data. We demonstrate the effectiveness of these techniques in the evaluation section.

3.6   Z-String

Consider the string of bytes corresponding to the sorted, rank ordered byte frequency of a model. Figure 4 displays a view of this process. The frequency distribution of payloads of length 185 is plotted in the top graph. The lower graph represents the same information by the plot is reordered to the rank ordering of the distribution. Here, the first bar in the lower plot is the frequency of the most frequently appearing ASCII character. The second bar is likewise the second most frequent, and so on. This rank ordered distribution surprisingly follows a Zipf-like distribution (an exponential function or a power law where there are few values appearing many times, and a large number of values appearing very infrequently.)

The rank order distribution also defines what we call a "Z-string". The byte values ordered from most frequent to least frequent serves as a representative of the entire distribution. Figure 5 displays the Z-String for the plot in Figure 4. Notice that for this distribution there are only 83 distinct byte values appearing in the distribution. Thus, the Z-string has length 83.

Furthermore, as we shall see later, this rank ordered byte value distribution of the new payload deemed anomalous also may serve as a simple representation of a "new worm signature" that may be rapidly deployed to other sites to better detect the appearance of a new worm at those sites; if an anomalous payload appears at those sites and its rank ordered byte distribution matches a Z-string provided from another site, the evidence is very good that a worm has appeared. This distribution mechanism is part of an ongoing project called "Worminator" [11, 22] that implements a "collaborative security" system on the internet. A full treatment of this work is beyond the scope of this paper, but the interested reader is encouraged to visit http://worminator. cs.columbia.edu/ for details.

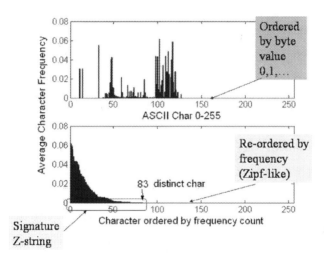

Fig. 4. Payload distribution appears in the top plot, re-ordered to the rank-ordered count frequency distribution in the bottom plot. Notice there are only 83 distinct characters used in the average payload for this service (port 80, http) for this length distribution of payloads (all payloads with length 185 bytes)

eto.c/a $\alpha\beta$ lsrw:imnTupgbhH|-
0AdxEPUCG3*vF@_fyR,~24RzMk9=();SDWIjL6B7Z8%?
Vq[]ONK+JX&

α : LF – Line feed β : CR – Carriage return

Fig. 5. The signature "Z-string" for the average payload displayed in Figure 4. "e" is the most frequent byte value, followed by "t" and so on. Notice how balanced characters appear adjacent to each other, for example "()" and "[]" since these tend to appear with equal frequency

4   Evaluation of the 1-Gram Models

We conducted two sets of experiments to test the effectiveness of the 1-gram models. The first experiment was applied to the 1999 DARPA IDS Data Set which is the most complete dataset with full payload publicly available for experimental use. The experiment here can be repeated by anyone using this data set to verify the results we report. The second experiment used the CUCS dataset which is the inbound network traffic to the web server of the computer science department of Columbia University. Unfortunately, this dataset cannot be shared with other researchers due to the privacy policies of the university. (In fact, the dataset has been erased to avoid a breach of anyone's privacy.)

4.1   Experiments with 1999 DARPA IDS Data Set

The 1999 DARPA IDS data set was collected at MIT Lincoln Labs to evaluate intrusion detection systems. All the network traffic including the entire payload of each packet was recorded in tcpdump format and provided for evaluation. In addition, there are also audit logs, daily file system dumps, and BSM (Solaris system call) logs. The data consists of three weeks of training data and two weeks of test data. In the training data there are two weeks of attack-free data and one week of data with labeled attacks.

This dataset has been used in many research efforts and results of tests against this data have been reported in many publications. Although there are problems due to the nature of the simulation environment that created the data, it still remains a useful set of data to compare techniques. The top results were reported by [10].

In our experiment on payload anomaly detection we only used the inside network traffic data which was captured between the router and the victims. Because most public applications on the Internet use TCP (web, email, telnet, and ftp), and to reduce the complexity of the experiment, we only examined the inbound TCP traffic to the ports 0-1023 of the hosts 172.016.xxx.xxx which contains most of the victims, and ports 0-1023 which covers the majority of the network services. For the DARPA 99 data, we conducted experiments using each packet as the data unit and each connection as the data unit. We used tcptrace to reconstruct the TCP connections from the network packets in the tcpdump files. We also experimented the idea of "truncated payload", both for each packet and each connection. For truncated packets, we tried the first N bytes and the tail N bytes separately, where N is a parameter. Using truncated payload saves considerable computation time and space. We report the results for each of these models.

We trained the payload distribution model on the DARPA dataset using week 1 (5 days, attack free) and week 3 (7 days, attack free), then evaluate the detector on weeks 4 and 5, which contain 201 instances of 58 different attacks, 177 of which are visible in the inside tcpdump data. Because we restrict the victims' IP and port range, there are 14 others we ignore in this test.

In this experiment, we focus on TCP traffic only, so the attacks using UDP, ICMP, ARP (address resolution protocol) and IP only cannot be detected. They include: smurf (ICMP echo-reply flood), ping-of-death (over-sized ping packets), UDPstorm, arppoison (corrupts ARP cache entries of the victim), selfping, ipsweep, teardrop (mis-fragmented UDP packets). Also because our payload model is computed from only the payload part of the network packet, those attacks that do not contain any payload are impossible to detect with the proposed anomaly detector. Thus, there are in total 97 attacks to be detected by our payload model in weeks 4 and 5 evaluation data.

After filtering there are in total 2,444,591 packets, and 49556 connections, with non-zero length payloads to evaluate. We build a model for each payload length observed in the training data for each port between 0-1023 and for every host machine. The smoothing factor is set to 0.001 which gives the best result for this dataset (see the discussion in Section 3.2). This helps avoid over-fitting and reduces the false positive rate. Also due to having an inadequate number of training examples in the DARPA99 data, we apply clustering to the models as described previously. Clustering the models of neighboring length bins means that similar models can provide more training data for a model whose training data is too sparse thus making it less sensitive and more accurate. But there is also the risk that the detection rate will be lower when the model allows more variance in the frequency distributions. Based on the models for each payload length, we did clustering with a threshold of 0.5, which means if the two neighboring model's byte frequency distribution has less than 0.5 Manhattan distance we merge their models. We experimented with both unclustered and clustered models. The results indicate that the clustered model is always better than the unclustered model. So in this paper, we will only show the results of the clustered models.

Different port traffic has different byte variability. For example, the payload to port 80 (HTTP requests) are usually less variable than that of port 25 (email). Hence, we set different thresholds for each port and check the detector's performance for each port. The attacks used in the evaluation may target one or more ports. Hence, we calibrate a distinct threshold for each port and generate the ROC curves including all appropriate attacks as ground truth. The packets with distance scores higher than the threshold are detected as anomalies.

Figure 6 shows the ROC curves for the four most commonly attacked ports: 21, 23, 25, and 80. For the other ports, eg. 53, 143, 513 etc., the DARPA99 data doesn't provide a large enough training and testing sample, so the results for those ports are not very meaningful.

For each port, we used five different data units, for both training and testing. The legend in the plots and their meaning are:

1) Per Packet Model, which uses the whole payload of each network packet;
2) First 100 Packet Model, which uses the first 100 bytes of each network packet;
3) Tail 100 Packet Model, which uses the last 100 bytes of each network packet;
4) Per Conn Model, which uses the whole payload of each connection;
5) Truncated Conn Model, which uses the first 1000 bytes of each connection.

From Figure 6 we can see that the payload-based model is very good at detecting the attacks to port 21 and port 80. For port 21, the attackers often first upload some malicious code onto the victim machine and then login to crash the machine or get root access, like casesen and sechole. The test data also includes attacks that upload/download illegal copies of software, like warezmaster and warezclient. These attacks were detected easily because of their content which were rarely seen executable code and quite different from the common files going through FTP. For port 80, the attacks are often malformed HTTP requests and are very different from normal requests. For instance, crashiis sends request "GET ../.."; apache2 sends request with a lot of repeated "User-Agent:sioux\r\n", etc. Using payload to detect these attacks is a more reliable means than detecting anomalous headers simply because their packet headers are all normal to establish a good connection to deliver their poison payload. Connection based detection has a better result than the packet based models for port 21 and 80. It's also important to notice that the truncated payload models achieve results nearly as good as the full payload models, but are much more efficient in time and space.

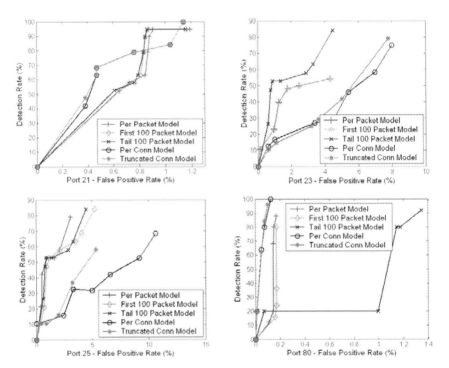

Fig. 6. ROC curves for ports 21, 23, 25, 80 for the five different models. Notice the x-axis scale is different for each plot and does not span to 100%, but limited to the worst false positive rate for each plot

For port 23 and port 25 the result is not as good as the models for port 21 and 80. That's because their content are quite free style and some of the attacks are well hidden. For example, the framespoofer attack is a fake email from the attacker that misdirects the victim to a malicious web site. The website URL looks entirely normal. Malformed email and telnet sessions are successfully detected, like the perl attack which runs some bad perl commands in telnet, and the sendmail attack which is a carefully crafted email message with an inappropriately large MIME header that exploits a buffer overflow error in some versions of the sendmail program. For these two ports, the packet-based models are better than the connection-based models. This is likely due to the fact that the actual exploit is buried within the larger context of the entire connection data, and its particular anomalous character distribution is swamped by the statistics of the other data portions of the connection. The per packet model detects this anomalous payload more easily.

There are many attacks that involve multiple steps aimed at multiple ports. If we can detect one of the steps at any one port, then the attack can be detected successfully. Thus we correlate the detector alerts from all the ports and plot the overall performance. When we restrict the false positive rate of each port (during calibration of the threshold) to be lower than 1%, we achieve about a 60% detection rate, which is pretty high for the DARPA99 dataset. The results for each model are displayed in the Table 1:

Table 1. Overall detection rate of each model when false positive rate lower than 1%

Per Packet Model	57/97 (58.8%)
First 100 Packet Model	55/97 (56.7%)
Tail 100 Packet Model	46/97 (47.4%)
Per Conn Model	55/97 (56.7%)
Truncated Conn Model	51/97 (52.6%)

Modeling the payload to detect anomalies is useful to protect servers against new attacks. Furthermore, careful inspection of the detected attacks in the tables and from other sources reveals that correlating this payload detector with other detectors increases the coverage of the attack space. There is large non-overlap between the attacks detected via payload and other systems that have reported results for this same dataset, for example PHAD [13]. This is obvious because the data sources and modeling used are totally different. PHAD models packet header data, whereas payload content is modeled here.

Our payload-based model has small memory consumption and is very efficient to compute. Table 2 displays the measurements of the speed and the resulting number of centroids for each of the models for both cases of unclustered and clustered. The results were derived from measuring PAYL on a 3GHz P4 Linux machine with 2G memory using non-optimized Java code. These results do not indicate how well a professionally engineered system may behave (re-engineering in C probably would gain a factor of 6 or more in speed). Rather, these results are provided to show the relative efficiency among the alternative modeling methods. The training and test time reported in the table is seconds per 100Mof data, which includes the I/O time. The number of centroids computed after training represents an approximation of the total amount of memory consumed by each model. Notice that each centroid has fixed size: two 256-element double arrays, one for storing averages and the other for storing the standard deviation of the 256 ASCII bytes. A re-engineered version of PAYL would not consume as much space as does a Java byte stream object. From the table we can see that clustering reduces the number of centroids, and total consumed memory by about a factor from 2 to 16 with little or no hit in computational performance. Combining Figure 6, Table 1 and Table 2, users can choose the proper model for their application according to their environment and performance requirements.

Table 2. Speed and Memory measurements of each model. The training and testing time is in units of seconds per 100M data, including the I/O time. The memory comsuption is measured in the number of centroids that were kept after clustering or learning

Unclustered /Clustered	Per Packet	First 100	Tail 100	Per Conn.	Trunc Conn.
Train time(uncl)	26.1	21.8	21.8	8.6	4.4
Test time(uncl)	16.1	9.4	9.4	9.6	1.6
No. centroid(uncl)	11583	11583	11583	16326	16326
Train tme(clust)	26.2	22.0	26.2	8.8	4.6
Test time(clust)	16.1	9.4	9.4	9.6	1.6
No. centroid(clust)	4065	7218	6126	2219	1065

This result is surprisingly good for such a simple modeling technique. Most importantly, this anomaly detector can easily augment existing detection systems. It is not intended as a stand alone detection system but a component in a larger system aiming for defense in depth. Hence, the detector would provide additional and useful alert information to correlate with other detectors that in combination may generate an alarm and initiate a mitigation process.   The DARPA 99 dataset was used here so that others can verify our results. However, we also performed experiments on a live stream that we describe next.

4.2   Experiments with CUCS Dataset

The CUCS dataset denotes Columbia University CS web server dataset, which are two traces of incoming traffic with full payload to the CS department web server (www.cs.columbia.edu). The two traces were collected separately, one in August 2003 for 45 hours with a size of about 2GB, and one in September 2003 for 24 hours with size 1GB. We denote the first one as A, the second one as B, and their union as AB. Because we did not know whether this dataset is attack-free or not, this experiment represents an unlabeled dataset that provides the means of testing and evaluating the unsupervised training of the models.

Table 3. Unsupervised learning result on CUCS dataset

Train	Test	Anomaly #	CR-II	Buffer
A	A	28(0.0084%)	----	----
A	B	2601(1.3%)	Yes	Yes
B	A	686(0.21%)	----	----
B	B	184(0.092%)	Yes	Yes
AB	AB	211(0.039%)	Yes	Yes

First we display the result of unsupervised learning in Table 3. We used an unclustered single-length model since the number of training examples is sufficient to adequately model normal traffic. Also the smoothing factor is set to 0.001 and 256 as the anomaly threshold. Dataset A has 331,236 non-zero payload packets, and B has

199,881. The third column shows the number and percentage of packets that are deemed anomalous packets. Surprisingly, when we manually checked the anomalous packets we found Code Red II attacks and extremely long query string buffer overflow attacks in dataset B. ("yes" means the attack is successfully detected.)

There is a high anomaly rate when we train on A and test on B; this is because there are many pdf file-uploads in B that did not occur in A. (Notice the dates. A was captured during the summer; B was captured later during student application time.) Because pdf files are encoded with many nonprintable characters, these packets are very different from other normal HTTP request packets. For the rest of those detected packets, more than 95% are truly anomalous. They include malformed HTTP headers like "~~~~~~:~~~~~~~~~", a string with all capital letter's, "Weferer" replacing the standard Referer tag (apparently a privacy feature of a COTS product), extremely long and weird parameters for "range", javascripts embedded html files sent to the CS server, etc. These requests might do no harm to the server, but they are truly unusual and should be filtered or redirected to avoid a possible attack. They do provide important information as well to other detectors that may deem their connections anomalous for other reasons.

Figure 7 displays a plot of the distance values of the normal packets against the attacks. For illustrative purposes, we selected some packets of the Code Red II attack and the buffer overflow attack, which has length 1460 and were detected to be anomalous, and compare these with the distances of the normal packets of the same length. The training and test data both use data set A for these plots.

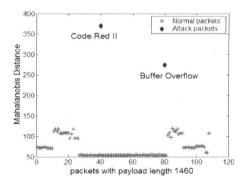

Fig. 7. The computed Mahalanobis distance of the normal and attack packets

We also tested some other packets collected from online sources of virus's as they appeared in the wild and within the DARPA 99 data set. These were tested against the CUCS dataset. They include Code Red I & II, Nimbda, crashiis, back, apache2 etc. All of these tcpdump packets containing virus's were successfully caught by our model.

For illustrative purposes, we also display in Table 4 the Z-strings of the Code Red II and, the buffer overflow attacks and the centroid Z-string to demonstrate how different each appears from the norm. Notice these are the Z-strings for one of the single malicious packets we captured at packet payload length 1460. Because the full Z-string is too long (more than 200 characters) and contains many nonprintable characters, we only display the first 20 characters' ASCII value in decimal for illustration. The buffer overflow packet only has 4 different characters, so its Z-string has length 4 and are all displayed in the table.

Table 4. Illustrations of the partial Z-strings. The characters are shown in ASCII

Code Red II (first 20 characters)									
88	0	255	117	48	85	116	37	232	100
100	106	69	133	137	80	254	1	56	51
Buffer Overflow (all)									
65	37	48	68						
Centroid (first 20 characters)									
48	73	146	36	32	46	61	113	44	110
59	70	45	56	50	97	110	115	51	53

5 Conclusion

The experimental results indicate that the method is effective at detecting attacks. In the 1999 DARPA IDS dataset, the best trained model for TCP traffic detected 57 attacks out of 97 with every port's false positive rate lower than 1%. For port 80, it achieves almost 100% detection rate with around 0.1% false positive rate. It also successfully detected the Code Red II and a buffer overflow attack from the unlabeled CUCS dataset. The payload model is very simple, state-free, and quick to compute in time that is linear in the payload length. It also has the advantage of being implemented as an incremental, unsupervised learning method. The payload anomaly detector is intended to be correlated with other detectors to mitigate against false alarms, and to increase the coverage of attacks that may be detected. The experiment also demonstrated that clustering of centroids from neighboring length bins dramatically reduce memory consumption up to a factor of 16.

The Z-string derived from the byte distributions can be used as a "signature" to characterize payloads. Each such string is at most 256 characters, and can be readily stored and communicated rapidly among sites in a real-time distributed detection system as "confirmatory" evidence of a zero-day attack. This can be accomplished faster than is otherwise possible by observing large bursts in probing activity among a large segment of the internet. This approach may also have great value in detecting slow and stealthy worm propagations that may avoid activities of a bursty nature!

In our future work, we plan to evaluate the technique in live environments, implement and measure the costs and speed of the Z-string distribution mechanism and most interestingly whether higher order n-grams provide added value or not in modeling payload. Furthermore, we plan to evaluate the opportunity or difficulty for mimicry attack by comparing the payload distributions across different sites. If, as we suspect, each site's payload distributions are consistently different (in a statistical sense), then the anomaly detection approach proposed here, based upon site-specific payload models, will provide protection for all sites.

Acknowledgments

We'd like to thank Nick Edwards, Phil Gross, Janak J. Parekh, Shlomo Hershkop, Morris Pearl, Wei-Jen Li for help on collecting data and the experimental set up, and for useful discussions and helpful comments on this paper.

References

1. D. Armstrong, S. Carter, G. Frazier, T. Frazier. A Controller-Based Autonomic Defense System. *Proc.* of DISCEX, 2003.
2. M. Damashek. Gauging similarity with n-grams: language independent categorization of text. *Science*, 267(5199):843--848, 1995.
3. S. Forrest, S. A. Hofmeyr, A. Somayaji, and T. A. Longstaff, A Sense of self for Unix Processes. *Proc. of IEEE Symposium on Computer Security and Privacy*, 1996.
4. A. K. Ghosh, A. Schwartzbard, A study in Using Neural Networks for Anomaly and Misuse Detection, *Proc. 8th USENIX Security Symposium* 1999.
5. J. Hoagland, SPADE, Silican Defense, http://www.silicondefense.com/software/spice, 2000.
6. H. S. Javits and A. Valdes. The NIDES statistical component: Description and justification. *Technical report, SRI International, Computer Science Laboratory*, 1993.
7. D. E. Knuth, the Art of Computer Programming, Vol 1 Fundamental Algorithms. *Addison Wesley*, 2nd edition, 1973.
8. C. Kruegel, T. Toth and E. Kirda, Service Specific Anomaly Detection for Network Intrusion Detection. In *Symposium on Applied Computing (SAC)*, Spain, March 2002.
9. W. Lee and S. Stolfo, A Framework for Constructing Features and Models for Intrusion Detection Systems. *ACM Transactions on Information and System Security*, 3(4), November 2000.
10. R. Lippmann, et al. The 1999 DARPA Off-Line Intrusion Detection Evaluation, *Computer Networks* 34(4) 579-595, 2000.
11. M. Locasto, J. Parekh, S. Stolfo, A. Keromytis, T. Malkin and V. Misra, Collaborative Distributed Intrusion Detection, *Columbia University Tech Report, CUCS-012-04*, 2004.
12. M. Mahoney. Network Traffic Anomaly Detection Based on Packet Bytes. *Proc. ACM-SAC* 2003.
13. M. Mahoney, P. K. Chan, Learning Nonstationary Models of Normal Network Traffic for Detecting Novel Attacks, *Proc. SIGKDD* 2002, 376-385.
14. M. Mahoney, P. K. Chan, Learning Models of Network Traffic for Detecting Novel Attacks, *Florida Tech, Technical report 2002-08*, http://cs.fit.edu/~tr.
15. M. Mahoney, P. K. Chan: An Analysis of the 1999 DARPA/Lincoln Laboratory Evaluation Data for Network Anomaly Detection. *RAID 2003*: 220-237.
16. D. Moore, C. Shannon, G. Voelker and S. Savage, Internet Quarantine: Requirements for Containing Selp-Propagating Code, *Proc. Infocom* 2003.
17. V. Paxson, Bro: A system for detecting network intruders in real-time, *USENIX Security Symposium*, 1998.
18. P. Porras and P. Neumann, EMERALD: Event Monitoring Enabled Responses to Anomalous Live Disturbances, *National Information Systems Security Conference*, 1997.
19. S. Robertson, E. Siegel, M. Miller, and S. Stolfo, Surveillance Detection in High Bandwidth Environments, *In Proceedings of the 2003 DARPA DISCEX III Conference*, 2003.

20. M. Roesch, Snort: Lightweight intrusion detection for networks, *USENIX LISA Conference*, 1999.
21. S. Staniford, V. Paxson, and N. Weaver, How to Own the Internet in Your Spare Time, *Proceedings of the 11th USENIX Security Symposium,* 2002.
22. S. Stolfo, Worm and Attack Early Warning: Piercing Stealthy Reconnaissance, *IEEE Privacy and Security,* May/June, 2004 (to appear).
23. C. Taylor and J. Alves-Foss. NATE – Network Analysis of Anomalous Traffic Events, A Low-Cost approach, *New Security Paradigms Workshop,* 2001.
24. G. Vigna and R. Kemmerer, NetSTAT: A Network-based intrusion detection approach, *Computer Security Application Conference,* 1998.
25. T. Lane and C. E. Broadley, Approaches to online learning and concept drift for user identification in computer security. 4th International Conference on Knowledge Discovery and Data Mining, 1998.

Anomaly Detection Using Layered Networks Based on Eigen Co-occurrence Matrix

Mizuki Oka[1], Yoshihiro Oyama[2,5], Hirotake Abe[3], and Kazuhiko Kato[4,5]

[1] Master's Program in Science and Engineering, University of Tsukuba
mizuki@osss.is.tsukuba.ac.jp
[2] Graduate School of Information Science and Technology, University of Tokyo
oyama@yl.is.s.u-tokyo.ac.jp
[3] Doctoral Program in Engineering, University of Tsukuba
habe@osss.is.tsukuba.ac.jp
[4] Graduate School of Systems and Information Engineering, University of Tsukuba
kato@is.tsukuba.ac.jp
[5] Japan Science and Technology Agency (JST) CREST

Abstract. Anomaly detection is a promising approach to detecting intruders masquerading as valid users (called masqueraders). It creates a user profile and labels any behavior that deviates from the profile as anomalous. In anomaly detection, a challenging task is modeling a user's dynamic behavior based on sequential data collected from computer systems. In this paper, we propose a novel method, called Eigen co-occurrence matrix (ECM), that models sequences such as UNIX commands and extracts their principal features. We applied the ECM method to a masquerade detection experiment with data from Schonlau et al. We report the results and compare them with results obtained from several conventional methods.

Keywords: Anomaly detection, User behavior, Co-occurrence matrix, PCA, Layered networks

1 Introduction

Detecting the presence of an intruder masquerading as a valid user is becoming a critical issue as security incidents become more common and more serious. Anomaly detection is a promising approach to detecting such intruders (masqueraders). It first creates a *profile* defining a normal user's behavior. It then measures the *similarity* of a current behavior with the created profile and notes any behavior that deviates from the profile. Various approaches for anomaly detection differ in how they create *profiles* and how they define *similarity*.

In most masquerade detection methods, a profile is created by modeling sequential data, such as the time of login, physical location of login, duration of user session, programs executed, names of files accessed, and user commands issued [1]. One of the challenging tasks in detecting masqueraders is to accurately model user behavior based on such sequential data. This is challenging because the nature of a user's behavior is dynamic and difficult to capture completely. In this paper, we propose a new method, called Eigen co-occurrence matrix (ECM), designed to model such dynamic user behavior.

E. Jonsson et al. (Eds.): RAID 2004, LNCS 3224, pp. 223–237, 2004.

One of the approaches to modeling user behavior is to convert a sequence of data into a *feature vector* by accumulating measures of either unary events (histogram) or n-connected events (n-grams) [2–4]. However, the former approach only considers the number of occurrences of observed events within a sequence, and thus sequential information will not be included in the resulting model. The latter approach considers n-connected neighboring events within a sequence. Neither of them considers any correlation between events that are not adjacent to each other.

Other approaches to modeling user behavior are based on converting a sequence into a network model. Such approaches include those based on an automaton [5–8], a Bayesian network [9], and an Hidden Markov Model (HMM) [10,11].

The nodes and arcs in an automaton can remember short- and long-range transition relations between events by constructing rules within a sequence of events. To construct an automaton, we thus require well-defined rules that can be transformed to a network. However, it is difficult to construct an automaton based on a set of user-generated sequences with various contexts, which does not have such well-defined rules. When an automaton can indeed be obtained, it is computationally expensive to learn on the automaton when a new sequence is added.

A node in a Bayesian network associates probabilities of the node being in a specific state given the states of its parents. The parent-child relationship between nodes in a Bayesian network indicates the direction of causality between the corresponding variables. That is, the variable represented by the child node is causally dependent on those represented by its parents. The topology of a Bayesian network must be predefined, however, and thus, the capability for modeling a sequence is dependent on the predefined topology.

An HMM can model a sequence by defining a network model that usually has a feed-forward characteristic. The network model is created by learning both the probability of each event emerging from each node and the probability of each transition between nodes by using a set of observed sequences. However, it is tough to build an adequate topology for an HMM by using ad hoc sequences generated by a user. As a result, the performance of a system based on an HMM varies depending on the topology and the parameter settings.

We argue that the dynamic behavior of a user appearing in a sequence can be captured by correlating not only connected events but also events that are not adjacent to each other while appearing within a certain distance (*non-connected* events). Based on this assumption, to model user behavior, the ECM method creates a so-called *co-occurrence matrix* by correlating an event in a sequence with any following events that appear within a certain distance. The ECM method then creates so-called *Eigen co-occurrence matrices*. The ECM method is inspired by the Eigenface technique, which is used to recognize humans facial images. In the Eigenface technique, the main idea is to decompose a facial image into a small set of characteristic feature images called eigenfaces, which may be thought of as the principal components of the original images. These eigenfaces are the orthogonal vectors of a linear space. A new facial image is then reconstructed by projecting onto the obtained space. In the ECM method, we consider the co-occurrence matrix and the Eigen co-occurrence matrices analogous to a facial image and the corresponding eigenfaces, respectively. The Eigen co-occurrence matrices are characteristic feature sequences, and the characteristic features of a new sequence converted to a co-occurrence matrix are obtained by projecting it onto the space defined by the Eigen co-occurrence matrices.

In addition, the ECM method constructs the extracted features as a *layered* network. The distinct principal features of a co-occurrence matrix are presented as layers. The layered network enables us to perform detailed analysis of the extracted principal features of a sequence.

In summary, the ECM method has three main components: (1) modeling of the dynamic features of a sequence; (2) extraction of the principal features of the resulting model; and (3) automatic construction of a layered network from the extracted principal features.

The reminder of the paper is organized as follows. In Section 2, the ECM method is described in detail by using an example set of UNIX commands. Section 3 applies the ECM method to detect anomalous users in a dataset, describes our experimental results, and compares them with results obtained from several conventional methods. Section 4 analyzes the computational cost involved in the ECM method. Section 5 discusses possible detection improvements in using the ECM method. Section 6 gives our conclusions and describes our future work.

2   The Eigen Co-occurrence Matrix (ECM) Method

The purpose of this study is to distinguish malicious users from normal users. To do so, we first need to model a sequence of user commands and then apply a pattern classifica-

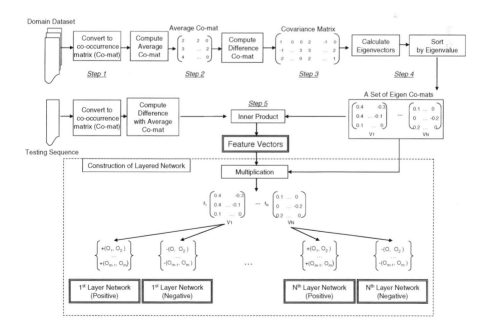

Fig. 1. Overall procedure of the ECM method

Table 1. Notation and terminology

l	length of an observation sequence
s	maximum distance over which correlations between events are considered (scope size)
O	set of observation events
m	number of events in O
D	set of sample observation sequences (*domain* dataset)
n	number of sample sequences in D
M	a co-occurrence matrix
V_i	ith Eigen co-occurrence matrix
F	a feature vector
f_i	ith component of F
N	dimension size of F
X_i	a matrix for producing ith *positive* network layer
Y_i	a matrix for producing ith *negative* network layer
h	threshold of elements in X_i (or Y_i) to construct a network layer
R	number of elements in $f_i V_i$ for constructing the ith network layer
r	number of nodes in a subnetwork

$$\overrightarrow{time}$$

```
User1    cd   ls less  ls  less cd  ls cd cd   ls
User2  emacs gcc gdb emacs  ls  gcc gdb ls ls emacs
User3  mkdir cp  cd   ls    cp   ls  cp cp cp   cp
```

Fig. 2. Example dataset of UNIX commands

tion method. To accurately classify a sequence as normal or malicious, it is necessary to extract its significant characteristics (*principal features*) and, if necessary, convert the extracted features into a form suitable for detailed analysis. In this section, we explain how the ECM method models a sequence, how it obtains the principal features, and how it constructs a model for detailed analysis, namely, a network model. The overall procedure of the ECM method is illustrated in Figure 1 and the notation and terminology used in the ECM method are listed in Table 1.

In the following sections, we explain each procedure in the ECM method by using a simple example of UNIX command sequences. Figure 2 shows an example dataset of UNIX commands for three users, designated as User1, User2, and User3. Each user issued ten UNIX commands, which are shown truncated (without their arguments) in the interest of simplicity.

2.1 Modeling a Sequence

The ECM method models a sequence by correlating an event with any following events that appear within a certain distance. The strength of the correlation between two events is defined by (a) the distance between events and (b) the frequency of their occurrence. In other words, when the distance between two events is short, or when they appear more frequently, their correlation becomes stronger. To model such strength of corre-

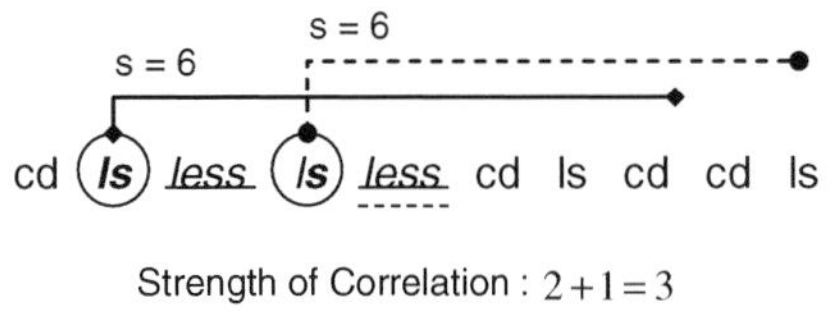

Strength of Correlation : $2 + 1 = 3$

Fig. 3. Correlation between *ls* and *less* for User1

	cd	ls	less	emacs	gcc	gdb	mkdir	cp
cd	4	7	2	0	0	0	0	0
ls	7	5	3	0	0	0	0	0
less	6	4	1	0	0	0	0	0
emacs	0	0	0	0	0	0	0	0
gcc	0	0	0	0	0	0	0	0
gdb	0	0	0	0	0	0	0	0
mkdir	0	0	0	0	0	0	0	0
cp	0	0	0	0	0	0	0	0

Fig. 4. Co-occurrence matrix of User1

lation between events, we construct a so-called *co-occurrence matrix* by counting the occurrence of every event pair within a certain distance (*scope size*). Thus, the correlations of both connected and non-connected events are captured for every event pair and subsequently represented in the matrix.

We define M_X as the co-occurrence matrix of a sequence $X (= x_1, x_2, x_3, \ldots, x_l)$ with length l. We define the unique events appearing in the sequence as a set of observation events, denoted as $O (= o_1, o_2, o_3, \ldots, o_m)$. In the example dataset of Figure 2, O is cd ls less emacs gcc gdb mkdir cp. The correlation between the ith and jth events in M_X, o_i and o_j, is computed by counting the number of occurrences of the event-pair within a scope size of s. Here, we did not change the strength of the correlations between events depending on their distance, but instead used a constant value 1 for simplicity. Doing this for every event pair generates a matrix representing all of the respective occurrences. Each element in the matrix represents the perceived strength of correlation between two events. For example, as illustrated in Figure 3, the events *ls* and *less* are correlated with a strength of three when s and l are defined as 6 and 10, respectively. Figure 4 shows the matrix generated from the sequence of User1.

2.2 Extracting the Principal Features

As explained earlier, to distinguish a malicious user from a normal user, it is necessary to introduce a pattern classification method. Measuring the distance between co-occurrence matrices is considered the simplest pattern classification method. A co-occurrence matrix is highly dimensional, however, and to make an accurate comparison, it is necessary to extract the matrix's principal features.

The ECM method uses principal component analysis (PCA) to extract the principal features, so-called *feature vectors*. PCA transforms a number of correlated variables into a smaller number of uncorrelated variables called principal components. It can thus reduce the dimensionality of the dataset while retaining most of the original variability within the data. The process for obtaining a feature vector is divided into the following five steps:

(Step 1) Take a domain dataset and convert its sequences to co-occurrence matrices: As a first step (*Step 1* in in Figure 1), we take a set of sample sequences, which we call a *domain* dataset and denote as D, and convert the sequences into corresponding co-occurrence matrices, $M_1, M_2, M_3, ..., M_n$, where n is the number of sample observation sequences and M is an $m \times m$ matrix (m: number of observation events). In the current example, the domain dataset consists of all the three users' sequences ($n = 3$), and M is an 8×8 matrix ($m = 8$).

(Step 2) Subtract the mean: We then take the set of co-occurrence matrices $M_1, M_2, M_3, ..., M_n$ and compute its mean co-occurrence matrix M_{mean} (*Step 2* in Figure 1). Here we introduce two different ways to compute M_{mean}. The first way is to compute it normally:

$$M_{mean} = \frac{1}{n} \sum_{k=1}^{n} M_k. \tag{1}$$

The second way is to compute M_{mean} by taking into account the fact that a co-occurrence matrix can be sparse. Let $m_{mean}(i, j)$ be the ith-row jth-column element of the mean co-occurrence matrix M_{mean}. We then compute $m_{mean}(i, j)$ by taking the sum of all the values in $m_1(i, j), m_2(i, j), m_3(i, j), \ldots, m_n(i, j)$ and dividing by the number of those values that are non-zero. In summary,

$$m_{mean}(i, j) = \frac{1}{K(i, j)} \sum_{k=1}^{n} m_k(i, j), \tag{2}$$

where $m_k(i, j)$ is the ith-row jth-column element of the kth co-occurrence matrix, and $K(i, j)$ and $\delta[x]$ are defined as

$$K(i, j) = \sum_{k=1}^{n} \delta[m_k(i, j)] \tag{3}$$

and

$$\delta[x] = \begin{cases} 1 & \text{if } x \text{ is not equal to zero} \\ 0 & \text{otherwise} \end{cases}, \tag{4}$$

respectively. The mean co-occurrence matrix M_{mean} is then subtracted from each event co-occurrence matrix,

$$A_k = M_k - M_{mean} \qquad \text{for } k = 1, 2, 3, \ldots, n, \tag{5}$$

where A_k is the kth co-occurrence matrix with the mean subtracted.

(Step 3) Calculate the covariance matrix: We then construct the covariance matrix as

$$P = \sum_{k=1}^{n} \hat{A}_k \hat{A}_k^{T}, \tag{6}$$

where $\hat{A}_k$ is created by taking each row in A_k and concatenating its elements into a single vector *(Step 3* in Figure 1). The dimension of $\hat{A}_k$ is $1 \times m^2$. In the example dataset, the dimension of $\hat{A}_k$ is 1×64.

The components of P, denoted by p_{ij}, represent the correlations between two event pairs q_i and q_j, such as the event pairs *(ls less)* and *(ls cd)* in the example dataset. An event pair q_i $(= o_x, o_y)$ can be obtained by

$$\begin{aligned} x &= \gamma[(i-1)/m] + 1 \\ y &= i - \gamma[(i-1)/m] \times m, \end{aligned} \tag{7}$$

where $\gamma[z]$ is the integer part of the value. The variance of a component indicates the spread of the component values around its mean value. If two components q_i and q_j are uncorrelated, their variance is zero. By definition, the covariance matrix is always symmetric.

(Step 4) Calculate the eigenvectors and eigenvalues of the covariance matrix: Since the covariance matrix P is symmetric (its dimension is $m^2 \times m^2$, or 64×64 in the example dataset), we can calculate an orthogonal basis by finding its eigenvalues and eigenvectors *(Step 4* in Figure 1). The eigenvector with the highest eigenvalue is the first principal component (the most characteristic feature) since it implies the highest variance, while the eigenvector with the second highest eigenvalue is the second principal component (the second most characteristic feature), and so forth. By ranking the eigenvectors in order of descending eigenvalues, namely $(v_1, v_2, ..., v_{m^2})$, we can create an ordered orthogonal basis according to significance. Since the eigenvectors belong to the same vector space as the co-occurrence matrices, v_i can be converted to an $m \times m$ matrix (8×8 in the example dataset). We call such a matrix an *Eigen co-occurrence matrix* and denote it as V_i.

Instead of using all the eigenvectors, we may represent a co-occurrence matrix by choosing N of the m^2 eigenvectors. This compresses the original co-occurrence matrix and simplifies its representation without losing much information. We define these N eigenvectors as the *co-occurrence matrix space*. Obviously, the larger N is, the higher the contribution rate of all the eigenvectors becomes. The contribution rate is defined as

$$\text{contribution rate} = \frac{\sum_{i=1}^{N} \lambda_i}{\sum_{i=1}^{m^2} \lambda_i}, \tag{8}$$

where λ_i denotes the ith largest eigenvalue.

(Step 5) Obtain a feature vector: We can obtain the *feature vector* of any co-occurrence matrix, M, by projecting it onto the defined co-occurrence matrix space *(Step 5* in Figure

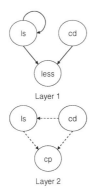

Fig. 5. Positive layered network for User1

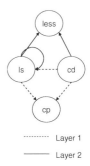

Fig. 6. Combined positive layered network of User1. The solid lines and dotted lines correspond to layer 1 and 2, respectively

1). The feature vector $F^T = [f_1, f_2, f_3, ..., f_N]$ of M is obtained by the dot product of vectors v_i and $\hat{A}$, where f_i is defined as

$$f_i = v_i^T \hat{A} \qquad \text{for } i = 1, 2, 3, ..., N \qquad (9)$$

The Components $f_1, f_2, f_3, ..., f_N$ of F are the coordinates within the co-occurrence matrix space. Each component represents the contribution of each respective Eigen co-occurrence matrix. Any input sequence can be compressed from m^2 to N while maintaining a high level of variance.

2.3 Constructing a Layered Network

Once a feature vector F is obtained from a co-occurrence matrix, the ECM method converts it to a so-called *layered network* (shown as *construction of layered network* in Figure 1) . The ith layer of a network is constructed from the corresponding ith Eigen co-occurrence matrix V_i multiplied by the ith coordinate f_i of F. In other words, the ith *layer* of the network represents the ith principal feature of the original co-occurrence matrix.

The layered network can be obtained from equation (9). Recall that this equation for obtaining a component f_i (for $i = 1, 2, 3, ..., N$) of a feature vector is

$$f_i = v_i^T \hat{A} \qquad \text{for } i = 1, 2, 3, ..., N,$$

where $\hat{A}$ is the vector representation of $A = (M - M_{mean})$. We can obtain an approximation to the original co-occurrence matrix M' with the mean M_{mean} subtracted from the original co-occurrence matrix M by isolating $\hat{A}$ from equation (9). In summary,

$$(M - M_{mean}) \simeq \sum_{i=1}^{N} f_i V_i = M', \qquad (10)$$

where $f_i V_i$ can be considered an adjacency matrix labeled by the set of observation events O. The ith network layer can be constructed by connecting the elements in the obtained matrix M'.

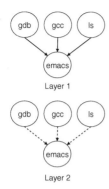

Layer 2

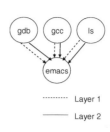

Fig. 8. Combined negative layered network for User1. The solid and dotted lines correspond to layers 1 and 2, respectively

Fig. 7. Negative layered network for User1

Each layer of the network constructed by $f_i V_i$ (for $i = 1, 2, 3, \ldots, N$) provides the distinct characteristic patterns observed in the approximated co-occurrence matrix. We can also express such characteristics *in relation to the average co-occurrence matrix* by separating it as

$$\sum_{i=1}^{N} f_i V_i = \sum_{i=1}^{N} (X_i + Y_i) = \sum_{i=1}^{N} X_i + \sum_{i=1}^{N} Y_i \qquad (11)$$

where X_i (or Y_i) denotes an adjacency matrix whose elements are determined by the corresponding positive (or negative) elements in $f_i V_i$. The matrix X_i (or Y_i) represents the principal characteristic of M' in terms of frequency (or rarity) in relation to the average co-occurrence matrix. We call the network obtained from X_i (or Y_i) a *positive* (or *negative*) network.

There may be elements in X_i (or Y_i) that are too small to serve as principal characteristics of M'. Thus, instead of using all the elements of X_i (or Y_i), we set a threshold h and choose elements that are larger (or smaller) than h (or $-h$) in order to construct the ith layer of the *positive* (or *negative*) network. Assigning a higher value to h reduces the number of nodes in the network and consequently creates a network with a different topology.

Figure 5 shows the first and second layers of the positive networks, obtained for User1 in the example dataset with h assigned to 0. We can combine these two layers to describe User1's overall patterns of principal frequent commands. The combined network is depicted in Figure 6, which indicates strong relations between the commands ls, cd, and less. This matches our human perception of the command sequence of User1 (i.e., cd ls less ls less cd ls cd cd ls).

Similarly, the first and second layers of the negative network and the combined network obtained for User1 are shown in Figures 7 and 8, respectively. These negative networks indicate the rarely observed command patterns in the command sequence of User1 relative to the average observed command patterns. We can observe strong correlations in the commands gdb, gcc, ls, and emacs. These relations did not appear in the command sequence.

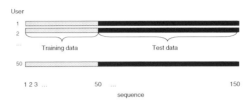

Fig. 9. Composition of the experimental dataset

3   Application of the ECM Method

3.1   Overview of the Experimental Data

We applied the ECM method to a dataset for masquerade detection provided by Schonlau et al. [12]. The dataset consists of 50 users' commands entered at a UNIX prompt, with 15,000 commands recorded for each user. Due to privacy arguments, the dataset includes no reporting of flags, aliases, arguments, or shell grammar. The users are designated as User 1, User 2, and so on. The first 5000 commands are entered by the legitimate user, and the masquerading commands are inserted in the remaining 10,000 commands. All the user sequences were decomposed into a sequence length of 100 commands ($l = 100$). Figure 9 illustrates the composition of the dataset.

3.2   Creation of a User Profiles (Offline)

For each user, we created a profile representing his normal behavior. Each decomposed sequence was converted into a co-occurrence matrix with a scope size of six ($s = 6$). We did not change the strength of the correlations between events on depending on their distance but instead used a constant value 1 for simplicity. We took all of the users' training dataset, consisting of 2500 (50 sequences × 50 users) decomposed sequences, and defined it as the *domain* dataset ($n = 2500$). The set of observation events ($O = o_1, o_2, o_3, \ldots, o_m$) was determined by the unique events appearing in the *domain* dataset, which accounted for 635 commands ($m = 635$). We took 50 Eigen co-occurrence matrices ($N = 50$), whose contribution rate was approximately 90%, and defined this as the co-occurrence matrix space.

The profile of a user was created by using his training dataset. We first converted all of his training sequences to co-occurrence matrices and obtained the corresponding feature vectors by projecting them onto the defined co-occurrence matrix space. Each feature vector was then used to reconstruct an approximated original co-occurrence matrix. This co-occurrence matrix was finally converted into a *positive* (or *negative*) layered network with a threshold of 0 ($h = 0$). We only used the *positive* layered network to define each user's profile.

3.3   Recognition of Anomalous Sequences (Online)

When a sequence seq_i of the User u was to be tested, we followed this procedure:

1. Construct a co-occurrence matrix from seq_i.
2. Project the obtained co-occurrence matrix on the co-occurrence matrix space and obtain its feature vector.

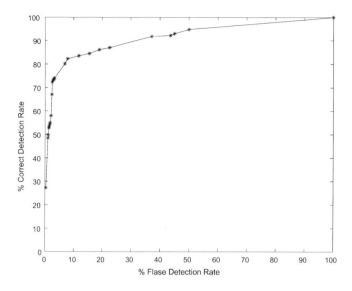

Fig. 10. ROC curves for the ECM method

3. Multiply the feature vector by the Eigen co-occurrence matrices to obtain a layered network.
4. Compare the layered network with the profile of User u.
5. Classify the testing sequence as anomalous or normal based on a threshold ϵ_u.

To classify a testing sequence seq_i as anomalous or normal, we computed the similarity between each network layer of seq_i and each networks layer in the user profile, where we chose the largest value as the similarity. If the computed similarity of seq_i was under a threshold ϵ_u for the User u, then the testing sequence was classified as anomalous; otherwise, it was classified as normal. We defined the similarity between the networks of two sequences, seq_i and seq_j, as,

$$Sim(seq_i, seq_j) = \sum_{k=1}^{N} \Gamma(T_k(i), T_k(j)), \qquad (12)$$

where $T_k(i)$ is the obtained network at the kth layer of seq_i and $\Gamma(T_k(i), T_k(j))$ is the number of subnetworks that $T_k(i)$ and $T_k(j)$ have in common. We extracted the 30 largest values to form a network ($R = 30$) and employed 3 connected nodes as the unit of a subnetwork ($r = 3$).

3.4 Results

The results illustrate the trade-off between correct detection (true positives) and false detection (false positives). A receiver operation characteristic curve (ROC curve) is often used to represent this trade-off. The percentages of true positives and false positives are shown on the y-axis and x-axis of the ROC curve, respectively. Any increase in

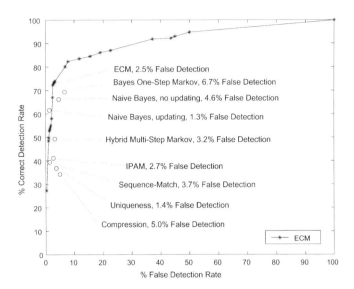

Fig. 11. ROC curve for the ECM method with the best results from other methods shown for comparison

the true positive rate will be accompanied by an increase in the false positive rate. The closer the curve follows the left-hand border and then the top border of the ROC space, the more accurate the results are, since they indicate high true positive rates and, correspondingly, low false positive rates.

Figure 10 shows the resulting ROC curve obtained from our experiment with the ECM method. We have plotted different correct detection rates and false detection rates by changing α in the expression:

$$\epsilon_u^{opt} + \alpha,$$

where ϵ_u^{opt} is the optimal threshold for User u. The optimal threshold ϵ_u^{opt} is defined by finding the largest correct detection rate with a false detection rate of less than $\beta\%$. We set β to 20 in this experiment and used the same values of ϵ_u throughout all the test sequences (no updating). As a result, the ECM method achieved a 72.3% correct detection rate with a 2.5% false detection rate.

Schonlau et al. [12] and Maxion et al. [13] have applied a number of masquerade detection techniques, including Bayes 1-Step Markov, Hybrid Multi-Step Markov, IPAM, Uniqueness, Sequence-Match, Compression, and Naive Bayes, to the same dataset used in this study. (See refs. [12] and [13] for detailed explanations of each technique.) Their results are shown in Figure 11 along with our results from the ECM method. As one can be seen from the data, the ECM method achieved one of the best scores among the various approaches.

4   Computational Cost

The ECM method has two computational phases, the offline and online phases. For the offline phase, the required computation processes are the following: transforming a set

Table 2. Changeable parameters in obtaining a feature vector

O	set of observation events.
l	length of sequence to be tested.
s	scope size
D	domain dataset.

Table 3. Changeable parameters in obtaining a layer of network

h	threshold of elements in X_i (or Y_i) for constructing a network.
R	number of elements in f_iV_i for constructing the ith network layer
r	number of nodes in a subnetwork.

training sequences of length w to co-occurrence matrices, calculating the N eigenvectors of the covariance matrix, projecting co-occurrence matrices onto the co-occurrence matrix space to obtain feature vectors, constructing layered networks with R nodes in each layer, and generating a lookup table containing subnetworks with r connected nodes.

We used the Linux operating system (RedHat 9.0) for our experiments. We implemented the conversion of a sequence to a co-occurrence matrix in Java SDK 1.4.2 [14] and the remaining processes in Matlab Release 13 [15]. The hardware platform was a Dell Precision Workstation 650 (Intel(R) Xeon (TM) CPU 3.20GHz, 4GB main memory, 120GB hard disk). With this environment, for the online phase, it took 26.77 minutes to convert all the user training sequences ($l = 100$, $s = 6$) to the co-occurrence matrices (average of 642 ms each), 23.60 minutes to compute the eigenvectors ($N = 50$), 6.76 minutes to obtain all the feature vectors (average of 162 ms each), 677.1 minutes to construct all the layered networks with 30 nodes in each layer (average of 16.25 s for each feature vector), and 106.5 minutes to construct the lookup table ($r = 3$).

For the online phase, the required computations are the following: transforming a sequence to a co-occurrence matrix, projecting the obtained co-occurrence matrix to the set of N Eigen co-occurrence matrices, obtaining the feature vector of the co-occurrence matrix, constructing a layered network with R nodes, generating subnetworks with r connected nodes, and comparing the obtained layered network with the corresponding user profile. For one testing sequence, using the same environment described above, it took 642 ms to convert the sequence ($l = 100$, $s = 6$) to the co-occurrence matrix, 162 ms to obtain the feature vector ($N = 50$), 16.25 s to construct the layered network ($R = 30$), 2.60 s to generate the subnetworks ($r = 3$), and 2.48 s to compare the subnetworks with the profile. In total, it took 22.15 s to classify a testing sequence as normal or anomalous.

5   Discussion

As noted above, we have achieved better results than the conventional approaches by using the ECM method. Modeling a user's behavior is not a simple task, however, and we did not achieve very high accuracy with false positive rates near to zero. There is room to improve the performance by varying the parameters of the ECM method, as shown in Tables 2 and 3.

Table 2 lists the parameters that can be changed when computing a feature vector from a co-occurrence matrix. The parameter O determines the events for which correlations with other events are considered. If we took a larger number of events (i.e., UNIX commands), the accuracy of the results would become better but the computational cost cost would increase. Thus, the number of events represents a trade-off between accuracy and computational cost.

Changing the parameter l results in a different length of test sequence. Although we set l to 100 in our experiment in order to compare the results with those of conventional methods, it could be changed by using a time stamp, for example. The parameter s determines the distance over which correlations between events are considered. If we assigned a larger value to s, two events separated by a longer time interval could be correlated. In our experiment, we did not consider the time in determining the values of l and s, but instead utilized our heuristic approach, as the time was not included in the dataset. Moreover, we did not change the strength of the correlations between events depending on their distance for simplicity. Considering the aspect of dividing the number of occurrences by the distance between events, for example, would influence the results.

Choosing more sequences for the *domain* dataset D would result in extracting of more precise features from each sequence, as in the case of the Eigenface technique. This aspect could be used to update the profile of each user: updating the *domain* dataset would automatically update its extracted principal features, since they are obtained by using Eigen co-occurrence matrices.

Table 3 lists the parameters that can be changed in constructing a network layer from a co-occurrence matrix. In our experiment, we set $h = 0$ and chose the largest 30 elements ($R = 30$) to construct a positive network. Nevertheless, the optimal values of these parameters are open for discussion.

Additionally, the detection accuracy would be increased by computing the mean co-occurrence matrix M_0 by using equation (2) instead of equation (1), since each original co-occurrence matrix is sparse. Moreover, normalization of $\Gamma(T_k(i), T_k(j))$ by the number of arcs (or nodes) in both $T_k(i)$ and $T_k(j)$ may improve the accuracy: let $|T_k(i)|$ be the number of arcs (or nodes) in network $T_k(i)$. Then the normalized $\Gamma(T_k(i), T_k(j))$ would be simply obtained by $\Gamma(T_k(i), T_k(j))/(|T_k(i)||T_k(j)|)$.

6   Conclusions and Future Work

Modeling user behavior is a challenging task, as it changes dynamically over time and a user's complete behavior is difficult to define. We have proposed the ECM method to accurately model such user behavior. The ECM method is innovative in three aspects. First, it models the dynamic natures of users embedded in their event sequences. Second, it can discover principal patterns of statistical dominance. Finally, it can represent such discovered patterns via layered networks, with not only frequent (*positive*) properties but also rare (*negative*) properties, where each layer represents a distinct principal pattern.

Experiments on masquerade detection by using UNIX commands showed that the ECM method achieved better results, with a higher correct detection rate and a lower false detection rate, than the results obtained with conventional approaches. This supports our assumption that not only connected events but also non-connected events within a certain scope size are correlated in a command sequence. It also shows that the principal features from the obtained model of a user behavior are successfully extracted by using PCA, and that detailed analysis by using layered networks can provide sufficient, useful features for classification.

Although we used the layered networks to classify test sequences as normal or malicious in our experiment, we should also investigate classification by using only the feature vectors. Furthermore, we need to conduct more experiments by varying the method's parameters, as described in Section 5, in order to improve the accuracy for masquerade detection. We must also try using various matching network algorithms to increase the accuracy.

References

1. Lunt, T.F.: A survey of intrusion detection techniques. Computers and Security **12** (1993) 405–418
2. Ye, N., Li, X., Chen, Q., Emran, S.M., Xu, M.: Probablistic Techniques for Intrusion Detection Based on Computer Audit Data. IEEE Transactions on Systems Man and Cybernetics, Part A (Systems & Humans) **31** (2001) 266–274
3. Hofmeyr, S.A., Forrest, S., Somayaji, A.: Intrusion Detection using Sequences of System Calls. Journal of Computer Security **6** (1998) 151–180
4. Lee, W., Stolfo, S.J.: A framework for constructing features and models for intrusion detection systems. ACM Transactions on Information and System Security (TISSEC) **3** (2000) 227–261
5. Sekar, R., Bendre, M., Bollineni, P.: A Fast Automaton-Based Method for Detecting Anomalous Program Behaviors. In: Proceedings of the 2001 IEEE Symposium on Security and Privacy, Oakland (2001) 144–155
6. Wagner, D., Dean, D.: Intrusion Detection via Static Analysis. In: Proceedings of the 2001 IEEE Symposium on Security and Privacy, Oakland (2001) 156–168
7. Abe, H., Oyama, Y., Oka, M., Kato, K.: Optimization of Intrusion Detection System Based on Static Analyses (in Japanese). IPSJ Transactions on Advanced Computing Systems (2004)
8. Kosoresow, A.P., Hofmeyr, S.A.: A Shape of Self for UNIX Processes. IEEE Software **14** (1997) 35–42
9. DuMouchel, W.: Computer Intrusion Detection Based on Bayes Factors for Comparing Command Transition Probabilities. Technical Report TR91, National Institute of Statistical Sciences (NISS) (1999)
10. Jha, S., Tan., K.M.C., Maxion, R.A.: Markov Chains, Classifiers and Intrusion Detection. In: Proc. of 14th IEEE Computer Security Foundations Workshop. (2001) 206–219
11. Warrender, C., Forrest, S., Pearlmutter, B.A.: Detecting Intrusions Using System Calls: Alternative Data Models. In: IEEE Symposium on Security and Privacy. (1999) 133–145
12. Schonlau, M., DuMouchel, W., Ju, W.H., Karr, A.F., Theus, M., Vardi, Y.: Computer intrusion: Detecting masquerades. In: Statistical Science. (2001) 16(1):58–74
13. Maxion, R.A., Townsend, T.N.: Masquerade Detection Using Truncated Command Lines. In: Prof. of the International Conference on Dependable Systems and Networks (DSN-02). (2002) 219–228
14. (Java) http://java.sun.com/
15. (Matlab) http://www.mathworks.com/

Seurat: A Pointillist Approach to Anomaly Detection

Yinglian Xie[1], Hyang-Ah Kim[1],
David R. O'Hallaron[1,2], Michael K. Reiter[1,2], and Hui Zhang[1,2]

[1] Department of Computer Science
[2] Department of Electrical and Computer Engineering
Carnegie Mellon University
{ylxie,hakim,droh,reiter,hzhang}@cs.cmu.edu

Abstract. This paper proposes a new approach to detecting aggregated anomalous events by correlating host file system changes across space and time. Our approach is based on a key observation that many host state transitions of interest have both temporal and spatial locality. Abnormal state changes, which may be hard to detect in isolation, become apparent when they are correlated with similar changes on other hosts. Based on this intuition, we have developed a method to detect similar, coincident changes to the patterns of file updates that are shared across multiple hosts. We have implemented this approach in a prototype system called *Seurat* and demonstrated its effectiveness using a combination of real workstation cluster traces, simulated attacks, and a manually launched Linux worm.

Keywords: Anomaly detection, Pointillism, Correlation, File updates, Clustering

1 Introduction

Correlation is a recognized technique for improving the effectiveness of intrusion detection by combining information from multiple sources. For example, many existing works have proposed correlating different types of logs gathered from distributed measurement points on a network (e.g., [1–3]). By leveraging collective information from different local detection systems, they are able to detect more attacks with fewer false positives.

In this paper, we propose a new approach to anomaly detection based on the idea of correlating host state transitions such as file system updates. The idea is to correlate host state transitions across both space (multiple hosts) and time (the past and the present), detecting similar coincident changes to the patterns of host state updates that are shared across multiple hosts. Examples of such coincident events include administrative updates that modify files that have not been modified before, and malware propagations that cause certain log files, which are modified daily, to cease being updated.

Our approach is based on the key observation that changes in host state in a network system often have both temporal and spatial locality. Both administrative updates and malware propagation exhibit spatial locality, in the sense that similar updates tend to occur across many of the hosts in a network. They also exhibit temporal locality in the sense that these updates tend to be clustered closely in time. Our goal is to identify atypical such aggregate updates, or the lack of typical ones.

E. Jonsson et al. (Eds.): RAID 2004, LNCS 3224, pp. 238–257, 2004.

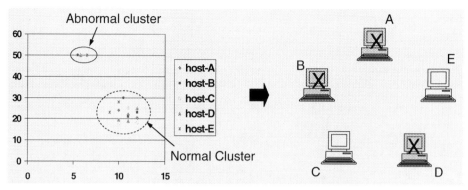

Fig. 1. Pointillist approach to anomaly detection: Normal points are clustered by the dashed circle. The appearance of a new cluster consisting of three points suggests anomalous events on host A, B, and D.

By exploring both the temporal and spatial locality of host state changes in a network system, our approach identifies anomalies *without foreknowledge of normal changes* and *without system-specific knowledge*. Existing approaches focus on the temporal locality of host state transitions, while overlooking the spatial locality among different hosts in a network system. They either define a model of normal host state change patterns through learning, or specify detailed rules about normal changes. The learning based approaches train the system to learn characteristics of normal changes. Since they focus only on the temporal locality of single-host state transitions, any significant deviation from the normal model is suspicious and should raise an alarm, resulting in a high false positive rate. Rule-based approaches such as Tripwire [4] require accurate, specific knowledge of system configurations and daily user activity patterns on a specific host. Violation of rules then suggests malicious intrusions. Although rule-based anomaly detection raises fewer false alarms, it requires system administrators to manually specify a set of rules for each host. The correlation capability of our approach across both space and time allows us to learn the patterns of normal state changes over time, and to detect those anomalous events correlated among multiple hosts due to malicious intrusions. This obviates the need for specific rules while eliminating the false alarms caused by single host activity pattern shifts.

The correlation is performed by clustering points, each representing an individual host state transition, in a multi-dimensional feature space. Each feature indicates the change of a file attribute, with all features together describing the host state transitions of an individual machine during a given period (e.g., one day). Over time, the abstraction of point patterns inherently reflects the aggregated host activities. For normal host state changes, the points should follow some regular pattern by roughly falling into several clusters. Abnormal changes, which are hard to detect by monitoring that host alone, will stand out when they are correlated with other normal host state changes. Hence our approach shares some flavor of *pointillism* – a style of painting that applies small dots onto a surface so that from a distance the dots blend together into meaningful patterns.

Figure 1 illustrates the pointillist approach to anomaly detection. There are five hosts in the network system. We represent state changes on each host daily as a point in a 2-dimensional space in this example. On normal days, the points roughly fall into the dash-circled region. The appearance of a new cluster consisting of three points (indicated by the solid circle) suggests the incidence of anomaly on host A, B, and D, which may all have been compromised by the same attack. Furthermore, if we know that certain hosts (e.g., host A) are already compromised (possibly detected by other means such as a network based IDS), then we can correlate the state changes of the compromised hosts with the state changes of all other hosts in the network system to detect more infected hosts (e.g., host B and D).

We have implemented a prototype system, called *Seurat*[1], that uses file system updates to represent host state changes for anomaly detection. Seurat successfully detects the propagation of a manually launched Linux worm on a number of hosts in an isolated cluster. Seurat has a low false alarm rate when evaluated by a real deployment. These alarms are caused by either system re-configurations or network wide experiments. The false negative rate and detection latency, evaluated with simulated attacks, are both low for fast propagating attacks. For slowly propagating attacks, there is a tradeoff between false negative rate and detection latency. For each alarm, Seurat identifies the list of hosts involved and the related files, which we expect will be extremely helpful for system administrators to examine the root cause and dismiss false alarms.

The rest of the paper is organized as follows: Section 2 describes Seurat threat model. Section 3 introduces the algorithm for correlating host state changes across both space and time. Section 4 evaluates our approach. Section 5 discusses the limitations of Seurat and suggests possible improvements. Section 6 presents related work.

2   Attack Model

The goal of Seurat is to automatically identify anomalous events by correlating the state change events of all hosts in a network system. Hence Seurat defines an anomalous event as an unexpected state change close in time across *multiple* hosts in a network system.

We focus on rapidly propagating Internet worms, virus, zombies, or other malicious attacks that compromise multiple hosts in a network system at a time (e.g., one or two days). We have observed that, once fast, automated attacks are launched, most of the vulnerable hosts get compromised due to the rapid propagation of the attack and the scanning preferences of the automated attack tools. According to CERT's analysis [5], the level of automation in attack tools continues to increase, making it faster to search vulnerable hosts and propagate attacks. Recently, the Slammer worm hit 90 percent of vulnerable systems in the Internet within 10 minutes [6]. Worse, the lack of diversity in systems and softwares run by Internet-attached hosts enables massive and fast attacks. Computer clusters tend to be configured with the same operating systems and softwares. In such systems, host state changes due to attacks have strong temporal and spatial locality that can be exploited by Seurat.

Although Seurat is originally designed to detect system changes due to fast propagating attacks, it can be generalized to detect slowly propagating attacks as well. This can be done by varying the time resolution of reporting and correlating the collective host state changes. We will discuss this issue further in Section 5. However, Seurat's

---

[1] Seurat is the 19th century founder of pointillism.

global correlation can not detect abnormal state changes that are unique to only a single host in the network system.

Seurat represents host state changes using *file system updates*. Pennington et al. [7] found that 83% of the intrusion tools and network worms they surveyed modify one or more system files. These modifications would be noticed by monitoring file system updates. There are many security tools such as Tripwire [4] and AIDE [8] that rely on monitoring abnormal file system updates for intrusion detection.

We use the file name, including its complete path, to identify a file in the network system. We regard different instances of a file that correspond to a common path name as a same file across different hosts, since we are mostly interested in system files which tend to have canonical path names exploited by malicious attacks. We treat files with different path names on different hosts as different files, even when they are identical in content.

For the detection of anomalies caused by attacks, we have found that this representation of host state changes is effective and useful. However, we may need different approaches for other applications of Seurat such as file sharing detection, or for the detection of more sophisticated future attacks that alter files at arbitrary locations as they propagate. As ongoing work, we are investigating the use of file content digests instead of file names.

3   Correlation-Based Anomaly Detection

We define a d-dimensional feature vector $H_{ij} = \langle v_1, v_2, \ldots, v_d \rangle$ to represent the file system update attributes for host i during time period j. Each H_{ij} can be plotted as a point in a d-dimensional feature space. Our pointillist approach is based on correlating the feature vectors by clustering. Over time, for normal file updates, the points follow some regular pattern (e.g., roughly fall into several clusters). From time to time, Seurat compares the newly generated points against points from previous time periods. The appearance of a new cluster, consisting only of newly generated points, indicates abnormal file updates and Seurat raises an alarm.

For clustering to work most effectively, we need to find the most relevant features (dimensions) in a feature vector given all the file update attributes collected by Seurat. We have investigated two methods to reduce the feature vector dimensions: (1) *wavelet-based selection*, and (2) *principal component analysis* (PCA).

In the rest of this section, we first present how we define the feature vector space and the distances among points. We then describe the methods Seurat uses to reduce feature vector dimensions. Finally, we discuss how Seurat detects abnormal file updates by clustering.

3.1   Feature Vector Space

Seurat uses binary feature vectors to represent host file updates. Each dimension in the feature vector space corresponds to a unique file (indexed by the full-path file name). As such, the dimension of the space d is the number of file names present on any machine in the network system. We define the *detection window* to be the period that we are interested in finding anomalies. In the current prototype, the detection window is one day. For each vector $H_{ij} = \langle v_1, v_2, \ldots, v_d \rangle$, we set v_k to 1 if host i has updated (added, modified, or removed) the k-th file on day j, otherwise, we set v_k to 0.

The vectors generated in the detection window will be correlated with vectors generated on multiple previous days. We treat each feature vector as an independent point in a set. The set can include vectors generated by the same host on multiple days, or vectors generated by multiple hosts on the same day. In the rest of the paper, we use $V = \langle v_1, v_2, \ldots, v_d \rangle$ to denote a feature vector for convenience. Figure 2 shows how we represent the host file updates using feature vectors.

$$
\begin{array}{ccccccc}
 & & & F_1 & F_2 & F_3 & F_4 & F_5 \\
V_1 = H_{11} = & < & 1, & 1, & 0, & 1, & 1 & > \\
V_2 = H_{21} = & < & 1, & 1, & 1, & 0, & 0 & > \\
V_3 = H_{12} = & < & 1, & 1, & 0, & 1, & 0 & > \\
\end{array}
$$

Fig. 2. Representing host file updates as feature vectors: F_1, F_2, F_3, F_4, F_5 are five different files (i.e., file names). Accordingly, the feature vector space has 5 dimensions in the example.

The correlation is based on the distances among vectors. Seurat uses a cosine distance metric, which is a common similarity measure between binary vectors [9, 10]. We define the distance $D(V_1, V_2)$ between two vectors V_1 and V_2 as their angle θ computed by the cosine value:

$$
D(V_1, V_2) = \theta = cos^{-1}\left(\frac{V_1 \cdot V_2}{|V_1||V_2|}\right)
$$

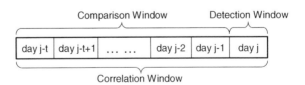

Fig. 3. Detection window, comparison window, and correlation window. The detection window is day j. The comparison window is from day $j - t$ to day $j - 1$. The correlation window is from day $j - t$ to day j.

For each day j (the detection window), Seurat correlates the newly generated vectors with vectors generated in a number of previous days $j - 1, j - 2, \ldots$. We assume that the same abnormal file update events on day j, if any, have not occurred on those previous days. We define the *comparison window* of day j as the days that we look back for comparison, and the *correlation window* of day j as the inclusive period of day j

and its comparison window. Vectors generated outside the correlation window of day j are not used to identify abnormal file updates on day j. Figure 3 illustrates the concepts of detection window, comparison window, and correlation window.

Since each vector generated during the comparison window serves as an example of normal file updates to compare against in the clustering process, we explore the temporal locality of normal update events by choosing an appropriate comparison window for each day. The comparison window size is a configurable parameter of Seurat. It reflects how far we look back into history to implicitly define the model of normal file updates. For example, some files such as /var/spool/anacron/cron.weekly on Linux platforms are updated weekly. In order to regard such weekly updates as normal updates, administrators have to choose a comparison window size larger than a week. Similarly, the size of the detection window reflects the degree of temporal locality of abnormal update events.

Since Seurat correlates file updates across multiple hosts, we are interested in only those files that have been updated by at least two different hosts. Files that have been updated by only one single host in the network system throughout the correlation window are more likely to be user files. As such, we do not select them as relevant dimensions to define the feature vector space.

3.2 Feature Selection

Most file updates are irrelevant to anomalous events even after we filter out the file updates reported by a single host. Those files become noise dimensions when we correlate the vectors (points) to identify abnormal updates, and increase the complexity of the correlation process. We need more selective ways to choose relevant files and reduce feature vector dimensions. Seurat uses a wavelet-based selection method and principal component analysis (PCA) for this purpose.

Wavelet-Based Selection. The wavelet-based selection method regards each individual file update status as a discrete time series signal S. Given a file i, the value of the signal

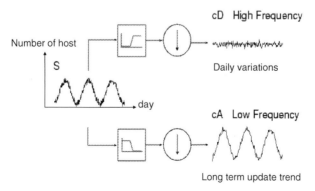

Fig. 4. Representing file update status with wavelet transformation: The original signal is S, which can be decomposed into a low frequency signal cA reflecting the long term update trend, and a high frequency signal cD reflecting the daily variations from the long-term trend.

on day n, denoted by $S_i(n)$, is defined as the total number of hosts that update file i on day n in the network system. Each such signal S_i can be decomposed into a low frequency signal cA_i reflecting the long term update trend, and a high frequency signal cD_i reflecting the day-to-day variation from the long term trend. (see Figure 4). If the high frequency signal cD_i shows a spike on a certain day, we know that a significantly larger number of hosts updated file i than on a normal day. We then select file i as a relevant feature dimension in defining the feature vector space.

Seurat detects signal spikes using the residual signal of the long-term trend. The same technique has been used to detect disease outbreaks[11]. To detect anomalies on day j, the algorithm takes as input the list of files that have been updated by at least two different hosts in the correlation window of day j. Then, from these files the algorithm selects a subset that will be used to define the feature vector space.

For each file i:

    1. Construct a time series signal:
        $S_i = cA_i + cD_i$
    2. Compute the residual signal value of day j:
        $R_i(j) = S_i(j) - cA_i(j-1)$
    3. If $R_i(j) >$ alpha, then select file i as a feature dimension

---

Fig. 5. Wavelet-based feature selection.

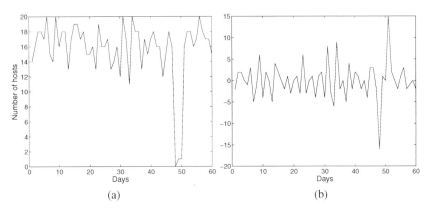

(a) (b)

Fig. 6. Wavelet transformation of file update status: (a) The original signal of the file update status (b) The residual signal after wavelet transformation.

Figure 5 shows the steps to select features by wavelet-based method. Given a fixed correlation window of day j, the algorithm starts with constructing a time series signal S_i for each file i, and decomposes S_i into cA_i and cD_i using a single-level wavelet transformation as described. Then we compute the residual signal value $R_i(j)$ of day j by subtracting the trend value $cA_i(j-1)$ of day $j-1$ from the original signal value $S_i(j)$ of day j. If $R_i(j)$ exceeds a pre-set threshold α, then the actual number of hosts who have updated file i on day j is significantly larger than the prediction $cA_i(j-1)$

based on the long term trend. Therefore, Seurat selects file i as an interesting feature dimension for anomaly detection on day j. As an example, Figure 6 shows the original signal and the residual signal of a file using a 32-day correlation window in a 22-host teaching cluster. Note the threshold value α of each file is a parameter selected based on the statistical distribution of historical residual values.

PCA-Based Dimension Reduction. PCA is a statistical method to reduce data dimensionality without much loss of information [12]. Given a set of d-dimensional data points, PCA finds a set of d' orthogonal vectors, called *principal components*, that account for the variance of the input data as much as possible. Dimensionality reduction is achieved by projecting the original d-dimensional data onto the subspace spanned by these d' orthogonal vectors. Most of the intrinsic information of the d-dimensional data is preserved in the d'-dimensional subspace.

We note that the updates of different files are usually correlated. For example, when a software package is updated on a host, many of the related files will be modified together. Thus we can perform PCA to identify the correlation of file updates.

Given a d-dimensional feature space $\mathcal{Z}_2^d$, and a list of m feature vectors $V_1, V_2, \ldots,$ $V_m \in \mathcal{Z}_2^d$, we perform the following steps using PCA to obtain a new list of feature vectors $V'_1, V'_2, \ldots, V'_m \in \mathcal{Z}_2^{d'} (d' < d)$ with reduced number of dimensions:

1. Standardize each feature vector $V_k = \langle v_{1k}, v_{2k}, \ldots, v_{dk} \rangle$ $(1 \le k \le m)$ by subtracting each of its elements v_{ik} by the mean value of the corresponding dimension $u_i (1 \le i \le d)$. We use $\overline{V}_k = \langle \overline{v}_{1k}, \overline{v}_{2k}, \ldots, \overline{v}_{nk} \rangle \in \mathcal{Z}_2^d$ to denote the standardized vector for the original feature vector V_k. Then,

$$\overline{v}_{ik} = v_{ik} - u_i \ \left(\text{where } u_i = \frac{\sum_{j=1}^m v_{ij}}{m}, \ 1 \le i \le d \right)$$

2. Use the standardized feature vectors $\overline{V}_1, \overline{V}_2, \ldots, \overline{V}_m$ as input data to PCA in order to identify a set of principal components that are orthogonal vectors defining a set of transformed dimensions of the original feature space $\mathcal{Z}_2^d$. Select the first d' principal components that count for most of the input data variances (e.g., 90% of data variances) to define a subspace $\mathcal{Z}_2^{d'}$.
3. Project each standardized feature vector $\overline{V}_k \in \mathcal{Z}_2^d$ onto the PCA selected subspace $\mathcal{Z}_2^{d'}$ to obtain the corresponding reduced dimension vector $V'_k \in \mathcal{Z}_2^{d'}$.

Note that PCA is complementary to wavelet-based selection. Once we fix the correlation window of a particular day, we first pick a set of files to define the feature vector space by wavelet-based selection. We then perform PCA to reduce the data dimensionality further.

3.3 Anomaly Detection by Clustering

Once we obtain a list of transformed feature vectors using feature selection, we cluster the vectors based on the distance between every pair of them.

We call the cluster a *new cluster* if it consists of multiple vectors only from the detection window. The appearance of a new cluster indicates possibly abnormal file updates occurred during the detection window and should raise an alarm.

There are many existing algorithms for clustering, for example, K-means [13, 14] or Single Linkage Hierarchical Clustering [10]. Seurat uses a simple iterative algorithm, which is a common method for K-means initialization, to cluster vectors without prior knowledge of the number of clusters [15]. The algorithm assumes each cluster has a hub. A vector belongs to the cluster whose hub is closest to that vector compared with the distances from other hubs to that vector. The algorithm starts with one cluster whose hub is randomly chosen. Then, it iteratively selects a vector that has the largest distance to its own hub as a new hub, and re-clusters all the vectors based on their distances to all the selected hubs. This process continues until there is no vector whose distance to its hub is larger than the half of the average hub-hub distance.

We choose this simple iterative algorithm because it runs much faster, and works equally well as the Single Linkage Hierarchical algorithm in our experiments. The reason that even the simple clustering algorithm works well is that the ratio of inter-cluster distance to intra-cluster distance significantly increases after feature selection. Since the current clustering algorithm is sensitive to outliers, we plan to explore other clustering algorithms such as K-means.

Once we detect a new cluster and generate an alarm, we examine further to identify the involved hosts and the files from which the cluster resulted. The suspicious hosts are just the ones whose file updates correspond to the feature vectors in the new cluster. To determine which files possibly cause the alarm, we only focus on the files picked by the wavelet-based selection to define the feature vector space. For each of those files, if it is updated by all the hosts in the new cluster during the detection window, but has not been updated by any host during the corresponding comparison window, Seurat outputs this file as a candidate file. Similarly, Seurat also reports the set of files that have been updated during the comparison window, but are not updated by any host in the new cluster during the detection window.

Based on the suspicious hosts and the selected files for explaining root causes, system administrators can decide whether the updates are known administrative updates that should be suppressed, or some abnormal events that should be further investigated. If the updates are caused by malicious attacks, administrators can take remedial counter measures for the new cluster. Furthermore, additional compromised hosts can be identified by checking if the new cluster expands later and if other hosts have updated the same set of candidate files.

4   Experiments

We have developed a multi-platform (Linux and Windows) prototype of Seurat that consists of a lightweight data collection tool and a correlation module. The data collection tool scans the file system of the host where it is running and generates a daily summary of file update attributes. Seurat harvests the summary reports from multiple hosts in a network system and the correlation module uses the reports for anomaly detection.

We have installed the Seurat data collection tool on a number of campus office machines and a teaching cluster that are used by students daily. By default, the tool scans the attributes of all system files on a host. For privacy reasons, personal files under user home directories are not scanned. The attributes of a file include the file name, type, device number, permissions, size, inode number, important timestamps, and a 16-byte MD5 checksum of file content. The current system uses only a binary bit to represent each file update, but the next version may exploit other attributes reported by the data collection tool. Each day, each host compares the newly scanned disk snapshot against that from the previous day and generates a file update summary report. In the current prototype, all the reports are uploaded daily to a centralized server where system administrators can monitor and correlate the file updates using the correlation module.

In this section, we study the effectiveness of Seurat's pointillist approach for detecting aggregated anomalous events. We use the daily file update reports from our real deployment to study the false positive rate and the corresponding causes in Section 4.1. We evaluate the false negative rate with simulated attacks in Section 4.2. In order to verify the effectiveness of our approach on real malicious attacks, we launched a real Linux worm into an isolated cluster and report the results in Section 4.3.

4.1   False Positives

The best way to study the effectiveness of our approach is to test it with real data. We have deployed Seurat on a teaching cluster of 22 hosts and have been collecting the daily file update reports since Nov 2003. The teaching cluster is mostly used by students for their programming assignments. They are also occasionally used by a few graduate students for running network experiments.

For this experiment, we use the file update reports from Dec 1, 2003 until Feb 29, 2004 to evaluate the false positive rate. During this period, there are a few days when a couple of hosts failed to generate or upload reports due to system failure or reconfigurations. For those small number of missing reports, we simply ignore them because they do not affect the aggregated file update patterns.

We set the correlation window to 32 days in order to accommodate monthly file update patterns. That is, we correlate the update pattern from day 1 to day 32 to identify abnormal events on day 32, and correlate the update pattern from day 2 to day 33 to detect anomalies on day 33, etc. Thus, our detection starts from Jan 1, 2004, since we do not have 32-day correlation windows for the days in Dec 2003.

Dimension Reduction.   Once we fixed the correlation window of a particular day, we identify relevant files using wavelet-based selection with a constant threshold $\alpha = 2$ to define the feature vector space for simplicity. We then perform PCA to reduce the data dimensionality further by picking the first several principal components that account for 98% of the input data variances.

Throughout the entire period of 91 days, 772 files with unique file names were updated by at least two different hosts. Figure 7 (a) shows the number of hosts that updated each file during the data collection period. We observe that only a small number files (e.g.,/var/adm/syslog/mail.log) are updated regularly by all of the hosts, while most other files (e.g., /var/run/named.pid) are updated irregularly, depending on the system usage or the applications running.

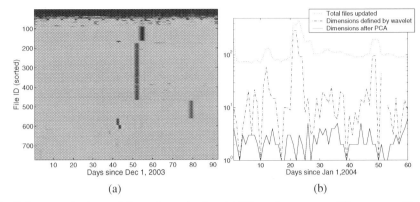

Fig. 7. Feature selection and dimension reduction: (a) File update patterns. Files are sorted by the cumulative number of hosts that have updated them throughout the 91 days. The darker the color is, the more hosts updated the corresponding file. (b) The number of feature vector dimensions after wavelet-based selection and PCA consecutively.

Figure 7 (b) shows the results of feature selection. There were, on average, 140 files updated by at least two different hosts during each correlation window. After wavelet-based selection, the average number of feature dimensions is 17. PCA further reduces the vector space dimension to below 10.

False Alarms. After dimension reduction, we perform clustering of feature vectors and identify new clusters for each day. Figure 8 illustrates the clustering results of 6 consecutive days from Jan 19, 2004 to Jan 24, 2004. There are two new clusters identified on Jan 21 and Jan 23, which involve 9 hosts and 6 hosts, respectively. Since Seurat outputs a list of suspicious files as the cause of each alarm, system administrators can tell if the new clusters are caused by malicious intrusions.

Based on the list of files output by Seurat, we can figure out that the new clusters on Jan 21 and Jan 23 reflect large scale file updates due to a system reconfiguration at the beginning of the spring semester. For both days, Seurat accurately pinpoints the exact hosts that are involved. The reconfiguration started from Jan 21, when a large number of binaries, header files, and library files were modified on 9 out of the 22 hosts. Since the events are known to system administrators, we treat the identified vectors as normal for future anomaly detection. Thus, no alarm is triggered on Jan 22, when the same set of library files were modified on 12 other hosts. On Jan 23, the reconfiguration continued to remove a set of printer files on 6 out of the 22 hosts. Again, administrators can mark this event as normal and we spot no new cluster on Jan 24, when 14 other hosts underwent the same set of file updates.

In total, Seurat raises alarms on 9 out of the 60 days under detection, among which 6 were due to system reconfigurations. Since the system administrators are aware of such events in advance, they can simply suppress these alarms. The 3 other alarms are generated on 3 consecutive days when a graduate student performed a network experiment that involved simultaneous file updates at multiple hosts. Such events are normal but rare, and should alert the system administrators.

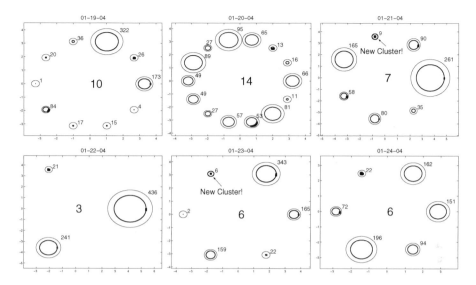

Fig. 8. Clustering feature vectors for anomaly detection: Each circle represents a cluster. The number at the center of the figure shows the total number of clusters. The radius of a circle corresponds to the number of points in the cluster, which is also indicated beside the circle. The squared dots correspond to the new points generated on the day under detection. New clusters are identified by a thicker circle.

4.2   False Negatives

The primary goal of this experiment is to study the false negative rate and detection latency of Seurat as the stealthiness of the attack changes. We use simulated attacks by manually updating files on the selected host reports, as if they were infected.

We first examine the detection rate of Seurat by varying the degree of attack aggressiveness. We model the attack propagation speed as the number of hosts infected on each day (the detection window), and model the attack stealthiness on a local host as the number of new files installed by this attack. Our simulation runs on the same teaching cluster that we described in Section 4.1. Since the aggregated file update patterns are different for each day, we randomly pick ten days in Feb 2004, when there was no intrusion. On each selected day, we simulate attacks by manually inserting artificial new files into a number of host reports on only that day, and use the modified reports as input for detection algorithm. We then remove those modified entries, and repeat the experiments with another day. The detection rate is calculated as the number of days that Seurat spots new clusters over the total ten days.

Figure 9 shows the detection rate of Seurat by varying the number of files inserted on each host and the number of hosts infected. On one hand, the detection rate monotonically increases as we increase the number of files inserted on each host by an attack. Since the inserted files do not exist before, each of them will be selected as a feature dimension by the wavelet-based selection, leading to larger distances between the points of infected host state changes and the points of normal host state changes. Therefore,

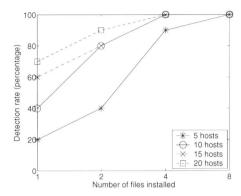

Fig. 9. Detection rate: We vary the number of hosts infected and the number of files inserted on each host by the simulated attacks.

the more new files are injected by an attack, the higher the detection rate gets. On the other hand, as we increase the number of infected hosts, the number of points for abnormal host state changes becomes large enough to create an independent new cluster. Thus, rapidly propagating attacks are more likely to be caught. Accordingly, detecting a slowly propagating attack requires a larger detection window, hence longer detection latency, in order to accumulate enough infected hosts. We revisit this issue in Section 5.

We further evaluate the detection rate of Seurat on six Linux worms with simulated attacks. To do so, we compile a subset of files modified by each worm based on the descriptions from public Web sites such as Symantec [16] and F-Secure information center [17]. We then manually modify the described files in a number of selected host reports to simulate the corresponding worm attacks. Again, for each worm, we vary the number of infected hosts, and run our experiments on the teaching cluster with ten randomly selected days.

Worms	Adore	Ramen-A	Ramen-B	Slapper-A	Slapper-B	Kork
Files modified	10	8	12	3	4	5
2 infected hosts	80%	80%	90%	30%	40%	30%
4 infected hosts	100%	100%	90%	70%	80%	70%
8 infected hosts	100%	100%	100%	100%	100%	100%

Fig. 10. Detection rate of emulated worms: We vary the number of hosts compromised by the attacks.

Table 10 shows the number of files modified by each worm and the detection rate of Seurat. In general, the more files modified by a worm, the more likely the worm will be detected. But the position of a file in the file system directory tree also matters. For example, both Slapper-B worm and Kork worm insert 4 new files into a compromised host. However, Kork worm additionally modifies /etc/passwd to create accounts with root privileges. Because there are many hosts that have updated /etc/passwd during a series of system reconfiguration events, the inclusion of such files in the feature vector space reduces the distances from abnormal points to normal points, resulting in higher false negative rates. We discuss this further in Section 5.

4.3   Real Attacks

Now we proceed to examine the efficacy of Seurat during a real worm outbreak. The best way to show this would be to have Seurat detect an anomaly caused by a new worm propagation. Instead of waiting for a new worm's outbreak, we have set up an isolated computer cluster where, without damaging the real network, we can launch worms and record file system changes. This way, we have full control over the number of hosts infected, and can repeat the experiments. Because the isolated cluster has no real users, we merge the data acquired from the isolated cluster with the data we have collected from the teaching cluster in order to conduct experiments.

We obtained the binaries and source codes of a few popular worms from public Web sites such as whitehats [18] and packetstorm [19]. Extensively testing Seurat, with various real worms in the isolated cluster, requires tremendous effort in setting up each host with the right versions of vulnerable software. As a first step, we show the result with the Lion worm [20] in this experiment.

The Lion worm was found in early 2001. Lion exploits a vulnerability of BIND 8.2, 8.2-P1, 8.2.1, 8.2.2-Px. Once Lion infects a system, it sets up backdoors, leaks out confidential information (/etc/passwd, /etc/shadow) via email, and scans the Internet to recruit vulnerable systems. Lion scans the network by randomly picking the first 16 bits of an IP address, and then sequentially probing all the 2^{16} IP addresses in the space of the block. After that, Lion randomly selects another such address block to continue scanning. As a result, once a host is infected by Lion, all the vulnerable hosts nearby (in the same IP address block) will be infected soon. Lion affects file systems: the worm puts related binaries and shell scripts under the /dev/.lib directory, copies itself into the /tmp directory, changes system files under the /etc directory, and tries to wipe out some log files.

We configured the isolated cluster with three Lion-vulnerable hosts and one additional machine that launched the worm. The vulnerable machines were running RedHat 6.2 including the vulnerable BIND 8.2.2-P5. The cluster used one C class network address block. Every machine in the cluster was connected to a 100Mbps Ethernet and was running named. The Seurat data collection tool generated a file system update report on every machine daily.

After we launched the Lion worm, all three vulnerable hosts in the isolated cluster were infected quickly one after another. We merge the file update report by the each compromised host with a different normal host report generated on Feb 11, 2004, when we know there was no anomaly. Figure 11 shows the clustering results of three consecutive days from Feb 10, 2004 to Feb 12, 2004 using the merged reports.

On the attack day, there are 64 files picked by the wavelet-based selection. The number of feature dimensions is reduced to 9 after PCA. Seurat successfully detects a new cluster consisting of the 3 infected hosts. Figure 12 lists the 22 files selected by Seurat as the causes of the alarm. These files provide enough hints to the administrators to confirm the existence of the Lion worm. Once detected, these compromised hosts as

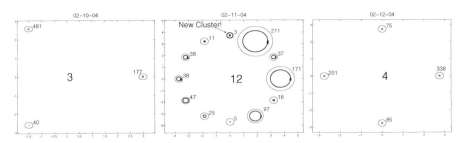

Fig. 11. Intrusion detection by Seurat: Seurat identified a new cluster of three hosts on Feb 11, 2004, when we manually launched the Lion worm.

File ID.	File name	File ID.	File name
1	/sbin/asp	12	/var/spool/mail
2	/dev/.lib	13	/dev/.lib/bindx.sh
3	/dev/.lib/star.sh	14	/tmp/ramen.tgz
4	/var/spool/mail/root	15	/dev/.lib/scan.sh
5	/dev/.lib/bind	16	/dev/.lib/pscan
6	/etc/hosts.deny	17	/var/spool/mqueue
7	/dev/.lib/randb	18	/dev/.lib/hack.sh
8	/sbin	19	/dev/.lib/.hack
9	/var/log	20	/dev/.lib/index.html
10	/dev/.lib/bindname.log	21	/dev/.lib/asp62
11	/dev/.lib/index.htm	22	/var/log/sendmail.st

Fig. 12. Suspicious files for the new cluster on Feb 11, 2004.

well as the list of suspicious files can be marked for future detection. If, in the following days, there are more hosts that are clustered together with the already infected machines, or experience the same file updates, then we may conclude they are infected by the same attack.

5   Discussion

5.1   Vulnerabilities and Limitations

By identifying parallel occurrences of coincident events, Seurat will be most successful in detecting virus or worm propagations that result in file modifications at multiple hosts. Certain attacks (e.g., password guessing attacks) that succeed only once or a few times in a network system may evade Seurat detection. The current prototype of Seurat also has limited detection capability to the following types of attacks.

Stealthy attack. Attackers may try to evade detection by slowing attack propagation. If an attacker is patient enough to infect only one host a day in the monitored network system, Seurat will not notice the intrusion with the current one-day detection window because Seurat focuses only on anomalous file changes common across multiple hosts.

A larger detection window such as a couple of days or a week can help to catch slow, stealthy attacks. Note, however, that Seurat notices the attacks only after multiple hosts in the network system are compromised. In other words, if an attack propagates slowly, Seurat may not recognize the attack for the first few days after the initial successful compromise. There is thus a tradeoff between detection rate and detection latency.

Mimicry attack. An attacker can carefully design his attack to cause file updates that look similar to regular file changes, and mount a successful *mimicry attack* [21]. There are two ways to achieve a mimicry attack against the current prototype. First, an attacker may try to fool Seurat's feature selection process by camouflaging all intrusion files as frequently, regularly updated files. Those concealed files, even when they are modified in an unexpected way (e.g., entries removed from append-only log files), will not be selected as feature vector dimensions because of current use of the binary feature representation. Note that Seurat's data collection tool provides additional information on file system changes, such as file size, file content digest, and permissions. By incorporating the extra information in representing host state transition, Seurat can make such mimicry attacks harder. Second, an attacker may find a way to cloak abnormal file updates with many normal but irregular changes during Seurat's clustering process. For example, in Section 4.2, we observed that the false negative rate of detecting the Kork worm was relatively higher due to the interference of irregular system reconfiguration. We leave it as future work to quantify this type of mimicry attack and the effectiveness of possible counter measures.

Random-file-access attack. Seurat correlates file updates based on their complete path names. Thus attackers can try to evade Seurat by installing attack files under different directories at different hosts, or replacing randomly chosen existing files with attack files. Many recent email viruses already change the virus file names when they propagate to a new host; we envision similar techniques could be employed by other types of attacks soon. Note, however, that even the random-file-access attack may need a few anchor files at fixed places, where Seurat still has the opportunity to detect such attacks. A more robust representation of a file, for example, an MD5 checksum, could help Seurat detect random-file-access attacks.

Memory-resident attack. Memory-resident and BIOS-resident only attacks make no file system updates. Thus Seurat will not be able to detect memory resident attacks by examining host file updates, nor those attacks that erase disk evidence before the Seurat data collection tool performs the scheduled disk scan.

Kernel/Seurat modification attack. The effectiveness of Seurat relies on the correctness of reports from the data collecting tools running on distributed hosts. So the host kernels and the Seurat data collection tools should run on machines protected by trusted computing platforms [22]. An alternative solution is to monitor file system changes in real time (will be discussed further in Section 5.2) and to protect file update logs using secure audit logging [23].

5.2   Future Work

Real-time anomaly detection. The current prototype periodically scans and reports file system updates with a 1-day cycle, which may be slow to detect fast propagating attacks. To shorten detection latency, we are enhancing the Seurat data collection module to monitor system calls related with file updates, and report the changes immediately to the correlation module. The reported file updates will be instantly reflected by setting the corresponding bits in the feature vectors at the Seurat correlation module, which continuously performs clustering of the new feature vectors for real time anomaly detection.

Distributed correlation module. Currently, Seurat moves the daily reports from distributed data collection tools to a centralized server, where the correlation module computes and clusters the host vectors. Despite the simplicity of centralized deployment, the centralized approach exposes Seurat to problems in scalability and reliability. First, the amount of report data to be transferred to and stored at the centralized server is large. In our experience, a host generates a file update report of 3K-140KBytes daily in a compressed format, so the aggregate report size from hundreds or thousands of hosts with a long comparison window will be large. The report size will be larger when Seurat's data collection tool reports the host state changes in real time. Second, the monitored hosts could be in different administrative domains (i.e., hosts managed by different academic departments or labs) and it is often impractical to transfer the detailed reports from all the hosts to one centralized server due to privacy and confidentiality issues. Third, the centralized server can be a single point-of-failure. It is important for Seurat to work even when one correlation server is broken or a part of network is partitioned. A distributed correlation module will cope with those issues. We are now investigating methods to correlate file update events in a distributed architecture such as EMERALD [1], AAFID [24], and Mingle [25].

Other applications. The approach of clustering coincident host state changes can be generalized to other types of applications such as detecting the propagation of spyware, illegal file sharing events, or erroneous software configuration changes. We are currently deploying Seurat on Planetlab [26] hosts for detecting software configuration errors by identifying host state vectors that do not fall into an expected cluster.

6   Related Work

Seurat uses file system updates to represent a host state change. File system updates have been known to be useful information for intrusion detection. Tripwire [4], AIDE [8], Samhain [27] are well-known intrusion detection systems that use file system updates to find intrusions. Recently proposed systems such as the storage-based intrusion detection systems [7] and some commercial tools [28] support real-time integrity checking. All of them rely on a pre-defined rule set to detect anomalous integrity violation, while Seurat diagnoses the anomaly using learning and correlation across time and space.

Leveraging the information gathered from distributed multiple measurement points is not a new approach. Many researchers have noticed the potential of the collective approaches for intrusion detection or anomaly detection. Graph-based Intrusion Detection System (GrIDS) [29] detects intrusions by building a graph representation of network activity based on the report from all the hosts in a network. Different from Seurat, GrIDS uses the TCP/IP network activity between hosts in the network to infer patterns of intrusive or hostile activities based on pre-defined rules. Other systems, such as Cooperative Security Managers (CSM) [30], Distributed Intrusion Detection System (DIDS) [31], also take advantage of a collective approach to intrusion detection. They orchestrate multiple monitors watching multiple network links and track user activity across multiple machines.

EMERALD (Event Monitoring Enabling Responses to Anomalous Live Disturbances) [1] and Autonomous Agents For Intrusion Detection (AAFID) [24] have independently proposed distributed architectures for intrusion detection and response capability. Both of them use local monitors or agents to collect interesting events and anomaly reports (from a variety of sources; audit data, network packet traces, SNMP traffic, application logs, etc.). The architectures provide the communication methods to exchange the locally detected information and an easy way to manage components of the systems. AAFID performs statistical profile-based anomaly detection and EMERALD supports a signature-based misuse analysis in addition to the profile-based anomaly detection. Note that Seurat starts with similar motivation. But Seurat focuses more on the technique for correlating the collective reports for anomaly detection, and infers interesting information on the system state from learning, rather than relying on a pre-defined set of events or rules. We envision Seurat as a complementary technique, not as a replacement of the existing architectures that provide global observation sharing.

Correlating different types of audit logs and measurement reports is another active area in security research. Many researchers have proposed to correlate multiple heterogeneous sensors to improve the accuracy of alarms [3, 32, 33, 2, 34]. In this work, we attempt to correlate information gathered by homogeneous monitors (especially, the file system change monitors) but we may enhance our work to include different type of measurement data to represent individual host status.

Wang et al. [35] also have noticed the value of spatial correlation of multiple system configurations and applied a collective approach to tackle misconfiguration trouble shooting problems. In their system, a malfunctioning machine can diagnose its problem by collecting system configuration information from other similar and friendly hosts connected via a peer-to-peer network. The work does not target automatic detection of the anomaly, but rather it aims at figuring out the cause of a detected problem.

7   Conclusions

In this paper, we presented a new "pointillist" approach for detecting aggregated anomalous events by correlating information about host file updates across both space and time. Our approach explores the temporal and spatial locality of system state changes through learning and correlation. It requires neither prior knowledge about normal host activities, nor system specific rules.

A prototype implementation, called *Seurat*, suggests that the approach is effective in detecting rapidly propagating attacks that modify host file systems. The detection rate degrades as the stealthiness of attacks increases. By trading off detection latency, we are also able to identify hosts that are compromised by slowly propagating attacks. For each alarm, Seurat identifies suspicious files and hosts for further investigation, greatly facilitating root cause diagnosis and false alarm suppression.

References

1. Porras, P.A., Neumann, P.G.: EMERALD: Event Monitoring Enabling Responses to Anomalous Live Disturbances. In: Proceedings of the 20th National Information Systems Security Conference. (1997)
2. Abad, C., Taylor, J., Sengul, C., Zhou, Y., Yurcik, W., Rowe, K.: Log Correlation for Intrusion Detection: A Proof of Concept. In: Proceedings of the 19th Annual Computer Security Applications Conference, Las Vegas, Nevada, USA (2003)
3. Kruegel, C., Toth, T., Kerer, C.: Decentralized Event Correlation for Intrusion Detection. In: International Conference on Information Security and Cryptology (ICISC). (2001)
4. Tripwire, Inc.: Tripwire. (http://www.tripwire.com)
5. CERT Coordination Center: Overview of Attack Trends. http://www.cert.org/archive/pdf/attack_trends.pdf (2002)
6. Moore, D., Paxson, V., Savage, S., Shannon, C., Staniford, S., Weaver, N.: Inside the Slammer Worm. IEEE Security and Privacy **1** (2003) 33–39
7. Pennington, A., Strunk, J., Griffin, J., Soules, C., Goodson, G., Ganger, G.: Storage-based intrusion detection: Watching storage activity for suspicious behavior. In: Proceedings of 12th USENIX Security Symposium, Washington, DC (2003)
8. Lehti, R., Virolainen, P.: AIDE - Advanced Intrusion Detection Environment. (http://www.cs.tut.fi/~rammer/aide.html)
9. Berry, M.W., Drmac, Z., Jessup, E.R.: Matrices, vector spaces, and information retrieval. SIAM Review **41** (1999)
10. Kamber, M.: Data mining: Concepts and techniques. Morgan Kaufmann Publishers (2000)
11. Zhang, J., Tsui, F., Wagner, M.M., Hogan, W.R.: Detection of Outbreaks from Time Series Data Using Wavelet Transform. In: AMIA Fall Symp., Omni Press CD (2003) 748–752
12. Jolliffe, I.T.: Principle component analysis. Spring-Verlag, New York (1986)
13. Forgy, E.: Cluster analysis of multivariante data: Efficiency vs. Interpretability of classifications. Biometrics **21** (1965)
14. Gersho, A., Gray, R.: Vector Quantization and Signal Compresssion. Kluwer Academic Publishers (1992)
15. Moore, A.: K-means and Hierarchical Clustering. http://www.cs.cmu.edu/~awm/tutorials/kmeans09.pdf (available upon request) (2001)
16. Symantec: Symantec Security Response. (http://securityresponse.symantec.com)
17. F-Secure: F-Secure Security Information Center. (http://www.f-secure.com/virus-info)
18. Whitehats, Inc.: Whitehats Network Security Resource. (http://www.whitehats.com)
19. PacketStorm: Packet Storm. (http://www.packetstormsecurity.org)
20. SANS Institute: Lion Worm. http://www.sans.org/y2k/lion.htm (2001)
21. Wagner, D., Dean, D.: Mimicry Attacks on Host-Based Intrusion Detection Systems. In: Proceedings of ACM Conference on Computer and Communications Security (CCS). (2002)
22. Trusted Computing Platform Alliance: Trusted Computing Platform Alliance. (http://www.trustedcomputing.org)
23. Schneier, B., Kelsey, J.: Cryptographic Support for Secure Logs on Untrusted Machines. In: The Seventh USENIX Security Symposium. (1998)
24. Balasubramaniyan, J.S., Garcia-Fernandez, J.O., Isacoff, D., Spafford, E., Zamboni, D.: An architecture for intrusion detection using autonomous agents. In: Proceedings of the 14th IEEE Computer Security Applications Conference. (1998)

25. Xie, Y., O'Hallaron, D.R., Reiter, M.K.: A Secure Distributed Search System. In: Proceedings of the 11th IEEE International Symposium on High Performance Distributed Computing. (2002)
26. Planetlab: PlanetLab. (http://www.planet-lab.org)
27. Samhain Labs: Samhain. (http://la-samhna.de/samhain)
28. Pedestal Software: INTACT^{TM}.
    (http://www.pedestalsoftware.com/products/intact)
29. Cheung, S., Crawford, R., Dilger, M., Frank, J., Hoagland, J., Levitt, K., Rowe, J., Staniford-Chen, S., Yip, R., Zerkle, D.: The Design of GrIDS: A Graph-Based Intrusion Detection System. Technical Report CSE-99-2, U.C. Davis Computer Science Department (1999)
30. White, G., Fisch, E., Pooch, U.: Cooperating security managers: A peer-based intrusion detection system. IEEE Network **10** (1994)
31. Snapp, S.R., Smaha, S.E., Teal, D.M., Grance, T.: The DIDS (distributed intrusion detection system) prototype. In: the Summer USENIX Conference, San Antonio, Texas, USENIX Association (1992) 227–233
32. Valdes, A., Skinner, K.: Probabilistic Alert Correlation. In: Recent Advances in Intrusion Detection, Volume 2212 of Lecture Notes in Computer Science, Springer-Verlag (2001)
33. Andersson, D., Fong, M., Valdes, A.: Heterogeneous Sensor Correlation: A Case Study of Live Traffic Analysis. Presented at IEEE Information Assurance Workshop (2002)
34. Ning, P., Cui, Y., Reeves, D.S.: Analyzing Intensive Intrusion Alerts Via Correlation. In: Recent Advances in Intrusion Detection, Volume 2516 of Lecture Notes in Computer Science, Springer-Verlag (2002)
35. Wang, H., Hu, Y., Yuan, C., Zhang, Z.: Friends Troubleshooting Network: Towards Privacy-Preserving, Automatic Troubleshooting. In: Proceedings of the 3rd International Workshop on Peer-to-Peer Systems (IPTPS). (2004)

Detection of Interactive Stepping Stones: Algorithms and Confidence Bounds

Avrim Blum, Dawn Song, and Shobha Venkataraman

Carnegie Mellon University, Pittsburgh, PA 15213
{avrim,shobha}@cs.cmu.edu, dawnsong@cmu.edu

Abstract. Intruders on the Internet often prefer to launch network intrusions indirectly, i.e., using a chain of hosts on the Internet as relay machines using protocols such as Telnet or SSH. This type of attack is called a *stepping-stone attack*. In this paper, we propose and analyze algorithms for stepping-stone detection using ideas from Computational Learning Theory and the analysis of random walks. Our results are the first to achieve provable (polynomial) upper bounds on the number of packets needed to confidently detect and identify encrypted stepping-stone streams with proven guarantees on the probability of falsely accusing non-attacking pairs. Moreover, our methods and analysis rely on mild assumptions, especially in comparison to previous work. We also examine the consequences when the attacker inserts chaff into the stepping-stone traffic, and give bounds on the amount of chaff that an attacker would have to send to evade detection. Our results are based on a new approach which can detect correlation of streams at a fine-grained level. Our approach may also apply to more generalized traffic analysis domains, such as anonymous communication.

Keywords: Network intrusion detection. Evasion. Stepping stones. Interactive sessions. Random walks.

1 Introduction

Intruders on the Internet often launch network intrusions indirectly, in order to decrease their chances of being discovered. One of the most common methods used to evade surveillance is the construction of *stepping stones*. In a stepping-stone attack, an attacker uses a sequence of hosts on the Internet as relay machines and constructs a chain of interactive connections using protocols such as Telnet or SSH. The attacker types commands on his local machine and then the commands are relayed via the chain of "stepping stones" until they finally reach the victim. Because the final victim only sees traffic from the last hop of the chain of the stepping stones, it is difficult for the victim to learn any information about the true origin of the attack. The chaotic nature and sheer volume of the traffic on the Internet makes such attacks extremely difficult to record or trace back.

To combat stepping-stone attacks, the approach taken by previous research (e.g., [1–4]), and the one that we adopt, is to instead ask the question "What

E. Jonsson et al. (Eds.): RAID 2004, LNCS 3224, pp. 258–277, 2004.

can we detect if we monitor traffic at the routers or gateways?" That is, we examine the traffic that goes in and out of routers, and try to detect which streams, if any, are part of a stepping-stone attack. This problem is referred to as the *stepping-stone detection problem*. A *stepping-stone monitor* analyzes correlations between flows of incoming and outgoing traffic which may suggest the existence of a stepping stone. Like previous approaches, in this paper we consider the detection of *interactive* attacks: those in which the attacker sends commands through the chain of hosts to the target, waits for responses, sends new commands, and so on in an interactive session. Such traffic is characterized by streams of packets, in which packets sent on the first link appear on the next a short time later, within some *maximum tolerable delay* bound Δ. Like previous approaches, we assume traffic is encrypted, and thus the detection mechanisms cannot rely on analyzing the content of the streams. We will call a pair of streams an *attacking pair* if it is a stepping-stone pair, and we will call a pair of streams a *non-attacking pair* if it is not a stepping-stone pair.

Researchers have proposed many approaches for detecting stepping stones in encrypted traffic. (e.g., [1–3]. See more detailed related work in Section 2.) However, most previous approaches in this area are based on ad-hoc heuristics and do not give any rigorous analysis that would provide provable guarantees of the false positive rate or the false negative rate [2, 3]. Donoho et al. [4] proposed a method based on wavelet transforms to detect correlations of streams, and it was the first work that performed rigorous analysis of their method. However, they do not give a bound on the number of packets that need to be observed in order to detect attacks with a given level of confidence. Moreover, their analysis requires the assumption that the packets on the attacker's stream arrive according to a Poisson or a Pareto distribution – in reality, the attacker's stream may be arbitrary. Wang and Reeves [5] proposed a watermark-based scheme which can detect correlation between streams of encrypted packets. However, they assume that the attacker's timing perturbation of packets is independent and identically distributed (*iid*), and their method breaks when the attacker perturbs traffic in other ways.

Thus, despite the volume of previous work, an important question still remains open: how can we design an efficient algorithm to detect stepping-stone attacks with (a) provable bounds on the number of packets that need to be monitored, (b) a provable guarantee on the false positive and false negative rate, and (c) few assumptions on the distributions of attacker and normal traffic?

The paper sets off to answer this question. In particular, in this paper we use ideas from Computational Learning Theory to produce a strong set of guarantees for this problem:

Objectives: We explicitly set our objective to be to distinguish attacking pairs from non-attacking pairs, given our fairly mild assumptions about each. In contrast, the work of Donoho et al. [4] detects only if a pair of streams is correlated. This is equivalent to our goal if one assumes non-attacking pairs are perfectly uncorrelated, but that is not necessarily realistic and our assumptions about non-attacking pairs will allow for substantial coarse-grained correlation among them. For example, if co-workers work and take breaks together, their typing behavior may be correlated at a coarse-grained level even though they are not part of any attack. Our models allow for this type of behavior on the part of "normal" streams, and yet we will still be able to distinguish them from true stepping-stone attacks.

Fewer assumptions: We make very mild assumptions, especially in comparison with previous work. For example, unlike the work by Donoho et al., our algorithm and analysis do not rely on the Poisson or Pareto distribution assumption on the behavior of the *attacking* streams. By modeling a non-attack stream as a sequence of Poisson processes with varying rates and over varying time periods, our analysis results can apply to almost any distribution or pattern of usage of non-attack and attack streams. This model allows for substantial high-level correlation among non-attackers.

Provable bounds: We give the first algorithm for detecting stepping-stone attacks that provides (a) provable bounds on the number of packets needed to confidently detect and identify stepping-stone streams, and (b) provable guarantees on false positive rates. Our bounds on the number of packets needed for confident detection are only quadratic in terms of certain natural parameters of the problem, which indicates the efficiency of our algorithm.

Stronger results with chaff: We also propose detection algorithms and give a hardness result when the attacker inserts "chaff" traffic in the stepping-stone streams. Our analysis shows that our detection algorithm is effective when the attacker inserts chaff that is less than a certain threshold fraction. Our hardness results indicate that when the attacker can insert chaff that is more than a certain threshold fraction, the attacker can make the attacking streams mimic two independent random processes, and thus completely evade any detection algorithm. Note that our hardness analysis will apply even when the monitor can actively manipulate the timing delay. Our results on the chaff case are also a significant advance from previous work. The work of Donoho et al. [4] assumes that the chaff traffic inserted by the attacker is a Poisson process independent from the non-chaff traffic in the attacking stream, while our results make no assumption on the distribution of the chaff traffic.

The type of guarantee we will be able to achieve is that given a confidence parameter δ, our procedure will certify a pair as attacking or non-attacking with error probability at most δ, after observing a number of packets that is only quadratic in certain natural parameters of the problem and logarithmic in $1/\delta$. Our approach is based on a connection to sample-complexity bounds in Computational Learning Theory. In that setting, one has a set or sequence of hypotheses $h_1, h_2, \ldots$, and the goal is to identify which if any of them has a low true error rate from observing performance on random examples [6–8]. The type of question addressed in that literature is how much data does one need to observe in order to ensure at most some given δ probability of failure. In our setting, to some extent packets play the role of examples and pairs of streams play the role of hypotheses, though the analogy is not perfect because it is the relationship *between* packets that provides the information we use for stepping-stone detection.

The high-level idea of our approach is that if we consider two packet streams and look at the *difference* between the number of packets sent on them, then this quantity is performing some type of random walk on the one-dimensional line. If these streams are part of a stepping-stone attack, then by the maximum-tolerable delay assumption, this quantity will never deviate too far from the origin. However, if the two streams are *not* part of an attack, then even if the streams are somewhat correlated, say because they are Poisson with rates that vary in tandem, this walk *will* begin to experience substantial deviation from the origin. There are several subtle issues: for example, our algorithm may not know in advance what an attacker's tolerable delay is. In addition, new streams may be arriving over time, so if we want to be careful not to have false-positives, we need to adjust our confidence threshold as new streams enter the system.

Outline. In the rest of the paper, we first discuss related work in Section 2, then give the problem definition in Section 3. We then describe the stepping-stone detection algorithm and confidence bounds analysis in Section 4. We consider the consequences of adding chaff in Section 5. We finally conclude in Section 6.

2   Related Work

The initial line of work in identifying interactive stepping stones focused on *content*-based techniques. The interactive stepping stone problem was first formulated and studied by Staniford and Heberlein [1]. They proposed a content-based algorithm that created thumbprints of streams and compared them, looking for extremely good matches. Another content-based approach, Sleepy Watermark Tracing, was proposed by Wang et al. [10]. These content-based approaches require that the content of the streams under consideration do not change significantly between the streams. Thus, for example, they do not apply to encrypted traffic such as SSH sessions.

Another line of work studies correlation of streams based on *connection timings*. Zhang and Paxson [2] proposed an algorithm for encrypted connection chains based on periods of activity of the connections. They observed that in stepping stones, the ON-periods and OFF-periods will coincide. They use this observation to detect stepping stones, by examining the number of consecutive OFF-periods and the distance of the OFF-periods. Yoda and Etoh [3] proposed a deviation-based algorithm to trace the connection chains of intruders. They computed deviations between a known intruder stream and all other concurrent streams on the Internet, compared the packets of streams which have small deviations from the intruder's stream, and utilize these analyses to identify a set of streams that match the intruder stream. Wang et al. [11] proposed another timing-based approach that uses the arrival and departure times of packets to correlate connections in real-time. They showed that the inter-packet timing characteristics are preserved across many router hops, and often uniquely identify the correlations between connections. These algorithms based on connection timings, however, are all vulnerable to active timing pertubation by the attacker – they will not be able to detect stepping stones when the attacker actively perturbs the timings of the packets on the stepping-stone streams.

We are aware of only two papers [4, 5] that study the problem of detecting stepping-stone attacks on encrypted streams with the assumption of a bound on the maximum delay tolerated by the attacker. In Section 1, we discuss the work of Donoho et al. [4] in relation to our paper. We note that their work does not give any bounds on the number of packets needed to detect correlation between streams, or a discussion of the false positives that may be identified by their method. Wang and Reeves [5] proposed a watermark-based scheme, which can detect correlation between streams of encrypted packets. However, they assume that the attacker's timing perturbation of packets is independent and identically distributed (*iid*). Our algorithms do not require such an assumption. Further, they need to actively manipulate the inter-packet delays in order to embed and detect their watermarks. In contrast, our algorithms require only passive monitoring of the arrival times of the packets.

Wang [12] examined the problem of determining the serial order of correlated connections in order to determine the intrusion path, when given the complete set of correlated connections.

3   Problem Definition

Our problem definition essentially mirrors that of Donoho et al. [4]. A *stream* is a sequence of packets that belong to the same connection. We assume that the attacker has a maximum delay tolerance Δ, which we may or may not know. That is, for every packet sent in the first stream, there must be a corresponding packet in the second stream between 0 and Δ time steps later. The notion of maximum delay bound was first proposed by Donoho et al. [4]. We also assume that there is a maximum number of packets that the attacker can send in a particular time interval t, which we call p_t. We note that p_Δ is unlikely to be very large, since we are considering interactive stepping-stone attacks. As in prior work, we assume that a packet on either stream maps to only one packet on the other stream (i.e., packets are not combined or broken down in any manner).

Similar to previous work, we do not pay attention to the content or the sizes of the packets, since the packets may be encrypted. We assume that the real-time traffic delay between packets is very small compared to Δ, and ignore it everywhere. We have a stepping-stone monitor that observes the streams going through the monitor, and keeps track of the total number of packets on each stream at each time of observation. We denote the total number of packets in stream i by time t as $N_i(t)$, or simply N_i if t is the current time step.

By our assumptions, for a pair of stepping-stone streams S_1, S_2, the following two conditions hold for the true packets of the streams, i.e., not including chaff packets:

1. $N_1(t) \geq N_2(t)$.
   Every packet in stream 2 comes from stream 1.

2. $N_1(t) \le N_2(t + \Delta)$.

All packets in stream 1 must go into stream 2 – i.e., no packets on stream 1 are lost enroute to stream 2, and all the packets on stream 1 arrive on stream 2 within time Δ.

If the attacker sends no chaff on his streams, then all the packets on a stepping stone pair will obey the above two conditions.

We will find it useful to think about the number of packets in a stream in terms of the total number of the packets observed in the union of two streams: in other words, viewing each arrival of a packet in the union of the two streams as a "time step". We will use $\overline{N}_i(w)$ for the number of packets in stream i, when there are a total of w packets in the union of the two streams.

In Section 4.1, we assume that a normal stream i is generated by a Poisson process with a constant rate λ_i. In Section 4.2, we generalize this, allowing for substantial high-level correlation between non-attacking streams. Specifically, we model a non-attacking stream as a "Poisson process with a knob", where the knob controls the rate of the process and can be adjusted arbitrarily by the user with time. That is, the stream is really generated by a sequence of Poisson processes with varying rates for varying lengths of time. Even if two non-attacking streams correlate by adjusting their knobs together – e.g., both having a high rate at certain times and low rates at others – our procedure will nonetheless (with high probability) not be fooled into falsely tagging them as an attacking pair.

The guarantees produced by our algorithm will be described by two quantities:

- a *monitoring time* M measured in terms of total number of packets that need to be observed on both streams, before deciding whether the pair of streams is an attack pair, and
- a *false-positive probability* δ, given as input to the algorithm (also called the confidence level), that describes our willingness to falsely accuse a non-attacking pair.

The guarantees we will achieve are that (a) any stepping-stone pair will be discovered after M packets, and (b) any normal pair has at most a δ chance of being falsely accused. Our algorithm will never fail to flag a true attacking pair, so long as at least M packets are observed. For instance, our first result, Theorem 1, is that if non-attacking streams are Poisson, then $M = \frac{8p_\Delta^2}{\pi} \log \frac{1}{\delta}$ packets are sufficient to detect a stepping-stone attack with false-positive probability δ. One can also adjust the confidence level with the number of pairs of streams being monitored, to ensure at most a δ chance of *ever* falsely accusing a normal pair.

All logarithms in this paper are base 2. Table 1 summarizes the notation we use in this paper.

Table 1. Summary of notation

Δ	maximum tolerable delay bound
p_Δ	maximum number of packets that may be sent in time interval Δ.
δ	false positive probability
S_i	stream i
M	number of packets that we need to observe on the union of the two streams in the detection algorithms
$N_i(t)$	number of packets sent on stream i in time interval t.
$\overline{N}_i(w)$	number of packets sent on stream i when a total of w packets is present on the union of the pair of stream under consideration.

4   Main Results: Detection Algorithms and Confidence Bounds Analysis

In this section, we give an algorithm that will detect stepping stones with a low probability of false positives. We only consider streams that have no chaff, which means that every packet on the second stream comes from the first stream, and packets can only be delayed, not dropped. We will discuss the consequences of adding chaff in Section 5.

Our guarantees give a bound on the number of packets that need to be observed to confidently identify an attacker. These bounds have a quadratic dependence on the maximum tolerable delay Δ (or more precisely, on the number of packets p_Δ an attacker can send in that time frame), and a logarithmic dependence on $1/\delta$, where δ is the desired false-positive probability. The quadratic dependence on maximum tolerable delay comes essentially from the fact that on average it takes $\Theta(p^2)$ steps for a random walk to reach distance p from the origin. Our basic bounds assume the value of p_Δ is given to the algorithm (Theorems 1 and 2); we then show how to remove this assumption, increasing the monitoring time by only an $O(\log \log p_\Delta)$ factor (Theorem 3).

We begin in Section 4.1 by considering a simple model of normal streams – we assume that any normal stream S_i can be modeled as a Poisson process, with a fixed Poisson rate λ_i. We then generalize this model in Section 4.2. We make no additional assumptions on the attacking streams.

4.1   A Simple Poisson Model

We first describe our detection algorithm and analysis for the case that p_Δ is known, and then later show how this assumption can be removed.

The Detection Algorithm. Our algorithm is simple and efficient: for a given pair of streams, the monitor watches the packet arrivals, and counts packets on both streams until the total number of packets (on both streams) reaches a certain threshold $\frac{8p_\Delta^2}{\pi}$ [1]. The monitor then computes the difference in the number

---

[1] The intuition for the parameters as well as the proof of correctness is in the analysis section.

DETECT-ATTACKS (δ, p_Δ)

    Set $m = \log \frac{1}{\delta}$, $n = \frac{8p_\Delta^2}{\pi}$.

    For m iterations

        Observe n packets on $S_1 \cup S_2$.

        Compute $d = N_1 - N_2$. If $d > p_\Delta$ return NORMAL.

    return ATTACK.

Fig. 1. Algorithm for stepping-stone detection (without chaff) with a simple Poisson model

of packets of the two streams – if the difference exceeds the packet bound p_Δ, we know the streams are normal; otherwise, it restarts. If the difference stays bounded for a sufficiently long time ($\log \frac{1}{\delta}$ such trials of $\frac{8p_\Delta^2}{\pi}$ packets), the monitor declares that the pair of streams is a stepping stone. The algorithm is shown in Fig. 1.

We note that the algorithm is memory-efficient – we only need to keep track of the number of packets seen on each stream. We also note that the algorithm does not need to know or compute the Poisson rates; it simply needs to observe the packets coming in on the streams.

Analysis. We first note that, by design, *our algorithm will always identify a stepping-stone pair, providing they send M packets*. We then show that the false positive rate of δ is also achieved by the algorithm. Under the assumption that normal streams may be modeled as Poisson processes, we show three analytical results in the following analysis:

1. When p_Δ is known, the monitor needs to observe no more than $M = \frac{8p_\Delta^2}{\pi} \log \frac{1}{\delta}$ packets on the union of the two streams under consideration, to guarantee a false positive rate of δ for any given pair of streams (Theorem 1).
2. Suppose instead that we wish to achieve a δ probability of false positive over *all* pairs of streams that we examine. For instance, we may wish to achieve a false positive rate of δ over an entire day of observations, rather than over a particular number of streams. When p_Δ is known, the monitor needs to observe no more than $M = \frac{8p_\Delta^2}{\pi} \log \frac{i(i+1)}{\delta}$ packets on the union of the ith pair of streams, to guarantee a δ chance of false positive among all pairs of streams it examines (Theorem 2).
3. When p_Δ is unknown, we can achieve the above guarantees with only an $O(\log \log p_\Delta)$ factor increase in the number of additional packets that need to observe (Theorem 3).

Below, we first give some intuition and then the detailed theorem statements and analysis.

Intuition. We first give some intuition behind the analysis. Consider two normal streams as Poisson processes with rates λ_1 and λ_2. We can treat the difference between two Poisson processes as a random walk, as shown in Fig. 2. Consider a sequence of packets generated in the union of the two streams. The probability that a particular packet is generated by the first stream is $\frac{\lambda_1}{\lambda_1+\lambda_2}$ (which we denote μ_1), and probability that it is generated by the second stream is $\frac{\lambda_2}{\lambda_1+\lambda_2}$ (which we call μ_2). We can define a random variable Z to be the difference between the number of packets generated by the streams. Every time a packet is sent on either S_1 or S_2, Z increases by 1 with probability μ_1, and decreases by 1 with probability μ_2. It is therefore a one-dimensional random walk. We care about the expected time for Z to exit the bounded region $[0, p_\Delta]$, given that it begins at some arbitrary point inside this range. If $Z < 0$, then the second stream has definitely a packet that the first stream did not; if $Z > p_\Delta$, then the delay bound is violated.

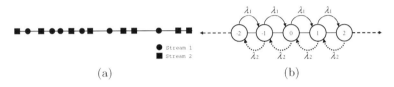

(a)   (b)

Fig. 2. (a) Packets arriving in the two streams. (b) Viewing the arrival of packets as a random walk with rates λ_1 and λ_2

Theorem 1. *Under the assumption that normal streams behave as Poisson processes, the algorithm* DETECT-ATTACKS *will correctly detect stepping-stone attacks with a false positive probability at most δ for any given pair of streams, after monitoring $\frac{8p_\Delta^2}{\pi} \log \frac{1}{\delta}$ packets on the union of the two streams.*

Proof. Let $0 \le \overline{N}_1(w) - \overline{N}_2(w) \le p_\Delta$ at total packet count w. Then, after n further packet arrivals, we want to bound the probability that the difference is still within $[0, p_\Delta]$. Let $Z = \overline{N}_1(w+n) - \overline{N}_2(w+n)$. For any given x, we have:

$$Pr[Z = x] = \binom{n}{\frac{n+x}{2}} \mu_1^{\frac{n+x}{2}} \mu_2^{\frac{n-x}{2}}.$$

Using Stirling's approximation, for $0 \le x \le p_\Delta \ll n$

$$Pr[Z = x] \le \frac{\mu_1^{n/2} \mu_2^{n/2}}{\left(\frac{1}{2}\right)^n \sqrt{\pi n/2}} \mu_1^x \mu_2^{-x} < \frac{1}{\sqrt{\pi n/2}}.$$

Therefore, over the interval of length p_Δ,

$$Pr[0 \le Z \le p_\Delta] \le \sum_{x=0}^{p_\Delta} Pr[Z = x] < \frac{p_\Delta}{\sqrt{\pi n/2}}.$$

Substituting $n = \frac{8p_\Delta^2}{\pi}$, we get $Pr[0 \le Z \le p_\Delta] < \frac{1}{2}$.

To ensure that this is bounded by the given confidence level, we take m such observations of n time steps, so that $\left(\frac{1}{2}\right)^m \leq \delta$, or

$$m \geq \log \frac{1}{\delta} \, .$$

We need to observe m sets of n packets; therefore, we need $\log \frac{1}{\delta}$ intervals.   □

We have just shown in Theorem 1 that our algorithm in Fig. 1 will identify any given stepping-stone pair correctly, and will have a probability δ of a false positive for any given non-attacking pair of streams. We can also modify our algorithm so that it only has a probability δ of a false positive among *all* the pairs of streams that we observe. That is, given δ, we distribute it over all the pairs of streams that we can observe, by allowing only $\frac{\delta}{i(i+1)}$ probability of false positive for the ith pair of streams, and using the fact that $\sum_{i=1}^{\infty} \frac{\delta}{i(i+1)} = \delta$. To see why this might be useful, suppose $\delta = 0.001$. Then, we would expect to falsely accuse one pair out of every 1000 pairs of (normal) streams. It could be more useful at times to be able to give a false positive rate of 0.001 over an entire month of observations, rather than give that rate over a particular number of streams.

Theorem 2. *Under the assumption that normal streams behave as Poisson processes, the algorithm* DETECT-ATTACKS *will have a probability at most δ of a false positive among all the pairs of streams it examines if, for the ith pair of streams, it uses a monitoring time of $\frac{8p_\Delta^2}{\pi} \log \frac{i(i+1)}{\delta}$ packets.*

Proof. We need to split our allowed false positives δ among all the pairs we will observe; however, since we do not know the number of pairs in advance, we do not split the δ evenly.

Instead, we allow the ith pair of streams a false positive probability of $\frac{\delta}{i(i+1)}$, and then use the previous algorithm with the updated false positive level. The result then follows from Theorem 1 and the fact that $\sum_{i=1}^{\infty} \frac{\delta}{i(i+1)} = \delta$.   □

The arguments so far assume that the algorithm *knows* the quantity p_Δ. We now remove this assumption by using a "guess and double" strategy. Let $p_j = 2^j$. When a pair of streams is "cleared" as not being a stepping-stone attack with respect to p_j, we then consider it with respect to p_{j+1}. By setting the error parameters appropriately, we can maintain the guarantee that any normal pair is falsely accused with probability at most δ, while guaranteeing that any attacking pair will be discovered with a monitoring time that depends only on the *actual* value of p_Δ. Thus, we can still obtain strong guarantees. In addition, even though this algorithm "never" finishes monitoring a normal pair of streams, the time between steps at which the monitor compares the difference $N_1 - N_2$ increases over the sequence. This means that for the streams that have been under consideration for a long period of time, the monitor tests differences less often, and thus does not need to do substantial work, so long as the stream counters are running continuously.

Theorem 3. *Assume that normal streams behave as Poisson processes. Then, even if p_Δ is unknown, we can use algorithm* DETECT-ATTACKS *as a subroutine and have a false positive probability at most δ, while correctly catching stepping-stone attacks within $O(p_\Delta^2(\log\log p_\Delta + \log\frac{1}{\delta}))$ packets, where p_Δ is the actual maximum value of $N_1(t) - N_2(t)$ for the attacker.*

Proof. As discussed above, we run DETECT-ATTACKS using a sequence of "p_Δ" values p_j, where $p_j = 2^j$, incrementing j when the algorithm returns NORMAL. As in Theorem 2, we use $\frac{\delta}{j(j+1)}$ as our false-positive probability on iteration j, which guarantees having at most a δ false-positive probability overall. We now need to calculate the monitoring time. For a given attacking pair, the number of packets needed to catch it is at most:

$$\sum_{j=1}^{\lceil \log p_\Delta \rceil} \frac{8 \cdot 2^{2j}}{\pi} \log \frac{j(j+1)}{\delta}.$$

Since the entries in the summation are more than doubling with j, the sum is at most twice the value of its largest term, and so the total monitoring time is $O(p_\Delta^2(\log\log p_\Delta + \log\frac{1}{\delta}))$. □

4.2   Generalizing the Poisson Model

We now relax the assumption that a normal process is Poisson with a fixed rate λ. Instead, we assume that a normal process can be modeled as a sequence of Poisson processes, with varying rates, and over varying time periods. From the point of view of our algorithm, one can view this as a Poisson process with a user-adjustable "knob" that is being controlled by an adversary to fool us into making a false accusation.

Note that this is a general model; we could use it to coarsely approximate almost any distribution, or pattern of usage. For example, at a high level, this model could approximately simulate Pareto distributions which are thought to be a good model for users' typing patterns [13], by using a Pareto distribution to choose our Poisson rates for varying time periods, which could be arbitrarily small. Correlated users can be modeled as having the same sequence of Poisson rates and time intervals: for example, co-workers may work together and take short or long breaks together.

Formally, for a given pair of streams, we will assume the first stream is a sequence given by $(\lambda_{11}, t_{11}), (\lambda_{12}, t_{12}), \ldots$, and the second stream by (λ_{21}, t_{21}), $(\lambda_{22}, t_{22}), \ldots$. Let $N_i(t)$ denote the number of packets sent in stream i by time t. Then, the key to the argument is that over any given time interval T, the number of packets sent by stream i is distributed according to a Poisson process with a single rate $\hat{\lambda}_{i,T}$, which is the weighted mean of the rates of all the Poisson processes during that time. That is, if time interval T contains a sequence of time intervals $j_{start}, \ldots, j_{end}$, then $\hat{\lambda}_{i,T} = \frac{1}{|T|}\sum_{j=j_{start}}^{j_{end}} \lambda_{ij}t_{ij}$ (breaking intervals if necessary to match the boundaries of T).

Theorem 4. *Assuming that normal streams behave as sequences of Poisson processes, the algorithm* DETECT-ATTACKS *will have a false positive rate of at most* δ, *if it observes at least* $\frac{7}{2} \log \frac{1}{\delta}$ *intervals of n packets each, where* $n = \frac{16p_\Delta^2}{\pi}$.

Proof. Let $S(t)$ be the number of packets on the union of the streams at time t. Let $D(t)$ be the difference in the number of packets at time t, i.e. $N_1(t) - N_2(t)$. Let $\hat{n} = \frac{8p_\Delta^2}{\pi}$.

We define T to be the time when $Pr[S(T) \geq \hat{n}] = \frac{1}{2}$, and let $T' \geq T$. Then,

$$
\begin{aligned}
Pr[D(T') \notin I] &= Pr[D(T') \notin I | S(T') \geq \hat{n}] Pr[S(T') \geq \hat{n}] \\
&\quad + Pr[D(T') \notin I | S(T') < \hat{n}] Pr[S(T') < \hat{n}], \\
&\geq Pr[D(T') \notin I | S(T') \geq \hat{n}] Pr[S(T') \geq \hat{n}], \\
&\geq \frac{1}{2} Pr[D(T') \notin I | S(T') \geq \hat{n}], \\
&= \frac{1}{2}(1 - Pr[D(T') \in I | S(T') \geq \hat{n}]).
\end{aligned}
$$

From the proof of Theorem 1, we know

$$
Pr[D(T') \in I | S(T') \geq \hat{n}] \leq \frac{p_\Delta}{\sqrt{\pi \hat{n}/2}}.
$$

$$
\text{Therefore, } Pr[D(T') \notin I] \geq \frac{1}{2}\left(1 - \frac{p_\Delta}{\sqrt{\pi \hat{n}/2}}\right).
$$

Substituting $\hat{n} = \frac{8p_\Delta^2}{\pi}$, we get $Pr[D(T') \notin I] \geq \frac{1}{4}$.
Now, note that $Pr[S(T) \geq k\hat{n}] \leq \frac{1}{2^k}$. Therefore, $Pr[t < T | S(t) \geq k\hat{n}] \leq \frac{1}{2^k}$. Then,

$$
\begin{aligned}
Pr[D(t) \notin I | S(t) \geq k\hat{n}] &= Pr[D(t) \notin I | t \geq T] Pr[t \geq T | S(t) \geq k\hat{n}] \\
&\quad + Pr[D(t) \notin I | t < T] Pr[t < T | S(t) \geq k\hat{n}] \\
&\geq Pr[D(t) \notin I | t \geq T] Pr[t \geq T | S(t) \geq k\hat{n}] \\
&\geq \frac{1}{4}\left(1 - \frac{1}{2^k}\right).
\end{aligned}
$$

Therefore, $Pr[D(t) \in I | S(t) \geq k\hat{n}] < 1 - \frac{1}{4}\left(1 - \frac{1}{2^k}\right)$.

To bound this by the given confidence level, we need to take m such observations of $k\hat{n}$ packets in the union of the streams, so that:

$$
\left(1 - \frac{1}{4}\left(1 - \frac{1}{2^k}\right)\right)^m \leq \delta.
$$

$$
\text{Setting } k = 2, \left(1 - \frac{1}{4}\left(\frac{3}{4}\right)\right)^m \leq \delta.
$$

$$
m \geq \frac{\log \frac{1}{\delta}}{\log\left(\frac{16}{13}\right)}.
$$

Since $\frac{1}{\log\left(\frac{16}{13}\right)} < \frac{7}{2}$, we set $m \geq \frac{7}{2} \log \frac{1}{\delta}$. $\qquad\square$

Likewise, we have the analogues of Theorem 2 and Theorem 3 for the general model. We omit their proofs, since they are very similar to the proofs of Theorem 2 and Theorem 3.

Theorem 5. *Assuming that normal streams behave as sequences of Poisson processes, the algorithm* DETECT-ATTACKS *will have a probability at most δ of a false positive over all pairs of streams it examines, if, for the ith pair of streams, it observes $\frac{7}{2} \log \frac{i(i+1)}{\delta}$ intervals of n packets each, where $n = \frac{16p_\Delta^2}{\pi}$.*

Theorem 6. *Assuming that normal streams behave as sequences of Poisson processes, then if p_Δ is unknown, we can use repeated-doubling and incur an extra $O(\log \log p_\Delta)$ factor in the number of packets over that in Theorem 5, to achieve false-positive probability δ.*

5   Chaff: Detection and Hardness Result

All the results in Section 4 rely on the attacker streams obeying two assumptions in Section 3 – in a pair of attacker streams, every packet sent on the first stream arrives on the second stream, and any packet that arrives on the second stream arrives from the first stream. In this section, we examine the consequences of relaxing these assumptions.

Notice that only the packets that must reach the target need to obey these two assumptions. However, the attacker could insert some superfluous packets into either of the two streams, that do not need to reach the target, and therefore, do not have to obey the assumptions. Such extraneous packets are called *chaff*. By introducing chaff into the streams, the attacker would try to ensure that the number of packets observed in his two streams appear less correlated, and thus reduce the chances of being detected.

Donoho et al. [4] also examine the consequences of the addition of chaff to attack streams. They show that under the assumption that the chaff in the streams is generated by a Poisson process that is independent of the non-chaff packets in the stepping-stone streams, it is possible to detect correlation between stepping-stone pairs, as long as the streams have sufficient packets. However, an attacker may not wish to generate chaff as a Poisson process. In this section, we assume that a clever attacker will want to optimize his use of chaff, instead of adding it randomly to the streams. In Section 5.1 we explain how to detect stepping stones using our algorithm when the attacker uses a limited amount of chaff (Theorem 7). In Section 5.2 we describe how an attacker could use chaff to make a pair of stepping-stone streams mimic two independent Poisson processes, and thus ensure that the pair of streams are not correlated. We then give upper bounds on the minimum chaff the attacker needs to do this (Theorems 8 and 9).

5.1   Algorithm for Detection with Chaff

Recall that our algorithm DETECT-ATTACKS is based on the observation that, with high probability, two independent Poisson processes will differ by any fixed distance given sufficient time. An attacker can, therefore, evade detection with our algorithm by introducing a sufficient difference between the streams all the time. Specifically, our algorithm checks if the two streams have a difference that is greater than p_Δ packets every time there are $\frac{8p_\Delta^2}{\pi}$ packets in the union of the streams. To evade our algorithm as it stands (in Fig. 1), all that the attacker might need to do is to send one packet of chaff on the faster stream.

Algorithm. We now modify DETECT-ATTACKS slightly, to detect stepping-stone attacks under a limited amount of chaff. Instead of waiting for a difference of p_Δ packets between the two streams, we could wait for a difference of $2p_\Delta$ packets. The independent Poisson processes would eventually get a difference of $2p_\Delta$, but now, the attacker would need to send at least p_Δ packets in chaff in order to evade detection. He could get away with exactly p_Δ packets if he sends all of the chaff packets in the same time interval, on the same stream. However, as long as he sends less than p_Δ packets of chaff in every time interval, the monitor will flag his streams as stepping stones[2]. The complete algorithm is shown in Fig. 3.

DETECT-ATTACKS-CHAFF (δ, p_Δ)

    Set $m = \log \frac{1}{\delta}$, $n = \frac{32p_\Delta^2}{\pi}$.
    For m iterations
        Observe n packets on $S_1 \cup S_2$.
        Compute $d = N_1 - N_2$. If $d \geq 2p_\Delta$ return NORMAL.
    return ATTACK.

Fig. 3. Algorithm for stepping-stone detection with with less than p_Δ packets of chaff every $\frac{32p_\Delta^2}{\pi}$ packets

Analysis. We now show that DETECT-ATTACKS-CHAFF will correctly identify stepping stones with chaff, as long as the attacker sends no more than p_Δ packets of chaff for every $\frac{32p_\Delta^2}{\pi}$ packets. Further, any given non-attacking pair of streams will have no more than a δ chance of being called a stepping stone.

Theorem 7. *Under the assumption that normal streams behave as Poisson processes, and the attacker sends less than p_Δ packets of chaff every $\frac{32p_\Delta^2}{\pi}$ packets, the algorithm DETECT-ATTACKS-CHAFF will have a false positive rate of utmost δ, if we observe $\log \frac{1}{\delta}$ intervals of $\frac{32p_\Delta^2}{\pi}$ packets each.*

Proof. Let $0 \leq \overline{N}_1(w) - \overline{N}_2(w) \leq p_\Delta$ at total packet count w. Then, after n further packet arrivals, we want to bound the probability that the difference is still within $[0, p_\Delta]$, for a normal pair. Let $Z = \overline{N}_1(w + n) - \overline{N}_2(w + n)$.

---

[2] We choose to wait for a difference of $2p_\Delta$ packets here, because it is the integral multiple of p_Δ that maximizes the rate at which the attacker may send chaff. We could replace it with the non-integral multiple of p_Δ that maximizes the rate at which the attacker must send chaff, but we omit the details here.

As in the proof of Theorem 1, for any x, we have:

$$Pr[Z = x] < \frac{1}{\sqrt{\pi n/2}}.$$

Therefore, over an interval of size $2p_\Delta$, we have:

$$Pr[0 \leq Z < 2p_\Delta] < \frac{2p_\Delta}{\sqrt{\pi n/2}}.$$

Substituting $n = \frac{32p_\Delta^2}{\pi}$, we get $Pr[0 \leq Z < 2p_\Delta] < \frac{1}{2}$.

To ensure that this is bounded by the given confidence level, we take m such observations of n time steps, so that $\left(\frac{1}{2}\right)^m \leq \delta$, which gives $m \geq \log \frac{1}{\delta}$.

Therefore, a normal pair will differ by at least $2p_\Delta$ with probability at least $1 - \delta$, in $\log \frac{1}{\delta}$ intervals of n packets.

On the other hand, for an attack pair with no chaff, we know that $\overline{N}_1(w) - \overline{N}_2(w) \leq p_\Delta$. When the attacker can add less than p_Δ packets of chaff in $\frac{32p_\Delta^2}{\pi}$ packets, $\overline{N}_1(w + n) - \overline{N}_2(w + n) < 2p_\Delta$, and thus, difference in packet count an attack pair cannot exceed $2p_\Delta$ in n packets.   □

Note that Theorem 7 is the analogue of Theorem 1 when the chaff rate is bounded as described above. The analogues to the other theorems in Section 4 can be obtained in a similar manner.

Obviously, the attacker can evade detection by sending more than p_Δ packets of chaff for every $\frac{32p_\Delta^2}{\pi}$ packets. Further, if we count in pre-specified intervals, the attacker would only need to send p_Δ packets of chaff in *one* of the intervals, since the algorithm only checks if the streams differ by the specified bound in *any* of the intervals.

We could address the second problem by sampling random intervals, and checking if the difference Z in those intervals is at least $2p_\Delta$. We could also modify our algorithm to check if the difference Z stays outside $2p_\Delta$ for at least a fourth of the intervals, and analyze the resulting probabilities with Chernoff bounds. To defeat this, the attacker would have to send at least $\frac{\pi}{32p_\Delta}$ fraction the total packets on the union (p_Δ packets of chaff every $\frac{32p_\Delta^2}{\pi}$ packets) in an independent interval, so that every (sufficiently long) interval is unsuspicious.

However, if the attacker just chooses to send a lot of chaff packets on his stepping-stone streams, then he will be able to evade the algorithm we proposed. This type of evasion is, to some extent, inherent in the problem, not just the detection strategy we propose. In the next section, we show how an attacker could successfully mimic two independent streams, so that no algorithm could detect the attacker. We also give upper bounds on the minimum chaff the attacker needs to add to his streams, so that his attack streams are completely masked as independent processes.

5.2   Hardness Result for Detection with Chaff

If an attacker is able to send a *lot* of chaff, he can in effect ride his communication on the backs of two truly independent Poisson processes. In this section, we analyze how much chaff this would require. This gives limitations on what we could hope to detect if we do not make additional assumptions on the attacker.

Specifically, in order to simulate two independent Poisson processes exactly, the attacker could first generate two independent Poisson processes, and then send packets on his streams to match them. He needs to send chaff packets on one of the streams, when the constraints on the other stream do not allow the non-chaff packet to be forwarded to/from it. In this way, he can mimic the processes exactly, and pair of streams will not appear to be a stepping-stone pair, to any monitor watching it. Note that even if the inter-packet delays were actively manipulated by the monitor, the attacker can still mimic two independent Poisson processes, and therefore, by our definition, will be able to evade detection.

Let λ_1 be the rate of the first Poisson process, and λ_2 be the rate of the second Poisson process. In our analysis, we assume $\lambda_1 = \lambda_2 = \lambda \gg \frac{1}{\Delta}$. If $\lambda_1 \gg \lambda_2$, or $\lambda_1 \ll \lambda_2$ the attacker will need to send many more chaff packets on the faster stream, so $\lambda_1 = \lambda_2$ will be the best choice for the attacker.

We model the Poisson processes as binomials. We choose to approximate the two independent Poisson processes of rate λ as two independent binomial processes, for cleaner analysis. To generate these processes, we assume that the attacker flips two coins, each with λ bias (of getting a head), at each time step[3]. He has to send a packet (either a real packet or chaff) on a stream when its corresponding coin turns up heads, and should send nothing when the coin turn up as tails. That way, he ensures that the two streams model two independent binomial processes exactly. Since the attacker generates the independent binomial processes, he could flip coins Δ or more time steps ahead, and then decide whether a non-chaff packet can be sent across for a particular coin flip that obeys all constraints, or if it has to be chaff.

We now show how the attacker could simulate two independently-generated binomial processes with minimum chaff. First, the attacker generates two sequences of independent coin flips. The following algorithm, BOUNDED-GREEDY-MATCH, then produces a strategy that minimizes chaff for the attacker, for any pair of sequences of coin flips. Given two sequences of coin flips, the attacker matches a head in first stream at time t to the first unmatched head in the second stream in the time interval $[t, t + \Delta]$. All matched heads become real (stepping-stone) packets, and all the remaining heads become chaff. An example of the operation of the algorithm is shown in Fig. 5.2.

The following theorem shows that BOUNDED-GREEDY-MATCH will allow the attacker to produce the minimum amount of chaff needed, when the attacker simulates two binomial processes that were generated independently.

---

[3] We could, equivalently, assume that the attacker flips a coin with $\frac{\lambda}{k}$ bias k times in a time step. As $k \to \infty$, the binomial approaches a Poisson process of rate λ.

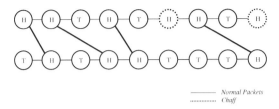

Normal Packets
Chaff

Fig. 4. An illustration of the matching produced by the algorithm BOUNDED-GREEDY-MATCH on two given sequences, with $\Delta = 2$

Theorem 8. *Given any pair of sequences of coin flips generated by two independent binomial processes,* BOUNDED-GREEDY-MATCH *minimizes the chaff needed for a pair of stepping-stone streams to mimic the given pair of sequences.*

Proof. Suppose not, i.e., suppose there exists a sequence pair of coin flips σ for which BOUNDED-GREEDY-MATCH is not optimal. Let S be the strategy produced by BOUNDED-GREEDY-MATCH for σ. Let S' be a better matching strategy, so that $Chaff(S) > Chaff(S')$. Then there exists a head in σ such that h is matched with a head h' through S', but not through S.

   Assume, wlog, that h is on the first stream at time t, and h' on the second stream. For S to be a valid match, h' should be in $[t, t + \Delta]$, and h' must be unmatched under S' to any other head. Let us suppose that h' is matched to another (earlier than t) head on the first stream under S (otherwise BOUNDED-GREEDY-MATCH would have generated a match between h and h' on S).

   We track chain of the matching heads in the sequence backwards (starting from h) in this way: we take the currently matched head in one strategy, and look for the head that matches it in the other strategy. When this chain of matchings stops, we must have an unmatched head, and one of following two cases (the manner in which we trace the chain of matching heads, along with the assumption that the unmatched head h is on the first stream, implies that we find only matched heads on the second stream of S, and the first stream of S'):

- *Case 1*: The unmatched head is in stream 1 of S'. In this case, an unmatched head in S correlates with an unmatched head in S', and therefore, this particular case is not our counterexample, since each unmatched head under S will correspond to an unmatched head under S'.
- *Case 2*: The unmatched head is in stream 2 of S. In this case, we have to have reached this head (call it g_0) from its matching head g_1 in S'; we have to reach g_1 from matched head g_2 in S. Since we are tracing backwards in time, time of g_2 is greater than the time of g_0. However, since g_0 can be matched to g_1, we have a contradiction, since we are not matching the head g_1 to the earliest available head g_0, as per BOUNDED-GREEDY-MATCH.

The analysis when h is on the second stream of S is similar.

Thus, with the algorithm BOUNDED-GREEDY-MATCH, every unmatched head in S must have a corresponding unmatched head in S', therefore, $Chaff(S) \leq Chaff(S')$, creating a contradiction.   □

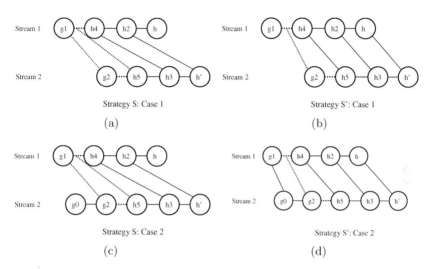

Fig. 5. The proof of Theorem 8. All the figures give an illustration of how the heads are traced back. (a) and (b) show case 1 of the proof, and (c) and (d) show case 2 of the proof. By assumption, h is unmatched in S and matched in S'. h is matched to h' in the strategy S'; in S, h' is matched to $h2$; then, we look at $h2$'s match in S', call it $h3$; use $h3$ to find $h4$ in S, $h4$ to find $h5$ in S', and so on. We continue tracing the matches of heads backwards in this manner until we stop, reaching either case 1 or case 2. In case 1, $g1$ is unmatched in strategy S', and in S, $g0$ is unmatched in S, but $g1$ is not matched greedily.

Now we examine upper bounds on the chaff that will need to be sent by the attacker, in terms of the total packets sent. We give an upper bound on the amount of chaff that the attacker must send in BOUNDED-GREEDY-MATCH. We note that our analysis shows how the attacker could do this if he mimics two independent Poisson processes, but it may not be necessary for him to do this in order to evade detection.

Theorem 9. *If the attacker ensures that his stepping-stone streams mimic two truly independent Poisson processes, then, under* BOUNDED-GREEDY-MATCH, *the attacker will not need to send more than* $\dfrac{1}{\sqrt{2\lambda\Delta - 2\sqrt{2\lambda(1-2\lambda)\Delta}}} + 0.05$ *fraction of packets as chaff in expectation, when the Poisson rates of the streams are equal with rate* λ.

Proof. We divide the total time (coin flips) into intervals that are Δ long, and examine the expected difference in one of these intervals. Notice that for the packets that are within a specific Δ interval, matches are not dependent on the times when they were generated. (i.e., any pair of packets in this interval is no further than Δ apart in time, and therefore, could be made a valid match). Many more packets than this can be matched, across the interval boundaries, but this gives us an easy upper bound.

Consider the packets in the union of the two streams in this interval. Each packet in this union can also be considered as though it were generated from a (different) unbiased coin, with heads as stream 1 and tails as stream 2; once again, we have a uniform random walk. Since every head can be matched to any available tail, the amount of chaff is the expected (absolute) difference in the number of heads and tails. Call this difference Z, and the packets on the union of the streams X. X is then a binomial with parameters 2λ, and Δ. Therefore, $E[X] = 2\lambda\Delta$. The expectation of $\frac{Z}{X}$ is then the following:

$$E[\frac{Z}{X}] = \sum_x \frac{1}{x} E[Z|X = x] P(X = x)$$

$$= \sum_x \frac{1}{\sqrt{x}} P(X = x)$$

$$\leq 0.05 + \frac{1}{\sqrt{2\lambda\Delta - 2\sigma}}, \text{ where } \sigma = \sqrt{2\lambda(1 - 2\lambda)\Delta}.$$

Since every interval of size Δ is identical, the attacker needs to send no more than $\frac{1}{\sqrt{2\lambda\Delta - 2\sqrt{2\lambda(1-2\lambda)\Delta}}} + 0.05$ fraction as chaff in expectation.   □

6   Conclusion

In this paper, we have proposed and analyzed algorithms for stepping-stone detection using techniques from Computational Learning Theory and the analysis of random walks. Our results are the first to achieve provable (polynomial) upper bounds on the number of packets needed to confidently detect and identify encrypted stepping-stone streams with proven guarantees on the probability of falsely accusing non-attacking pairs. Moreover, our methods and analysis rely on very mild assumptions, especially in comparison with previous work. We also examine the consequences when the attacker inserts chaff into the stepping-stone traffic, and give bounds on the amount of chaff that an attacker would have to send to evade detection. Our results are based on a new approach which can detect correlation of streams at a fine-grained level. Our approach may apply to more generalized traffic analysis domains, such as anonymous communication.

Acknowledgements

This work was supported in part by NSF grants CCR-0105488 and NSF-ITR CCR-0122581.

References

1. Staniford-Chen, S., Heberlein, L.T.: Holding intruders accountable on the internet. In: Proceedings of the 1995 IEEE Symposium on Security and Privacy, Oakland, CA (1995) 39–49
2. Zhang, Y., Paxson, V.: Detecting stepping stones. In: Proceedings of the 9th USENIX Security Symposium. (August 2000) 171–184
3. Yoda, K., Etoh, H.: Finding a connection chain for tracing intruders. In: F. Guppens, Y. Deswarte, D. Gollmann and M. Waidner, editors, 6th European Symposium on Research in Computer Security – ESORICS 2000 LNCS-1895, Toulouse, France (October 2000)
4. Donoho, D., Flesia, A.G., Shankar, U., Paxson, V., Coit, J., Staniford, S.: Multiscale stepping-stone detection: Detecting pairs of jittered interactive streams by exploiting maximum tolerable delay. In: Fifth International Symposium on Recent Advances in Intrusion Detection, Lecture Notes in Computer Science 2516, New York, Springer (2002)
5. Wang, X., Reeves, D.: Robust correlation of encrypted attack traffic through stepping stones by manipulation of inter-packet delays. In: Proceedings of the 2003 ACM Conference on Computer and Communications Security (CCS 2003), ACM Press (2003) 20–29
6. Kearns, M., Vazirani, U.: An Introduction to Computational Learning Theory. MIT Press (1994)
7. Valiant, L.: A theory of the learnable. Communications of the ACM **27** (1984) 1134–1142
8. Blumer, A., Ehrenfeucht, A., Haussler, D., Warmuth, M.K.: Occam's razor. Information Processing Letters **24** (1987) 377–380
9. Stoll, C.: The Cuckoo's Egg: Tracking a Spy through the Maze of Computer Espionage. Pocket Books (2000)
10. Wang, X., Reeves, D., Wu, S., Yuill, J.: Sleepy watermark tracing: An active network-based intrusion response framework. In: Proceedings of the 16th International Information Security Conference (IFIP/Sec'01). (2001) 369–384
11. Wang, X., Reeves, D., Wu, S.: Inter-packet delay-based correlation for tracing encrypted connections through stepping stones. In D.Gollmann, G.Karjoth, M.Waidner, eds.: 7th European Symposium on Research in Computer Security (ESORICS 2002), Lecture Notes in Computer Science 2502, Springer (2002) 244–263
12. Wang, X.: The loop fallacy and serialization in tracing intrusion connections through stepping stones. In: Proceedings of the 2004 ACM Symposium on Applied Computing, Nicosia, Cyprus, ACM Press (2004) 404–411
13. Paxson, V., Floyd, S.: Wide-area traffic: The failure of poisson modeling. IEEE/ACM Transactions on Networking **3** (1995) 226–244

Formal Reasoning
About Intrusion Detection Systems

Tao Song[1], Calvin Ko[2], Jim Alves-Foss[3], Cui Zhang[4], and Karl Levitt[1]

[1] Computer Security Laboratory, University of California, Davis
{tsong,knlevitt}@ucdavis.edu
[2] NAI Labs, Network Associates Inc., Santa Clara, CA
calvin_ko@nai.com
[3] Center for secure and dependable system, University of Idaho
jimaf@cs.uidaho.edu
[4] Computer Science Department, California State University, Sacramento
zhangc@ecs.csus.edu

Abstract. We present a formal framework for the analysis of intrusion detection systems (IDS) that employ declarative rules for attack recognition, e.g. specification-based intrusion detection. Our approach allows reasoning about the effectiveness of an IDS. A formal framework is built with the theorem prover ACL2 to analyze and improve detection rules of IDSs. SHIM (System Health and Intrusion Monitoring) is used as an exemplary specification-based IDS to validate our approach. We have formalized all specifications of a host-based IDS in SHIM which together with a trusted file policy enabled us to reason about the soundness and completeness of the specifications by proving that the specifications satisfy the policy under various assumptions. These assumptions are properties of the system that are not checked by the IDS. Analysis of these assumptions shows the beneficial role of SHIM in improving the security of the system. The formal framework and analysis methodology will provide a scientific basis for one to argue that an IDS can detect known and unknown attacks by arguing that the IDS detects all attacks that would violate a policy.

Keywords: Intrusion detection, verification, formal method, security policy

1 Introduction

Intrusion detection is an effective technology to supplement traditional security mechanisms, such as access control, to improve the security of computer systems. To date, over 100 commercial and research products have been developed and deployed on operational computer systems and networks. While IDS can improve the security of a system, it is difficult to evaluate and predict the effectiveness of an IDS with respect to the primary objective users have for the deployment of such a system: the ability to detect large classes of attacks (including variants of known attacks and unknown attacks) with a low false alarm rate. In addition,

E. Jonsson et al. (Eds.): RAID 2004, LNCS 3224, pp. 278–295, 2004.

it is difficult to assess, in a scientific manner, the security posture of a system with an IDS deployed. So far, experimental evaluation and testing have been the only approaches that have been attempted. There is a critical need to establish a scientific foundation for evaluating and analyzing the effectiveness of IDSs.

This paper presents an approach to formal analysis of IDSs. Our approach is primarily applicable to IDSs that employ declarative rules for intrusion detection, including signature-based detection and specification-based detection [16] [18] [3] [8] [4] [5] [22]. The former matches the current system or network activities against a set of predefined attack signatures that represent known attacks and potential intrusive activities. The latter recognizes attacks as activities of critical objects that violate their specifications. Testing is currently being used to evaluate the effectiveness of the rules. Nevertheless, testing is usually performed according to the tester's understanding of known attacks. It is difficult to verify the effectiveness of an IDS in detecting unknown attacks.

Our approach is inspired by the significant body of formal methods research in designing and building trusted computer systems. Briefly, the process of designing and building a trusted system involves the development of a security model, which consists of a specification of a security policy (the security requirements or what is meant by security) and an abstract behavioral model of the system. Usually, the security policy can be stated as a mapping from system states to *authorized* (secure) and *unauthorized* (insecure) states [14]or as a property (often stated as an invariant) of the system (e.g., noninterference). The model is an abstraction of the actual system that provides a high level description of the major entities of the system and operations on those entities. There may be layers of abstractions within the model, each a refinement of the higher level abstraction. Given the security policy and model, one should be able to prove that the model satisfies the security policy, assuming some restrictions on the state transition functions (e.g., the classical Bell and LaPadula model).

Our framework consists of an abstract behavioral model, specifications of high-level security properties, and specifications of intrusion-detection rules. The abstract behavioral model captures the real behavior of the targeted system. In addition to common abstractions such as access control lists, processes, and files, the abstract behavioral model will capture the auditing capabilities of the targeted system(i.e., given an operation, it will be decided whether or not an audit event will be generated and what information about the operation will be visible). The specifications of intrusion-detection rules describe formally when the rules will produce IDS alarms given the sequence of audit events generated. Intrusion detection rules can be viewed as constraints on the audit trace of the system (e.g., the sequence of observable state changes).

We employ the formal framework to analyze the properties of SHIM, a specification-based IDS that focuses on the behaviors of privileged programs. In SHIM, specifications are developed to constrain the behaviors of privileged programs to the least privilege that is necessary for the functionality of the program.

ACL2 [15] is employed to describe an abstract system model that can be used as the basis for different IDSs. A hierarchical model is built to generalize the verification of specifications. As an example, we formalize specifications of SHIM and a security policy (e.g, a trusted file access policy). And we prove that these specifications can satisfy the policy with various assumptions. Again, the assumptions represent activities that the SHIM IDS does not monitor, although it could if the IDS designer believes an attacker could cause the assumptions to be violated.

The rest of the paper is structured as follows: Section 2 introduces and analyzes intrusion detection rules, primarily used in a specification-based IDS such as SHIM. Section 3 describes a hierarchical framework of verification. Section 4 shows an example of our verification approach. We formalize specifications of SHIM and prove that these specifications together with assumptions satisfy trusted file access policies. In Section 5 we discuss our results and the limitations of the verification method we developed. We conclude and provide recommendations for future work in Section 6.

2   Analysis of Intrusion-Detection Rules

Development of correct intrusion-detection rules is a very difficult and error-prone task: it involves extensive knowledge engineering on attacks and most components of the system; it requires a deep and correct understanding of most of the components in a system and how they work together; it requires the rule developers to be cautious and careful to avoid mistakes and gaps in coverage. Often, crafting of intrusion-detection rules is performed by human security experts based on their knowledge and insights on attacks and security aspects of a system. Therefore, it is very difficult to assess whether a given set of intrusion-detection rules is correct (they detect the attacks). Furthermore, the complexity and subtlety of systems and attacks make it a challenging task to judge whether changes to the rules actually improve or degrade their efficacy with respect to their ability to detect new attacks.

We discuss the subtleties involved in writing valid behavior specifications for a program. Traditionally, in specification-based IDSs, a valid behavior specification for a program declares what operations and system calls are allowed for the program. Whether an operation is allowed or not depends on the attributes of the process and the object reference, and attributes of the system calls. In SHIM, a specification for a program is a list of rules describing all the operations valid for the program. For example, the following rule in the line printer daemon (lpd) specification allows the program to open any file in the */var/spool/hp* directory to read and write.

$$(open, \$flag == O\_RDWR \&\& InDir(\$F.path, ``/var/spool/hp"))$$

The expression formally describes a set of valid operations: any *open()* system call with the flag argument equal to *O_RDWR* (open the file for read and write) with an absolute path name subordinate to the */var/spool/hp* directory.

One way to develop a specification for a program is to first identify what operations and accesses the program needs to support its functionality. Based on an examination of the code or its behaviors, one writes rules in the specification to cover the valid operations of the program. The "draft" specification will be tested against the actual execution of the program. Often, the draft specification, when used to monitor the program execution, will produce false positives (i.e., valid operations performed by the program reported as erroneous because they are *not* included in the specification). Then, one augments the specification to include rules to cover these operations. In general, one needs to be very careful in writing the specification for a program to avoid errors.

For example, given the above rule, if */var/spool/hp* somehow is writable by attackers, they can create a link from */var/spool/hp/file* to the */etc/passwd* file. A specification-based IDS with this rule in the specification of *lpd* will permit this operation and the attack will go undetected. Therefore, we augment the rule to check the number of links to the file and to generate a warning if the number of links to the file is greater than one,thus preventing this attack from using hard links. This also works for soft links in our system because the audit record for an *open()* operation will provide the absolute pathname of the file being opened, if the path is a symbolic link. Based on our experience, writing specifications for a program is subtle and tricky, thus demanding an approach to rule validation.

Little research has been done on analyzing intrusion-detection rules. Different approaches have been taken to specify and analyze the intrusion signatures and detection rules [12] [19] [17], primarily for signature-based IDSs. A declarative language, MuSigs, is proposed in [12] to describe the known attacks. Temporal logic formulas with variables are used to express specifications of attack scenarios [19]. Pouzol and Ducasse formally specified attack signatures and proved the soundness and completeness of their detection rules. In addition, data mining techniques and other AI techniques such as neutral network are used to refine and improve intrusion signatures [6] [13] [21].

Our approach is different from these approaches in various ways. First of all, we developed a framework to evaluate detection rules of different IDSs. We formalized security-relevant entities of an UNIX-like system as well as access logs. Detection rules including intrusion signatures and specifications can be formalized and reasoned about in the framework.

Second, we proposed a method to verify security properties of IDSs together with assumptions, with respect to security policies. Security polices are always satisfied with sufficiently strong assumptions. So the key is to identify assumptions that are strong enough but not too strong. An attack can violate a security policy by breaking its assumptions. So it is possible to verify the improvement of security by proving the weakening of assumptions. For example, assuming a policy P is satisfied with assumption A and with the deployment of the mechanism m , and P is satisfied with assumption B where A implies B, then we can say m improves the security because attacks violating assumption B will also violate A, but attacks that violate assumption A may not violate B .

As our preliminary results, we have verified a significant property of specification-based IDSs: the capability to detect unknown attacks. In our verification, the specifications of SHIM satisfy a *passwd* file access policy with assumptions.

This means *any* attacks, including known attacks and unknown attacks, that violate the policy can be detected by SHIM.

3   Framework

We present a framework for analyzing detection rules in IDSs. Our goal is to answer the question of whether a given set of intrusion detection rules can satisfy the security requirements of the system. Security polices and properties of attacks are used to describe the security requirements of the system. The satisfaction of the security requirements determines whether violations of security policies or instances of attacks can be detected by the detection rules.

3.1   Hierarchical Framework of Verification

Figure 1 depicts the verification model, which consists of an abstract system model, an auditing model, detection rules, assumptions, and security requirements. The basis of the model is the abstract system model (S) in which security-critical entities of the system are formalized. The auditing model (L) is necessary for the model because almost all IDSs are based on the analysis of the audit trails from operating systems, applications and network components. Detection rules (R) vary dependent on the IDS. In SHIM, detection rules are specifications of normal behaviors of privileged programs. Security Requirements (SR) define properties that should be satisfied to guarantee the security of the system. Assumptions (H) are necessary for the verification. Security properties that we are not sure of and more important, properties that cannot be efficiently monitored will be declared as assumptions (e.g, kernel of the system is not subject to attack). Note that all of our assumptions could be checked by monitoring but at a substantial performance penalty to the IDS.

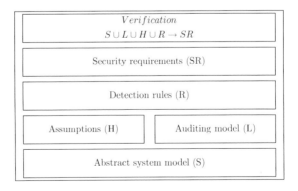

Fig. 1. Verification Hierachy

3.2   Formalization of the Model

In this section, we describe how to construct the components of the framework. We start with the abstract system model.

The abstract system model plays an important role in the framework. It provides a general basis to formalize security requirements, detection rules of IDSs and assumptions, and makes it possible to verify security properties of detection rules. To develop a simplified abstract model, we only formalize security-critical parts of UNIX-like systems. The model can be defined as a tuple $(F,\ U,\ E,\ P,\ S)$ where F describes a file system, U shows user and group mechanisms, E corresponds to environment variables, P describes a list of processes, and S describes system call interfaces of the kernel. Our preliminary experiment focuses on the access control mechanism, so we define access permissions of file objects and privileges of subjects.

Because of the importance of the auditing component in IDSs, we formalize it separately from the abstract system model. We model the auditing component at the system call level. Assume Σ is a set of all system calls, let $B \subseteq \Sigma^*$ be all sequences of operations of a program A. A trace $b \in B$ presents a sequence of operations of A. For each operation of a program, we use a tuple $(p,\ f,\ c,\ n)$ to indicate that a process p invokes a system call c on object f and assigns a new property n to f (e.g. a new owner for a file).

Detection rules vary according to different IDSs. In a specification-based IDS, detection rules are specifications which are used to describe normal behaviors of systems. Conversely, in a signature-based IDS, detection rules are signatures that identify different attacks. In this paper, we focus on the specification-based approach. Suppose the set of all possible behaviors of a program is defined as B, a specification $spec()$ can identify a set of valid behaviors VB where $VB \subseteq B$ and for any trace $b \in VB$, iff $spec(b) = true$.

Security requirements are used to describe properties necessary to satisfy the security of the system. There are basically two ways to present the security requirements: one is to define security policies, the other is to describe attack scenarios. Security policies can map the behavior of a system into two states: *authorized* or *unauthorized*. In this way, a security policy *security-policy()* separates the behavior of a system into an authorized behavior set AB and an unauthorized behavior set UB where $AB \subseteq B$, $UB \subseteq B$. For any trace b, $b \in AB$ iff *security-policy(b)* = "*authorized*". Attacks are behaviors that violate the security policy. We can use functions to define characterizations of attacks. An attack function *attack()* can define a set of dangerous behaviors DB where $DB \subseteq B$ and for any trace b, $b \in DB$ iff *attack(b)=true*.

In the verification, we try to answer two questions: Can some security policies be satisfied by IDSs? And can some attacks remain undetected by IDSs? The first question can be formalized as follows. Given specification s and security policy p, is the valid behavior set VB that is defined by s a subset of the "authorized" behavior set AB defined by p. We describe this relation as $VB \subseteq AB$ or for any trace b, *spec(b)* = *true implies security-policy(b)*= "*authorized*". In some cases, assumptions are introduced in proving whether a security policy is satisfied by a specification. The verification can be described as: for any trace

$b \in B$, *(assumption(b) = true)* $\land$ *(spec(b) = true)* $\vdash$ *(sr(b)= "authorized")*.

The second question can be formalized as follows. Given an attack ab or a set of attacks DB, is ab a member of the valid behavior set VB or does DB share elements with VB. It can be described as $ab \notin VB$ or $DB \cap VB = \phi$.

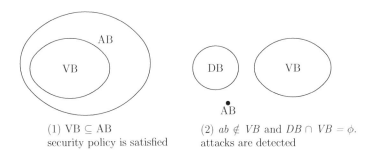

(1) $VB \subseteq AB$
security policy is satisfied

(2) $ab \notin VB$ and $DB \cap VB = \phi$.
attacks are detected

Fig. 2. Relationship among security policy, specifications and attacks

3.3   Mechanization of the Model

ACL2 is used in the mechanization of the framework. Structures and functions in ACL2 are used to formalize declarative components of the framework, including an abstract system model, audit data, detection rules of IDSs, assumptions, and security requirements. To perform the verifications we define the appropriate theorems in ACL2 and prove them using mathematical induction and the other proof mechanism of ACL2.

Introduction of ACL2. ACL2 is a significant extension of Nqthm [1], intended for large scale verification projects. The ACL2 system consists of a programming language based on Common Lisp, a logic of total recursive functions, and a mechanical theorem prover [15]. The syntax of ACL2 is that of Common Lisp. In addition, ACL2 supports the macro facility of Common Lisp. The following data types are axiomatized: rational and complex numbers, character objects, strings, symbols and lists. Common Lisp functions on these data types are axiomatized or defined as functions or macros in ACL2 [9]. Several functions that are used in our verification are listed in table 1. The ACL2 logic is a first order logic of recursive functions providing mathematical induction on the ordinals up to $\epsilon 0$ and two extension principles: one for recursive definition and one for the constrained introduction of new function symbols. Each preserves the consistency of the extended logic.

The ACL2 theorem prover has powerful and effective heuristics controlling the application of the following proof techniques: preprocessing including tautology checking using ordered binary decision diagrams(OBDDs) under user direction; simplification by primitive type checking and rewriting; destructor elimination; cross-fertilization using equivalence reasoning; generalization; elimination of irrelevant hypotheses; and mathematical induction.

Table 1. Important functions of ACL2

Functions	Descriptions
Nil	The empty list or False in Boolean contexts
T	True
(if x y z)	If x not equal to nil, return y, otherwise z
(equal x y)	If x and y have the same value, return t, otherwise nil
(and x y)	"And"operation in Boolean contexts
(car l)	First element of list l
(cdr l)	All but the first element of list l
(consp x l)	Add x onto the front of list l
(implies x y)	If x is nil or y is t, return t; otherwise return f

Abstract System Model. The abstract system model is formalized as a structure *sys* in ACL2. Security-critical components are defined as fields of the structure. For each field, *asserts* are defined to check the integrity of values of the fields. A predicate *sys-p* is defined to recognize values that have the required structural form and whose fields satisfy the assertions. The predicate *weak-sys-p* is defined to recognize values that have the required structural form, but does not require the field assertions to be satisfied. Functions are defined to get, put or check values from specific fields. In our verification, we can use instances of the structure to tell whether a statement is true in a system with specific settings. On the other hand, the system model can appear in a theorem without specific values to indicate a general condition in which the statement is held.

```
(defstructure sys
(proglist (:assert (and (not (endp proglist))(proglistp proglist))))
;list of programs, e.g. privileged programs
(calllist (:assert (and (not (endp calllist))(calllistp calllist))))
;list of system calls, e.g. open, read, write etc.
(filelist (:assert (and (not (endp filelist))(filelistp filelist))))
;list of files, e.g. /etc/passwd file
(userlist (:assert (and (not (endp userlist))(userlistp userlist))))
;list of system users
(envlist (:assert (and (not (endp envlist))(envlistp envlist)))))
;list of environment variables, e.g. home directories in a UNIX system
```

Audit Trail. The auditing capability of a system is formalized as a list of audit records and an audit record is formalized as a structure *logrec* in ACL2. We reference Sun Solaris BSM audit subsystem and simplify the audit record structure to four fields: process, file object, system call and new properties to the file object.

```
(defstructure logrec
(pobj (:assert (and (consp pobj)(proc-obj-p pobj))))
;object of the process
(fobj (:assert (and (consp fobj)(file-obj-p fobj))))
;object of the target file
```

```
(callobj (:assert (and (consp callobj)(syscall-obj-p callobj))))
;object of the system call
(newattrobj (:assert (newattr-obj-p newattrobj))))
;new properties of the target file
```

Security Requirements. In our verification, different classes of attacks and security policies are formalized to analyze detection rules of IDSs.

There are two ways to verify whether an attack can be detected by a specific IDS. The first method is to formalize possible audit trails, which include the attack scenarios, and then analyze the audit data according to the specification of the program for the violation. Such verification can be used to prove the capabilities of the specifications to detect *known* attacks. A more general way is to describe the security property that will be violated by the attacks instead of particular audit trails. Then we develop a proof based on the property that the formalized specifications will always result in the system being monitored for that property. For example, in an ftp-write attack, an attacker takes advantage of a normal anonymous *ftp* misconfiguration. If the *ftp* directory and its subdirectories are owned by the *ftp* account or in the same group as the *ftp* account, the attacker will be able to add files (such as the .rhosts file) and eventually gain local access to the system.

Security policies are also formalized to allow reasoning about the security properties of specifications. Trusted file access policies are security policies that we developed to keep trusted files from unauthorized access. In UNIX systems, a discretionary access control(DAC) mechanism defines whether a subject can access an object or not depending on the privilege of the subject and the access permission of the object. Some files are intended to be accessed by specific users or using specific programs. For example, the *passwd* file of a UNIX system should be editable by root using any program or by an ordinary user using the *passwd* program. Thus, file access policies are defined in our format as: *(trusted file, authorized user, program, access)* where *trusted file* is the file to be protected, *authorized user* defines the user that can access the file with any programs and *program* defines the program that can be used by other users to access the file.

As an example, the *passwd* file access policy is defined as: *(/etc/passwd, root, passwd, (open-wr,create, chmod, chown, rename))*. This policy is used in the verifications of the next section. The policy is formalized as a function in ACL2.

Assumptions. Our verificatio methodology rests on assumptions. A system specification will have assumptions on how the system and programs behave. The specifications cannot be declared as complete before all assumptions of the specifications are identified. In some cases, once the assumptions are declared as required by the verification approach, an IDS does not have to monitor the properties asserted in these assumptions. There are two different kinds of assumptions in our verification: general assumptions of the system and specific assumptions of verifications.

System assumptions are very important although they are not formalized in our verification. Some general assumptions of the system model are listed as follows:

– System kernel is not vulnerable to attack

The security of system kernel is beyond the scope of this paper. We simply assume that system kernel is not vulnerable to attack.

– DAC mechanism of the system is correctly implemented

Access control is a concern of our verification. So correct implementation of the DAC mechanism is an assumption for the security of the system. If the access control mechanism is not well implemented and a user can access objects for which he is not authorized, it is impossible to protect these objects by only constraining behaviors of privileged programs.

– Completeness on log data

As a hypothesis of the IDS, audit logs should record the trace of attacks so that analysis of the audit logs may detect such attacks. Therefore, log data should include all important operations with their correct sequence. If an attacker can successfully eliminate his traces before an IDS analyzes them, it is impossible to detect this activity by an IDS.

The specific assumption of verification will be discussed in section 4, in the context of the verifications of specific IDS and security policies.

4   Specification and Verification of SHIM

We formalized the specifications of a specification-based IDS, SHIM, and analyzed them according to different security policies and attacks.

4.1   Introduction of SHIM

SHIM is a specification-based IDS. Specification-based IDSs are based on the creation of specifications that describe desired functionality for security-critical entities [7] [8] [20] [10] [23]. The security specifications in SHIM mainly focus on the valid operations of a UNIX privileged program. Privileged programs are analyzed because of their significant impact on system security. The effective user of a privileged program has root privileges, and attacks against a privileged program often exploit the privilege to access security-critical objects that are not intended to be accessed by the victim program. For example, in a *ftp* buffer overflow attack, an attack can invoke a shell with root privilege and use it to access any files of the system [2]; that the attack is a buffer overflow is incidental to the specification.

During program operation, the system accesses associated with the operation of a program are recorded in audit logs and matched against the specifications by SHIM. Mismatches are reported and almost always indicate an attack. Theoretically, SHIM is capable of detecting unknown attacks or variants of known attacks, and a report is issued as soon as a specification violation occurs. If the program was compromised by an attack (e.g. buffer overflow) and attempted to invoke any system calls that violated the specifications, an alert would be raised.

4.2   Formalization of Specifications

In SHIM, a language, Parallel Environment Grammar (PE grammar), is developed to define specifications that describe all valid operations of a program. The language permits the parameterization of the language syntax and environment variables that aid in parsing efficiency. PE grammar can be used to specify the valid execution traces of programs. The specification of *ftp* daemon is listed to show how the language works:

```
        SE: <prog>
        <prog> -> <validop> *;
        <validop>
        -> (OPEN_RD, WorldReadable($F.mode))
;the program can read a file that is world-readable
           | (OPEN_RD, CreatedByProc($P.pid, &$F))
;the process can read a file that is created by itself
           | (OPEN_RD, $F.ouid == $S.uid)
;the process can read a file whose owner is the current user
           | (OPEN_WR, CreatedByProc($P.pid, &$F))
           | (OPEN_WR, $F.path == "/var/log/wtmp")
;the process can write to a file a specific path
           | (OPEN_WR, $F.path == "/var/log/xferlog")
           | (OPEN_RW, $F.path == "/var/run/ftp.pids-all")
           | (open, $F.path == "/dev/null")
           | (unlink,  CreatedByProc($P.pid, &$F))
           | (CHMOD,   CreatedByProc($P.pid, &$F))
           | (CHOWN,   CreatedByProc($P.pid, &$F))
           | (fork||vfork)
           | (OPEN_RD, InDir($F.path, getHomeDir($S.uid)))
;the process can read a file situated on a specific directory
           | (OPEN_WR, InDir($F.path, getHomeDir($S.uid)))
           | (read,  IsSocket($F.mode) && $K.lport == 21)
;the process can get information from specific port
           | (write, IsSocket($F.mode) && $K.lport == 21)
           | (CREAT, InDir($F.path, getHomeDir($S.uid)))
           | (EXEC, $path == "/bin/tar" || $path == "/bin/compress" ||
                       $path == "/bin/ls"  || $path == "/bin/gzip") ;END;
```

In this specification, valid operations are defined with a term *validop*. Eighteen valid operations are included in this specification and each valid operation is a function of system calls and environment variables. For example the operation *(OPEN_RD, WorldReadable($F.mode))* means this programs can open a file in read mode when the file is readable by all users. PE grammar is capable of defining a multi-state specification, but in this specification, only one state is used, namely the state associated with the invocation of the program. This specification shows a balance between expressiveness and detection efficiency.

In our verification, a function is defined to check whether audit trails of a *ftp* daemon process violates the specification. The function accepts an audit trail as a parameter. If any operation of the audit trail violates the specification, the function will return *false* otherwise *true*. All valid operations are defined with two functions: operation and property restriction. The operation function defines the operation on an object and the property restriction function defines the condition in which the operation will be performed. For example, the valid operation *(OPEN_RD, WorldReadable($F.mode))* can be formalized as *(and (operate 'openrd logrec) (WorldReadable (logrec-fobj logrec)))*. In the definition, the function *operate* gets the correct operation, and function *WorldReadable* determines whether the permission of the file is *world readable*.

4.3   Verifications

Our verification focuses on the effectiveness of specifications of SHIM in satisfying security requirements, including attacks and security policies. We attempt to address the issue whether, with specific detection rules, SHIM can detect specific attacks or detect attacks that cause specific security policies to be validated.

Detection of Attacks. Attacks are modeled as sequences of operations. We use two ways to describe attack scenarios: an audit trail that contains an attack or a characterization of attacks. According to the characteristic of specification-based IDS, SHIM cannot detect any attacks that do not change the behavior of victim programs. So here we introduce an assumption about attack:

Assumption: an attack cannot cause any damage without changing the behavior of a victim program.

Then we can claim that SHIM is capable of detecting attacks before or at least "as" they cause damage to the system.

For known attacks, we can always simulate their audit trails. Considering the buffer overflow attack against wuftpd 2.4.2-beta-18. The program can be compromised by overflowing a buffer in *strcat()*. We simulated an audit trail which invoked a shell after penetration of *strcat()*. Then we used the specification of *ftp* daemon to check this audit trail. A violation is reported and this indicates that the attack can be detected by SHIM. A further analysis shows that the violation is revealed by the audit record that indicates invocation of the shell. The call to the library function *strcat()* does not reveal aviolation. This result proves that the specification of SHIM can detect this buffer overflow attack if the attacker tries to invoke a shell after penetration.

For unknown attacks, we can consider a group of similar attacks that invoke shells after they successfully compromise an *ftp* daemon program. We indicate a theorem which shows any audit trail with an operation invoking a shell will be detected by the specification of *ftp* daemon. The theorem is defined as :

```
(defthm attack-ftp
(implies
(member 'exec "/bin/bash" log sys)
;any operation invoking a shell
(not(spec_ftpd sys log nil))
;violate the specification of ftp program
))
```

This theorem demonstrates an important feature of SHIM: detection of unknown attacks. Any unknown attacks against the *ftp* daemon will be detected if an operation of invoking shells is observed. The proof of the theorem is straightforward because */bin/bash* is not a valid path for the *exec* system call in the specification.

Proving a Specification Satisfies a Security Policy. In this section, we carry out a verification that indicates the trusted file access policy is satisfied by specifications of SHIM with some assumptions.

We use the *passwd* file access policy as an example in this verification. As we defined in section 3, the *passwd* file access policy defines how the *passwd* file should be accessed. According to the DAC mechanism of UNIX systems, any user without root privilege cannot modify the *passwd* file except through a privileged program. If the DAC mechanism is well implemented, no user except root can use unprivileged programs, like vi, to change the *passwd* file. So, we only focus on the behavior of privileged programs in verifying that the system satisfies the policy.

Given an audit trail of a specific privileged program, we try to prove that any audit trail that passes the check of the specification will satisfy the *passwd* file access policy. We use *ftp* deamon as an example to show how it works.

The proof is defined as a theorem which is indicated below. The formalization of the abstract system model *sys* and audit data *log* are used in this theorem. We may notice that some assumptions are added to complete the proof. Two important verification assumptions are made in this proof.

The first assumption is about the access permissions of the *passwd* file. The *passwd* file can only be protected when it has proper access permission. If the *passwd* file is set world writeable, the integrity of the file cannot be protected because any user has the privilege to change the *passwd* file.

The other assumption is concerned with the setting of the home directory of the user who attempts to access the *passwd* file. A user can access the *passwd* file if his home directory is set as */etc*. The reason is that the specification of the *ftp* deamon allows the user to access the files under his home directory. In fact, this assumption can be guaranteed by deploying some configuration checking tools such as KUANG [24]. But in SHIM, such a property of the system is not monitored. With these assumptions, any audit data that passes the specification check of the *ftp* deamon will satisfy the *passwd* file access policy.

```
(defthm passwd-ftp
(implies
(and(not (member '(/ etc passwd) created))
;passwd file was not created by the process
    (consp log)(consp sys)(logp log)(consp created)(sys-p sys)
;format checking
    (validuser sys log)
;assumption: no invalid user as determined by the audit data
    (passwdsafe log)
```

```
;assumption: passwd file has proper permissions
   (homedirsafe sys)
;assumption: home diretory settings are correct
(spec_ftpd sys log created))
;the specification is not violated by any operations
(not-access-passwd log)
;then, thepasswd access policy is satisfied
))
```

Using a similar method, we have proved that the specification of the *lpd* program satisfies the *passwd* file access policy with the assumption that the environment variable *printerspool* is not misconfigured. Changes to environment variables are not monitored by SHIM, so this assumption clearly covers a property that SHIM cannot check.

Composition of Specifications Satisfies the Policy. A further question is whether the composition of different specifications will satisfy the *passwd* file access policy. In this section, we consider concurrent execution of different privileged programs. We use *ftp* daemon and *lpd* as examples to show that the composition of specifications of these two programs satisfying the policy.

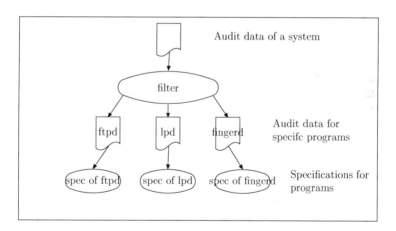

Fig. 3. Mechanism of SHIM to filter concurrent execution audit log

As shown in figure 3, in SHIM, the audit filter is used to separate the audit trail of individual programs from the audit data of the system. We simulate the filter using a function *filter(prog, log)* in ACL2, where *prog* is the name of the program and *log* is the audit trail of the system. A question is whether the filter will change the security property of the audit trail. If the filter maps the data trail of a few privileged programs to the audit trail of each program and all subsets of the data trail satisfy the *passwd* file access policy, does this means the audit trail satisfies the policy?

Suppose *log* is the audit trail of *ftpd* and *lpd*. We have proved that if the audit trail of *ftpd*, *filter('ftpd, log)*, can pass the specification check of ftpd and if the audit trail of *lpd*, *filter('lpd, log)*, can pass the specification check of *lpd*, the audit trails of *ftpd* and *lpd* satisfy the *passwd* file access policy.

```
(defthm passwd-specs
(implies
(not (member '(/ etc passwd) created))
;passwd file was not created by the process
(implies
(and (logp log) (consp log) (consp sys) (sys-p sys) (procsafe log)
;format checking
(passwdsafe log) (homedirsafe sys) (validuser sys log)
;assumptions for ftpd program
(validenv sys 'printerspool)
;assumptions for lpd program
(spec_ftpd sys (filter 'ftpd log) created)
;the specification of ftpd is not violated by any operations
(spec_lpd sys (filter 'lpd log) created))
;the specification of lpd is not violated by any operations
(not-access-passwd log)))    )
;then, the passwd access policy is satisfied
```

We notice that the assumptions in this verification are the union of assumptions in these two verifications that have been proved priviously. All theorems appearing in this section have been proved automatically by the ACL2 theorem prover using rewriting and mathematical induction.

4.4   Performance

We measure the performance of ACL2 in carrying out the proofs described above. We formalize the abstract system model, detection rules and security policies with 174 functions and 13 data structures. We defined and proved 56 lemmas and theorems to complete the verification. It took three weeks to develop all the functions and complete the verification. On a 450MHZ Pentium machine with 384 MB memory, ACL2 spent 15.21 minutes to complete the verification. This suggests that using ACL2 to formalize and verify security properties of IDSs is a feasible approach.

5   Discussion

The assumptions of the verification process may, in some cases, be guaranteed through other tools. In the exemplary verification, we introduced assumptions needed to satisfy the passwd file access policy. These assumptions relate to access permissions of target objects (e.g., the *passwd* file cannot be world-writable), proper configurations (e.g., home directories of users cannot be /etc/), etc. SHIM is not capable of monitoring these static properties of the system. But these assumptions can be checked by deploying other security tools such as Tripwire [11] [25] .

In our verification, the soundness and completeness of detection rules of IDSs are not yet completely proved. If the soundness of the detection rules could be verified, the false positive rate of IDSs would theoretically be proved to be zero. In SHIM, the detection rules are specifications of the system. It is feasible, in principle, to prove the soundness of specifications by comparing the specifications with the implementation of the system. Automatic generation and verification of specifications can be achieved by associating formal methods with code analysis. As an extreme but practically useless example, it is easy to prove a specification rejecting all possible behaviors is sound. Considering the huge false negative rate, this specification is clearly not an acceptable solution even with a zero false positive rate. If the completeness of detection rules can be verified, the false negative rate of IDSs will be zero. Similarly, a specification accepting all behaviors can be proved complete.

The ACL2 theorem prover is used in our verification. It provides reliable verification by using well-accepted deduction rules, e.g., mathematical induction. By describing properties of attacks, we can prove that all the attacks (including known attacks and unknown attacks) with specific operations (e.g. invoking shell) can be detected by SHIM. This verifies an important and often-cited claim of specification-based intrusion detection: detection of unknown attacks. There are a few limitations about mechanical theorem provers. First, proof creation of almost any practical properties correct in theorem provers is not totally automatic. Although theorem provers help find missing steps in proofs, it is still impossible for a theorem prover to create proofs without human interaction. Second, even if a proposition cannot be proved by a theorem prover, it doesn't indicate the proposition is wrong. Also it is difficult to find a counter-example to show conditions under which a property is incorrect.

6   Conclusions and Future Work

In this paper, we present a formal framework that can be used to evaluate detection rules of IDSs. ACL2 is used to formalize declarative components of the framework and to carry out the verifications. An abstract system model is built as the basis for verifications. Trusted file access policies are developed to define authorized access on security-critical objects of a system. We also report on our experience with a preliminary implementation of this framework in reasoning about security properties of SHIM, a specification-based IDS. We have formalized all detection rules of SHIM, specifications for privileged programs, and addressed two important issues about SHIM (and specification-based IDS, in general): what attacks can be detected by SHIM and whether abstract security policies can be satisfied by SHIM. An important feature of SHIM, its ability to detect unknown attacks, is actually verified by specifying properties of attacks.

Potential future work includes analyzing misuse detection systems (i.e. signature-based IDSs) and network IDSs; generating specification using code analysis;

verifying soundness of specifications; and developing realistic security policies for network protocols.

Acknowlegements

We thank Steven Cheung, Jeff Rowe, Poornima Balasubramanyam, Tye Stallard and Marcus Tylutki for helpful discussion on security policy, verification and intrusion detection. We are grateful to Patty Graves for her valuable help. This material is based upon work supported by the National Science Foundation under Grant No 0341734. Any opinions, findings, and conclusions or recommendations expressed in this material are those of the author(s) and do not necessarily reflect the views of the National Science Foundation.

References

1. R. S. Boyer and J S. Moore, A computational logic, Academic Press, New York, 1979.
2. Cert coordination center, advisory ca-1999-03, http://www.cert.org/advisories/CA-99-03.html
3. C.C.W. Ko , "Execution Monitoring of Security-Critical Programs in a Distributed System: A Specification-Based Approach", Ph.D. Thesis, August 1996
4. C. Ko, "Logic induction of valid behavior specifications for intrusion detection", Proc. of IEEE Symposium on Security and Privacy 2000
5. C. Ko, J. Rowe, P. Brutch, K. Levitt, "System Health and Intrusion Monitoring Using a hierarchy of Constraints", Proceeding of 4th International Symposium, RAID, 2001
6. Anup K. Ghosh and Aaron Schwartzbard , "A Study in Using Neural Networks for Anomaly and Misuse Detection", Proc. of USENIX Security Symposium, 1999
7. C. Ko, G. Fink, and K. Levitt. "Automated detection of vulnerabilities in privileged programs by execution monitoring". In Proceedings of the Tenth Computer Security Applications Conference, pages 134-144, Orlando, FL, Dec. 1994. IEEE Computer Society Press.
8. C. Ko, M. Ruschitzka, and K. Levitt, "Execution Monitoring of Security-critical Programs in Distributed Systems: A Specification-based Approach," Proc. of the 1997 IEEE Symposium on Security and Privacy, Oakland, California, May 1997, pp. 134-144.
9. M. Kaufmann, P. Manolios, J S. Moore, "Computer-Aided Reasoning : An Approach", Kluwer Academic Publishers, 2000
10. C. Ko, J. Rowe, P. Brutch, K. Levitt, "System Health and Intrusion Monitoring Using a hierarchy of Constraints," Proceeding of 4th International Symposium, RAID, 2001
11. G. Kim, E. H. Spafford, "The design of a system integrity monitor: Tripwire," Technical report CSD-TR-93-071, Purdue University, November 1993
12. Jia-Ling Lin; Wang, X.S.; Jajodia, S., "Abstraction-based misuse detection: high-level specifications and adaptable strategies", Proc. of IEEE Computer Security Foundations Workshop, 2002.

13. Wenke Lee; Stolfo, S.J.; Mok, K.W., "A data mining framework for building intrusion detection models", Proc. of IEEE Symposium on Security and Privacy, 1999

14. Matthew A. Bishop, Computer Security: Art and Science, Addison Wesley Longman 2002

15. Matt Kaufmann, Panagiotis Manolios, and J Strother Moore, "Computer-Aided Reasoning: An Approach", Kluwer Academic Publishers, June, 2000

16. M. Roesch, "Snort: Lightweight Intrusion Detection for Networks", Proc. of USENIX LISA '99, Seattle, Washington, November 1999, pp. 229-238.

17. J.P. Pouzol, M. Ducasse, "Formal specication of intrusion signatures and detection rules", Proc. of IEEE Computer Security Foundations Workshop, 2002.

18. P.A. Porras and P.G. Neumann, "EMERALD: Event Monitoring Enabling Responses to Anomalous Live Disturbances", Proc. of the 20th National Information Systems Security Conference, Baltimore, Maryland, October 1997, pp. 353-365.

19. Roger, M.; Goubault-Larrecq, J., "Log auditing through model-checking", Page(s): 220-234, proc.of 14th IEEE Computer Security Foundations Workshop, 2001.

20. R. Sekar,Yong Cai, Mark Segal, "A Specification-Based Approach for Building Survivable Systems," Proc. 21st NIST-NCSC National Information Systems Security Conference 1998

21. Schultz, M.G.; Eskin, E.; Zadok, F.; Stolfo, S.J., "Data mining methods for detection of new malicious executables", Proc. of IEEE Symposium on Security and Privacy,2001

22. P. Uppuluri, R. Sekar, "Experiences with Specification-based intrusion detection," Proc of Recent Advances in Intrusion detection, 2001

23. David Wagner, Drew Dean: Intrusion Detection via Static Analysis. IEEE Symposium on Security and Privacy 2001.

24. D. Zerkle, K. Levitt, "NetKuang-A Multi-host Configuration Vulnerability Checker," Proc of Sixth USENIX Security Symposium, 1996

25. A. Mounji, B. Le Charlier, "Continuous Assessment of a Unix Configuration: Integrating Intrusion Detection and Configuration Analysis," Proc.of the ISOC' 97 Symposium on Network and Distributed System Security. 1997.

RheoStat: Real-Time Risk Management

Ashish Gehani[*] and Gershon Kedem

Department of Computer Science, Duke University

Abstract. As the frequency of attacks faced by the average host connected to the Internet increases, reliance on manual intervention for response is decreasingly tenable. Operating system and application based mechanisms for automated response are increasingly needed. Existing solutions have either been customized to specific attacks, such as disabling an account after a number of authentication failures, or utilize harsh measures, such as shutting the system down. In contrast, we present a framework for systematic fine grained response that is achieved by dynamically controlling the host's exposure to perceived threats.

This paper introduces a formal model to characterize the risk faced by a host. It also describes how the risk can be managed in real-time by adapting the exposure. This is achieved by modifying the access control subsystem to let the choice of whether to grant a permission be delegated to code that is customized to the specific right. The code can then use the runtime context to make a more informed choice, thereby tightening access to a resource when a threat is detected. The running time can be constrained to provide performance guarantees.

The framework was implemented by modifying the Java Runtime. A suite of vulnerable Jigsaw servlets and corresponding attacks was created. The following were manually added: code for dynamic permission checks; estimates of the reduction in exposure associated with each check; the frequencies with which individual permissions occurred in a typical workload; a global risk tolerance. The resulting platform disrupted the attacks by denying the permissions needed for their completion.

1 Introduction

This paper presents a new method of intrusion prevention. We introduce a mechanism to dynamically alter the exposure of a host to contain an intrusion when it occurs. A host's exposure comprises the set exposures of all its resources. If access to a resource is to be controlled, then a permission check will be present to safeguard it. The set of permissions that are utilized in the process of an intrusion occurring can thus be viewed as the system's exposure to that particular threat.

By performing auxiliary checks prior to granting a permission, the chance of it being granted in the presence of a threat can be reduced. By tightening the access control configuration, the system's exposure can be reduced. By relaxing the configuration, the exposure can be allowed to increase. The use of auxiliary checks will introduce runtime overhead. In addition, when permissions are denied, applications may be prevented from functioning correctly. These two factors require that the use of the auxiliary checks must be minimized.

---

[*] Supported by a USENIX Association Research Grant and a North Carolina Networking Initiative Graduate Fellowship.

We first investigate how the auxiliary checks can be performed by modifying the access control subsystem. After that we introduce a model for measuring and managing the risk by dynamically altering the host's exposure. Finally, we demonstrate how the approach can be used to contain attacks in real-time.

2 Predicated Permissions

One approach is to use a subset of the security policy that can be framed intuitively. While this method suffers from the fact that the resulting specification will not be complete, it has the benefit that it is likely to be deployed. The specific subset we consider is that which constitutes the authorization policy. These consist of statements of the form $(\sigma \Rightarrow p)$. Here p is a permission and σ can be any legal statement in the policy, L. If σ holds true, then the permission p can be granted. The reference monitor maintains an access control matrix, M, which represents the space of all combinations of the set of subjects, S, set of objects, O, and the set of authorization types, A.

$$M = S \times O \times A, \quad \text{where} \quad p(i,j,k) \in M \tag{1}$$

Traditionally, the space M is populated with elements of the form:

$$p(i,j,k) = 1 \tag{2}$$

if the subject $S[i]$ should be granted permission $A[k]$ to access object $O[j]$, and otherwise with:

$$p(i,j,k) = 0 \tag{3}$$

In our new paradigm, we can replace the elements of M with ones of the form:

$$p(i,j,k) = \sigma, \quad \text{where} \quad \sigma \in L \tag{4}$$

Thus, a permission check can be the evaluation of a predicate framed in a suitable language, L, which will be required to evaluate to either true or false, corresponding to 1 or 0, instead of being a lookup of a binary value in a static configuration.

3 Active Monitoring

To realize our model of evaluating predicates prior to granting permissions, we augment a conventional access control subsystem by interceding on all permission checks and transferring control to our **ActiveMonitor** as shown in Figure 1[1]. If an appropriate binding exists, it delegates the decision to code customized to the specific right. Such bindings can be dynamically added and removed to the running **ActiveMonitor** through a programming interface. This allows the restrictiveness of the system's access control configuration to be continuously varied in response to changes in the threat level.

Our prototype was created by modifying the runtime environment of Sun's Java Development Kit (JDK 1.4), which runs on the included stack-based virtual machine. The runtime includes a reference monitor, called the **AccessController**, which we altered as described below.

[1] The impact of interceding alone (without counting the effect of evaluating predicates) does not impact the running time of SPECjvm98 [SPECjvm98] with any statistical significance.

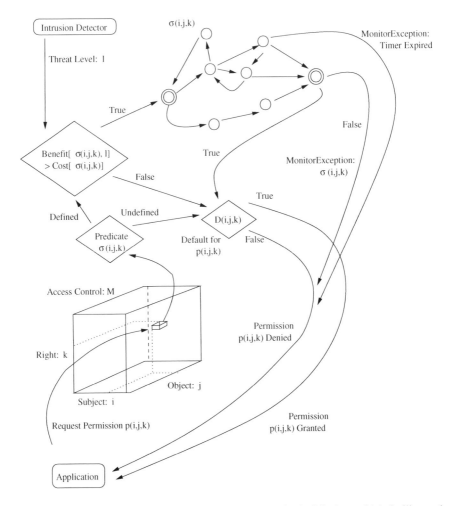

Fig. 1. Static permission lookups are augmented using an **ActiveMonitor** which facilitates the use of runtime context in deciding whether to grant a permission. **ActiveMonitor** predicated permissions have 3 distinguishing features: (i) Constant running time, (ii) Dynamic activation if expected benefit exceeds cost, (iii) Interrogatable for cause of denial.

3.1   Interposition

When an application is executed, each method that is invoked causes a new frame to be pushed onto the stack. Each frame has its own access control context that encapsulates the permissions granted to it. When access to a controlled resource is made, the call through which it is made invokes the **AccessController**'s *checkPermission()* method. This inspects the stack and checks if any of the frames' access control contexts contain permissions that would allow the access to be made. If it finds an appropriate permission it returns silently. Otherwise it throws an exception of type **AccessControlException**. See [Koved98] for details.

We altered the *checkPermission()* method so it first calls the active **ActiveMonitor**'s *checkPermission()* method. If it returns with a `null` value, the **AccessController**'s *checkPermission()* logic executes and completes as it would have without modification. Otherwise, the return value is used to throw a customized subclass of **AccessControlException** which includes information about the reason why the permission was denied. Thus, the addition of the **ActiveMonitor** functionality can restrict the permissions, but it can not cause new permissions to be granted. Note that it is necessary to invoke the **ActiveMonitor**'s *checkPermission()* first since the side-effect of invoking this method may be the initiation of an exposure-reducing response. If it was invoked after the **AccessController**'s *checkPermission()*, then in the cases that an **AccessControlException** was thrown, control would not flow to the Active Monitor's *checkPermission()* leaving any side-effect responses uninitiated.

Code that is invoked by the **ActiveMonitor** should not itself cause new **ActiveMonitor** calls, since this could result in a recursive loop. To avoid this, before the **ActiveMonitor**'s *checkPermission()* method is invoked, the stack is traversed to ensure that none of the frames is an **ActiveMonitor** frame, since that would imply that the current thread belonged to code invoked by the **ActiveMonitor**. If an **ActiveMonitor** frame is found, the **AccessController**'s *checkPermission()* returns silently, that is it grants the permission with no further checks.

3.2 Invocation

When the system initializes, the **ActiveMonitor** first creates a hash table which maps permissions to predicates. It populates this by loading the relevant classes, using Java *Reflection* to obtain appropriate constructors and storing them for subsequent invocation. At this point it is ready to accept delegations from the **AccessController**.

```
public abstract class PredicateThread extends Thread{

    protected PredicateThread(Permission permission,
                                        Object lock);
    public void run(){

        if(condition) result=true;

        synchronized(lock){
            lock.notify();
        }
    }

    public boolean getResult();
}
```

Fig. 2. Skeletal version of **PredicateThread**

When the **ActiveMonitor**'s *checkPermsission()* method is invoked, it uses the permission passed as a parameter to perform a lookup and extract any code associated with the permission. If code is found, it is invoked in a new thread and a timer is started. Otherwise, the method returns `null`, indicating the **AccessController** use the static configuration decide if the permission should be granted. The code must be a subclass of the abstract class **PredicateThread**. A skeletal version is presented in Figure 2. This ensures that it will store the result in a shared location when the thread completes and notify the **ActiveMonitor** of its completion via a shared synchronization lock.

The shared location is inspected when the timer expires. If the code that was run evaluated to `true`, then a `null` is returned by the **ActiveMonitor**'s *checkPermission()* method. Otherwise a string describing the cause of the permission denial is returned.

If the code had not finished executing when the timer expired, a string denoting this is returned. As described above, when a string is returned, it is used by the modified **AccessController** to throw an **ActiveMonitorException**, our customized subclass of **AccessControlException**, which includes information about the predicate that failed. The thread forked to evaluate code can be destroyed once its timer expires. Care must be taken when designing predicates so that their destruction midway through an evaluation does not affect subsequent evaluations.

Finally, the **ActiveMonitor**'s own configuration can be dynamically altered. It exposes *enableSafeguard()* and *disableSafeguard()* methods for this. These can be used to activate and deactivate the utilization of the auxiliary checks for a specific permission. If a piece of code is being evaluated prior to granting a particular permission and there is no longer any need for this to occur, it can be deactivated with the *disableSafeguard()* method. Subsequently that permission will be granted using only the **AccessController**'s static configuration using a lookup of a binary value. Similarly, if it is deemed necessary to perform extra checks prior to granting a permission, this may be enabled by invoking the *enableSafeguard()* method.

4   Risk

Given the ability to predicate permissions the successful verification of auxiliary conditions, we now consider the problem of how to choose when to use such safeguards.

The primary goal of an intrusion response system is to guard against attacks. However, invoking responses arbitrarily may safeguard part of the system but leave other weaker areas exposed. Thus, to effect a rational response, it is necessary to weigh all the possible alternatives. A course of action must then be chosen which will result in the least damage, while simultaneously assuring that cost constraints are respected. Risk management addresses this problem.

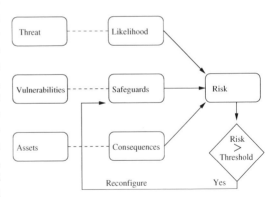

Fig. 3. Risk can be analyzed as a function of the threats, their likelihood, the vulnerabilities, the safeguards, the assets and the consequences. Risk can be managed by using safeguards to control the exposure of vulnerable resources.

4.1   Risk Factors

Analyzing the risk of a system requires knowledge of a number of factors. Below we describe each of these factors along with its associated semantics. We define these in the context of the operating system paradigm since our goal is host-based response.

The paradigm assumes the existence of an operating system augmented with an access control subsystem that mediates access by subjects to objects in the system using predicated permissions. In addition, a host-based intrusion detection system is assumed to be present and operational.

Threats. A *threat* is an agent that can cause harm to an asset in the system. We define a threat to be a specific attack against any of the application or system software that is running on the host. It is characterized by an intrusion detection signature. The set of threats is denoted by $T = \{t_1, t_2, \ldots\}$, where $t_\alpha \in T$ is an intrusion detection signature. Since t_α is a host-based signature, it is comprised of an *ordered set* of events $S(t_\alpha) = \{s_1, s_2, \ldots\}$. If this set occurs in the order recognized by the rules of the intrusion detector, it signifies the presence of an attack.

Likelihood. The *likelihood* of a threat is the hypothetical probability of it occurring. If a signature has been partially matched, the extent of the match serves as a predictor of the chance that it will subsequently be completely matched. A function μ is used to compute the likelihood of threat t_α. μ can be threat specific and will depend on the history of system events that are relevant to the intrusion signature. Thus, if $E = \{e_1, e_2, \ldots\}$ denotes the ordered set of all events that have occurred, then:

$$\mathcal{T}(t_\alpha) = \mu(t_\alpha, E \overset{\prec}{\cap} S(t_\alpha)) \tag{5}$$

where $\overset{\prec}{\cap}$ yields the set of all events that occur *in the same order* in each input set. Our implementation of μ is described in Section 7.1.

Assets. An *asset* is an item that has value. We define the assets to be the data stored in the system. In particular, each file is considered a separate object $o_\beta \in O$, where $O = \{o_1, o_2, \ldots\}$ is the set of assets. A set of objects $A(t_\alpha) \subseteq O$ is associated with each threat t_α. Only objects $o_\beta \in A(t_\alpha)$ can be harmed if the attack that is characterized by t_α succeeds.

Consequences. A *consequence* is a type of harm that an asset may suffer. Three types of consequences can impact the data. These are the loss of confidentiality, integrity and availability. If an object $o_\beta \in A(t_\alpha)$ is affected by the threat t_α, then the resulting costs due to the loss of confidentiality, integrity and availability are denoted by $c(o_\beta)$, $i(o_\beta)$, and $a(o_\beta)$ respectively. Any of these values may be 0 if the attack can not effect the relevant consequence. However, all three values associated with a single object can not be 0 since in that case $o_\beta \in A(t_\alpha)$ would not hold. Thus, the consequence of a threat t_α is:

$$\mathcal{C}(t_\alpha) = \sum_{o_\beta \in A(t_\alpha)} c(o_\beta) + i(o_\beta) + a(o_\beta) \tag{6}$$

Vulnerabilities. A *vulnerability* is a weakness in the system. It results from an error in the design, implementation or configuration of either the operating system or application software. The set of vulnerabilities present in the system is denoted by $W = \{w_1, w_2, \ldots\}$. $W(t_\alpha) \subseteq W$ is the set of weaknesses exploited by the threat t_α to subvert the security policy.

Safeguards. A *safeguard* is a mechanism that controls the exposure of the system's assets. The reference monitor's set of permission checks $P = \{p_1, p_2, \ldots\}$ serve as safeguards in an operating system. Since the reference monitor mediates access to all objects, a vulnerability's exposure can be limited by denying the relevant permissions. The set $P(w_\gamma) \subseteq P$ contains all the permissions that are requested in the process of exploiting vulnerability w_γ. The static configuration of a conventional reference monitor either grants or denies access to a permission p_λ. This *exposure* is denoted by $v(p_\lambda)$, with the value being either 0 or 1. The active reference monitor can reduce the exposure of a statically granted permission to $v'(p_\lambda)$, a value in the range $[0, 1]$. This reflects the nuance that results from evaluating predicates as *auxiliary safeguards*.)

Thus, if all auxiliary safeguards are utilized, the total exposure to a threat t_α is:

$$\mathcal{V}(t_\alpha) = \sum_{p_\lambda \in \hat{P}(t_\alpha)} \frac{v(p_\lambda) \times v'(p_\lambda)}{|\hat{P}(t_\alpha)|} \tag{7}$$

where:

$$\hat{P}(t_\alpha) = \bigcup_{w_\gamma \in W(t_\alpha)} P(w_\gamma) \tag{8}$$

5   Runtime Risk Management

The risk to the host is the sum of the risks that result from each of the threats that it faces. The risk from a single threat is the product of the chance that the attack will occur, the exposure of the system to the attack, and the cost of the consequences of the attack succeeding [NIST800-12]. Thus, the cumulative risk faced by the system is:

$$\mathcal{R} = \sum_{t_\alpha \in T} \mathcal{T}(t_\alpha) \times \mathcal{V}(t_\alpha) \times \mathcal{C}(t_\alpha) \tag{9}$$

If the risk posed to the system is to be managed, the current level must be continuously monitored. When the risk rises past the threshold that the host can tolerate, the system's security must be tightened. Similarly, when the risk decreases, the restrictions can be relaxed to improve performance and usability. This process is elucidated below.

The system's risk can be reduced by reducing the exposure of vulnerabilities. This is is effected through the use of auxiliary safeguards prior granting a permission. Similarly, if the threat recedes, the restrictive permission checks can be relaxed.

5.1   Managed Risk

The set of permissions P is kept partitioned into two disjoint sets, $\Psi(P)$ and $\Omega(P)$, that is $\Psi(P) \cap \Omega(P) = \phi$ and $\Psi(P) \cup \Omega(P) = P$. The set $\Psi(P) \subseteq P$ contains the permissions for which auxiliary safeguards are currently active. The remaining permissions $\Omega(P) \subseteq P$ are handled conventionally by the reference monitor, using only static lookups rather than evaluating associated predicates prior to granting these permissions.

At any given point, when the set of safeguards $\Psi(P)$ is in use, the current risk $\mathcal{R}'$ is calculated with:

$$\mathcal{R}' = \sum_{t_\alpha \in T} \mathcal{T}(t_\alpha) \times \mathcal{V}'(t_\alpha) \times \mathcal{C}(t_\alpha) \tag{10}$$

where:

$$\mathcal{V}'(t_\alpha) = \sum_{p_\lambda \in \hat{P}(t_\alpha) \cap \Omega(P)} \frac{v(p_\lambda)}{|\hat{P}(t_\alpha)|} \tag{11}$$

$$+ \sum_{p_\lambda \in \hat{P}(t_\alpha) \cap \Psi(P)} \frac{v(p_\lambda) \times v'(p_\lambda)}{|\hat{P}(t_\alpha)|}$$

5.2 Risk Tolerance

While the risk must be monitored continuously, there is a computational cost incurred each time it is recalculated. Therefore, the frequency with which the risk is estimated must be minimized to the extent possible. Instead of calculating the risk synchronously at fixed intervals in time, we exploit the fact that the risk level only changes when the threat to the system is altered.

An intrusion detector is assumed to be monitoring the system's activity. Each time it detects an event that changes the extent to which a signature has been matched, it passes the event e to the intrusion response subsystem. The level of risk $\mathcal{R}_b$ before e occurred is noted, and then the level of risk $\mathcal{R}_a$ after e occurred is calculated. Thus, $\mathcal{R}_a = \mathcal{R}_b + \epsilon$, where ϵ denotes the change in the risk. Since the risk is recalculated only when it actually changes, the computational cost of monitoring it is minimized.

Each time an event e occurs, either the risk decreases, stays the same or increases. Each host is configured to tolerate risk upto a threshold, denoted by $\mathcal{R}_0$. After each event e, the system's response guarantees that the risk will return to a level below this threshold. As a result, $\mathcal{R}_b < \mathcal{R}_0$ always holds. If $\epsilon = 0$, then no further risk management steps are required.

If $\epsilon < 0$, then $\mathcal{R}_a < \mathcal{R}_0$ since $\mathcal{R}_a = \mathcal{R}_b + \epsilon < \mathcal{R}_b < \mathcal{R}_0$. At this point, the system's security configuration is more restrictive than it needs to be. To improve system usability and performance, the response system must deactivate appropriate safeguards, while ensuring that the risk level does not rise past the threshold $\mathcal{R}_0$.

If $\epsilon > 0$ and $\mathcal{R}_a \leq \mathcal{R}_0$, then no action needs to be taken. Even though the risk has increased, it is below the threshold that the system can tolerate, so no further safeguards need to be introduced. In addition, the system will not be able to find any set of unused safeguards whose removal will increase the risk by less than $\mathcal{R}_0 - \mathcal{R}_b - \epsilon$, since the presence of such a combination would also mean that the set existed before e occurred. It is not possible that such a combination of safeguards existed before e occurred since they would also have satisfied the condition of being less than $\mathcal{R}_0 - \mathcal{R}_b$ and would have been utilized before e occurred in the process of minimizing the impact on performance in the previous step.

If $\epsilon > 0$ and $\mathcal{R}_a > \mathcal{R}_0$, then action is required to reduce the risk to a level below the threshold of tolerance. The response system must search for and implement a set of safeguards to this end. Since the severity of the response is dependent on the current risk level, the risk recalculation can not be delayed despite the additional overhead it imposes at a point when the system is already stressed.

5.3   Recalculating Risk

When the risk is calculated the first time, Equation 9 is used. Therefore, the cost is $O(|T| \times |P| \times |O|)$. Since the change in the risk must be repeatedly evaluated during real-time reconfiguration of the runtime environment, it is imperative the cost is minimized. This is achieved by caching all the values $\mathcal{V}'(t_\alpha) \times \mathcal{C}(t_\alpha)$ associated with threats $t_\alpha \in T$ during the evaluation of Equation 9. Subsequently, when an event e occurs, the change in the risk $\epsilon = \delta(\mathcal{R}', e)$ can be calculated with cost $O(|T|)$ as described below.

The ordered set E refers to all the events that have occurred in the system prior to the event e. The change in the likelihood of a threat t_α due to e is:

$$\delta(\mathcal{T}(t_\alpha), e) = \mu(t_\alpha, (E \cup e) \overset{\prec}{\cap} S(t_\alpha)) - \mu(t_\alpha, E \overset{\prec}{\cap} S(t_\alpha)) \tag{12}$$

The set of threats affected by e is denoted by $\Delta(T, e)$. A threat $t_\alpha \in \Delta(T, e)$ is considered to be affected by e if $\delta(\mathcal{T}(t_\alpha), e) \neq 0$, that is its likelihood changed due to the event e. The resultant change in the risk level is:

$$\delta(\mathcal{R}', e) = \sum_{t_\alpha \in \Delta(T, e)} \delta(\mathcal{T}(t_\alpha), e) \times \mathcal{V}'(t_\alpha) \times \mathcal{C}(t_\alpha) \tag{13}$$

6   Cost / Benefit Analysis

After an event e occurs, if the risk level $\mathcal{R}_a$ increases past the threshold of risk tolerance $\mathcal{R}_0$, the goal of the response engine is to reduce the risk by $\delta_g \geq \mathcal{R}_a - \mathcal{R}_0$ to a level below the threshold. To do this, it must select a subset of permissions $\rho(\Omega(P)) \subseteq \Omega(P)$, such that adding the safeguards will reduce the risk to the desired level. By ensuring that the permissions in $\rho(\Omega(P))$ are granted only after relevant predicates are verified, the resulting risk level is reduced to:

$$\mathcal{R}'' = \sum_{t_\alpha \in T} \mathcal{T}(t_\alpha) \times \mathcal{V}''(t_\alpha) \times \mathcal{C}(t_\alpha) \tag{14}$$

where the new vulnerability measure, based on Equation 7, is:

$$\mathcal{V}''(t_\alpha) = \sum_{p_\lambda \in (\hat{P}(t_\alpha) \cap \Omega(P) - \rho(\Omega(P)))} \frac{v(p_\lambda)}{|\hat{P}(t_\alpha)|} \tag{15}$$

$$+ \sum_{p_\lambda \in (\hat{P}(t_\alpha) \cap \Psi(P) \cup \rho(\Omega(P)))} \frac{v(p_\lambda) \times v'(p_\lambda)}{|\hat{P}(t_\alpha)|}$$

Instead, after an event e occurs, if the risk level $\mathcal{R}_a$ decreases, the goal of the response engine is to allow the risk to rise by $\delta_g \leq \mathcal{R}_0 - \mathcal{R}_a$ to a level below the threshold of risk tolerance $\mathcal{R}_0$. To do this, it must select a subset of permissions $\rho(\Psi(P)) \subseteq \Psi(P)$, such that removing the safeguards currently in use for the set will yield the maximum improvement to runtime performance. After the safeguards are relaxed, the risk level will rise to:

$$\mathcal{R}'' = \sum_{t_\alpha \in T} \mathcal{T}(t_\alpha) \times \mathcal{V}''(t_\alpha) \times \mathcal{C}(t_\alpha) \tag{16}$$

where the new vulnerability measure, based on Equation 7, is:

$$\mathcal{V}''(t_\alpha) = \sum_{p_\lambda \in \hat{P}(t_\alpha) \cap \Omega(P) \cup \rho(\Psi(P))} \frac{v(p_\lambda)}{|\hat{P}(t_\alpha)|} \tag{17}$$

$$+ \sum_{p_\lambda \in \hat{P}(t_\alpha) \cap \Psi(P) - \rho(\Psi(P))} \frac{v(p_\lambda \times v'(p_\lambda))}{|\hat{P}(t_\alpha)|}$$

There are $O(2^{|P|})$ ways of choosing subsets $\rho(\Omega(P)) \subseteq \Omega(P)$ for risk reduction or subsets $\rho(\Psi(P)) \subseteq \Psi(P)$ for risk relaxation. When selecting from the possibilities, the primary objective is the maintenance of the bound $\mathcal{R}'' < \mathcal{R}_0$, where $\mathcal{R}'' = \mathcal{R}_a - \delta_g$ in the case of risk reduction, and $\mathcal{R}'' = \mathcal{R}_a + \delta_g$ in the case of risk relaxation.

The choice of safeguards also impacts the performance of the system. Evaluating predicates prior to granting permissions introduces latency in system calls. A single interrogation of the runtime, such as checking how much swap space is free, takes about 1ms. When file permission checks were protected with safeguard code that ran for 150ms, 5 of 7 applications in [SPECjvm98] took less than 2% longer to run on average, while the other 2 applications took 37% longer. Hence, the choice of subsets $\rho(\Omega(P))$ or $\rho(\Psi(P))$ is subject to the secondary goal of minimizing the overhead introduced. (In practice, the cumulative effect is likely to be acceptable since useful predicate functionality can be created with code that runs in just a few milliseconds.)

The adverse impact of a safeguard is proportional to the frequency with which it is utilized in the system's workload. Given a typical workload, we can count the frequency $f(p_\lambda)$ with which permission p_λ is requested in the workload. This can be done for all permissions. The cost of utilizing subset $\rho(\Omega(P))$ for risk reduction can then be calculated with:

$$\zeta(\rho(\Omega(P))) = \sum_{p_\lambda \in \rho(\Omega(P))} f(p_\lambda) \tag{18}$$

Similarly, if the safeguards of subset $\rho(\Psi(P))$ are relaxed, the resulting reduction in runtime cost can be calculated with:

$$\zeta(\rho(\Psi(P))) = \sum_{p_\lambda \in \rho(\Psi(P))} f(p_\lambda) \tag{19}$$

The ideal choice of safeguards will minimize the impact on performance, while simultaneously ensuring that the risk remains below the threshold of tolerance. Thus, for risk reduction we wish to find:

$$\min \zeta(\rho(\Omega(P))), \quad \mathcal{R}'' \leq \mathcal{R}_0 \tag{20}$$

In the context of risk relaxation, we wish to find:

$$\max \zeta(\rho(\Psi(P))), \quad \mathcal{R}'' \leq \mathcal{R}_0 \tag{21}$$

Both these problems are equivalent to the NP-complete *0-1 Knapsack Problem*. Although approximation algorithms exist [Kellerer98], they are not suitable for our use since we need to make a choice in real-time. Instead, we will use a heuristic which guarantees that the risk is maintained below the threshold. The heuristic is based on the greedy algorithm for the *0-1 Knapsack Problem* which picks the item with the highest benefit-to-cost ratio repeatedly till the knapsack's capacity is reached. This yields a solution that is always within a factor of 2 of the optimal choice [Garey79].

6.1 Response Heuristic

When the risk needs to be reduced, the heuristic uses the greedy strategy of picking the response primitive with the highest benefit-to-cost ratio repeatedly till the constraint is satisfied. By maintaining the choices in a *heap* data structure keyed on the benefit-to-cost ratio, each primitive in the response set can be chosen in $O(1)$ time. This is significant since implementing a single response primitive is often sufficient for disrupting an attack in progress. When the risk needs to be relaxed, the active safeguards with the highest cost-to-benefit ratios can be selected since these will be yield the best improvement to system performance. A separate *heap* is utilized to maintain these.

Risk Reduction. We outline the algorithm for the case where the risk needs to be reduced. The first two steps constitute pre-processing and therefore only occur during system initialization. Risk relaxation is analogous and therefore not described explicitly.

Step 1 The benefit-to-cost ratio of each candidate safeguard permission $p_\lambda \in \Omega(P)$ can be calculated by:

$$\kappa(p_\lambda) = \frac{\displaystyle\sum_{t_\alpha : p_\lambda \in (\hat{P}(t_\alpha) \cap \Omega(P))} \left\{ \mathcal{T}(t_\alpha) \times \dfrac{v(p_\lambda) \times (1 - v'(p_\lambda))}{|\hat{P}(t_\alpha)|} \times \mathcal{C}(t_\alpha) \right\}}{f(p_\lambda)} \tag{22}$$

Step 2 The response set is defined as empty, that is $\rho(\Omega(P)) = \phi$.
Step 3 The single risk reducing measure with the highest benefit-to-cost can be selected, that is:

$$p_{max} = \max \ \kappa(p_\lambda), \quad p_\lambda \in \Omega(P) \tag{23}$$

The permission is added to $\rho(\Omega(P))$.
Step 4 The risk before the candidate responses were utilized is $\mathcal{R}_a$. If the responses were activated the resulting risk $\mathcal{R}''$ is given by:

$$\mathcal{R}'' = \mathcal{R}_a \quad - \sum_{p_\lambda \in \rho(\Omega(P))} \kappa(p_\lambda) \times f(p_\lambda) \tag{24}$$

This is equivalent to using Equations 14 and 15. While the worst case complexity is the same, when few protective measures are added the cost of the above calculation is significantly lower.

Step 5 If $\mathcal{R}'' > \mathcal{R}_0$ then the system repeats the above from Step 3 onwards. If $\mathcal{R}'' \le \mathcal{R}_0$ then proceed to the next step.

Step 6 The set of safeguards $\rho(\Omega(P))$ must be activated and $\rho(\Omega(P))$ should be transferred from $\Omega(P)$ to $\Psi(P)$.

The time complexity is $O(|\rho(\Omega(P))|)$. In the worst case, this is $O(|\Omega(P)|) \le O(|P|)$. Unless a large variety of attacks are simultaneously launched against the target, the response set will be small.

Risk Relaxation. In the case of risk relaxation, the algorithm becomes:

Step 1 For $p_\lambda \in \Psi(P)$ calculate:

$$\kappa(p_\lambda) = \sum_{t_\alpha : p_\lambda \in (\hat{P}(t_\alpha) \cap \Psi(P))} \{\mathcal{T}(t_\alpha) \times \qquad (25)$$

$$\frac{\dfrac{v(p_\lambda) \times (1 - v'(p_\lambda))}{|\hat{P}(t_\alpha)|} \times \mathcal{C}(t_\alpha)\}}{f(p_\lambda)}$$

Step 2 Set $\rho(\Psi(P)) = \phi$.

Step 3 Find the safeguard which yields the least risk reduction per instance of use:

$$p_{min} = \min \ \kappa(p_\lambda), \quad p_\lambda \in \Psi(P) \qquad (26)$$

Add it to $\rho(\Psi(P))$.

Step 4 Calculate $\mathcal{R}''$:

$$\mathcal{R}'' = \mathcal{R}_a \ + \sum_{p_\lambda \in \rho(\Psi(P))} \kappa(p_\lambda) \times f(p_\lambda) \qquad (27)$$

Step 5 If $\mathcal{R}'' < \mathcal{R}_0$, repeat from Step 3. If $\mathcal{R}'' = \mathcal{R}_0$, proceed to the next step. If $\mathcal{R}'' > \mathcal{R}_0$, undo the last iteration of Step 3.

Step 6 Relax all measures in $\rho(\Psi(P))$ and transfer them to $\Omega(P)$.

7   Implementation

Our prototype augments Sun's Java Runtime Environment (version 1.4.2) running on Redhat Linux 9 (with kernel 2.4.20). Security in the Java 2 model is handled by the **AccessController** class, which in turn invokes the legacy **SecurityManager**. We instrumented the latter to invoke an **Initialize** class which constructs and initializes an instance of the **RheoStat** class [Gehani03]. A shutdown hook is also registered with the **SecurityManager** so that the intrusion detector is terminated when the user application exits. The **ActiveMonitor** class initializes the first time the **AccessController**'s *checkPermission()* method is invoked.

   RheoStat implements a limited state transition analysis intrusion detector, based on the methodology of [Ilgun95]. It adds a *pre-match timer* and *post-match timer* for each signature. The first handles false partial matches by reseting the signature if the match doesn't complete in a pre-determined interval. The second is used to reset the system after a signature match completes and sufficient time has elapsed to deem that the threat has passed.

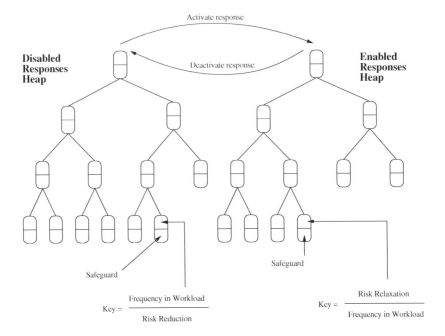

Fig. 4. When the Risk Manager needs to activate a response to effect risk reduction, it attempts to select the one which will minimize the runtime overhead while maximizing the risk reduction.

7.1   Risk Manager

A **RiskManager** class uses events generated by **RheoStat** and invokes the **ActiveMonitor**'s *enableSafeguard( )* and *disableSafeguard( )* methods as required. The μ matching function, described in Section 4.1, is used for estimating the threat from a partial match. We use:

$$\mu(t_\alpha, E \overset{\prec}{\cap} S(t_\alpha)) = \frac{|E \overset{\prec}{\cap} S(t_\alpha)|}{|S(t_\alpha)|} \tag{28}$$

The new risk level is calculated with the updated threat levels. If the risk level increases above or decreases below the risk tolerance threshold, the following course of action occurs.

The **RiskManager** maintains two heap data structures as illustrated in Figure 4. The first one contains all the permissions for which the **ActiveMonitor** has predicates but are currently unused. The objects are stored in the heap using the cost-to-benefit ratios as the keys. The second heap contains all the permissions for which the **ActiveMonitor** is currently evaluating predicates before it grants permissions. The objects in this heap are keyed by the benefit-to-cost ratios. When the risk level rises, the **RiskManager** extracts the minimum value element from the first heap, and inserts it into the second heap. The corresponding predicate evaluation is activated. The risk level is updated. If it remains above the risk tolerance threshold the process is repeated until the risk has reduced sufficiently. Similarly, when an event causes the risk to drop, the **RiskManager** extracts the minimum element repeatedly from the second heap, inserting it into the first heap, disabling predicate checks for the permission, while the risk remains below the threshold of tolerance. In this manner, the system is able to adapt its security posture continuously.

8 Evaluation

The NIST ICAT database [ICAT] contains information on over 6, 200 vulnerabilities in application and operating system software from a range of sources. These are primarily classified into seven categories. Based on the database, we have constructed a suite of attacks, with each attack illustrating the exploitation of a vulnerability from a different category. In each case, the system component which includes the vulnerability is a Java servlet that we have created and installed in the W3C's Jigsaw web server (version 2.2.2) [Jigsaw]. While our approach is general, we focus below only on 4 categories for brevity. We describe a scenario that corresponds to each attack, including a description of the vulnerability that it exploits, the intrusion signature used to detect it and the way the system responds. The global risk tolerance threshold is set at 20.

8.1 Configuration Error

A *configuration error* introduces a vulnerability into the system due to setting that are controlled by the user. Although the configuration is implemented faithfully by the system, it allows the security policy to be subverted. In our example, the servlet authenticates the user before granting access to certain documents. The password used is a permutation of the username. As a result, an attacker can guess the password after a small number of attempts. The flaw here is the weak configuration.

When the following sequence of events is detected, an attack that exploits this vulnerability is deemed to have occurred. First, the web server accepts a connection to port 8001. Second, it serves the specific HTML document which includes the form which requests authentication information as well as the desired document. Third, the server receives another connection. Fourth, the servlet that verifies if the file can be served to the client, based on the authentication information provided, will execute. Fifth, the decision to deny the request is logged. If this

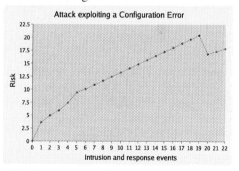

Fig. 5. Attack exploiting a configuration error.

sequence of events repeats twice again within the pre-match timeout of the signature, which is 1 minute, an intrusion attempt is deemed to have occurred.

In Figure 5, events $7 - 18$ and $20 - 22$ correspond to this signature. Events $1 - 6$ are of other signatures that cause the risk level to rise. Event 18 causes the risk threshold to be crossed. As a result, the **RiskManager** searches for and finds the risk reduction measure which has the lowest cost-benefit ratio. The system enables a predicate for the permission that controls whether the servlet can be executed. This is event 19 and reduces the risk. The predicate checks whether the current time is within the range of business operating hours. It allows the permission to be granted only if it evaluates to `true`. During operating hours, it is likely that the intrusion will be flagged and seen by an administrator and it is possible that the event sequence occurred accidentally, so the permission continues to be granted. Outside those hours, it is likely that this is an attack attempt and no administrator is present, so the permission is denied thereafter, till the post-match timer expires after one hour and the threat is reset.

8.2   Design Error

A *design error* is a flaw that introduces a weakness in the system despite a safe config-uration and correct implementation. In our example, the servlet allows a remote node to upload data to the server. The configuration specifies the maximum size file that can be uploaded. The servlet implementation ensures that each file uploaded is limited to the size specified in the configuration. However, the design of the restriction did not ac-count for the fact that repeated uploads can be performed by the same remote node. This effectively allows an attacker to launch the very denial-of-service (that results when the disk is filled) that was being guarded against when the upload file size was limited.

When the following sequence of events is detected, an attack that exploits this vul-nerability is deemed to have occurred. First, the web server accepts a connection to port 8001. Second, it serves the specific HTML document which includes the form that allows uploads. Third, the server receives another connection. Fourth, it executes the servlet that accepts the upload and limits its size. Fifth, a file is written to the uploads directory. If this sequence of events repeats twice again within the pre-match timeout of the signature, which is 1 minute, an intrusion attempt is deemed to have occurred.

In Figure 6, events $7 - 21$ correspond to this signature. Events $1 - 6$ are of other signatures that cause the risk level to rise. Event 21 causes the risk thresh-old to be crossed. The system responds by enabling a predicate for the permission that controls whether files can be writ-ten to the uploads directory. This is event 22 and reduces the risk. The predicate checks whether the current time is within the range of business operating hours. It allows the permission to be granted only

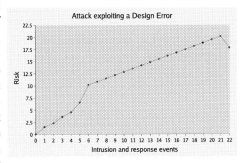

Fig. 6. Attack exploiting a design error.

if it evaluates to `true`. During operating hours, it is likely that the denial-of-service attempt will be flagged and seen by an administrator, so the permission continues to be granted on the assumption that manual response will occur. Outside those hours, it is likely that no administrator is present, so the permission is denied thereafter, till the post-match timer expires after one hour and the threat is reset.

8.3   Environment Error

An *environment error* is one where an assumption is made about the runtime environ-ment which does not hold. In our example, the servlet authenticates a user, then stores the user's directory in a cookie that is returned to the client. Subsequent responses utilize the cookie to determine where to serve files from. The flaw here is that the server assumes the environment of the cookie is safe, which it is not since it is exposed to manipulation by the client. An attacker can exploit this by altering the cookie's value to reflect a directory that they should not have access to.

When the following sequence of events is detected, an attack that exploits this vulnerability is deemed to have occurred. First, the web server accepts a connection to port 8001. Second, it serves the specific HTML document which includes the form that authenticates a user. Third, the server receives another connection. Fourth, it executes the servlet that authenticates the user and maps users to the directories that they are allowed to access. It sets a cookie which includes the

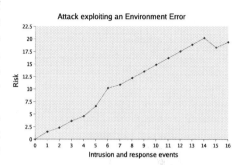

Fig. 7. Attack exploiting an environment error.

directory from which files will be retrieved for further requests. Fifth, the server receives another connection. Sixth, it serves the specific HTML document that includes the form which accepts the file request. Seventh, the server receives another connection. Eighth, the servlet that processes the request, based on the form input as well as the cookie data, is executed. Ninth, a file is served from a directory that was not supposed to be accessible to the user. The events must all occur within the pre-match timeout of the signature, which is 1 minute.

In Figure 7, event 3, events $8 - 14$ and event 16 correspond to this signature. Events $1 - 2$ and $4 - 7$ are of other signatures. Event 14 causes the risk threshold to be crossed. The system responds by enabling a predicate for the permission that controls whether the file download servlet can be executed. This is event 15 and reduces the risk. The predicate simply denies the permission. As a result, the attack can not complete since no more files can be downloaded till the safeguard is removed when the risk reduces at a later point in time (when a threat's timer expires).

8.4   Input Validation Error

An *input validation error* is one that results from the failure to conduct necessary checks on the data. A common example of this type of error is the failure to check that the data passed in is of length no greater than that off the buffer in which it is stored. The result is a buffer overflow which can be exploited in a variety of ways. In our example, the servlet allows a file on the server to be updated remotely. The path of the target file is parsed and a check is performed to verify that it is in a directory that can be updated. The file 'Password.cfg' is used in each directory to describe which users may access it. By uploading a file named 'Password.cfg', an attacker can overwrite and alter the access configuration of the directory. As a result, they can gain unlimited access to the other data in the directory.

When the following sequence of events is detected, an attack that exploits this vulnerability is deemed to have occurred. First, the web server accepts a connection to port 8001. Second, it serves the specific HTML document which includes the form that allows uploads to selected directories. Third, the server receives another connection. Fourth, it executes the servlet that checks that the uploaded file is going to a legal directory. Fifth, the 'Passwords.cfg' file in the uploads directory is written to. The events must all occur within the pre-match timeout of the signature, which is 1 minute.

In Figure 8, event 1 and events $7 - 10$ correspond to this signature. Events $2 - 6$ are of other signatures. Event 10 causes the risk threshold to be crossed. The system responds by enabling a predicate for the permission that controls write access to the 'Passwords.cfg' file in the uploads directory. This is event 11 and reduces the risk. The predicate simply denies the permission. As a result, the attack can not complete since the last step requires this permission to upload and overwrite the 'Passwords.cfg' file. Enabling this safeguard does not affect legitimate uploads since they do not need to write to this file.

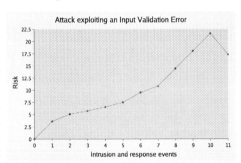

Fig. 8. Attack exploiting an input validation error.

9   Related Work

We describe below the relationship of our work to previous research on intrusion detectors and risk management systems.

9.1   Intrusion Detection

Early systems developed limited ad-hoc responses, such as limiting access to a user's home directory or logging the user out [Bauer88], or terminating network connections [Pooch96]. This has also been the approach of recent commercial systems. For example, BlackICE [BlackICE] allows a network connection to be traced, Intruder Alert [IntruderAlert] allows an account to be locked, NetProwler [NetProwler] can update firewall rules, NetRanger [Cisco] can reset TCP connections and RealSecure [ISS] can terminate user processes.

Frameworks have been proposed for adding response capabilities. DCA [Fisch96] introduced a taxonomy for response and a tool to demonstrate the utility of the taxonomy. EMERALD's [Porras97] design allows customized responses to be invoked automatically, but does not define them by default. AAIR [Carver01] describes an expert system for response based on an extended taxonomy.

Our approach creates a framework for systematically choosing a response in real-time, based on the goal of reducing exposure by reconfiguring the access control subsystem. This allows an attack to be contained automatically instead of being limited to raising an alarm, and does not require a new response subsystem to be developed for each new class of attack discovered.

9.2 Risk Management

Risk analysis has been utilized to manage the security of systems for several decades [FIPS31]. However, its use has been limited to offline risk computation and manual response. [SooHoo02] proposes a general model using decision analysis to estimate computer security risk and automatically update input estimates. [Bilar03] uses reliability modeling to analyze the risk of a distributed system. Risk is calculated as a function of the probability of faults being present in the system's constituent components. Risk management is framed as an integer linear programming problem, aiming to find an alternate system configuration, subject to constraints such as acceptable risk level and maximum cost for reconfiguration.

In contrast to previous approaches, we use the risk computation to drive changes in the operating system's security mechanisms. This allows risk management to occur in real-time and reduces the window of exposure.

10 Future Directions

We utilized a simple μ function that assumed independent probabilities for successive events. However, μ functions can be defined even when pre-conditions are known. By measuring the frequencies of successive events occurring in typical and attacked workloads, conditional probabilities can be derived. A tool to automate the process could be constructed.

The exposure reduction values, workload frequencies, consequence costs and risk threshold were all manually calculated in our prototype. All such parameters will need to be automatically derived for our approach to be practical. The frequencies with which permissions are utilized can be estimated by instrumenting the system to measure these with a typical workload.

A similar approach could be used to determine the average inherent risk of a workload. An alternative would be the creation of a tool to visualize the effect of varying the risk threshold on (i) the performance of the system and (ii) the cost of intrusions that could successfully occur below the risk threshold. Policy would then dictate the trade-off point chosen.

The problem of labeling data with associated consequence values can be addressed with a suitable user interface augmentation - for example, it could utilize user input when new files are being created by application software. The issue could also be partially mitigated by using pre-configured values for all system files.

Finally, some attacks may utilize few or no permission checks. Such scenarios fall into two classes. In the first case, this points to a design shortcoming where new permissions need to be introduced to guard certain resources such as critical subroutines in system code. The other case is when the attack has a very small footprint, in which case our approach will fail (as it can't recognize the threat in advance).

11 Conclusion

We have introduced a formal framework for managing the risk posed to a host. The model calculates the risk based on the threats, exposure to the threats and consequences of the threats. The threat likelihoods are estimated in real-time using output from an intrusion detector. The risk is managed by altering the the exposure of the system. This is done by dynamically reconfiguring the modified access control subsystem. The utility of the approach is illustrated with a set of attack scenarios in which the risk is managed in real-time and results in the attacks being contained. Automated configuration of the system's parameters, either analytically or empirically, remains an open research area.

References

[Bauer88]   D. S. Bauer and M. E. Koblentz, NIDX - A Real-Time Intrusion Detection Expert System, Proc. of USENIX Technical Conference, p261-273, 1988.

[Bilar03]   Daniel Bilar, Quantitative Risk Analysis of Computer Networks, PhD thesis, Dartmouth College, 2003.

[BlackICE]   http://documents.iss.net/literature/BlackICE/BISP-UG_36.pdf

[Carver01]   Curtis Carver, Adaptive, Agent-based Intrusion Response, PhD thesis, Texas A and M University, 2001.

[Cisco]   http://www.cisco.com/application/pdf/en/us/guest/products/ps2113/c1626/ ccmi-gration_09186a00800ee98e.pdf

[FIPS31]   Guidelines for Automatic Data Processing Physical Security and Risk Management, National Bureau of Standards, 1974.

[Fisch96]   Eric Fisch, Intrusive Damage Control and Assessment Techniques, PhD thesis, Texas A and M University, 1996.

[Garey79]   M.R. Garey and D.S. Johnson, Computers and Intractability: A Guide to the Theory of NP-Completeness, Freeman, San Francisco, 1979.

[Gehani03]   Ashish Gehani, Support for Automated Passive Host-based Intrusion Response, PhD thesis, Duke University, 2003.

[ICAT]   http://icat.nist.gov/icat.cfm

[Ilgun95]   Koral Ilgun, Richard A. Kemmerer and Phillip A. Porras, State Transition Analysis: A Rule-Based Intrusion Detection Approach, IEEE Transactions on Software Engineering, 21(3), p181-199, March 1995.

[IntruderAlert] http://enterprisesecurity.symantec.com/content/ProductJump.cfm? Product=171

[ISS]   http://documents.iss.net/literature/RealSecure/RSDP-UG_70.pdf

[Jigsaw]   http://www.w3.org/Jigsaw

[Kellerer98]   H. Kellerer and U. Pferschy, A new fully polynomial approximation scheme for the knapsack problem, Proceedings of the APPROX 98, Lecture Notes in Computer Science, v1444, p123-134, Springer, 1998.

[Koved98]   Larry Koved, Anthony J. Nadalin, Don Neal, and Tim Lawson, The Evolution of Java Security, IBM Systems Journal 37(3), p349-364, 1998.

[NetProwler]   http://symantec.com

[NIST800-12]   Guidelines for Automatic Data Processing Physical Security and Risk Management, National Institute of Standards and Technology, 1996.

[Pooch96]   U. Pooch and G. B. White, Cooperating Security Managers: Distributed Intrusion Detection System, Computer and Security, (15)5, p441-450, September/October 1996.

[Porras97]   P.A. Porras and P.G. Neumann, EMERALD: Event Monitoring Enabling Responses to Anomalous Live Disturbances, Proceedings of the Nineteenth National Computer Security Conference, p353-365, Baltimore, MD, October 1997.

[SooHoo02]   Kevin Soo Hoo, Guidelines for Automatic Data Processing Physical Security and Risk Management, PhD Thesis, Stanford University, 2002.

[SPECjvm98]   http://www.specbench.org/osg/jvm98/

Author Index

Lecture Notes in Computer Science

For information about Vols. 1–3104

please contact your bookseller or Springer